ST. SYMEON
THE NEW THEOLOGIAN
AND SPIRITUAL FATHERHOOD

BYZANTINA NEERLANDICA

EDENDA CURAVERUNT

G.H. BLANKEN · H.J. SCHELTEMA · H. HENNEPHOF

Ab actis: H. Hennephof, Gortestraat 48, 2311 NM Leiden

FASCICULUS 11

ST. SYMEON
THE NEW THEOLOGIAN
AND SPIRITUAL FATHERHOOD

BY

H.J.M. TURNER

E.J. BRILL
LEIDEN · NEW YORK · KØBENHAVN · KÖLN
1990

BX
382.5
.T87
1990

Library of Congress Cataloging-in-Publication Data

Turner, H.J.M.
   St. Symeon the New Theologian and spiritual fatherhood / by H.J.M.
Turner.
      p.   cm. -- (Byzantina Neerlandica, ISSN 0525-4507 : fasc. 11)
   Revision of author's thesis (University of Manchester, 1985).
   Includes bibliographical references and index.
   ISBN 9004091661
      1. Spiritual direction--History of doctrines--Middle Ages,
   600-1600.   2. Orthodox Eastern Church--Doctrines--History.
   3. Monasticism and religious orders. Orthodox Eastern--History.
   4. Symeon, the New Theologian, Saint, 949-1022--Contributions in
   doctrine of spiritual direction.   I. Title.   II. Title: Saint
   Symeon the New Theologian and spiritual fatherhood.   III. Series.
   BX382.5.T87   1990
   253.5'3'092--dc20   90-39223
                                                                CIP

ISSN 0525-4507
ISBN 90 04 09166 1

CONTENTS

PREFACE

This book is the revised version of a thesis presented to the University of Manchester in 1985. I have for many years been fascinated by St. Symeon the New Theologian, and I am very grateful to Dr. Rosemary Morris, my supervisor, and to all who have helped me to study him and his background in Byzantium. I wish also to thank my son, Francis Turner, for instructing me in the use of the word-processor by means of which the final text has been produced.

H.J.M. Turner.

Frinton-on-Sea,
Essex.

May, 1988.

SELECT BIBLIOGRAPHY

St. Symeon the New Theologian: —

Catecheses
    Catéchèses, t. I, II, III, Sources Chrétiennes 96, 104, 113, Paris, 1963, 1964, 1965; edited by B. Krivochéine, French translation and additional notes by J. Paramelle.

Chapters
    Chapitres théologiques, gnostiques et pratiques. Sources Chrétiennes 51, Paris, 1st edit. 1957, 2nd 1980; edited, with French translation, by J. Darrouzès, L. Neyrand collaborating in 2nd edit.

Hymns
    Hymnes, t. I, II, III, Sources Chrétiennes 156, 174, 196, Paris, 1969, 1971, 1973; *I*, edited by J. Koder, French translation by J. Paramelle, *II*, text edited by J. Koder, French translation and notes by L. Neyrand, *III*, text edited by J. Koder, French translation and notes by J. Paramelle and L. Neyrand.

    Hymnen: Prolegomena, kritischer Text, Indices; edited by A. Kambylis, *Supplementa Byzantina* 3, Berlin/New York, 1976.

Treatises
    Traités théologiques et éthiques, t. I, II, Sources Chrétiennes 122, 129, Paris, 1966, 1967; edited, with French translation, by J. Darrouzès.

Epistles
    Epistle 1 (De Confessione), text printed by K. Holl, q.v. below, *Enthusiasmus und Bussgewalt*, pp. 110–127.

    Epistles 2 and 3; text in *Coislin 292* and *Vaticanus graecus 1782*, photocopies of which were lent by B. Krivochéine.

    Epistle 4; transcript of text in *Coislin 292*, made by B. Krivochéine.

Nicetas Stethatos
    Life of our holy father Symeon the New Theologian, priest and hegumen of St. Mamas of Xerocercos. (Edited by I. Hausherr, with a French translation of the text made in collaboration with G. Horn, and published with the title: — *Un grand mystique byzantin: Vie de Syméon le Nouveau Théologien. Orientalia Christiana* XII, 45, Rome, 1928.)

R.J. Barringer
    Ecclesiastical Penance in the Church of Constantinople: A Study of the Hagiographical Evidence to 983 A.D., Oxford D. Phil. thesis, 1979.
N.H. Baynes and H.St.L.B. Moss (edd.)
    Byzantium, Oxford, 1948 (including, G. Buckler, 'Byzantine Education' and H. Delehaye, 'Byzantine Monasticism').
H.-G. Beck
    Kirche und theologisch Literatur im byzantinischen Reich, Munich, 1959.
H.M. Biedermann
    'Novizenunterweisung in Byzanz um die Jahrtausendwende,' *Ostkirkliche Studien*, I, (1952), pp. 16–31.

P. Brown
  'The Rise and Function of the Holy Man in Late Antiquity,' *Journal of Roman Studies*,
  LXI, (1971), pp. 80–101.
D.J. Chitty
  The Desert a City, Oxford, 1966.
V.C. Christophorides
  ἡ πνευματικὴ πατρότης κατὰ Συμεῶν τὸν Νέον Θεόλογον, (*Spiritual Fatherhood according
  to Symeon the New Theologian*), Thessalonica, 1977.
Cosmas
  Le traité contre les Bogomiles de Cosmas le prêtre, edited and translated by H.-C. Puech
  and A. Vaillant, Paris, 1945.
St. Dorotheus of Gaza
  Dorothée de Gaza: Oeuvres spirituelles, Sources Chrétiennes 92, edited with a French trans-
  lation by L. Regnault and J. de Préville, Paris, 1963. (Includes *Life* of St. Dositheus)
H. Dörries
  'The Place of Confession in Ancient Monasticism,' *Texte und Untersuchungen* 80,
  Berlin, (1962), pp. 284–311.
Euchologion
  ed. Zerbos, Venice, 6th edit., 1891.
F.W. Faber
  Growth in Holiness, London, 3rd edit., 1859, reprinted 1928.
B. Fraigneau-Julien
  Les sens spirituels et la vision de Dieu selon Syméon le Nouveau Théologien, Paris, 1985.
P. Gautier
  'Le *typikon* de la *Théotokos Évergétis*,' *Revue des Études Byzantines*, 40, (1982), pp. 5–101.
J. Gouillard
  '*Constantin Chrysomallos sous le masque de Syméon le Nouveau Théologien*,' *Travaux et Mémoires
  V*, Centre de recherche d'histoire et civilisation de Byzance, 1973, pp. 313–328.
J. Gouillard
  'Quatre Procès de mystiques à Byzance (vers 960–1143),' *Revue des Études Byzantines*,
  36, (1978), pp. 5–81.
J. Gouillard
  '*Syméon le Jeune, le Théologien, ou le Nouveau Théologien*,' article in *Dictionnaire de Théologie
  Catholique*, XIV, 2, Paris, 1941.
H. Graef
  'The Spiritual Director in the Thought of Symeon the New Theologian,' *Kyriakon—
  Festschrift Johannes Quasten*, (edd. P. Cranfield and J.A. Jungmann), Münster, 1970,
  II, 608–614.
S. Hackel (ed.)
  The Byzantine Saint, London, 1981, (including R. Morris, 'The Political Saint of the
  Eleventh Century,' P. Magdalino, 'The Byzantine Holy Man of the Twelfth Cen-
  tury' and L. Rydén, 'The Holy Fool').
F. Halkin
  Saints moines d'Orient, London (Variorum Reprints), 1973.
I. Hausherr
  Direction spirituelle en Orient autrefois, Orientalia Christiana Analecta, 144, (1955), Rome.
K. Holl
  *Enthusiasmus und Bussgewalt beim griechischen Mönchtum: Eine Studie zu Symeon dem Neuen
  Theologen*, Leipzig, 1898 (reprinted 1969).
J.M. Hussey
  'Ascetics and Humanists in 11th century Byzantium,' *Friends of Dr. Williams' Library
  Lecture 13*, 1960.
J.M. Hussey
  The Byzantine Empire: Government Church and Civilisation, Cambridge Medieval History,
  IV, ii, Cambridge, 1967.

J.M. Hussey
The Byzantine World, London, 1957.
J.M. Hussey
Church and Learning in the Byzantine Empire, 867–1185, Oxford, 1937.
R. Janin
La géographie ecclésiastique de l'empire byzantin—Première partie: Le siège de Constantinople et le patriarcat oecuménique; III, Les églises et les monastères, Paris, 2nd edit., 1969.
St. John Climacus
Liber ad Pastorem, Patrologia Graeca 88, Paris, 1864, cols. 1165–1210.
St. John Climacus
Scala Paradisi, Patrologia Graeca 88, Paris, 1864, cols. 623–1164. (English translation by C. Luibheid and N. Russell, *The Ladder of Divine Ascent*, with notes by N. Russell, introduction by K. Ware, preface by C. Luibheid, London, 1982.)
A. Kazhdan and G. Constable
People and Power in Byzantium, Dumbarton Oaks, 1982.
B. Krivochéine
'The Brother-Loving Poor Man,' *The Christian East*, N.S. II, (1953–54), pp. 216–227.
B. Krivochéne
Dans la lumière du Christ: Saint Syméon le Nouveau Théologien, 949–1022: Vie, spiritualité, doctrine, Chevetogne, 1980. (English translation by A.P. Gythiel, *In the Light of Christ*, St. Vladimir's Seminary, New York, 1987; translation into modern Greek, Μέσα στὸ φῶς τοῦ Χριστοῦ, Thessalonica, 1983.)
B. Krivochéine
'The Most Enthusiastic Zealot,' *Ostkirkliche Studien*, IV, (1955), pp. 108–128.
B. Krivochéine
'The Writings of St. Symeon the New Theologian,' *Orientalia Christiana Periodica*, 20, (1954), pp. 323–326.
G.W. Lampe
A Patristic Greek Lexicon, Oxford, 1961.
P. Lemerle
Le premier humanisme byzantin, Paris, 1971.
G.A. Maloney
The Mystic of Fire and Light, Denville, N.J., 1975.
C. Mango
Byzantium: the Empire of New Rome, London, 1980.
E.A. de Mendieta
L'ascèse monastique de S. Basile, Maredsous, 1949.
E.A. de Mendieta
Mount Athos, the Garden of the Panaghia, Berlin, 1972.
N.F. Robinson
Monasticism in the Orthodox Churches, London, 1916.
I. Rosenthal-Kamarinea
'Symeon Studites, ein heiliger Narr,' *Akten des XI internationale Byzantinisten Kongresses*, 1958, pp. 515–520.
I. Rosenthal-Kamarinea
'Symeon der Neue Theologe und Symeon Studites,' *Oekumenische Einheit* 3, (1952), pp. 103–120.
P. Rousseau
Ascetics, Authority and the Church, Oxford, 1973.
J. van Rossum
'Priesthood and Confession in St. Symeon the New Theologian,' *St. Vladimir's Theological Quarterly*, 20, (1976), pp. 220–228.
J. Saward
Perfect Fools: Folly for Christ's Sake in Catholic and Orthodox Spirituality, Oxford, 1980.

Symeon the Studite
    Chapters—v. under Abbreviations/ Method of Citation, and chapter IV, pp. 64–65.
W. Völker
    Praxis und Theoria bei Symeon dem Neuen Theologen: *Ein Beitrag zur byzantinischen Mystik*,
    Wiesbaden, 1974.
A. Vööbus
    History of Asceticism in the Syrian Orient—II: *Early Monasticism in Mesopotamia and Syria*
    (*Corpus Scriptorum Christianorum Orientalium*, Vol. 197, Subsidia 17), Louvain, 1960.
B. Ward
    The Wisdom of the Desert Fathers—Apophthegmata Patrum (*The Anonymous Series*), (trans-
    lated and with introduction), Fairacres, Oxford, 1975.
K. Ware
    'The Spiritual Father in Orthodox Christianity,' *Cross Currents* XXIV, (1974),
    pp. 296–313.

For quotations from the Bible the Revised Standard Version has normally been used; the
LXX reference is given first, when there is a difference in numbering, and that of the
English Bible follows in brackets.

ABBREVIATIONS/METHOD OF CITATION

The works of Symeon published in the *Sources Chrétiennes* series (*SC*) have been treated as follows: —

Cat I, etc. (followed by Arabic figures) denotes the *Catéchèse* (and line or lines) so numbered in *SC* 96 (*Cats I–V*), 104 (*Cats VI–XXII*) and 113 (*Cats XXIII–XXXVI*). Krivochéine, *SC* 96, intr. p. . . ., (n. . . .), refers to B. Krivochéine's introduction specifying page (and note), Krivochéine, *SC* . . ., p. . . ., n. . . ., relates to his notes on matters in the text, and Paramelle, p. . . . similarly to J. Paramelle's additional notes.

Ch I, 1 etc. (followed by Arabic figures) denotes the 'century' (I, II or III) and *Chapitre* (and line or lines) so numbered in *SC* 51 (*Chapitres Théologiques, Gnosqitues et Pratiques*). Darrouzès, *SC* 51, intr. p. . . ., (n. . . .), refers to J. Darrouzès' introduction, specifying page (and note). Darrouzès, *SC* 51, p. . . ., n. . . ., relates to his notes on matters in the text. (Although L. Neyrand co-operated in this 2nd edition, there is no clear indication of exactly what comes from his pen.)

Hymn I, etc. (followed by Arabic figures) denotes the *Hymne* (and line or lines) so numbered in *SC* 156 (*Hymns I–XV*), 174 (*Hymns XVI–XL*) and 196 (*Hymns XLI–LVIII*). The method of referring to J. Koder's introduction, and to notes on matters in the text by him, L. Neyrand and J. Paramelle, is the same as that used for the *Catéchèses*.

Tr Th/Eth I etc. (followed by Arabic figures) denotes the *Tr Th/Eth* (and line or lines) so numbered in *SC* 122 (*Trs Th I–III, Trs Eth I–III*) and 129 (*Trs Eth IV–XV*). The method of referring to J. Darrouzès' introduction, and to his notes on matters in the text, is the same as that used for the *Chapitres*.

Ep 1 denotes Epistle 1 (*De Confessione*), edited by K. Holl in *Enthusiasmus und Bussgewalt*, the figures following p. . . ., indicating line(s) on the page.

Ep 2 (or *3*) denotes *Epistle 2* (or *3*), with pages in the manuscript *Vaticanus Graecus* 1782 indicated by 206r etc.

Ep 4 denotes *Epistle 4*, the figures following indicating line(s) in Krivochéine's handwritten transcript of *Coislin* 292.

Nicetas, *Life*, denotes Nicetas' *Life of Symeon* (ed. Hausherr), with the first figure(s) following indicating chapter(s) and the next line(s).

Hausherr, *Life*, denotes Hausherr's introduction to the above, with p. I etc. indicating the page(s), which are numbered in Roman figures.

A.V.
    Bible, Authorised Version.
Barringer, *Penance*
    R.J. Barringer, *Ecclesiastical Penance in the Church of Constantinople.*
Climacus, *ad Pastorem*
    St. John Climacus, *Liber ad Pastorem.*
Climacus, *Sc. Par.*
    St. John Climacus, *Scala Paradisi.* (Luibheid, Russell, Ware, *Climacus* refer to their respective contributions to John Climacus, *The Ladder of Divine Ascent.*)

C.S.E.L.
  Corpus Scriptorum Ecclesiasticorum Latinorum.
C.S.H.B.
  Corpus Scriptorum Historiae Byzantinae.
Cosmas, *Traité*
  Le traité contre les Bogomiles de Cosmas le prêtre.
Dorotheus, *Doctrinae, Epistolae, Sententiae*
  St. Dorotheus of Gaza, works so named, cited from *SC* 92.
Dörries, 'Confession'
  H. Dörries, 'The Place of Confession in Ancient Monasticism.'
Graef, 'Spiritual Director'
  H. Graef, 'The Spiritual Director in the Thought of Symeon the New Theologian.'
Hausherr, *Direction spirituelle*
  I. Hausherr, *Direction spirituelle en Orient autrefois.*
Hausherr, *Life*
  I. Hausherr, *Un grand mystique byzantin: Vie de Syméon le Nouveau Théologien.*
Holl, *Enthusiasmus*
  K. Holl, *Enthusiasmus und Bussgewalt beim griechischen mönchtum: Eine Studie zu Symeon
  dem Neuen Theologen.*
Janin, *Églises et monastères*
  R. Janin, *La géographie ecclésiastique . . . III: Les églises et les monastères.*
J.R.S.
  Journal of Roman Studies.
Krivochéine, *Lumière*
  B. Krivochéine, *Dans la lumière du Christ*
Lampe, *Lexicon*
  G.W. Lampe, *A Patristic Greek Lexicon.*
Lemerle, *Premier humanisme*
  P. Lemerle, *Le premier humanisme byzantin.*
Mango, *Byzantium*
  C. Mango, *Byzantium: The Empire of New Rome.*
N.E.B.
  New English Bible.
O.C.A.
  Orientalia Christiana Analecta.
O.C.P.
  Orientalia Christiana Periodica.
R.E.B.
  Revue des Études Byzantines.
Regnault and de Préville, *Dorotheus, SC* 92
  L. Regnault and J. de Préville, introduction/notes to *Dorothée de Gaza: Oeuvres
  spirituelles, SC* 92.
Rousseau, *Ascetics*
  P. Rousseau, *Ascetics, Authority and the Church.*
Studite, *Ch(s)* . . .
  Symeon the Studite, *Chapters*, numbered as 120–152 in *PG* 668C–685C. N.B. *Ch* 36,
  which is not in *PG*, is cited from Hausherr's French translation, *Life*, pp. XLIXf.
T.U.
  Texte und Untersuchungen.
Völker, *Praxis*
  W. Völker, *Praxis und Theoria bei Symeon dem Neuen Theologen: Ein Beitrag zur byzan-
  tinischen Mystik.*
Vööbus, *Early Monasticism*
  A. Vööbus, *History of Asceticism . . . II: Early Monasticism in Mesopotamia and Syria.*
Ward, *Desert Fathers*
  B. Ward, *The Wisdom of the Desert Fathers—Apophthegmata Patrum (The Anonymous Series).*

GLOSSARY

A few Greek terms, which are important in a study of Symeon, present difficulties for the translator, or seem to require some explanatory comment. They are here collected together in a short glossary, from which, however, words fully discussed in the text have mostly been excluded.

ἅγιος—'holy', 'saint'. Difficulty arises because the Greek corresponds to two English words, the latter being used as a title, eg. 'Saint' Andrew. It must thus be remembered that when Symeon insisted that his spiritual father was ἅγιος, the word, which after all is also used of the Holy Spirit, conveyed to him and to his hearers or readers both the idea of 'holy' and also that of 'saint'.

ἀπάθεια (ἀπαθής)—'dispassion' ('dispassionate'). This rendering, which is that of Luibheid and Russell in *Climacus*, has the advantage of being able to convey a meaning different from that of the Stoics' 'passionlessness'. For a discussion of the meaning in Christian writers, v. chapter VII, iii).

ἐκκοπὴ θελήματος—'elimination of one's own will.' In spite of its not being an exact translation of ἐκκοπή, this translation seems to convey well the general meaning. θέλημα, however, requires further comment, which is provided by a quotation referring to St. Dorotheus of Gaza: "Like most of the holy fathers of Eastern monasticism, [he] understands by one's own will not only, as do many modern spiritual authorities, attachment to one's own will, but also the whole range of wills, or rather of desires, which spontaneously arise in the soul and are usually the result of a *logismos*." (J.M. Ezymusiak and J. Leroy, *Dictionnaire de Spiritualité*, III, Paris, 1957, col. 1659).

ἡσυχία—has been left untranslated and untransliterated. It denotes in this book a withdrawal from normal community life and its accompanying responsibilities, in order to be free to experience spiritual reality more directly and intensely.

ἰδιορρυθμία—the disparaging implications of living 'without direction' are well brought out in a scholium to Climacus, where it is described as 'having one's own life-style (ἰδία τάξις) and accomplishing one's own will.' *Sc. Par.* 27, PG 88, 1117 BC. As a type of monasticism, idiorrhythmism, "appeared on Mount Athos about the year 1374". (N.F. Robinson, *Monasticism in the Orthodox Churches*, London, 1916, p. 8) From that time onwards, at least by those who approve of idiorrhythmic monasteries, the word can be used in a good sense. (cf. Hausherr, *Direction spirituelle*, p. 122)

λογισμός—'thought'. This rendering appears inevitable, even though in some respects it is quite inadequate. Ware (*Climacus*, p. 38) rightly states that λογισμοί "may be neutral or God-inspired as well as sinful," but there is a distinct tendency for them to be regarded with suspicion by the writers quoted in this book. "In the language of monasticism this term has almost always a pejorative sense." (Paramelle and Neyrand, *SC* 196, p. 186, n. 2).

μεσίτης—Lampe's *Lexicon* gives examples of this word's being used, in the sense of 'mediator', not only of Christ, but also of others who may play a part in the reconciling of people to God, for example clergy, and holy men (saints), both living and departed. Thus, although 'mediator' will seem strange to those accustomed theologically to apply the word solely to Christ, it is best to retain it in all cases as the rendering of μεσίτης.

μετάνοια—'repentance' or 'prostration'. The context alone can determine which is the correct translation. (It is to be noted that γονυκλισία, 'genuflexion', is less reverential than μετάνοια used in the sense of 'prostration')

νοῦς (νοερός, νοητός)—the rendering 'intellect' ('intellectual') has generally been avoided, and instead 'spirit' ('spiritual') has been preferred. There is no single English word which gives the exact flavour of the Greek, relating as it does to that element in mankind "by origin or nature fitted to receive the knowledge of God." (Hausherr, 'Ignorance infinie,' *O.C.A.*, 176, (1966), p. 44).

πίστις—a uniform translation is impossible, and the context has to determine whether this word is to be rendered 'faith', 'trust', 'faithfulness' or 'loyalty'.

Transliteration—A Note

In the transliteration of Greek words, there is no attempt to differentiate between 'ε' and 'η', or 'o' and 'ω', while 'ου' is represented by 'u', and 'υ' by 'y'. Apart from the foregoing, all Greek letters are represented by those which most nearly correspond to them in English. Thus 'τυπικόν' is written '*typikon*', and 'ἡγούμενος' has been Anglicised as 'hegumen', without a case-ending. Exceptions to these principles will be found in cases in which custom has come to dictate a different rendering, and also in quotations, where the author's method of transliteration has been followed.

CHAPTER ONE

INTRODUCTORY

"He is the greatest of Byzantine mystical writers"—such is the verdict on Symeon in the *Oxford Dictionary of the Christian Church*,[1] and there is no doubt that it is because of his importance in the history of mysticism that he has mostly been studied. There is, however, no reason why interest in him should be limited to that single aspect, an aspect which in this book is, so far as possible, being deliberately left to one side. Instead, attention is to be focused on his life and work in connection with spiritual father-hood, and although spiritual fatherhood in itself is too vast a subject to be fully discussed here, it is of course bound to come under scrutiny to the extent that is necessary for the purpose of illuminating Symeon's experience and his writings.

Such an approach to Symeon might be thought unduly restricted, but in fact he provides more than ample material for examination. Moreover, it is worthwhile to attempt a study of this nature, in which his experience of spiritual fatherhood will be looked at in conjunction with his teaching about it, because through Symeon it is possible to gain important insights into the theory and practice of this ministry, in which there is nowadays a growing interest.

This interest is shown by the publication of several books, two of which may be taken as examples. In *Soul Friend*, in which Symeon is referred to, K. Leech states that he has attempted

> to provide some nourishment for this important ministry by drawing on the teachings of the great spiritual guides,

and the work demonstrates the significant place which spiritual father-hood holds in the Christian tradition. M. Thornton's *Spiritual Direction*, where Symeon's only appearance is in a diagram, is intended as a professional course of study for those embarking on

> this much needed form of pastoral ministry ... who are prepared to work at it seriously and continuously.

It is interesting, in view of what we shall discover in studying Symeon, that one aspect of the director's work specifically mentioned in Thornton's

---

[1] F.L. Cross and E.A. Livingstone, *The Oxford Dictionary of the Christian Church*, Oxford, 2nd edit. 1974, p. 1275.

book is "to guide prayer, to deepen the relationship between God and man in Christ." At a time when matters such as these are increasingly being discussed, it is not a waste of effort to investigate Symeon's experience and his teaching.[2]

From passages in Symeon's own works, supplemented by (and interpreted in connection with) his biography written by Nicetas Stethatos, we can learn a good deal about his relationship with his spiritual father, another Symeon and a monk of the Studios monastery. (In order to avoid confusion the latter will henceforth normally be referred to as 'the Studite'.) For the period when Symeon in his turn became a spiritual father himself, much evidence is available, partly from the biography, but mostly from his own writings, both about the way in which he sought to fulfil the duties pertaining to this role and also about his teaching on the subject. We can moreover trace, to a considerable extent, how Symeon's personal experience interacted both with his original ideas about spiritual fatherhood, and with what he received from the traditional wisdom of the past as he became familiar with it. All this can provide insights and suggestions which arise from the career and the teaching of a great personality of long ago, but are far from irrelevant to the interests and concerns of to-day.

Much scholarly work in connection with Symeon has been undertaken, particularly in recent years, but as already stated, it is as a mystic that he has attracted most attention. While there have been, as we shall see in what follows, various articles or single chapters referring to his experience as the Studite's disciple and to his work as a spiritual father, there has apparently as yet been only one longer attempt to study Symeon primarily from this angle. A brief review of a selection of works illustrates the way in which the theme of spiritual fatherhood has hitherto, especially by writers in English, been accorded only a relatively minor place in studies of Symeon.

I. Hausherr's important edition of Nicetas' *Life of Symeon* will be discussed when we come to deal with sources. For the moment it is sufficient simply to call attention to the lengthy introduction in which Hausherr dealt *inter alia* with the chronology of the lives of Symeon and of the Studite, with Symeon's character and with the conflicts in which he was

---

[2] Other books recently published and dealing with similar subjects include: M.T. Kelsey, *Companions of the Inner Way: The Art of Spiritual Guidance*, New York, 1983; W. Barry and W. Connolly, *The Practice of Spiritual Direction*, London, 1984; T.C. Oden, *Care of Souls in the Classic Tradition*, Philadelphia, 1984; and G.H. Jeff, *Spiritual Direction for Every Christian*, London, 1987. In an article in *Theology*, September 1987, R. Greenwood wrote of the need for spiritual directors.

engaged, as well giving a convincing description of Nicetas as a writer, his purpose and his methods.

Under the heading of sources something will also have to be said about K. Holl's *Enthusiasmus und Bussgewalt beim griechischen Mönchtum*, inasmuch as it contains the text of one of Symeon's letters, *De Confessione*, classified as *Ep 1*. But the very title of Holl's book might seem to suggest that, contrary to what has just been stated, at least one aspect of the work of a spiritual father was studied in a major piece of scholarship published as long ago as 1898. However, in spite of all that he did to rescue Symeon from the general ignorance about him which prevailed in Western Europe and America, Holl did not examine in any detail the actual ways in which as a spiritual father he undertook the task of guiding others in accordance with his ideals. Holl's concern was chiefly to set forth his own interpretation of the history of monasticism and of the penitential system in the Eastern Church. As he sought to find support for Symeon's contention that monks who are truly spiritual, even though they may be unordained, have divine authority to hear confessions and to bestow absolution, he came naturally to emphasise the significance of holiness and charismatic gifts, and the important place which they held in the monastic tradition among the qualities needed by a spiritual father. All this led Holl to attempt to depict monks as ''enthusiasts'', ever likely to come into conflict with an ecclesiastical hierarchy which naturally tends to stress the requirement of submission to duly constituted authority. Holl's was, of course, a work of great value, not least for the subsequent interest in Symeon which it excited, but it scarcely entered upon the areas relating to the actual conduct of a father towards his spiritual children, clients or disciples (and *vice versa*), which are to be investigated in the following chapters. (To avoid monotony, 'spiritual children,' 'clients' and 'disciples' are used as synonyms throughout this book.)

The concentration of interest upon Symeon as a mystic is shown in the titles of three books which must next be mentioned. W. Völker's *Praxis und Theoria bei Symeon dem Neuen Theologen*: *Ein Beitrag zur byzantinischen Mystik* contains only one chapter which specifically treats of Symeon in the role of spiritual father, but is important as demonstrating his many affinities with John Climacus. G.A. Maloney's *The Mystic of Fire and Light*: *St. Symeon the New Theologian* is notable as being apparently the first full-length book on Symeon to be written in English, but by the first words of its title reveals the main object of its author's interest. It may be added that this impression of where Maloney's sympathies lie is confirmed by a reading of the introduction which he contributed to a later work, the translation of Symeon's *catecheses* into English. Here not only is there no mention whatever of spiritual fatherhood in all that is written about Symeon, but even when discussing his exile Maloney fails to mention that the cause of this was, in part at least, the controverted question of the sanctity or lack of sanctity observable in the behaviour of his father the Studite. Lastly, B. Fraigneau-Julien's *Les sens spirituels et la vision de Dieu selon Syméon le Nouveau Théologien* is a detailed study of particular aspects of Symeon's mysticism.[3]

B. Krivochéine's full-scale study of Symeon, *Dans la lumière du Christ: Saint Syméon le Nouveau Théologien, 949–1022: Vie—Spiritualité—Doctrine*, amply justifies its title, but contains no more than one chapter dealing explicitly with spiritual direction and spiritual fatherhood. As well as this, however, there are also many important observations with a bearing on these subjects, which can be found scattered throughout the book.[4]

A work in modern Greek which does treat of Symeon as a spiritual father was published in 1977 by V.C. Christophorides as a doctoral dissertation for the Theological School of the University of Thessalonica. It is entitled ἡ πνευματικὴ πατρότης κατὰ Συμεὼν τὸν Νέον Θεολόγον (*Spiritual Fatherhood according to Symeon the New Theologian*), and inevitably refers to many of the topics which will be considered in this present work. However, as a contemporary member of the Orthodox Church in Greece, Christophorides naturally writes from his own standpoint which leads him into questions which may be of little interest to non-Orthodox readers, as when, for instance, he inserts a chapter in which he discusses, on the basis of ecclesiastical authority, whether a spiritual father ought of necessity to be a priest and a hegumen. Furthermore as his title suggests, Christophorides starts from spiritual fatherhood as an institution, whereas in this book our attention will be concentrated on Symeon himself, so that his background, his experience and his writings, particularly those parts of them which have to do with training, will be considered in much more detail than in Christophorides' work. The result is that in spite of the similarity suggested by the titles, the two books differ from one another in very many respects. It is interesting, nevertheless, that already in 1977 spiritual fatherhood was being seen as a matter in need of discussion,

---

[3] Völker had previously written *Scala Paradisi: Eine Studie zu Johannes Climacus und zugleich eine Vorstudie zu Symeon dem Neuen Theologen*, Wiesbaden, 1968. In 1976 there appeared Maloney's translation of the *Hymns of Divine Love by St. Symeon the New Theologien*. He also wrote the introduction to *Symeon the New Theologien—The Discourses*, (1980) C.J. de Catanzaro's translation of the *catecheses*. It is appropriate also to notice here: *Symeon the New Theologian: The Practical and Theological Chapters and the Three Theological Discourses*, translated by P. McGuckin (1982). A great many of Symeon's works are thus now available in English.

[4] As noted in the Bibliography, an English translation has now appeared, but since it was not available until this book was nearly completed, quotations from Krivochéine's work are my own renderings of the French original.

and one concerning which much can be gained from a study of Symeon.

Passing from full-length studies to articles and similar material, we must notice first that in 1952 H.M. Biedermann, in *Novizenunterweisung in Byzanz um die Jahrtausendwende*, described Symeon's method of training monastic novices, a matter closely connected with the work of a hegumen as his monks' spiritual father. Biedermann drew in particular on *Cat XXVI*, though unfortunately at the date of writing he did not have access to the Greek original, but only to Pontanus' Latin version printed by Migne as *Oratio XXV*. The brevity of the article, as well as the fact that it concentrates upon novices, means that although interesting it can make only a limited contribution to the understanding of Symeon and spiritual fatherhood.[5]

The Spiritual Director in the Thought of Symeon the New Theologian, an even shorter article, was written in 1970 by H. Graef. She touched on the relationship of Symeon with the Studite, on the question of the latter's sanctity, on the "identification of the spiritual director with Christ" in *Cat XX*, and on other topics including the qualifications for spiritual fatherhood prescribed in *Cat XXVIII*. In a brief space, however, it was not possible for her to do justice to all these important points.

J. van Rossum was the author of another and more recent article, the title of which suggests that it bears directly on our subject, though in fact *Priesthood and Confession in St. Symeon the New Theologian* does so only marginally. Van Rossum's concern was to discuss the contention of Symeon, notably in *Ep 1* but also in *Cat XXVIII*, that to hear confessions and grant absolution it is not necessary to have been ordained priest, but that what is indispensable is to have truly and consciously received the Holy Spirit. By treating the subject exclusively from this point of view van Rossum did not enter upon most of the matters which we are to consider.

Two articles by I. Rosenthal-Kamarinea must also be mentioned: in *Symeon der Neue Theologe und Symeon Stylites* she examined the relationship between the two men on the basis chiefly of Nicetas' biography and of passages in some of Symeon's *Hymns*. Her somewhat fanciful and very sentimental picture of the New Theologian was justly criticised by Krivochéine.[6] However, the other article, *Symeon Studites, ein heiliger Narr*, is an important contribution to our understanding of the Studite, for in it she produces strong reasons for thinking that he ought to be regarded

---

[5] *Oratio XXV*, *PG* 120, 4400–4478. Biedermann had previously written *Das Menschenbild bei Symeon dem Jungeren, dem Theologen (949–1022)*, in *Das Östliche Christentum*, New Series 9, 1949.

[6] Krivochéine's comments on Rosenthal-Kamarinea are to be found in his article, *The Most Enthusiastic Zealot*, referred to in the next paragraph.

as a "holy fool," in spite of the fact that nowhere is he explicitly so styled.

The way that interest in Symeon as a mystic has predominated is exemplified by J. Gouillard's article in the *Dictionnaire de Théologie Catholique* which concentrated on his greatness in this field and devoted only a few sentences to him in connection with spiritual fatherhood. Somewhat similarly J.M. Hussey, in her *Church and Learning in the Byzantine Empire, 867–1185*, referred many times to Symeon, especially when treating of monastic life, and included a whole chapter dealing with him as a mystic. Again, Krivochéine in his article, *The Brother-Loving Poor Man*, after a short account of the earlier part of Symeon's career, dealt almost entirely with his mystical experiences, albeit emphasising his desire that the spiritual treasures he had discovered should be shared by his monks. Subsequently, in *The Most Enthusiastic Zealot*, Krivochéine studied Symeon's activities as hegumen and the way in which "he endeavoured to accomplish his 'apostolate of mysticism'." In this article he made valuable comments concerning the tensions to which this endeavour gave rise, but he was of course in no sense attempting to describe the full extent of Symeon's work as a spiritual father.

Naturally, references to Symeon can be found in much material not specifically dealing with him. It may suffice to notice here Hausherr's *Direction spirituelle en Orient autrefois* in which, as might be expected, he is often mentioned, although his activity is not described in the detailed manner now to be attempted.

This short survey of items written in the course of the last ninety years reveals that Symeon's contribution to our understanding of spiritual fatherhood has only once been studied in any depth, and in particular has failed to attract much attention amongst scholars writing in English. It must not, of course, be supposed that Symeon is the only patristic writer whom it would be profitable to study along these lines. Much could be learned, for instance, if the letters of Barsanuphius and John the Prophet to Dorotheus of Gaza, their spiritual child, were examined in connection with Dorotheus' own writings.[7] But although the latter contain several autobiographical touches, there is nothing in them comparable with the many passages in which Symeon reveals so clearly what he felt about his relationship with the Studite and his consciousness of the immense debt that he owed him. There is therefore good reason for claiming that

---

[7] cf. L. Regnault, P. Lemaire and B. Outtier, *Barsanuphe et Jean de Gaza: Correspondance*, Solesmes, 1972. But it is interesting that M.B. Pennington (*O Holy Mountain*, London, 1980, p. 100) remarks that on a visit to Mount Athos he was recommended, "in regard to the role of the spiritual father" to read "St. Symeon the New Theologian and the chapter to pastors at the end of St. John Climacus' *Ladder*."

Symeon occupies an important place in the history of spiritual fatherhood, and for examining, both in the records of his experience and in the teaching which he gave, as much as possible of the large amount of valuable material that is available. This can greatly increase understanding of the subject, and of what it has involved and may involve both in theory and practice.

For this reason, then, St. Symeon the New Theologian has been chosen as our theme, and it is desirable now to say a little about the method of proceeding. The necessary background material will first be presented in order to provide a general frame of reference. We shall begin with a description of the sources of our information, followed by an outline of Symeon's life, and an examination of his inheritance from the past and of the chief influences which can be seen to have affected him. All this will be undertaken not in order to produce a total study of Symeon, but with the intention of highlighting matters which may have a bearing on his experience of spiritual fatherhood and his teaching concerning it.

Thereafter these themes will be approached from a variety of angles. Traditional points of view will be delineated so as to provide a standard with which to compare Symeon as different aspects are investigated in turn. Since John Climacus can be shown to have greatly influenced Symeon, he will therefore be utilised as a principal, though not as the only, representative of the traditional wisdom concerning spiritual direction. Anecdotes found in Climacus, in the Desert Fathers and elsewhere, will be cited because they were often the vehicles by which teaching was conveyed. Since Symeon and his contemporaries had no difficulty in accepting accounts of miracles and similar happenings, there will be no need to spend time on an investigation of their factual reliability; traditional material will be used for the purpose of providing a criterion whereby Symeon's debt to the past, and therefore also his originality, can be estimated.[8]

In order to illustrate Symeon's experience and his teaching, it will be necessary to include many quotations.[9] These will be presented along with the necessary explanations and comments, so that they may take their proper place in an ordered exposition of the themes of the successive

---

[8] Regarding miracles, cf. Hausherr's remark about the Fathers: "Qu'ils aient cru aux miracles, c'est l'évidence même, Mais ils n'ont pas attribué à un miracle toutes les merveilles qu'ils opéraient ou voyaient opérer." (*Direction spirituelle*, p. 47)

[9] Quotations in the text are almost always given in translation, and unless otherwise stated the renderings from whatever language are my own, although in interpreting the Greek I have often found assistance in the French translations provided in the *Sources Chrétiennes* series. In quotations, nouns substituted for pronouns or words added to clarify the meaning are enclosed in brackets [. . .].

chapters. These themes are, of course, interconnected, and in consequence the division into chapters and sections cannot but appear rather
artificial, necessary though it is for the sake of clarity. The plan is thus
that, after preliminary matters have been dealt with in the next three
chapters, there will follow, in chapters V to IX, a full investigation of
Symeon's teaching about spiritual fatherhood in its various aspects. His
teaching will be assessed in the light of his experience, and examples will
be given of his actual practice and its results. It is inevitable that a great
many of the quotations will relate to the life of monks, for there is an abundance of material connected with monasticism but comparatively little
evidence that reveals how spiritual fathers dealt with their clients or disciples living in the world. However, some valuable information can be
gathered from Symeon's *Epistles*, and it will be found that this has been
utilised as much as possible in order to counterbalance the monastic
character of so much of the source-material.

To round off the detailed examination of what can be gathered from
Symeon, a concluding chapter will offer some reflections on the findings.
In this way it is hoped to demonstrate that Symeon, while a man of his
own place and time, does nevertheless provide real illumination both for
all who seek to understand what is involved in spiritual fatherhood in any
age, and for those who are involved in the study and practice of it to-day.

CHAPTER TWO

THE SOURCES

Our knowledge of Symeon is drawn essentially from his own writings and from the *Life* written by Nicetas, his disciple. Apart from these, there is in the fourteenth century a reference to him by David Dishypatos as a mystic who had suffered persecution, while St. Gregory of Sinai recommended him as an author to be read along with Climacus and others.[1]

Nicetas

Although known to Holl, Nicetas' *Life* was not edited and published until 1928, when this was done by I. Hausherr, who, assisted by G. Horn, provided a French translation. It is impossible to say anything very definite about the date of the *Life*, though Hausherr believes that it was probably not written until well after 1054. Whenever he wrote, Nicetas, having in his youth been one of Symeon's disciples and acted as his secretary, came to possess, as he claims, "all his writings." He was able, too, as his narrative makes clear, to draw material from various people who had known Symeon. However, we shall discover that in spite of these advantages he is not always to be relied on, for his purpose in writing was rather to edify than to be exact, or in other words he was not so much a biographer as a hagiographer.[2]

Symeon

Catecheses. Our consideration of Symeon's own writings begins with these, which for the most part originated as spoken discourses to his monks. One or two, however, appear from the first to have been written works, as for example *Cats XVII* and *XX*, and *Cat XXXV*. The latter has much in common with *Cat XXXVI*, and both are primarily addressed to God in thanksgiving for his guidance, being thus similar to St. Augustine's *Confessions*, though on a much smaller scale. The two are included by Krivochéine as *Catecheses*—in *XXXV* at one point Symeon does address "fathers and brethren"—, but are also designated *Eucharistiae 1* and *2*.

---

[1] Dishypatos, *Poem on Akindynos*, 231–241 (ed. R. Browning), *Byzantion*, XXV–XXVII, 1955–57, pp. 713–745; Gregory, *PG* 150, 1324D.

[2] Hausherr, *Life*, pp. XIX–XXI; Nicetas, *Life*, 133, 1–3, 131, 11–12, 140, 7–12.

There is no means of dating individual *Catecheses* other than by internal evidence, and the same holds true for almost all of Symeon's works. Krivochéine points to features of *Cats I, IV, X, XVII, XXI* and *XXIV* which give some indication of their respective dates, and it may be added that *Cat XVIII*, the last third of which is addressed to a newly-appointed hegumen, could well, so far as this part of it goes, have actually been spoken by Symeon at the installation of his disciple and successor Arsenius, in favour of whom he resigned the hegumenate of St. Mamas' monastery in 1005.[3]

The two *Eucharistiae* provide some valuable information about Symeon's life and spiritual development, which supplements or corrects what we learn from Nicetas. Apart from these, which are written in the first person, and apart too from incidental remarks appearing at various points in the *Catecheses* which give glimpses of himself and of his relationship with the Studite, there are some lines in *Cat VI* and most of *XVI* and *XXII*, which though ostensibly referring to persons other than himself, deserve to be regarded as autobiographical. The Studite had taught that when speaking of one's own experiences one should do so very humbly, presenting them as if they were those of another, and we might well expect Symeon to follow this rule when addressing his monks.[4]

In *Cat VI* Symeon's disguise is little more than formal, since he begins with the words "I know a man . . . ," a clear echo of St. Paul, who writes "I know a man in Christ . . ." and continues with a description of a mystical experience which he almost openly claims as his own. Much of *Cat XXII* is in the form of a narrative, the latter part reproduced in direct speech, which Symeon claims to have been told him by "George", a young man who later became a monk, while the account in *Cat XVI* is stated to come from the lips of an unnamed youth, apparently a novice in a monastery.[5]

While the few lines in *Cat VI* can easily be accepted as a shorter form of the narrative in *Cat XXII*, it is not quite so easy to harmonize one feature of the latter with what we find in *Cat XVI*. The difficulty is that towards the end of *Cat XXII*, "George" is represented as saying, after he

---

[3] Krivochéine, *Cats SC* 96, intr. pp. 165f.; *Cat XVIII* begins, "Brother, if you have been appointed hegumen," but then describes the intrigues which may precede an election, before continuing as a charge—Nicetas uses much of the last part as the address which he puts into Symeon's mouth at the installation of Arsenius. (*Life*, 60–67)

[4] Studite, *Ch* 143, 680CD.

[5] *Cat VI*, 121–131; *II Corinthians* 12, 2–5; *Cat XXII*, 22–128, 270–320 (it is possible that in *Cat XXII* Symeon was deliberately adopting a transparent disguise as in *Cat VI*, and if so it might be surmised that before he became a monk, his name in the world had been George); *Cat XVI*, 8–144.

had been a monk for "three or four years," that he had never again had a vision comparable with that vouchsafed to him while still in the world; he had only been "judged worthy so see indistinctly a poor little ray of that most sweet divine light." In *Cat XVI*, on the contrary, the novice describes a wonderful vision granted him in the early days of his monastic life. In spite of this discrepancy, Krivochéine maintains that reliance on *Cat XVI* is defensible, arguing that it is a mistake to look for overmuch precision in these descriptions of mystical phenomena, and that visions involving light may be stronger or weaker without its being easy always to judge of them exactly.[6] Moreover, there is a further argument against giving too much weight to what is said in *Cat XXII*: "George" there admits that he did not act in the right way after the vision but relapsed into worldliness, and Symeon, desirous of impressing on his monks the gravity of this fault, may well have wished to indicate that it had lasting consequences, and therefore deliberately have decided to falsify the actual facts. In spite of some uncertainty, then, *Cat XVI*, may justifiably still be used as a source of autobiographical information.

The *Catecheses* for the most part, however, will concern us for reasons other than their contribution to what may be known about Symeon's personal life; through them we can, as it were, listen to him instructing his monastic spiritual children, and so they can all be claimed as valuable sources for an understanding of his objectives and his methods as a father.

Theological and Ethical Treatises. These, apparently written works from the outset, were addressed to a wider public than the monks of Symeon's monastery, and Darrouzès has shown that in several places they relate to issues raised in the conflict between Symeon and the syncellus, Stephen of Nicomedia. They are on the whole much less lively than the *Catecheses*, and in general of less importance for our purpose in this study, although they do furnish some material which we shall find useful. It is, again, only on internal evidence that attempts at dating can be made, but in view of the controversial elements which can be detected in them, Darrouzès is justified in assigning most of these works to the early years of the eleventh century, when Symeon was being compelled to defend himself against attacks from the syncellus.[7]

---

[6] *Cat XVI*, SC 104, pp. 236–239, n. 2; v. also p. 249, n. 1.

[7] As an example of the wider public, Darrouzès (*Trs SC* 122, intr. p. 13, n. 1) gives *Tr Eth II*, 2, 5, where Symeon addresses "all believers in Christ, both monks and lay-folk." It is nevertheless possible that some of the material now in the *Treatises* may have originated in *Catecheses* no longer extant, cf. *Tr Eth VII*, 22ff., referring to "those who have renounced the world and the things of the world," and *Tr Eth X*, 606, 612, where the vocative, "brethren" occurs twice. For the controversy with Stephen of Nicomedia, v. next chapter and Darrouzès, *op. cit.*, pp. 8–13.

Chapters. Under this heading there are three sections: the first is entitled "One hundred practical and theological Chapters (κεφάλαια πρακτικὰ καὶ θεολογικά);" the second, "Twenty-five other Chapters, both gnostic and theological (κεφάλαια γνωστικά τε καὶ θεολογικά);" and the third, "One hundred other theological and practical Chapters (θεολογικὰ καὶ πρακτικά)." The literary form of "Chapters", which are often no more than brief paragraphs or even single sentences, is common amongst ascetic writers, and the epithets attached to these collections of Symeon's are not unusual. Those styled "practical" are so called because they relate to the practising of the different virtues, the "gnostic" because they have to do with the acquiring of that knowledge which leads from natural enlightenment to enlightenment by the Holy Spirit, and the "theological" because they deal with the contemplation of God, which for Symeon, as for many of his predecessors, is what "theology" really signifies.[8]

Darrouzès has noted some resemblances between certain of the *Chapters* and *Cat XXVIII*, and less striking ones between others and *Trs Eth IV* and *X*. There is, however, no means of telling whether one is original and the other dependent, and if so, which, and there are no internal indications that would help to date the *Chapters* either individually or collectively. Apart from the examples of Symeon's ascetical teaching which they contain, the *Chapters* are useful as sources of information concerning his views on spiritual fatherhood, and this is particularly true of two groups in the first section, I, 24 – 30 and 58 – 62. The perspective from which they were written is definitely monastic, or, as Symeon put it, he intended them for those who were "fleeing from from the world."[9]

Hymns. In spite of their title, these writings in verse are not liturgical compositions; they are, in the main, records of Symeon's personal religious experiences, in several cases colloquies with Christ. A few, however, are didactic or controversial. The *Hymns* furnish much information about Symeon's inner life, and because this and his experience of spiritual fatherhood reacted on one another, we shall discover in them a great deal that is relevant to our theme. One of them can be given an approximate dating, *Hymn XXI*, Symeon's letter in verse to Stephen of Nicomedia, which Koder puts at about 1003, when the conflict between the two was beginning. In other *Hymns* there are various allusions to events in Symeon's life, but none that afford more than a general indication of date, such as references for instance to his work as hegumen.[10]

---

[8] cf. Darrouzès *Chs SC* 51, intr. pp. 40f., n. 1.
[9] Darrouzès, *op. cit.*, pp. 28f.; Symeon, *Ch* I, 15.
[10] Koder, *Hymns SC* 156, intr. pp. 74 – 76.

Epistles. Of the known letters of Symeon, four in number, only the first (edited by Holl, as mentioned in chapter I), has so far appeared in print. Holl demonstrated, on the basis of the evidence in two manuscripts, that it was indeed written by Symeon, in spite of the fact that Lequien had attributed it to St. John of Damascus, on account of its title in the only manuscript available to him. The attempt to father *Ep 1* (*De Confessione*) on John was no doubt inspired by the wish of some editor or scribe to claim an author of unimpeachable orthodoxy for a work that both challenged a commonly accepted view-point and also attacked the conduct of many who belonged to the hierarchy.[11] The contents of the letter are, of course, of great importance in any consideration of spiritual fatherhood, and use will therefore be made of it in this book. At the same time it should be noted—and this is an incidental tribute to its authenticity—that expressions not at all unlike those found in this letter can be discovered also in the *Catecheses* and elsewhere, so that there is no question of our having to rely on *Ep 1* as the sole authority for the kind of teaching it contains, even though it is now generally accepted as a genuine work of Symeon's.

The remaining three letters are still only available in manuscript form, although Holl included in a foot-note some lines from *Ep 2* and Krivochéine presented several extracts from all three.[12] For the purpose of this book, use has been made of photocopies of manuscripts for *Epp 2* and *3*, and of a transcript of the text of *Ep 4* made by Krivochéine. Between them these three letters contain very much that is relevant to the matters we shall be investigating.

Other Works. There are other works which for the sake of completeness ought to be mentioned, in spite of the fact that they will not be used as source-material for reasons which will readily be understood. First to be noticed is one which in all probability was written by Symeon, but the contents of which are irrelevant as far as our present purpose is concerned: this is a short piece, called by Darrouzès "*Dialogue with the Scholastic*," and published by des Places at the end of his edition of the works of Diadochus of Photice. Some manuscripts attribute it to Diadochus, but by far the greater number to Symeon.[13] While this, then, may be regarded as authentic, the "*Method of holy prayer and attentiveness*," or "*Concerning the*

---

[11] Holl, *Enthusiasmus*, pp. 1f., 30–36, 106–109.

[12] Holl—in the original—, *Enthusiasmus*, p. 318, n. 1; Krivochéine—in translation—, *Lumière*, *passim*, but especially in chapter VI. (However, when Krivochéine's book was translated into modern Greek with the title Μέσα στό φῶς τοῦ Χριστοῦ, quotations from Symeon were given in the original.)

[13] Darrouzès, *Chs SC* 51, intr. p. 11; E. des Places, *Diadoque de Photicé: Œuvres spirituelles*, *SC* 5 (2nd edit., 1955), pp. 28f., 80f., 180–183.

three ways of prayer,'' though ascribed to Symeon by some manuscripts, is almost certainly not by him and so will be disregarded.[14]

Finally, reference must be made to the *Orations* and *Alphabetical Orations*, the former of which appear in Migne in Pontanus' Latin translation. Both collections are based on the *Catecheses*, but with frequent alterations, omissions and additions to the original texts. The procedure apparently involved has been described by Krivochéine, who suggests that Nicetas, after preparing his edition of the *Catecheses*, took the further step of adapting them in this way for "a larger circle of readers and one less concerned with monastic matters." The additions will either have been composed by Nicetas himself or else taken by him from the "rough drafts," written by Symeon, which came into his possession. It is noteworthy, as Krivochéine remarks, that the manuscripts do not describe the *Orations* and *Alphabetical Orations* as actual works by Symeon, but as extracts from his writings.[15]

However the responsibility for the additions just referred to cannot be ascribed solely to Nicetas. Gouillard found that there were clear resemblances between passages in the *Orations* and matter taken from the writings of Constantine Chrysomallos, which were condemned by the Synod shortly after the latter's death in 1140. Various theories might be propounded to account for the situation thus brought to light, but what must here be emphasised is that it in no way casts suspicion on the text of the *Catecheses*, since the Chrysomallos material is found only in *Orations*, or parts of an *Oration*, which do not correspond with any *Catechesis*. It is, nevertheless, very interesting that, as Gouillard justifiably argues, the evidence points to some of Chrysomallos' disciples being so convinced that he was a true spiritual descendant of Symeon that they sought to disseminate their master's teaching as if it emanated from the New Theologian and was thus guaranteed by his authority—an ironical quasi-parallel with what occurred, as we saw above, in the case of *Ep 1*.[16]

Manuscripts

Particulars concerning the actual manuscripts on which the published

---

[14] The arguments against authenticity are well presented by Krivochéine, *Lumière*, p. 81, n. 2.

[15] *Cats CS* 96, intr. pp. 172–174; cf. the preceding pages, 166ff., for Nicetas' edition, and v. Nicetas, *Life*, 131, 11–13, 140, 7–18, for his own words about τὰ σχεδιαζόμενα, and about publishing Symeon's works.

[16] J. Gouillard, 'Constantin Chrysomallos sous le masque de Syméon le Nouveau Théologien,' *Travaux et Mémoires*, 5, (1973), pp. 313–317; the writings were condemned as a mixture of enthusiasm, Messalianism and Bogomilism, cf. V. Grumel, *Les Regestes des Actes du Patriarcat de Constantinople*, Vol. I, Fasc. III, no. 1007; regarding the *Catecheses*, cf. Gouillard's citations with the tables given by Krivochéine, *Cats CS* 96, pp. 194–199.

texts are based can be found in the works referred to in this chapter or cited in the Bibliography, and there is no need for further discussion here. Although the variant readings afford valuable material for studies relating to the editing and transmission of the text of Symeon's writings, for the purposes of our present investigation they are of little significance apart from one or two cases which will be discussed as they arise. With regard to the as yet unpublished *Epp 2 – 4*, it should be said that Krivochéine made his transcript of *Ep 4* from *Coislin* 292, and his photocopies of the same manuscript and of *Vaticanus graecus* 1782 have been used for the study of *Epp 2* and *3*. In several places the two manuscripts have been compared with each other, and as far as our theme is concerned no important differences have been found between them. In fact, as will be seen, it is *Vaticanus* that has for the most part been utilised as the authority when quotations have been made.

CHAPTER THREE

SYMEON: BIOGRAPHICAL

Early Life

Before entering upon a detailed study of Symeon in connection with spiritual fatherhood, it seems desirable to give an outline account of his life and career, with some attempt to set these in the context of the history of his time. Since the intention is essentially to provide a background to the particular aspect of Symeon with which we shall be concerned, much that might otherwise have been included will be omitted as being irrelevant to our purpose.

Holl calculated that Symeon was born between 963 and 969 and died in 1041 or 1042. Hausherr, however, found that Holl had for various reasons been mistaken, and argued that 949 was the real date of his birth and 1022 that of his death. These dates in fact accord with all the evidence, apart from one sentence in Nicetas in which Symeon is stated to have been a priest for 48 years, whereas on Hausherr's reckoning 42 years is the required length of time. Hausherr, nevertheless, is able to point out that a confusion between μη′ (48) and μβ′ (42) could very easily have occurred at a time when numbers were written in this way in manuscripts, and that 42 fits exactly with the remainder of his calculations. These were indeed later questioned by Chrestou, an editor of Nicetas' mystical writings, but the objections he raised were convincingly answered by Grumel, and 949–1022 are now generally accepted as Symeon's dates.[1]

We have already seen that we are almost totally dependent on Nicetas for information about Symeon, apart from what can be inferred from his own writings. With regard to these we observed also that the information they provide is not of a kind that can be used as a basis for exact dating, though in other respects they are of course invaluable as autobiography. Concerning Nicetas, Hausherr concludes after a careful investigation:

> We shall accept the material facts which he gives us; but we shall mistrust the way in which he presents them, because this may well conceal some trick; we shall challenge his explanations, since he is capable of omitting

---

[1] Holl, *Enthusiasmus*, pp. 23–26; Hausherr, *Life*, pp. LXXX–XCI; Nicetas, *Life*, 30, 18; Hausherr, *ibid.*, p. XCI; P.K. Chrestou, Νικήτα Στηθάτου μυστικὰ συγγράμματα, Thessalonica, 1957, pp. 9–11; V. Grumel, 'Nicolas II Chrysobergès et la chronologie de la vie de Syméon le Nouveau Théologien,' *R.E.B.*, 22, (1964), pp. 253f.

needful pieces of information, while at times providing what does not really square with his conclusions.[2]

None the less it may be claimed that despite some problems and uncertainties, and although it would be good to have fuller information on various matters, it is still by no means impossible to attempt a reasonable portrayal of Symeon's personality and of the main events of his life.

Although Symeon himself gives no direct description of his childhood and education, he does just mention his family,[3] and we shall discover later that we can learn something from his writings about his attitude towards book-learning. Nicetas, too, supplies only a minimum of information about his hero's early life with his family and about his education, a mere three chapters out of one hundred and fifty-two. He does, however, tell us that Symeon was the son of Basil and Theophano, who bore the surname Galaton, derived from their native town Galate, in Paphlagonia. He adds that they were well-born and wealthy people, something of a *topos* in hagiography, but one which in this case is probably an accurate description.[4]

Nicetas never gives any indication that Symeon, before becoming a monk, had been called by any other name, neither does he state that for Symeon an exception was made to the usual custom that, when a monk was tonsured, he received a new name with the same initial as his former one. It would seem most likely, in view of the intense loyalty and deep veneration which was such a feature of his relationship with Symeon the Studite, that he took Symeon as his name on becoming a monk, but, if so, there is no means of knowing what he had previously been called. The most that can be said is that, as we have seen, it may be conjectured that his name had originally been George. If this was so, he must have deliberately set aside the usual custom in order to adopt the name of his spiritual father, but given a man of Symeon's temperament there would be nothing surprising in that.[5]

To assist in the understanding of his early life, it is useful to compare what we know of him with a similar account which supplies interesting

---

[2] Hausherr, *Life*, p. LXVII.

[3] For references, v. n. 12.

[4] Nicetas, *Life*, 2, 3–6.

[5] For the custom, v. N.F. Robinson, *Monasticism in the Orthodox Churches*, London, 1916, p. 58, but exceptions to the taking of a new name with the same initial certainly occur, and Nicetas, *Life*, 116, 2–5, tells of the adoption of the name Symeon by a certain Nicephorus, one of the New Theologian's disciples; "George", *Cat XXII*, 22, cf. Krivochéine, *Lumière*, p. 13, n. 4, *Cats SC* 96, intr. p. 18, n. 1, and L. Bouyer, *A History of Christian Spirituality*, London, 1968, II, 560.

parallels, the *Life of St. Nicephorus*.[6] This man was an older contemporary of Symeon, became a monk of Latmos, and eventually bishop of Miletus. Lemerle points out that his *Life* was written soon after he had died by one who had known him personally. The hagiographer states that Nicephorus was born into a well-to-do family at Basileion in Galatia, and that his parents made 'him a eunuch at a tender age. We are given to understand that this was done with a view to his having a career in the Church, but Lemerle observes that

> it was a better preparation for other careers . . . and Nicephorus' precocious ecclesiastical vocation may well be only a hagiographical *topos*.

Anyhow, at the age of seven Nicephorus was sent to Constantinople to be educated, and was later joined there by his mother. In accordance with convention it is maintained that his education was limited to instruction in the Scriptures, a statement elaborated in a way which might suggest that he went to a school which gave only a 'religious' education. But Lemerle argues that no such schools existed and that this is simply another *topos*: "from his early childhood a saint has attended solely to what is sacred." In fact it appears that Nicephorus was a pupil at an ordinary school in the city.

Nicetas, who was probably writing at least thirty years after Symeon's death, is much less informative than Nicephorus' biographer on the subject of early days. He implies, but never directly states, that Symeon was made a eunuch, perhaps because such men, although many of them held high positions in the Byzantine world, did not enjoy an entirely good reputation, and were in fact banned from some monasteries, including those on Mount Athos.[7] But Nicetas does say that as a young man Symeon was honoured by being made a *spatharocubicularius*, a dignity restricted to eunuchs,[8] and also, when describing how after death he was seen in a vision by a certain Philotheos, writes of his appearing as a "white-haired, handsome and venerable eunuch."[9] Moreover the *Life*

---

[6] v. Lemerle, *Premier Humanisme*, pp. 243–246, based on *Analecta Bollandiana*, 14, (1895), pp. 129–160.

[7] v. *tragos*, i.e. *typikon* of John Tzimiskes, *Archives de l'Athos VII, Actes du Protaton*, ed. D. Papachryssanthou, Paris, 1975, p. 212, XVI; cf. *Acta Sanctorum*, March III, Paris, 1865, p. *21, where, when St. Basil the Younger accuses Samonas of being secretly a sodomite, it is explained: ἦν γὰρ . . . φύσει ἐυνοῦχος καὶ ὡραῖος τῇ ὄψει. ("George" also was ὡραῖος and "some people entertained base suspicions about him," according to Symeon in *Cat XXII*, 24–26; v. also Nicetas, *Life*, 3, 1f.)

[8] Nicetas, *Life*, 3, 9f.; P.A. Yannopoulos, *La société profane dans l'empire des VIIe, VIIIe et IXe siècles*, Louvain, 1975, p. 36, lists *spatharocubicularius* amongst *Dignités des Eunuques*.

[9] Nicetas, *Life*, 147, 6f.—a eunuch could often be recognised by the absence of a beard.

significantly contains no mention of any attempt to arrange a marriage for Symeon, in spite of the fact that one of the *topoi* of hagiography is an account of how the future saint resists such parental efforts.[10] If then it was hoped that Symeon would have a career in the imperial service (as Nicetas unlike Nicephorus' biographer admits), we may reasonably assume that he was in fact castrated in childhood by parents eager for his future advancement.[11]

There is, however, a difficulty about this supposition, since it is hard to imagine even the most ambitious parents intentionally depriving themselves of all hope of direct descendants, and it is possible that Symeon was an only child. Thus, according to Nicetas, Symeon's father, in the course of an appeal to his son not to become a monk, said: "You know that I have no one but you to be a staff for me in my old age." This is in harmony with the absence of any mention by Nicetas of his having any brothers or sisters, although Symeon himself speaks of "father, brothers, mother."[12] The upshot is that if, as seems most probable, he was like Nicephorus a eunuch, we could assume either that his brothers had all died by the time he decided to enter a monastery, or that Nicetas simply used the kind of language which he felt appropriate to the occasion. The latter is the most reasonable solution of the problem in the light of Symeon's actual words.

Like Nicephorus, Symeon is said to have been sent at "a tender age" to Constantinople in order to be educated.[13] This was doubtless because only there could a boy, whose parents intended him to have a distinguished career, obtain the appropriate type of education. In those days, as Lemerle writes with reference to Nicephorus, "it was only in the capital that one could receive a formation of that kind."[14]

An important part of the training consisted in being taught to write classical Greek, since the spoken language of ordinary folk had by now become something very different from this. But "both church and state

---

[10] For this as a *topos*, cf. Mango, *Byzantium*, pp. 247f.

[11] Evidence against Symeon's having been a eunuch might be adduced from *Cat XXXV*, 141–146, where he speaks of himself as on one occasion narrowly escaping nocturnal pollution (πάθος ῥεύσεως) in his sleep, but medical authorities state that castration can be performed in such a way as not to render an occurrence of this kind impossible; for his family's connection with the court and for what was intended for Symeon, v. Nicetas, *Life*, 2, 8f., and 3, 5–8.

[12] Nicetas, *Life*, 8, 11f.—that this is not a mere hagiographical convention is evidenced by *Ch* I, 15f., where Symeon finds it needful to warn a person "fleeing from the world" against spurious pity for his family; for "brothers," v. *Hymn XVIII*, 126, *Hymn XX*, 98f.

[13] Nicetas, *Life*, 2, 6–10.

[14] Lemerle, *Premier humanisme*, pp. 243f.; significantly he also observes that an education of this sort was designed for "a restricted social class," with "a role to play in the state," and "defined by its ambitions or its ideal." (*ibid.*, p. 260)

required officials proficient in Attic or Atticist prose,"[15] and so the gaining of this proficiency held an important place in the education of boys
whose parents resembled those of Nicephorus and Symeon. In Mango's
words,

> access to the ancient language was conditional on a rhetorical education,
> which after the disaster of the seventh century, was limited to a small group
> of prospective civil servants and clergymen.[16]

Indeed, as Magdalino puts it, "education was commonly a means of
social advancement," and he notes how Michael Choniates remarked that
he was regarded as eccentric because he enjoyed learning for its own
sake.[17]

It is against this background that the conventional statements of
hagiographers need to be looked at. Thus we may doubt whether it was
really intended that Nicephorus should be "educated in nothing but Holy
Scripture," and although Nicetas does not say anything quite as sweeping
about his hero's education, we may suspect that it was not necessarily the
case that Symeon

> having learnt what is called grammar, would have nothing to do with the
> rest, one might say with the whole, of non-Christian education.[18]

At this point there is no need to examine further the content of Symeon's
education—this will be attempted in the next chapter—, but the subject
has been touched on here because a training such as he received was an
essential element in his parents' ambitions for him, and to obtain it he had
to be sent to Constantinople.

In the case of Nicephorus, leaving home to be educated seems to have
meant a temporary separation from his family, for he was lodged in the
house of a *magistros*, who is not stated to have been a relation. Some
time later, we are told, his mother joined him in the capital. Symeon,
on the contrary, had close relatives with whom to stay, his grand-parents,
who according to Nicetas at that time held high rank at court. After a
single mention, nothing more is said about them, but we next hear of a
paternal uncle, who was *persona grata* with Basil II and Constantine VIII,
a chamberlain (κοιτωνίτης), and therefore presumably himself a eunuch

---

[15] B. Baldwin, 'Photius and Poetry,' *Byzantine and Modern Greek Studies*, 4, (1978), p. 9.
[16] Mango, *Byzantium*, p. 236, but as will be seen in the next chapter, although Symeon
learnt "the ancient language," his education was not in fact "rhetorical".
[17] P. Magdalino, 'The Byzantine Holy Man in the 12th Century,' *The Byzantine Saint*,
London, 1981, p. 57, with ref. to Michael Choniates in n. 32.
[18] Nicephorus, cited by Lemerle, *Premier humanisme*, p. 244; Symeon, Nicetas, *Life*, 2,
24–26.

also. Nicetas later mentions as a γάμβρος of Symeon a certain John ὁ δεήσεων, the holder that is to say of an important office, responsible for studying petitions addressed to the emperor.[19] Symeon's family was therefore one that moved in the highest circles, and it has been remarked that in his writings there are not infrequent references of life in a royal household.[20]

But we must not be misled by what would be natural to us in our own culture when we are thinking of the plans for Symeon's future which his family may have made. Whereas nowadays in the West there is concern about enabling a boy to realise his full potential, in Byzantium emphasis would much more be put on how the family's interests could best be served. The 10th and 11th centuries were times when, as Herman expressed it,

> the great landed proprietors were using all possible means to enlarge their possessions at the expense of small properties . . . As long as the Macedonian dynasty reigned, the *basileis*, who were for the most part strong and clever men, succeeded in slowing down the victory of the great lords . . .[21]

It seems, then, a reasonable supposition that to further its own interests a well-to-do provincial family, such as that into which Symeon was born, would take steps to see that, if possible, at least one of its members held an influential post in the imperial service in Constantinople. It is quite likely that the intention was that at the proper time Symeon should succeed his uncle in this position, and such an intention may plausibly be assumed to lie behind Nicetas' statement that this uncle "considered presenting him to the monarch and promoting his close acquaintance with him." However, though the family, it may be supposed, did form a plan of the kind suggested, nothing came of it, for we are next told that "[Symeon] with tears rejected what was intended by his uncle, being unwilling to be on terms of friendship with those then in power."[22]

Hausherr explains this refusal by the fact that the ruler in question will have been Romanus II (959–963), notorious for his sexual immorality, and thus

---

[19] Nicephorus—Lemerle, *Premier humanisme*, p. 244, inc. n. 6, and p. 245, n. 10; Symeon—Nicetas, *Life*, 2, 8f. and 3, 1–5; on κοιτωίτης, cf. R. Morris, 'The Political Saint,' *The Byzantine Saint*, London, 1981, p. 44, n. 9; John—Nicetas, *Life*, 113, 25f.

[20] cf. Darrouzès, *Ch SC* 51, pp. 106f., n. 1; Paramelle, *Cat V SC* 96, p. 381, n. 1, notes Symeon's liking for imaginary scenes which place a monarch in a ludicrous or humiliating position; other references to royalty include *Cat II*, 109–112 (where v. Krivochéine's note), *Cat IV*, 470–472 and *Cat V*, 573–636.

[21] E. Herman, 'Ricerche sulle instituzioni monastiche bizantine: Typika ktetorika, caristicari e monasteri liberi,' *O.C.P.*, 6, (1940), p. 372.

[22] Nicetas, *Life*, 3, 5–8.

one can understand why a young man, even one not specially virtuous, would have been horrified at the idea of becoming closely acquainted with such a monarch.[23]

If then we combine this explanation with what was suggested in the preceding paragraph, we reach the not improbable conclusion that the young Symeon felt that he was being asked to sacrifice his self-respect for the sake of promoting the interests of his family, and refused to do so. This supposition is supported by his own words in which he thanks God that

> by thine ineffable judgements thou didst deliver me from kings and rulers who desired to use me as a dishonoured vessel in the service of their own wills.[24]

A Career in the World?

Nicetas a few lines further on records in a somewhat mysterious way the disappearance of Symeon's uncle from the scene—"suddenly [he] was ushered out of this present life by no ordinary death"—, and Hausherr surmises that this is a veiled reference to the events of 963, "the troubles by which the capital was agitated after the fall of Joseph Bringas."[25] (Hausherr further speculates as to the possibility that this unnamed uncle may in fact have been no other than Bringas himself, though he adds that this is not really a question of great importance.)

At all events, according to Nicetas,

> Symeon seized the opportunity, and, abandoning everything, fled from the world and the things of the world, making haste towards God.

After some pious reflections there follows the statement that Symeon betook himself to the Studios monastery, sought out the Studite, his spiritual father "since his early childhood (ἐκ νεότητος)," and demanded to become a monk immediately. The Studite, however, refused to permit this on the ground of Symeon's youth, since he was not yet fourteen.[26]

This last statement in fact involves Nicetas in an inconsistency, in that

---

[23] Hausherr, *Life*, p. LXXXVIII; cf. Leo Diaconus, *Historiae* I, 2, *C.S.H.B.* XI, Bonn, 1828, p. 6.

[24] *Cat XXXVI*, 32–35, using language reminiscent of *Romans* 9, 21 and *II Timothy* 2, 20; cf. in the same sense *Hymn XX*, 156–164.

[25] Nicetas, *Life*, 3, 16f.; Hausherr, *Life*, pp. LXXXVIIIf. It is interesting in this connection that Skylitzes states that Joseph Bringas was first banished to Paphlagonia (Symeon's place of origin) and afterwards sent to a monastery where he died—v. Skylitzes, ed. J. Thurn, *Corpus Fontium Historiae Byzantinae*, V, 260, 68–71, Berlin/New York, 1973. Leo Diaconus (*ibid.*, III, 4, p. 40) calls Bringas ἀγεννής, which, if true, tells against Hausherr, since Symeon's family could hardly have been so described.

[26] Nicetas, *Life*, 3, 17–19, 4, 1–12.

he elsewhere asserts that he himself had been no more than fourteen when he renounced the world and ceased to pursue his studies, but clearly, writing as a hagiographer, he was concerned to depict Symeon as precociously devout. Thus he was eager to make the most of the visit to the monastery at this time, whilst also being obliged to confess that it was not really until some years later that Symeon became a postulant there.[27]

Furthermore, we can detect in Nicetas a desire to minimise the significance of the time which Symeon spent in the world, a period during which, as the latter himself tells us, he did not unswervingly pursue the path of holiness. It is interesting that in the scholia to the *Hymns*, which Koder has shown may with good reason be ascribed to Nicetas' hand, there is found an even more emphatic assertion of juvenile sanctity:

> He was fourteen when thanks to Symeon the Studite, his holy spiritual father, he was set apart from all these [worldly] things.''[28]

On the basis of *Cat XXII* as providing a guide to the interpretation of Nicetas' narrative, Hausherr reconstructs the actual course of events in Symeon's life after the death of his uncle:

> He took refuge in the Studios monastery, but neither could nor wished to stay there. He went to live in the house of another patrician . . . When a little over twenty, he had his first vision, and then attempted to join the monastery, but was prevented by some unknown obstacle. He thus remained in the world and even found it so attractive that he completely forgot the good advice of his spiritual father . . . He actually entered Studios when he was about twenty-seven, six years after the vision . . .[29]

Generally speaking, this makes good sense, for a study of *Cat XXII* reveals facts which Nicetas, writing as a hagiographer, would naturally wish to gloss over, even if by doing so he lapsed into inconsistency or absurdity. Thus he says nothing about where Symeon lived after this visit to the monastery at about the age of fourteen, but having mentioned the Studite he provides us with an example of the spiritual direction given by the latter, not specifying the date, but implying that Symeon was at the time still in his uncle's house. It is true that, in his account of the same matter, Symeon says that he was living in Constantinople without specifying where, but when like Nicetas he comes a little later to describe the first vision vouchsafed to him, he mentions that he

---

[27] For the inconsistency, v. *ibid.*, 135, 23–25; cf. Hausherr, *Life*, p. LXII.

[28] Koder, *Hymns SC* 156, intr. pp. 46, 68–70, with quotation from scholium at *Hymn XVIII*, 130.

[29] Hausherr, *Life*, pp. LXXXIXf.; instead of Hausherr's ''senator'', we should probably use the phrase, ''member of the senatorial order,'' v. R. Guilland, *Byzantion*, XXIV, (1954), p. 573.

was superintending the household of a certain patrician, and going daily to the palace.[30]

Krivochéine therefore identified this patrician with the uncle spoken of by Nicetas, though he admitted that the fact of the uncle's death having already been recorded must render this uncertain. It would seem better to accept Hausherr's view that the patrician was a different person.[31]

Hausherr was surely right also in supposing that it was about this time that Symeon became a *spatharocubicularius* and "one of the Senate," whereas Nicetas refers to the bestowal of these dignities immediately after telling of Symeon's refusal to become intimate with "those in power," thus implying the unlikely appointment to these positions of a boy of under fourteen. The improbability is all the greater in the light of the refusal just mentioned, whereas some time after the death of Romanus II there is nothing incredible about these titles being conferred on a young man who was "going daily to the palace" and who occupied a prominent position in a patrician's household.

Further, Nicetas is misleading his readers when he insists that Symeon had had the Studite for his spiritual father "since his early childhood,"[32] even though it is not possible to say precisely when or how he first made his acquaintance. As we shall see, it was as an adult that Symeon became concerned to find a saintly spiritual father, though then hoping for no more from him than a guarantee of salvation at the last. In *Cat XXXV*, where the first vision is described in not quite the same terms as in *Cat XXII*, Symeon says that in the course of it he saw the Studite looking just as he ordinarily appeared, and that thereby he was convinced that God had designated this man as his spiritual father. It is nevertheless possible that Nicetas may be not wholly incorrect, since, as we learn from *Cat XVI*, the Studite had numerous disciples living in the city whom he visited from time to time, and in the course of such visits some contact might much earlier have been established between him and Symeon. But quite apart from any intrinsic improbability in Nicetas' picture of a child so pious as to have a spiritual father, Symeon's own words make it plain that he was not sure that he ought to commit himself to the Studite before he was convinced by the vision.[33]

According to Nicetas, Symeon had first asked to be tonsured when not yet fourteen, immediately after his uncle's death, and some time must

[30] Nicetas, *Life*, 4, 15–21; Symeon, *Cat XXII*, 23, 34–51, 70–72.
[31] Krivochéine, *Cat XXII SC* 104, pp. 370f., n. 1; Nicetas, *Life*, 3, 16f. and 5, 1–31; Hausherr, *Life*, pp. LXXXIXf.
[32] Nicetas, *Life*, 4, 2f.
[33] *Cat XXXV*, 100–113; *Cat XXII*, 88–104; *Cat XVI*, 31–34.

then be supposed to have elapsed before the vision and its consequence that "he was insistent in his requests to his [spiritual] father to tonsure him." These requests, we are told, were refused, because the Studite judged that the young man was not yet strong enough to support the rigours of asceticism.[34]

It is thus clear that for an understanding of this phase of Symeon's life we cannot rely on Nicetas; on the basis of the *Catecheses*, Hausherr's summary may be expanded in the following manner. While, some time after his uncle's death, Symeon "was superintending the household of a certain patrician," he became concerned about his sins and sought for a living saint to be his spiritual father, in order that through the intercession of such a man he might be assured of forgiveness and ultimate salvation. Somehow the Studite became "acquainted with him"—the first contact may perhaps have been made at an earlier date—, and it would seem at least a plausible speculation that the introduction was effected by means of one of his future father's existing spiritual children in the city.[35]

Symeon then received and followed the spiritual direction given him by the Studite,[36] but though sincere, was not yet fully committed as a disciple, because he was not completely certain that he had found the saint he was seeking. His uncertainty, however, was ended by his first vision, in the course of which he saw the Studite. There is nothing inherently improbable in Nicetas' assertion that he then again tried to become a monk but was not permitted to do so by his spiritual father, but unfortunately this edifying statement is not corroborated by what Symeon actually says:

> I am convinced . . . that it was solely for this purpose that [God] was pleased to appear to me, namely that in spite of all my unworthiness he might draw me to himself and might set me apart from all the world. But since I had not the strength to act promptly, little by little I became oblivious of all I have just recounted and reached the point of being in total darkness, so that of the matters I have spoken about I recalled nothing, small or great, not even giving them a bare thought.[37]

This Nicetas totally though understandably omits, but we cannot ignore Symeon's plain confession that the vision had no lasting effect on him, something which he later felt to have been his own fault, in that at the

---

[34] Nicetas, *Life*, 4, 1–12, 6, 1–6.

[35] *Cat XXII*, 70f., *Cat XXXV*, 19–21, 73–80; cf. an example given by Nicetas (*Life*, 54, 1–21, 55, 1–8): a Western bishop, eager to do penance, came to Constantinople, conversed with Symeon's spiritual child Genesios, and was introduced by him to Symeon.

[36] *Cat XXII*, 29–38.

[37] *Cat XXII*, 281–288; "had not the strength" (οὐκ ἴσχυσα) suggests some personal deficiency.

critical time he had lacked sufficient resolution to abandon the world and become a monk. He ascribes this fault in one place to "constant temptations" and in another to "slackness and negligence," and confesses that in consequence of it he began to regard the Studite "as a mere ordinary man" and no longer "observed his injunctions." Nevertheless he still kept in touch with him.[38]

In language that is picturesque, but not specific, Symeon tells how God, with the Studite as his agent, then came to the rescue: from this "pit of perdition" he was delivered "by [the Studite's] prayers."[39] In *Cat XXXV*, when giving thanks to God, he sketches the kind of existence from which he had been set free.

> By means of him, the saint (ἅγιος) thou didst convert me, and didst condescend to allow me to fall down at his holy (ἅγιος) feet, when by thy strong hand and thine exalted arm thou leddest me forth from the deceitful world and its affairs and pleasures, and didst set me apart from them all, as regards both body and soul ... and didst place me in the ranks of those who serve thee.[40]

The last words contain an obvious reference to his entering a monastic community, and it is interesting to observe that just as Symeon here emphasises the Studite's active role—"by means of him"—, so Nicetas, in spite of his unwillingness to admit that his hero had needed to be rescued from a sinful life, none the less at this point represents the older man as taking an initiative and saying to his potential disciple:

> Lo, now is the time, my child, to change your dress and your mode of life, if you wish to do so.[41]

We should also notice how, with regard to the occasion to which he ascribes these words, Nicetas contrives to use, but to put a different complexion on, information which he could have gained from Symeon: the latter, referring to the time when after his vision he relapsed into worldliness, had said:

> I did not completely hold aloof from [the Studite] ... but ... would frequently go to his cell, when I chanced to be in the city."[42]

Nicetas tells us that when preparing to undertake a journey to his native Paphlagonia, "[Symeon] came to take leave of his holy father in the famous monastery of Studios," and was then invited to prepare to "change [his] dress" and become a monk. There is no difficulty in believing that

---

[38] *Cat XXII*, 277f., 293, 304–308, *Cat XXXV*, 115, cf. *Cat VI*, 121–131.
[39] *Cat XXII*, 296, 302f.
[40] *Cat XXXV*, 118–125, cf. *Cat XXII*, 303f., *Hymn XVIII*, 124–130.
[41] Nicetas, *Life*, 6, 10f.
[42] *Cat XXII*, 304–307.

the Studite did say something not unlike the words Nicetas put into his mouth, and we need not doubt either the occasion or the fact that, as stated a few lines later, the journey was a duty to be undertaken in the imperial service, for Symeon's own words, "when I chanced to be in the city," suggest that he may on various occasions have been sent away on missions of one kind or another.[43]

Thus, by giving the weight to Symeon's confessions, we can envisage and understand the situation: although his first vision assured him that the Studite was the saint he had been seeking as his spiritual father, the very fact that Symeon's motives for undertaking the quest were inadequate made it easy for him to succumb soon afterwards to "slackness and negligence;" still he was sufficiently impressed by the Studite to want to keep in touch with him, even though he did not remain a committed disciple. Equally, part of the Studite's skill as a spiritual father consisted, as we shall consider later, in his willingness to tolerate this kind of relationship and to continue praying for the wayward youth. He also perceived the right moment at which to intervene effectively, so as to bring about both his real conversion and his entrance upon the monastic life. This took place when Symeon was about twenty-seven, and thus in the year 976 or 977.[44]

Before proceeding further with our sketch of Symeon's life, we must try to see if it is possible to determine what sins weighed most heavily on his conscience, both when he was first trying to find an authentic saint whom he might have for his spiritual father, and also when later he came to accuse himself of the way he had behaved during the period when he was estimating the Studite "as a mere ordinary man." At once we encounter the difficulty that in various places Symeon accuses himself of breaking every one of God's commandments. Modern minds will be tempted to dismiss this impatiently as morbid fantasy, but for it two reasons may be suggested, either or both of which will lead us to discounting his actual words: the first, which will receive further mention in another chapter, is that Symeon hoped by this means to encourage others to reveal their thoughts to him, giving them confidence that they would find a sympathetic listener in a father who admitted himself to be so sinful; the other possible reason is that, as Koder suggests, he was deliberately combating his own temptations to pride by behaving as a holy fool (σαλός), in speech if not in action. Some of the scholia to the *Hymns*, support this view, for example:

---

[43] For Nicetas' account, v. *Life*, 6, 6–18.
[44] Symeon's age, and thus the date, is calculated on the basis of *Cat XXII*, 270–273.

> Wishing to have his soul ever illuminated by the Holy Spirit . . . and afraid of falling through pride, he would call himself a perpetrator of vile deeds and swear to it, as he does in detail in *Hymn XXIV* with what are really lies that proceed from his deep humility.[45]

When, however, Symeon uses less wide-ranging language in his self-accusations, it is reasonable to assume that his confessions are referring more closely to his actual conduct. At these times he appears mostly concerned about what used to be castigated as 'worldliness', the excessive preoccupation with wealth, status and the other merchandise displayed to tempt pilgrims on their way through Vanity Fair. Thus both intrinsic probability, and the motives we have suggested for his use of exaggerated language, will lead us to discount a good deal of his self-accusation and to class him not as some notorious sinner, but as a normally ambitious young man enjoying the opportunity of taking his first steps in a successful secular career.[46]

Our discussion of Symeon's confessions, however, cannot omit some reference to the possibility that his conscience was disquieted also by his having been somehow involved in homosexual practices. We have shown that he was almost certainly a eunuch, and have noted both that eunuchs had a bad reputation and that there are good reasons for supposing that it was for licentious purposes that Symeon's uncle intended "presenting him to [Romanus II] and promoting his close acquaintance with him." Symeon, as we saw, successfully resisted this attempt and afterwards thanked God for his deliverance, but on the other hand he elsewhere gives the impression that, either then or perhaps later, he had not escaped totally unsullied.

> As for impure thoughts and indecent desires, thou, my God, didst wipe my heart clean from them and didst inspire my soul with hatred for them, even though I did by choice incline towards them.[47]

These lines are at least somewhat ambiguous, whilst elsewhere, in the middle of one of those catalogues of self-accusation which we have just discussed, there are words which suggest something more than unfulfilled desires.

---

[45] Koder, *Hymns SC* 156, intr. pp. 70f.; scholium to *Hymn XVIII*, 92, quoted from *SC* 174, p. 82; more information about holy fools will be given in the next chapter.

[46] cf. *Cat XXXV*, 121f., *Cat XXXVI*, 35–38, *Hymn XX*, 120f., 131–133; Christophorides, *op. cit.*, p. 73 ascribes Symeon's language to humility and to a desire to encourage his monks by minimising the difference between himself and them.

[47] *Hymn XX*, 134–137.

[48] *Hymn XXIV*, 74f.—μοιχὸς τῇ καρδίᾳ (cf. *St. Matthew* 5. 28), but σοδομίτης ἔργῳ καὶ προαιρέσει.

Alas, I have also been in heart an adulterer and a sodomite in deed and by choice.[48]

The evidence is thus somewhat contradictory, and whether we decide that Symeon was in reality guilty or innocent of homosexual activities, it is in either case necessary to interpret some of his words so as to make them fit the decision taken. Tentatively one might suggest that he was conscious of having at some time had homosexual inclinations, and had perhaps been initiated into some mild form of homosexual behaviour, but nevertheless could honestly claim that, in spite of everything, he had never indulged in it with full understanding and with the full consent of his will. To sum up, then, we may say that Symeon, in spite of his vehement self-accusations, was far from being addicted to gross and flagrant sins, while at the same time he was clearly not the paragon of all the virtues depicted by Nicetas. What caused him at first to seek for a spiritual father was a conviction that the kind of life he was living was one which would not in the end lead to his salvation.

Studios

About the year 977 then, Symeon, delivered as he believed by God from the deceits of the world, returned from his journey to Paphlagonia and was admitted to the Studios monastery as a postulant. According to Nicetas, he did not technically become a monk there, for his tonsuring is not recounted until later, when in circumstances shortly to be described, he had been forced to move to another monastery, that of St. Mamas.[49] Symeon obviously went to Studios because his spiritual father was a monk of that community, and to begin with he must have considered himself fortunate in that lack of other accommodation resulted in his being told to live and sleep in a confined space under the staircase of the Studite's cell.[50]

We are not at this point concerned with the training Symeon received, and therefore can pass at once to what led to his having to leave the monastery after a very brief sojourn. Nicetas says that his piety and rapid progress gave the demons the opportunity of enlisting jealousy (φθόνος) in their struggle against him, and that they stirred up this feeling in the hearts of the less zealous monks, and even in that of the hegumen, Peter. This jealousy, moreover, led to an attempt being made to cause Symeon to lose confidence in the Studite.[51]

---

[49] Nicetas, *Life*, 10, 3–10, and 11, 1–4. As opposed to tonsuring, which is not mentioned while Symeon was at Studios, there is a reference in the latter passage to his being clothed in the σάκκος τῆς γυμνασίας τῶν ἀρετῶν.

[50] Nicetas, *Life*, 11, 4–11.

[51] Nicetas, *Life*, 16, 3–5, 17–23.

As regards this latter point, Nicetas is supported by some words of Symeon which will be cited in a subsequent chapter, but his ascribing everything simply to jealousy is open to some suspicion. What Symeon says suggests that there were some who in good faith held the Studite to be "a buffoon and a deceiver,"[52] for as we shall see his conduct did in fact lay itself open to misunderstanding. Furthermore, as will also be explained, Peter in seeking to regulate and control Symeon's choice of a spiritual father

> was only striving to secure the effective operation of a tradition which had become a customary law, if indeed it was not sanctioned by legislative texts. St. Theodore Studite ... would no doubt have given his approval.[53]

It is with this background in mind that we must read Nicetas' statement that the hegumen "now by promises and now by threats made every effort to detach [Symeon] from his teacher and to attach him to himself." At last, as Symeon proved inflexible, he was expelled from the monastery.[54]

How long had he actually spent there? Hausherr concludes that "his stay ... only lasted a very short time, a few weeks or a few months at most."[55] There is no reason to dispute this verdict, arrived at by careful examination of the texts, and additionally confirmed, it may be added, by the fact that, as we have noticed, Symeon is not stated to have received the tonsure before his expulsion from Studios. He must, however, have remained in the same monastery as the Studite long enough to enable the events to have occurred which he relates in *Cat XVI*, concerning both the training given him by his spiritual father and another vision which he was granted.[56] Incidentally, if Nicetas is accurate in his statement about Symeon's having at first been lodged in the Studite's cell, the *Catechesis* (and by implication Nicetas' account which is based on it) makes it clear that this was indeed merely a temporary arrangement, for Symeon describes how he had the visionary experience after he had been dismissed to his own cell for the night.[57] At any rate there is no need on this account to postulate a stay of many weeks in Studios, nor is this necessitated by the efforts which Nicetas records as having been made by people in the world, including Symeon's father, to persuade him to

---

[52] *Cat XXXVI*, 102–116.

[53] Hausherr, *Direction spirituelle*, p. 120; cf. also R. Janin, 'Le monachisme byzantin au moyen âge,' *R.E.B.* 22, (1964), pp. 24f. for details of the regulations according to the *typika* of a number of monasteries.

[54] Nicetas, *Life*, 21, 5–12.

[55] Hausherr, *Life*, p. LXXXVII.

[56] *Cat XVI*, 8–144, cf. Nicetas, *Life*, 12, 18 and 19.

[57] *Cat XVI*, 75, cf. Nicetas, *Life*, 19, 10–12.

give up his determination to be a monk, Nicetas, in any case, may be here simply writing what he feels to be demanded by the conventions of hagiography.[58]

St. Mamas'

The Studite now arranged for Symeon to be received in the "nearby monastery of St. Mamas," but after his arrival there, renewed attempts were made to draw him back into the world. It is interesting that on this occasion his father is stated to have been joined by "some who belonged to the Senate," a further piece of evidence about the social *milieu* to which Symeon's family belonged. His resolution, however, remained unshaken, and he was fortified by the frequent visits paid him by his spiritual father, who himself—in Nicetas' words—"tonsured him and clothed him in the tunic of gladness."[59]

We are next told of the ascetic life which Symeon lived and the rapid spiritual progress that he made in his new surroundings. St. Mamas' was very different from the famous and flourishing Studios monastery, for it was in a ruinous condition and contained only a few monks. This, no doubt, was the reason why the hegumen, Antony, did not hesitate to accept Symeon and did not object to his remaining under the Studite's spiritual tutelage. This relationship, of course, rather than his physical surroundings, was what mattered to Symeon.[60]

The decayed state of St. Mamas' monastery, and the fact that Symeon in spite of being a newcomer was clearly in many respects superior to most of his fellow monks, whom Nicetas characterizes as "spiritually neglected (ἀγεώργητος)"—this renders it not unexpected that on the death of Antony, when Symeon had only been a member of the community for two or three years, he was chosen as the new hegumen "by the vote of the Patriarch, Nicholas Chrysoberges, and of the monks of St. Mamas'." In accordance with what had in practice become a general rule, on succeeding to this office he was ordained priest.[61]

As hegumen he set about vigorously on the work which needed to be done to restore the monastery. Nicetas says that he rebuilt the whole of it, apart from the church. This had come to be used as a burial-place, and

---

[58] Nicetas, *Life*, 17, 2–6.

[59] Nicetas, *Life*, 22, 1–11, 24, 1–4; cf. for the language of the latter *Isaiah* 61, 10 (LXX); for the monastery of St. Manas, its history and its site, v. Janin, *Églises et monastères*, pp. 314–319.

[60] Nicetas, *Life*, 34, 2–6, describes the condition of the buildings of St. Mamas' and of its monks a little later, when Symeon became hegumen.

[61] Nicetas, *Life*, 34, 5, 30, 3–6; for hegumens usually being priests, v. G. Da Costa-Louillet, 'Saints de Constantinople,' *Byzantion*, *XXIV*, (1954), p. 234.

so he removed from it the dead bodies, covered the floor with marble, and adorned the building with icons and candelabra. But Nicetas emphasises, as we should anyhow gather from Symeon's writings, that his main concern was with the spiritual reformation of his monks.[62]

During his first few years as hegumen he had encouragement and support, since the Studite was still alive and could both help him as his own spiritual father and also supervise him when he acted in this capacity towards his monks. But on the Studite's death, which as Hausherr has calculated took place in 986 or 987, Symeon felt himself

> an utter orphan, utterly isolated, utterly without help from anybody, while yet—alas!—the leader and shepherd of a flock.[63]

In Symeon's writings there are several indications of tensions arising between him and his monks, and it would be tempting to assign these difficulties to the period after his spiritual father's death, when he no longer had the benefit of wise advice and guidance. Unfortunately, however, since there is no means of dating accurately the various items contained in Symeon's works, this suggestion is not supported by concrete evidence.

Anyhow, at a date which Hausherr places between 995 and 998, matters came to a head.[64] Nicetas recounts a revolt on the part of some thirty monks on an occasion when Symeon was delivering one of his *Catecheses*. Restrained from making a physical attack by "the grace which indwelt him," they ran off and complained to the patriarch (Sisinnios), who after hearing Symeon's version of the event decided in his favour.[65] Nicetas uses the occurrence to illustrate and extol Symeon's magnanimity towards those who had sought to injure him, but the narrative testifies incidentally to two other matters: under Symeon, numbers at St. Mamas' must have considerably increased, since the thirty or so disaffected monks did not constitute the whole of the community, those "who lived devout lives" remaining with their hegumen; on the other hand, a revolt on this scale is a clear indication that Symeon had either lost, or perhaps had never won, the whole-hearted support of many of those for whom he had, *ex officio*, to function as spiritual father.

If, as suggested above, the death of the Studite perhaps contributed something to the worsening of the relationship between Symeon and his monks and so to his troubles within the monastery, it certainly had a

---

[62] Nicetas, *Life*, 34, 12–22, 35, 1–6, 38, 1f.; Symeon, *passim*, especially *Cats I, III, IV, V*.

[63] Hausherr, *Life*, p. XC; *Hymn XXXVII*, 48–50.

[64] Hausherr, *Life*, p. XC.

[65] Nicetas, *Life*, 38, 7–19, 39, 1–22.

connection with the difficulties which some years later began to press on him from without. Not surprisingly, he had initiated a cult of his dead father as a saint, composing hymns, getting an icon painted, and celebrating an annual festival in his honour. This attracted the attention of Patriarch Sergius II, but, according to Nicetas, on reading what Symeon had written in praise of the Studite, he so far approved as to send candles and perfume to enhance the splendour of the festival. Matters continued thus for about sixteen years.[66]

According to Nicetas' account, which for lack of other evidence cannot at this point be checked, no trouble would in fact ever have arisen, had not Symeon's reputation for wisdom and sanctity provoked the jealousy of the patriarch's syncellus, Stephen, who had formerly been metropolitan of Nicomedia, but had resigned his see. (Jealousy, we may notice, is again how Nicetas seeks to explain opposition to Symeon.)[67]

Stephen, in order to discredit him, attempted to trap Symeon into uttering heresy on the subject of the Trinity, and received in reply an explanation in verse, containing many expressions designed to irritate a person such as himself. (This reply is preserved among Symeon's writings as *Hymn XXI*.)[68] Unable to win a victory here, the syncellus next tried to unearth in Symeon's personal life something on which to base an accusation, but was unable to succeed in this. Accordingly, he finally selected the 'canonisation' of the Studite as the ground for an attack. Nicetas says that to begin with the patriarch and the other bishops rejected the charges, but after two years—that is in 1005, according to Hausherr—Stephen at last managed to get Symeon arraigned before the Synod, accused of honouring as a saint one who in reality was far from saintly. Having rejected the patriarch's suggestion that he should compromise by keeping the Studite's festival as a private observance within the monastery, Symeon was condemned to go into exile in January 1009.[69]

In the course of his narrative Nicetas, as one might expect, blackens Stephen in every possible way, accusing him not only of being motivated

---

[66] Nicetas, *Life*, 72, 24–26, 73, 1–12.

[67] Concerning Stephen, v. Hausherr, *Life*, pp. LI–LVI, and additionally Leo Diaconus, *Historiae*, X, 6 (*C.H.S.B.*, XI, Bonn, 1828, pp. 168f.) for his reputation as an interpreter of celestial portents, and J. Darrouzès, *Documents inédits d'ecclésiologie byzantine*, Paris, 1966, pp. 250–252, for his resignation from the see of Nicomedia; what is very likely a letter from him, as well as three (and probably also a fourth) to him, can be found in J. Darrouzès, *Epistoliers byzantins du Xe siècle*, Paris, 1960, pp. 192f., 219f., 221, 222, 244–247.

[68] Nicetas, *Life*, 75, 76, 77; on *Hymn XXI*, v. L. Neyrand's note *SC* 174 pp. 130f., n. 1.

[69] For the remainder of Stephen's campaign, leading to Symeon's condemnation and exile, v. Nicetas, *Life*, 78–95; for the date 1009, v. Hausherr, *Life*, p. LXXXV.

by jealousy, but also of thoroughgoing iconoclasm, similar to that of
Constantine V (Copronymus), because he caused icons of the Studite to
be destroyed. But it is possible to view Stephen somewhat differently, and
Hausherr succeeds in depicting him and his actions in a much more
favourable light.[70] In any case his triumph was, as we shall see, very
limited.

By the time that Symeon's exile began, he had ceased to be hegumen
of St. Mamas', having resigned some four years previously in favour of
his disciple Arsenius. Nicetas represents this as being a voluntary act,
undertaken in order that he might devote himself to contemplation; but
this was perhaps not the sole reason, for it may be conjectured that the
patriarch, whom Nicetas specifically mentions as agreeing with Symeon's
decision, had suggested resignation in the hope of averting further conflict.[71] If this was Sergius II's hope, the plan did not meet with success.
Symeon, however, will not have been reluctant to resign, for we shall later
observe how burdensome he found the temporal concerns with which
inevitably a hegumen had to be involved. His resignation, it should be
added, does not seem to have entailed his abdicating from the position of
spiritual father.[72]

The Oratory of St. Marina

It was thus no longer as hegumen that Symeon went into exile. Nicetas
makes the most of his sufferings, but in reality he was able to establish himself at no great distance from Constantinople at a place called Palukiton
in Asia Minor. There he found a ruined oratory, dedicated to St. Marina,
on land which belonged to a highly-placed personage, Christopher
Phagura. This man was one of Symeon's spiritual children, not a monk
but a devout secular, for by now several such people were numbered
among his disciples. Christopher, on hearing of his father's exile, at once
visited him and presented the oratory to him. Furthermore, other influential spiritual children, including the patrician Genesios, busied themselves
on Symeon's behalf and made representations to the patriarch.[73]

The upshot was that Sergius II, "fearing that the matter might come
before the emperor," revoked the sentence of exile at a meeting of the
Synod and announced his intention of first re-establishing Symeon in
St. Mamas' and of later consecrating him as archbishop of one of the most
important metropolitan sees. In return he would only ask him to observe

---

[70] Hausherr, *Life*, p. LXXIXf., and cf. Krivochéine, *Lumière*, pp. 45ff.

[71] Nicetas, *Life*, 59, 4–15; Hausherr, *Life*, p. LXXV.

[72] Nicetas, *Life*, 59, 20–23.

[73] Nicetas, *Life*, 95, 6–24, 96, 1f., 100, 1–9, 24–26, 102, 7–13.

some degree of restraint for the time being in his celebration of the Studite's festival. Characteristically, Symeon refused to compromise, and this, says Nicetas, led the patriarch to exclaim, "You are genuinely a Studite and devoted to your father ..." He then gave him permission to live where he would and celebrate the festival as he wished.[74]

Symeon decided to return to St. Marina's oratory, where he restored the ruins and in effect founded a small monastic community of like-minded disciples who were glad to have him as their spiritual father. Amongst these there came to be included his future biographer, Nicetas. Here Symeon remained for some eleven or twelve years, until his death in 1022.[75] In this period he composed *Hymns*, so Nicetas tells us, having earlier mentioned that some of these had been written during the time when he was at St. Mamas'. Koder holds that most of the *Hymns* were in fact produced in these closing years of Symeon's life. Nicetas refers to other literary activity during this period, and describes how he himself would copy out on parchment what Symeon had drafted, and then give back his handiwork.[76]

Even though Nicetas tells us that Symeon did not escape hostility from some people in the neighbourhood,[77] we gain the impression that these last years were the happiest period of his life. Those who joined his community did so because they were attracted by his personality and teaching, and he did not therefore encounter the problems which he had met with at St. Mamas' when his monks included several who proved recalcitrant. Moreover as a voluntary exile, Symeon could be true to himself and at the same time avoid coming into conflict directly with those who represented contemporary aspects of ecclesiastical life with which he was at variance.

> The Byzantine Church—Krivochéine writes—was at that time developing in the direction of regulating its liturgical patterns so that they were both more outwardly splendid and less diverse. The same period saw the ecclesiastical festivals and the calendar settled by the Emperor Basil II's 'Menologion'. At that time also Symeon Metaphrastes expurgated and re-edited the Lives of the Saints, in order to render them more uniform by getting rid of irregularities in the language and eccentricities in the stories.

---

[74] Nicetas, *Life*, 102, 15–21, 103, 104, 107, 15–27, 108; "a Studite," cf. *ibid.*, 61, 20–23, 63, 15–17, where Nicetas records Symeon's claims to follow the precepts of Theodore, and, in explanation of the patriarch's words, "that policy of uncompromising opposition [which] their master Theodore handed on to the Studites," H. Delehaye, 'Byzantine Monasticism' *Byzantium*, (edd. N.H. Baynes and H.St.L.B. Moss), Oxford, 1948, p. 162.

[75] Nicetas, *Life*, 109, 12–19, 110, 128, 129; for dates (including that of Symeon's death), v. Hausherr, *Life*, pp. LXXXIVf., XC.

[76] Nicetas, *Life*, 111, 8–17, 131, 6–15, cf. 37, 11–15; Koder, *Hymns SC* 156, intr. p. 77.

[77] Nicetas, *Life*, 110, 1–15, 112.

After mentioning St. Theodore and his monastery, Krivochéine significantly concludes:

> One may say that Symeon's spirituality was a kind of reaction against the formal cenobitism which developed at Studios under Theodore's successors.[78]

This verdict on the era not only sheds light on the whole of Symeon's stormy career, but also helps us to understand why he was content to end his days in semi-seclusion and away from Constantinople.

ADDITIONAL NOTES

A. *"The New Theologian."* The meaning of Νέος Θεολόγος as a title given to Symeon has provoked much discussion—v. Hausherr, *Life*, p. LXXIX, Krivochéine. *Cats SC* 96, intr. p. 53, n. 1 and pp. 155–157, also 'The Writings of St. Symeon the New Theologian,' *O.C.P.*, 20, (1954), pp. 323–326, Darrouzès, *Chs SC* 51, pp. 92f., n. 1, and P. Wirth, καινὸς Θεολόγος, *Oriens Christianus*, 45, (1961), pp. 127f. That it was felt liable to cause offence is indicated by the fact that in some manuscripts it is altered to Νέος καὶ Θεολόγος (Krivochéine, *Cats SC* 96, p. 169). It seems reasonable to follow Hausherr in supposing that it was first applied derisively to Symeon by some who were jealous of his reputation, and later adopted by his disciples as a title of honour. (We shall see in the next chapter a parallel with regard to the Studite.) For those who understood it in a good sense, it will naturally have carried the implied suggestion that Symeon was a true successor to St. Gregory of Nazianzus, the Theologian.

B. *The Intercession of a Living Saint.* It is tempting to suggest that Symeon's insistence on discovering a living saint to intercede for his salvation owed something to what he knew about the treatment of petitions submitted to the emperor. This knowledge he could have gained through his γαμβρός John ὁ δεήσεων (Nicetas, *Life*, 113, 25f.), or as one "going daily to the palace" he might himself have had opportunities of observing that it was important for petitioners to secure a well-placed patron. We have also seen that it is probable that his family found it advantageous to have a member representing their interests at the imperial court. It is easy to understand that for a person with this kind of background it would appear essential to secure an effective patron in the heavenly court, "a friend of God" (*Ep 1*, p. 115, 9), enjoying παρρησία ("confidence in intercession") in his approach to the Deity (cf. *Ch* I, 101, 23 and Barringer, *Penance*, p. 47 and *passim*).

This desire is something of a *topos*, appearing for example in the words of a certain Thomas to St. John the Eremopolite, "I want only this from you, the obtaining of pardon for my sins through your hallowed prayers to God" ('Life of St. John the Eremopolite,' ed. F. Halkin, *Saints moines d'orient*, London, 1973, V, 19, 4). P. Brown, (*The Cult of the Saints*, London, 1981, pp. 64f.) writes of the concept of a (dead) saint as *patronus*, and elsewhere illustrates the importance attached to the intercession of a living holy man, who might be a πατὴρ πνευματικός ('The Rise and Function of the Holy Man in Late Antiquity,' *J.R.S.*, LXI, (1971), pp. 97–99).

Even though by the 10th century in Constantinople it had come to be frequently assumed, as we shall see, that there were no longer any living saints, Symeon was determined to discover one. His reluctance to rely on the help of one in the next world can be explained as the result of his anxiety to be sure that he had found a patron who really would accept him and intercede for him.

---

[78] Krivochéine, *Cats SC* 96, intr. pp. 40f., and in almost identical words, *Lumière*, p. 32; cf. J. Gouillard, *Dictionnaire de Théologie Catholique*, 14 (ii), col. 2957.

CHAPTER FOUR

SYMEON: HERITAGE AND INFLUENCES

Education

Symeon's education was glanced at in the context of the story of his life, but it must now be considered in somewhat greater detail as an element in what the French would call his *formation*, the overall theme of this chapter.

There is no reason for doubting what Nicetas has to say, namely that on his arrival in Constantinople he was sent to γραμματιστής for προπαιδεία, that he then proceeded as he grew older to τελεωτέρα μαθήματα, and soon learnt the skill of the ταχυγράφοι as well as acquiring "the beautiful hand-writing of which the books written by him afford clear evidence." After this it remained for him to become perfectly at home in the classical language "by familiarising himself with pagan culture and gaining a mastery of rhetorical speech."[1]

At this point, however, as we saw, Symeon refused to pursue his studies any further—or so Nicetas asserts, introducing a hagiographical *topos* and furnishing it with the typical comment that his hero thus "escaped the harm which might have befallen him from his fellow-students."[2] Such a remark reveals him as writing what convention dictated and so may give rise to suspicion, but apart from its hagiographical embellishment there is no reason to doubt the basic accuracy of Nicetas' account. Education is known to have comprised two, or at times, three stages, and although the demarcation between these is not made very clear in what he says, Nicetas employs terms which were definitely in current use.[3]

---

[1] Nicetas, *Life*, 2, 9–21; Lemerle, *Premier humanisme*, pp. 99–103 gives examples showing how educational terms were used, προπαιδεία commonly denoting 'elementary instruction,' i.e. reading and writing, with γραμματιστής often employed for the teacher at this level and the subjects styled γράμματα, while those belonging to the next stage were called μαθήματα; on ταχυγράφοι ('stenographers'), v. *ibid.*, p. 50, n. 15 and pp. 102f., n. 91, the second reference providing an example of a clear distinction "between the tachygrapher (or 'oxygrapher') and the calligrapher," although Nicetas, by the construction of his sentence, seems to blur the difference in his remarks about Symeon; there appear to be no known examples of still extant manuscripts written by Symeon, so that it is impossible to confirm Nicetas' statement.

[2] Nicetas, *Life*, 2, 21–26.

[3] G. Buckler, 'Byzantine Education,' *Byzantium*, (edd. N.H. Baynes and H.St.L.B. Moss), pp. 205f., cites Psellus for three stages: *encyclios paideusis*, entailing elementary instruction in language and in the outlines of *grammatiké*, which itself formed the second

Furthermore, while it is tempting to treat as conventional hagiography the statement that Symeon refused to extend his studies into the realm of "non-Christian education (ἡ ἔξωθεν παιδεία),"[4] to do so is probably to be unfair to Nicetas.

In support of this claim, it can be shown that while Symeon was himself conversant with the principles of educational practice, he insisted that his "own speech [was] powerless and lacking in non-Christian learning."[5] This is in harmony both with a description of his *Hymns* as early examples of "a growing body of texts written in literary Koine—which by this time had to be learnt at school—without Atticizing pretentions,"[6] and also with an assessment of his prose style as owing "very little to the rhetoric which was so highly esteemed by his contemporaries in Byzantium."[7]

In fact these verdicts are confirmed by a reading of Symeon's works which in general are tolerably correct so far as grammar is concerned, and are written in a straightforward manner, far removed from the artificialities of contemporary "rhetorical speech." His style is a proof of the possibility in the tenth century of a boy's getting enough education to be able to write "literary Koine," without being immersed in that kind of pedantic study of classical authors which resulted in mannerisms and affectations.

Thus Nicetas is probably to be trusted in his apparently conventional assertion about Symeon's refusal to complete his education; he depicts quite fairly the attitude of the mature Symeon, who though at home in a language "deliberately different from the *speech* in use at the time,"[8] still felt it necessary to protest that the Holy Spirit was not sent "to orators or philosophers or students of the writings of the Greeks," whereas "those with [him] as their teacher have no need of the learning (μάθησις) imparted by men."[9]

This conclusion about the limits of Symeon's education would be invalidated if he could be shown to have made use of, or to have been influenced

---

stage, and was followed by 'higher learning,' i.e. rhetoric and philosophy. Lemerle—v. n. 1 – distinguishes two stages only, the second of which might be styled τελειωτέρα μάθησις, and remarks that fluctuation and confusion are found in the terminology. Nicetas may imply two stages: προπαιδεία, the first, and the second, τελεωτέρα μαθήματα, perhaps subdivided into γραμματική and rhetoric (*Life*, 2, 10–25).

[4] Nicetas, *Life*, 2, 25f.; on ἡ ἔξωθεν, v. Lemerle, *op. cit.*, pp. 47f., n. 11; cf. also what is said of Theodore Studite, *PG* 99, 117CD.

[5] Symeon, *Ch* III, 24; *Hymn LVIII*, 3f., with probably a reminiscence of *II Corinthians* 10. 10—τὸ ἀσθενὲς τοῦ λόγου καὶ ἀμέτοχον μαθήσεως τῆς ἔξω.

[6] R. Browning, 'The Language of Byzantine Literature,' *The 'Past' in Medieval and Modern Greek Culture*, (ed. S. Vryonis, jr.), Malibu, 1978, p. 122.

[7] Darrouzès, *Trs SC* 122, intr. p. 72.

[8] Lemerle, *op. cit.*, p. 260 (his italics).

[9] Symeon, *Hymn XXI*, 55f., 102f.

by, the writings of non-Christian authors. Of this, however, there is practically no trace: the indices in the *Sources Chrétiennes* editions of his works contain no names of secular writers apart from that of Aelian, with one of whose works it is just conceivable that he may have been acquainted.[10] Kambylis, it is true, in his edition of the *Hymns* does give a number of what he regards as possible parallels with lines from the classics,[11] but on examination these prove to be either so very remote, or else so commonplace in their substance, that it would be highly precarious to assume from them that Symeon really had any direct knowledge of the authors in question. Thus though one may feel it necessary to be cautious about accepting the statements of Nicetas and even of Symeon himself, the actual evidence of his writings strongly supports the conclusion that his education had conveyed to him practically nothing of the literary inheritance of pagan Hellenism.

The Bible

Into the inheritance of the Scriptures, on the other hand, Symeon entered with the greatest eagerness. He quotes a maxim of the Studite's "Gain God, and you will have no need of a book,"[12] but naturally this was never intended to refer to the Bible. In fact when reading Symeon's works one cannot but be struck by the number of Biblical quotations and the frequent use of language alluding to Scriptural texts or reminiscent of them. He can be shown to have drawn upon every book of the New Testament and upon forty of those which make up the Old Testament and Apocrypha. The extent to which he uses individual books does, of course, vary considerably; it ranges from 858 counted examples in the case of *St. Matthew's Gospel* to no more than one in the case of *III John*.[13]

---

[10] Aelian, *De Natura Animalium*, X, 13—Symeon, *Tr Eth VIII*, 73f., where Darrouzès comments that "Symeon had probably never read Aelian; his explanation [of pearls] must have been current and used in preaching" (*SC* 129, p. 207, n. 2).

[11] For example in his note Kambylis on p. 164 compares Homer, *Iliad* II, 488f. (πληθὺν δ' οὐκ ἂν ἐγὼ μυθήσομαι οὐδ' ὀνομήνω, οὐδ' εἴ μοι δέκα μὲν γλῶσσαι, δέκα δὲ στόματ' εἶεν), with *Hymn XX*, 167f. (εἰ γὰρ μυρίαι γλῶσσαι μοι δοθήσονται καὶ χεῖρες, οὐκ ἂν ἰσχύσω ἐξειπεῖν ἢ περὶ πάντων γράψαι), and on p. 183 Aeschylus, *Seven against Thebes*, 593 (βαθεῖαν ἄλοκα διὰ φρενὸς καρπούμενος), with *Hymn XXI*, 427 (γλυκεῖαν αὔλακα τέμνων τοῦ λόγου)—in neither case is the alleged parallel convincing.

[12] Symeon, *Cat VI*, 192.

[13] It is not to be expected that there will be complete agreement as to the exact number of reminiscences of Scripture in Symeon. Kambylis (cf. n. 11) is more ready to see possible allusions in the *Hymns* than is Koder. The figures given in this section are derived essentially from the *SC* editors, but to some of the totals calculated on the basis of their indices a small number of additions has been made, because a few extra examples of convincing allusions have been noticed. The statistics are intended to do no more than give a general indication of how far Symeon can be seen to have known and used the different books of the Bible.

Without giving complete statistics, which would be an unnecessary elaboration, it is of interest to present in tabular form figures which will indicate the differing degrees of frequency with which Symeon, in his quotations from, or allusions to, the Bible, drew upon some of the individual books: —

Old Testament and Apocrypha		New Testament	
Genesis	184	St. Matthew	858
Exodus	63	St. Mark	138
Psalms	458	St. Luke	439
Proverbs	44	St. John	684
Canticles	12	Acts	120
Isaiah	89	Romans	298
Jeremiah	32	I Corinthians	340
Ezekiel	25	II Corinthians	221
Minor Prophets	52	Galatians	111
Wisdom	45	Ephesians	199
Ecclesiasticus	32	I Timothy	117
		Hebrews	117
		I John	122

From these tables it is clear that of the books of the Old Testament it was the *Psalms* which had the deepest influence on Symeon, the total for quotations from or allusions to them being only exceeded by the figures for *St. Matthew* and *St. John* in the New Testament. This figure for the *Psalms* is easily explicable in view of the important place which the recitation of the psalter holds in the daily round of services in a monastery, in consequence of which its contents could not fail to be extremely well-known to Symeon. Because of the great emphasis which he came to lay on repentance, something which will be illustrated in a later chapter, it is also not surprising to discover that out of the total of 458 references, no fewer than 27 are to *Psalm* 50 (51), the classic appeal by a penitent sinner for forgiveness and a clean heart.

Next to the *Psalms*, *Genesis* is the Old Testament book most often quoted or alluded to by Symeon. It is interesting that 72 of his references are to the creation narratives of chapters 1 and 2, while there are 46 to chapter 3, the account of the archetypal sin committed by Adam and Eve. In the light of what has just been said about Symeon's stress on the necessity of repenting, it is only to be expected that he would find frequent occasion to allude to these chapters which tell of what man was intended to be, and of his sinful failure to live in obedience to his Creator. It is noteworthy that at one place Symeon has a long passage in which, after hinting at his knowledge of a shorter but similar treatment of *Genesis* 3 by St. Dorotheus of Gaza, he re-tells the story in a lively manner and uses it to enforce the lesson of the vital importance of repentance, maintaining that it was the refusal of Adam and Eve to repent while they had the opportunity which led to their expulsion from the Garden of Eden.[14]

In our calculations regarding the use made by Symeon of the books of the Old Testament, it will be noticed that the figure for *Isaiah* is the next highest after that for *Genesis*. It should be added that of the total of 89 citations or allusions, 53 are to be found in chapters 1 – 39 (commonly known as "*First Isaiah*"), and 36 in the remaining chapters, 40 – 66. The influence of the Church's conviction that the Isaianic writings, particularly *Isaiah* 7, 10 – 14, 9, 1 – 7, and 11, 1 – 9, are especially prophetic of Christ's coming, will be the reason for their importance to Symeon, although he appears actually to have confined himself to *Isaiah* 9 and not to quote from or allude to either chapter 7 or chapter 11. It is striking also that only once does he seem to refer to *Isaiah* 53, the great chapter understood as prophesying Christ's passion, and here the verse in question is cited also by a New Testament writer, who might thus be Symeon's source.[15]

The figures show that Symeon was influenced much less by the other prophetic books. Moreover it is noteworthy that of the 52 instances given for the twelve *Minor Prophets*, no less than 12 are references to *Malachi*, and this can again to a large extent be accounted for by his Christocentric devotion: he was impressed by verses such as *Malachi* 4. 2, which speaks of the advent of the Sun of Righteousness and has been understood by Christians as foretelling the coming of Christ.

Symeon's fairly frequent use of *Exodus* is understandable when one remembers that this book contains a wealth of typology for the Christian expositor, while the extent to which he drew on the Wisdom literature for practical counsel is shown by the figures for *Proverbs*, *Wisdom* and *Ecclesiasticus*, 121 references in all. It is rather surprising that, though a mystic, Symeon cites or alludes to *Canticles* (*Song of Songs*) only 12 times, an indication that it did not deeply affect him, in spite of its being, as is well-known, a favourite source of inspiration to many mystical writers.[16]

Passing to the New Testament, we can readily account for the large number of references to *St. Matthew*, since

---

[14] Symeon, *Cat V*, 171 – 466, where basing himself on *Genesis* 3. 9 – 19, he extends the discussion to cover sin, repentance and redemption generally; for Dorotheus' treatment of the chapter, v. *Doctrinae* I, 9, and also Krivochéine's note on *Cat V*, 172, *SC* 96, pp. 390f., n. 2.

[15] Symeon, *Tr Eth VI*, 365f., *Isaiah* 53. 9 (*I Peter* 2. 22); *Tr Eth VII*, 358 might be taken to allude to *Isaiah* 53. 4, but since the LXX version is very different from that of the quotation in *St. Matthew* 8. 17, Symeon probably depends on the latter, as it is of this that his language is reminiscent.

[16] St. Gregory of Nyssa in the East and St. Bernard in the West are notable examples of mystical theologians who have been inspired to write at length about *Canticles*.

at least from the time of Irenaeus and early canonical witnesses, Matthew was for seventeen centuries the 'first Gospel' in a most real sense.[17]

With regard to *St. John*, it has been stated that "the Johannine Christ may ... be described as himself the one true mystic,"[18] and there is thus nothing surprising when we find its words being quoted or implicitly alluded to as many as 684 times by one who was a mystic himself. The figure of 122 instances for *I John*, a work by the same writer or at least emanating from the same school, is of course similarly explicable.

However, if we add up the figures given for works from the Pauline corpus given in the table (*Romans* to *Ephesians*,—omitting *I Timothy* which is often held to be pseudonymous, and the certainly non-Pauline *Hebrews*), we shall find that the total is 1,169, a figure which suggests that Symeon was profoundly influenced not only by the theology and mysticism of the Johannine writings, but also by the works of St. Paul which, though theological and mystical, have a very different ethos.[19]

The conclusion to be drawn from this survey is obvious: Symeon knew the Bible intimately and many of its books exercised a very marked influence on him. To illustrate what this could mean in practice we shall now look at two of the *Catecheses* which, as will be shown afterwards, also furnish us with good examples of his treatment of other Christian literature. In the *Sources Chrétiennes* edition *Cat IV* runs to 720 lines in which there can be discovered 12 quotations from, and 65 allusions to, or reminiscences of, Scriptural texts, that is an average of more than one reference to the Bible in every 10 lines; *Cat VI*, with 370 lines, is even more Biblical, for there are 20 quotations and 52 allusions in this much shorter work, which includes a kind of paraphrase of the Gospels in a passage dealing with our Lord's trial and crucifixion.

There is further evidence of the profound way in which the Bible influenced Symeon in the very fact that he evidently relied largely on memory when quoting from it, since he often does not quote accurately and at times conflates two or more texts.[20] The frequent, and perhaps half unconscious, reminiscences of Scriptural phrases were the result of his

---

[17] K. Stendahl in Peake's Commentary (revised edition), London, 1962, p. 769.

[18] C.K. Barrett, *The Gospel according to St. John*, London, 1955, p. 73.

[19] Although scholars are divided as to whether *Ephesians* was actually written by St. Paul, all would agree that it belongs to the Pauline corpus in a way which cannot be asserted of *I Timothy*.

[20] A good example of Symeon's conflation of texts can be found at *Cat VI*, 237–239, where *II Corinthians* 1. 3 and 11. 31 are conflated and the language has also been influenced by *Romans* 9. 1 or *I Timothy* 2. 7. It is amusing, incidentally, to find him twice (*Hymn XV*, 35f., and *Hymn L*, 220f.) attributing *St. James* 2. 26 to St. Paul, clearly the result of relying upon memory.

familiarity not only with the *Psalms*, but also with many other books of the Bible. This familiarity he will have gained by private reading as well as through the liturgical use of Scripture, and when delivering his *Catecheses* he probably assumed a like familiarity on the part of his hearers.

Cats IV and *VI* also provide examples of how Symeon made use of the authority attaching to the Bible: sometimes he would appeal to it in illustration of a point he wished to make, as when in *Cat IV* he recalled the description of the two thieves crucified on Calvary, one penitent and the other not, and used this to prove that we are justified or condemned through our choices and our thoughts; alternatively, he could quote from the Bible in support of his assertions as he did in *Cat VI*, supporting his claim about what he had received from the Studite by verses cited from *St. John*.[21]

Nevertheless, important as the Bible was for Symeon, Darrouzès has arrived at a convincing verdict in his comment about the nature of its significance for him.

> In his infrequent citations of the fathers, and in his citations of the Bible, it is not the thought of someone else that he is seeking, but it is an echo of his own inner life that he is rediscovering.[22]

That this is in general true, and that for Symeon the Scriptures proved valuable for reasons of this kind, can be well illustrated by examining how the parable of the Prodigal Son haunted him when writing his *Hymns*, which were largely compositions inspired by his spiritual experiences. The well-known story relates how the younger of two brothers journeyed to a far country, squandered his possessions ζῶν ἀσώτως, and was reduced to poverty and near-starvation. When he at last came to his senses and returned home, his father welcomed him with a feast, thus leading the elder brother to complain about such kindness being shown to one whom he described as καταφαγών σου τὸν βίον μετὰ τῶν πορνῶν (πορνῶν being here treated as a feminine plural and translated 'harlots' in the A.V.).[23] Symeon found in this parable an echo of his own experience as a sinner, totally unworthy but yet welcomed home by God. This is clearly suggested by the fact that in the *Hymns* he no fewer than nineteen times describes himself as ἄσωτος and once confesses to having lived ἀσώτως.[24]

---

[21] Symeon, *Cat IV*, 81–91, cf. *St. Luke* 23. 29–43, and *Cat VI*, 198–220, in the concluding lines of which *St. John* 4. 13f. and 7. 39 are cited.

[22] Darrouzès, *Chs SC* 51, intr. pp. 33f.

[23] *St. Luke* 15. 11–32.

[24] Symeon, *Hymns I*, 5, *II*, 3, *XI*, 28, 93, *XIII*, 54, *XIV*, 51, *XV*, 18, *XVII*, 75, *XVIII*, 178, *XIX*, 130, *XX*, 67, 115, *XXII*, 2, *XXIV*, 34, 48, *XXV*, 145f., *XXVIII*, 170, *XLI*, 21 (ἀσώτως), *XLII*, 53, *LVI*, 18. In view of the use in *St. Luke* 15. 22 of στολὴν τὴν πρώτην,

44 SYMEON: HERITAGE AND INFLUENCES

Moreover on five occasions he couples with the description of himself as ἀσώτως the word πόρνος (masculine), which in New Testament and patristic Greek has the primary meaning of 'fornicator', but can also be used more generally for an 'unchaste, sensual person.' One wonders whether instead of, or in addition to, this general sense, πόρνος had for Symeon something of its meaning in classical Greek, namely 'sodomite', for as we have already seen it is not improbable that he may earlier in his life have been involved in some form of homosexual misconduct.[25] At all events, these repeated echoes of the parable of the Prodigal Son make it clear that in this story Symeon felt that he encountered something which was closely akin to his own experience. It should be added that he once joins to his description of himself as ἄσωτος the word τελώνης ('tax-collector', or, as A.V., 'publican'), and also in another place lays stress on Christ's willingness to associate and eat with ἄσωτοι and τελῶναι, that is with those who were outcastes in the eyes of the Jewish religious leaders.[26]

To highlight the way in which for Symeon personal experience and the Scriptures were inter-related, we may contrast with him Dorotheus of Gaza: in the latter's writings the editors of the *Sources Chrétiennes* series[27] have noticed no allusions to, or quotations from, *St. Luke* 15, the chapter in which the parable of the Prodigal Son occurs; they give a single instance of the use of ἀσωτία by Dorotheus, one of ἄσωτος and two—both in the same context—of τελώνης. Moreover, in spite of the fact that he suffered much from temptations to sexual impurity, the word πόρνος does not seem to be found in Dorotheus' vocabulary. He, like Symeon, was a monk, and so both were men who had the opportunity of becoming very familiar with the Bible through their daily worship and by studying it in their cells. Symeon, however, could not help unconsciously revealing through his utterances that for him the Scriptures were a treasury of words and themes that reflected and interpreted the experiences of his life, and that he did not simply accept them in an external fashion as writings pronounced authoritative by the Church.

---

it is interesting to find in proximity to one of the above στολισάτω με φαιδρῶς (*Hymn XXV*, 151).
[25] Symeon, *Hymn I*, 3, *XIV*, 51, *XVIII*, 178, *XXV*, 145f., *XXVIII*, 170; on πόρνος v. Lampe, *Lexicon*; Aristophanes, Demosthenes and Xenophon use the word in the sense of 'sodomite', v. πόρνος in H.G. Liddell and R. Scott, *Greek—English Lexicon* (new edition, revised and augmented by H.S. Jones), Oxford, 1940.
[26] Symeon as τελώνης, *Hymn XX*, 67, cf. *St. Luke* 18. 9–14; reference to Christ's associating with ἄσωτοι and τελῶναι, *Hymn XLI*, 49, cf. *St. Matthew* 11. 19 (or parallel in *St. Luke*, 7. 34), though the Biblical writers link ἁμαρτωλοί and not ἄσωτοι with τελῶναι.
[27] L. Regnault and J. de Préville, *Dorotheus*, SC 92.

The Fathers

As we turn to consider the influence which non-Biblical writers exercised on Symeon, the evidence of course being found in the use he made of them, we must first of all take note of Holl's comment that "only to a very moderate extent was he acquainted with the literature of his Church."[28] This is certainly the impression that anyone would get by counting the number of occasions on which Symeon explicitly quotes a named author. But a closer inspection of his writings will lead to some modification of this verdict, for Symeon not infrequently betrays by his language the influence of an earlier author, without naming him or indicating that he is indebted to someone other than himself. In this respect there is often little difference between his treatment of the Biblical writers and of the Fathers.

His relationship with St. John Climacus is instructive. Nicetas recounts how Symeon, while visiting his home in Paphlagonia shortly before his admission at Studios, found a copy of the *Scala Paradisi* in the family library, and on reading it was extremely receptive to its teaching.[29] If there were any doubt as to whether afterwards a copy of this work, "the manuscripts [of which] are innumerable,"[30] was available to him at St. Mamas', the fact that it could be had there is virtually established by Symeon's own words in *Cat IV*, when he invites any of his hearers to read the book from which he has just quoted a few words.[31] But apart from this occasion there is only one other instance of his mentioning Climacus by name, when he cites *Sc. Par.* 5 as authority for what he himself has to say about repentance. In addition there are just two places noted in the nine *Sources Chrétiennes* volumes where possible reminiscences can be detected in his language.[32] Thus, in spite of Climacus' immense reputation, and in spite of Nicetas' comment that Symeon, on first reading the book, "like good soil received the seed of the word in his heart," one might be tempted to suppose that the *Scala Paradisi* actually influenced him very little.[33]

However, through an analysis of subjects dealt with by both writers, Völker has demonstrated that in fact Symeon was, not surprisingly,

---

[28] Holl, *Enthusiasmus*, p. 37.

[29] Nicetas, *Life*, 6, 21–39.

[30] L. Petit, *Dictionnaire de Théologie Catholique* 8 (i), col. 692.

[31] Symeon, *Cat IV*, 540–543.

[32] Symeon, *Cat XXX*, 140–142, quoting the first words of the title, περὶ μετανοίας, at *PG* 88, 764B; possible reminiscences at *Cat VI*, 146 of *Sc. Par.* 27, 1100D, and at *Ch* I, 70 of *Sc. Par.* 21, 945B; in addition, at *Tr Eth XI*, 94ff. he is writing of a ladder (κλῖμαξ) of ascent to heaven, "an allusion to the well-known work of John Climacus" (Darrouzès, note *ad loc.*).

[33] Nicetas, *Life*, 6, 23f., cf. *St. Luke* 8. 11, 15.

greatly influenced by Climacus in his treatment of the matters which we
are to examine in succeeding chapters. The relevant section of Völker's
book has, as its title suggests, a good deal to say about spiritual fatherhood, and towards the end of it, after a detailed comparison of the two
writers comes the assertion that Symeon

> presents nothing original in his ideas, but merely reproduces those of Clima-
> cus even down to precise phrases and terms.[34]

At a later stage we shall produce instances which demonstrate that this
judgment is too sweeping and that as well as his knowledge of Climacus,
Symeon's experience as a disciple of the Studite is something that one
must take into account in order to assess his teaching about spiritual
fatherhood. But what Völker says can with qualifications be accepted, and
we may agree on the basis of the evidence he has accumulated that Symeon
had so absorbed many of Climacus' ideas that he reproduced them in his
own words, having in fact made them his own. To take a single example,
Climacus gives a warning against "self-direction (ἰδιορρυθμία)," describing it as a temptation to leave the short but rough road that leads to one's
journey's end; Symeon has an admonition with the same meaning, but
he uses the expression "living by self-direction (ἰδιορρύθμως) and gathering in the worthless fruits of one's own will."[35] It may then safely be concluded, in the case of the *Scala Paradisi*, that neither failure to name his
source nor the absence of exact verbal parallels can avail as arguments for
Symeon's having remained ignorant of Climacus or uninfluenced by him.

Although therefore with regard to Climacus Holl's estimate of Symeon
cannot really be sustained, the position is somewhat different when other
writers are considered. If we turn to St. Gregory of Nazianzus, the Father
whom he quotes or refers to by name more than any other, it is again
instructive to compare Symeon's practice with that of Dorotheus of Gaza.
The latter in the one *SC* volume which contains his works quotes Gregory
no fewer than eight times, while Symeon in nine volumes has only twenty-
nine quotations and one definite allusion.

There will inevitably be scope for disagreement among editors when it
is a question not of the cases where an author is mentioned by name, but
of those where there appears to be a more or less certain reminiscence of
something in his works. Thus for the *Hymns*, Kambylis in his edition on
the one hand, and on the other Koder, Paramelle and Neyrand in the

---

[34] Völker, *Praxis*, section entitled '*Der Verzicht auf den eigenen Willen und der* Πατὴρ
πνευματικός,' pp. 111–129.
[35] Völker, *ibid.*, p. 112, n. 1 and p. 116, n. 5, referring to *Sc. Par.* 4, 680C and *Cat XX*,
53f.

Sources Chrétiennes series, often fall to agree, with the result that what is designated in one edition as an allusion to Gregory may be ignored in the other. We are, however, compelled for what follows to depend on the *Sources Chrétiennes*, since in them we have available all Symeon's works, apart from the *Epistles*, whereas Kambylis has only produced an edition of the *Hymns*. With this in mind, we may add ten possible reminiscences to the twenty-nine quotations and one allusion already mentioned.

Of this total of forty instances in Symeon, no fewer than twenty-five[36] are found to come from a mere three of Gregory's works, *Orations XXXVIII, XXXIX* and *XL*, known respectively as *In Theophania, In Sancta Lumina*, and *In Sanctum Baptisma*, being sermons preached at Christmas, Epiphany and on the day after Epiphany. In these can be found themes which, as we shall see, were dear to Symeon, for example the healing power of tears, the deification or 'christification' of the redeemed and the conscious realisation of grace received. But if it was by these three works of Gregory that Symeon was chiefly influenced, he can be shown to have had knowledge possibly of a further nine, and certainly at least of a further six. He appears, indeed, also to have been particularly impressed by *Oration XXI, In Laudem S. Athanasii*.[37]

Symeon only rarely names Gregory as his source: in connection with his favourite *Orations XXXVIII–XL*, we find that on no more than three occasions does he actually refer to him by name, while twice he says that he is quoting from "a theologian" and three times merely indicates that he is citing the words of another.[38] In the remaining cases, which are sometimes no more than reminiscences of notable words or phrases, he gives no overt indication that he is borrowing. Furthermore—and this presents an additional parallel with his way of using the Bible—, it is interesting that in one of the three places where Gregory is specifically named, Symeon has a "quotation" that is far from exact: its source indeed cannot be definitely identified.[39] (Alternatively, it is possible that it was taken from a work now lost.)

---

[36] The twenty-five instances might be reduced to twenty, since in five cases the same or very similar wording occurs elsewhere in Gregory. Our purpose in any case is simply to give a general picture.

[37] *Or. XXI, PG* 35, 1084B, v. Symeon *Ch* II, 17; *ibid.*, 1104A, v. *Hymn XLIX*, 34; *ibid.*, 1104B, v. *Tr Eth XV*, 170, where although Gregory is specifically named, there is merely some resemblance in thought and very little in actual language—cf. Darrouzès' note (*SC* 129, p. 456 n.c.).

[38] Gregory is named in *Cat IV*, 686, *Cat XXII*, 179, and *Hymn XXIII*, 415f.; reference to "a theologian" at *Cat XXVIII*, 417 and *Tr Eth IV*, 801; quotation indicated at *Tr Eth V*, 221, *Ch* I, 5, 15, III, 21, 15.

[39] *Hymn XXIII*, 415–418, where Neyrand comments that "Symeon is perhaps thinking of *Or. XXXIX*." (*PG* 36, 344A).

As can be seen from the references given in the notes, Symeon's predilection for Gregory manifests itself throughout his works. On occasion, he seems to cite him as an authority even though he omits his name and simply introduces the quotation by a formula which denotes it as such. However he scarcely attempts to expound or develop the thought contained in what he quotes: a good illustration of his attitude of mind is to be seen in *Tr Eth V* where, without naming Gregory, he quotes from *Oration XXXVIII* to substantiate what he has just said, prefacing his quotation by κατὰ τό. But in point of fact it is some echo of his own thought that has led him to Gregory's words, which really have to do with God's method of creating the universe, whereas Symeon uses them to justify his oft-repeated demand that Christians ought consciously to know God and be aware of possessing the Holy Spirit.[40]

A passage in *Cat IV* is instructive as revealing something of the influence of *Oration XL* upon Symeon. In lines 686–688 occur the words, "as Gregory the theologian says," and there follows an almost exact quotation which is quite fairly cited as authority for the proposition which Symeon is upholding, namely that if we fail to allow our spiritual sight to be purified in this life, we cannot expect to be capable of seeing God in the life to come. A few lines later (702f.) we can see further indications of Gregory's influence when Symeon, in speaking about readiness to meet the Bridegroom, uses language marked by a pronounced verbal reminiscence of that which can be found in the same *Oration XL*, not far from the words he has recently quoted explicitly. Then at line 705 we can discover another phrase which occurs at a much earlier point in Gregory, while an additional possible reminiscence can be noticed considerably nearer the beginning of *Cat IV*.[41] Taken together these instances provide a good illustration of the influence on Symeon of a single work of Gregory's, and incline one to speculate as to whether he had recently been reading or re-reading it at the time when he was composing this *Catechesis*.

The general impression we can thus gain from our attempt to study how he was influenced by Gregory is that Symeon must have read quite widely in the works of this Father and must have become familiar enough with parts of them for sentences and phrases to have lodged themselves in his mind; on the other hand, he shows no signs of having been so inspired by Gregory that he was ever moved to try to enter deeply into his thought and build upon it.

---

[40] *Tr Eth V*, 221, quoting from Gregory, *Or. XXXVIII*, *PG* 36, 320C.

[41] Gregory, quotation from *PG* 36, 424C; influence of *ibid.*, 425B; phrase from earlier in the *Or.*, (λαμπροὶ λαμπρῶς) *ibid.*, 393AB; possible reminiscence of *ibid.*, 388B, πᾶν εἶδος κακίας διεξελθόντες, Symeon, *Cat IV*, 99f., πᾶν εἶδος κακίας . . . μετελθόντων.

It is not, of course, remarkable that he should have been fairly well acquainted with Gregory, one of "the Christian classics," who "judging by the number of preserved manuscripts, were read more than any other authors."[42] Nevertheless it is noteworthy that during Symeon's lifetime two of the monasteries in Constantinople are definitely known to have acquired newly-made copies of Gregory's works.[43] It is reasonable also to suppose that interest in Gregory was stimulated by the bringing of his relics from Cappadocia to the imperial capital at a date either a few years after, or a few years before, the birth of Symeon.[44] Highly regarded by all, however, as Gregory undoubtedly was, the way he is used by Symeon only illustrates the truth of Darrouzès' remark, quoted in the previous section; Symeon did not really seek to comprehend the thought of this great theologian—indeed, he does not appear to have assimilated it to the extent to which he assimilated much of the thought of Climacus.[45]

St. John Chrysostom stands next to St. Gregory of Nazianzus in the list of Fathers with whom Symeon appears to have been chiefly acquainted. This is not surprising, inasmuch as he too is reckoned to have been one of the "Christian classics." Works by Chrysostom, or ascribed to him, can be detected as perhaps influencing Symeon to the following extent: one reminiscence noted by Kambylis, which however he qualifies by calling it "*locus communis apud patres Graecos*," and according to the *Sources Chrétiennes* editors fourteen possible or probable reminiscences, one somewhat general allusion and one instance where, although Symeon explicitly claims to be quoting Chrysostom on *Psalm* 50 (51), it has proved impossible to identify the source of the alleged quotation.[46]

It is striking that no less than eleven of these fourteen reminiscences are to be found in the *Hymns*, and indeed in only seven of these, though there

---

[42] Mango, *Byzantium*, p. 240.

[43] Janin, *Eglises et monastères*, records (p. 396) that the Μονὴ τοῦ Πελεκάνου owned one dated 5 June 975, and (p. 299) the Μονὴ τοῦ ἁγίου Λαζάρου one dated 14 May 1007.

[44] Lemerle, *Premier humanisme*, putting the date at 955/6 or possibly 944.

[45] There is one instance, not included in the totals given in the text, where perhaps Symeon adopted and expanded an idea of Gregory's: in *Tr Eth VI*, 276–311, a passage which will be examined later, he has a full description of a spiritual physician's skilful treatment (ἔντεχνος ἰατρεία) of a sinner, which might have been inspired by Gregory's ὥσπερ οἱ ἰατροὶ τοῖς ἀρρωστοῦσιν, ἵν' ἡ φαρμακεία παραδεχθῇ διὰ τῆς τέχνης ... Or. XXXI, *PG* 36, 161AB, and there is also in *Or. II*, *PG* 35, 425A–441B, a long passage comparing physicians of the body and of the soul. However, the idea is somewhat commonplace and, as we shall see in chapter VI, may have come to Symeon from Climacus.

[46] Kambylis, *op. cit.*, on *Hymn II*, 13f., referring to *In Johannem hom.* 46, *PG* 59, 260— Koder, on *Hymn V*, 8 notes an allusion to the same passage in Chrysostom, and compares *Hymn II*, 12ff., although there he does not remark on the possible reminiscence; Symeon has a general allusion at *Hymn XIX*, 80, where Neyrand writes that he has in mind *De Sacerdotio*, particularly books II and III, *PG* 48, 631–660; *Psalm* 50 (51), *Cat V*, 126–135, and v. Paramelle's notes (*SC* 96, p. 387, n. 1 and n. 2).

are fifty-eight *Hymns* in all. Furthermore, seven of these allusions are to Chrysostom's homilies *De Incomprehensibili* and occur in *Hymns XIX, XXI, XXIX, XXX*, and *XXXI*. From this it is reasonable to deduce that it was when composing his *Hymns* that Symeon was most influenced by Chrysostom, and at the time of his writing the five just enumerated, the homilies *De Incomprehensibili* were particularly in his mind. This suggestion resembles that made earlier about his use of Gregory of Nazianzus' *Oration XL* in *Cat IV*.[47]

Other earlier writers, of whom Symeon apparently had some knowledge, and who may therefore have exercised some influence on him, include St. Basil the Great (three citations, two definite allusions and seven possible reminiscences, on the basis of the *Sources Chrétiennes* indices), and St. Gregory of Nyssa (one allusion, five possible reminiscences in the same indices, and two others noticed in addition). Völker, moreover, has demonstrated that Maximus the Confessor (and, through him, Evagrius) had some influence on Symeon's thought, and Krivochéine observed a striking resemblance between the opening part of *Cat XXXIV* and the second part of the *Epistula Magna* of pseudo-Macarius, although Symeon characteristically gives no indication of indebtedness.[48] It is somewhat surprising that he never definitely quotes pseudo-Dionysius, although at times one can detect him using similar language, and although Nicetas explicitly refers to the *Divine Names* as authoritative support for the teaching contained in the *Hymns*.[49] It is also remarkable that while in an autobiographical passage Symeon recounts how as a young man he was given by the Studite a work of St. Mark the Hermit to read, and in the same context cites three sentences from this author by which he was impressed, yet apart from these he never quotes him directly and indeed has no more than a few possible, but not certain, reminiscences of him.[50]

As well as all the above-mentioned works, Symeon has some fifteen quotations from or references to the *Lives* of various saints and martyrs.

---

[47] Chrysostom, *De Incomprehensibili*, PG 48, 701–748.

[48] Völker, *Praxis*, pp. 266–272; on Symeon's *Cat XXXIV* and pseudo-Macarius, v. Krivochéine SC 113, pp. 270f., n. 1, with notes on subsequent pages detailing the parallels; for the *Epistula Magna*, v. W. Jaeger, *Two Rediscovered Works of Ancient Christian Literature—Gregory of Nyssa and Macarius*, Leiden, 1954.

[49] For similarities between pseudo-Dionysius and Symeon, cf. *Divine Names* 1, 1; 4, 32, (*PG* 3, 588B; 732D) and *Tr Th I*, 79–81, *Tr Th III*, 108–111; for Nicetas' statement, v. *Preface to Hymns*, 84–86 (*SC* 156, p. 114); v. B. Fragneau-Julien's full discussion in *Les sens spirituels et la vision de Dieu selon Syméon le Nouveau Théologien*, pp. 176–181.

[50] St. Mark the Hermit, *Cat XXII*, 34–51, cf. Nicetas, *Life*, 4, 16–19, the work in question being *De Lege Spirituali*, PG 65, 905–929, which Symeon must have known in a manuscript in which there was no division between it and *De his qui putant se ex operibus justificari, ibid.*, 929–965—v. Krivochéine's notes, SC 104, p. 367, n. 3, and pp. 368f., notes 1, 2 and 3.

These are books of the kind one might expect to be available for edifying reading in a monastery, and Symeon indeed on one occasion explicitly told his monks to read "the lives" of "our holy fathers," instancing their prowess as support for his own teaching.[51] Krivochéine remarked that "he appears to have been deeply moved by" the *Life* of St. Mary of Egypt which he three times cites, while on another occasion he employs language reminiscent of it though without mentioning his source.[52] In *Cat V*,[53] as well as that of St. Mary of Egypt, he mentions the *Lives* of St. Pelagia, St. Theodora, St. Euphrosyne, and St. Xene, and in *Cat VI*[54] those of St. Antony, St. Arsenius, St. Euthymius and St. Sabas. He was thus sufficiently familiar with a good many examples of hagiography to be able to allude to them in his teaching, and it is interesting that when he did so he appeared to assume that the monks he was addressing would also know these works and would be able to read them for themselves.[55]

The Words of the Studite

The general influence of the Studite on Symeon will be considered in a later section, but *Cat VI*, at some of which we have been looking, provides good evidence that however much Symeon might revere the writings of the saints of former days, none of them inspired in him anything approaching the devotion which he felt for the utterances of his spiritual father, whom he unhesitatingly regarded as a contemporary saint. It is appropriate, therefore, to glance now at the response which the Studite's words elicited from Symeon.

This *Catechesis* runs to 370 lines, and it is in line 102 that we find Euthymius and Sabas mentioned by Symeon, but merely as being of the company of those who had performed "superhuman deeds," whereas considerably more details about Antony and Arsenius have previously been given. In lines 164f. Symeon refers eulogistically to the Studite by name,[56] while shortly afterwards he quotes an enigmatic saying of his to the effect that a monk in his monastery should be

---

[51] Symeon, *Cat VI*, 18–20.
[52] *Life* of St. Mary of Egypt cited *Cats V*, 562, *IX*, 61–84, *XII*, 179f., and a reminiscence of its language in *XVI*, 10f.; v. also *SC* 96, p. 424, n. 1 for Krivochéine's remarks from which a few words have been quoted.
[53] Symeon, *Cat V*, 560–566.
[54] Symeon, *VI*, 40–69 (Antony), 70–98 (Arsenius), 102 (Euthymius and Sabas).
[55] Incidents in the *Lives* of Antony and Arsenius are referred to in a way that suggests that the hearers are familiar with them, and at *Cat V, 18–21* can be found an explicit injunction to read the *Lives* of "our holy Fathers."
[56] Symeon's words are: ὁ ἅγιος καὶ μακαριώτατος εὐλαβὴς Συμεών, ὁ λάμψας δίκην ἡλίου μέσον τῆς περιωνύμου μονῆς τῶν Στουδίου.

as one who is and is not and does not appear, or rather does not even make his existence known.[57]

After giving the explanation of this as the Studite himself had interpreted it, Symeon bursts into a display of enthusiasm far greater than any that he manifested when speaking of the saints of old,

> O blessed words, by means of which his superhuman angelic mode of life is proclaimed . . .[58]

This comes not quite half-way through the *Catechesis*, and of the remainder the greater part is devoted to the Studite. There are three more quotations of his words, and the last of these is followed by another enthusiastic comment:

> O blessed voice, or rather blessed soul, judged worthy to become like this, and altogether separated from the world.[59]

Cat VI thus illustrates vividly the difference for Symeon between what he received from writers of the past and what he was given by his spiritual father: he valued, used and paid tribute to the former, but it was the latter which really touched his heart.

Remarks to the same effect will be found recurring at several points in subsequent pages, for we shall often have occasion to notice the overwhelming importance for Symeon of his actual experience as a spiritual child of the Studite, and various instances of this will be commented on as they arise. But this experience of his cannot, of course, be isolated from the general concept of spiritual fatherhood, which must therefore be discussed next as a constituent of the heritage into which Symeon entered.

Spiritual Fatherhood

Is it possible to determine when, in Christianity, there arose the ideas and practices characteristic of what came to be called spiritual fatherhood? Holl carries us to a time before the commencement of the monastic movement when Clement of Alexandria advised anyone who, though a Christian, was wealthy and haughty, to submit himself to some "man of God" who would be his director and trainer.[60] There is no trace here of anything in the nature of a recognised institution, but in a saying ascribed to St. Antony, often regarded as the founder of monasticism, we seem to be hearing of something in process at least of becoming a regulated system:

---

[57] The Studite quoted by Symeon, *Cat VI*, 172–174.
[58] Symeon, *ibid.*, 178f.
[59] Symeon, *ibid.*, 273–275.
[60] Holl, *Enthusiasmus*, pp. 228f., citing Clement, *Quis dives salvetur?*, *PG* 9, 645C.

> The monk ought, if possible, to confide to the elders how many steps he takes or how many drops [of water] he drinks in his cell, so as to avoid making a mistake in these matters.

Here, as Hausherr noted,[61] we find the first explicit enunciation of what was to become a central feature of the spiritual father's work, the receiving from his disciple of an account of the latter's every thought, word and deed.

Before a spiritual father's activity is described and discussed—something to which every subsequent chapter will contribute—, it is first necessary to speak of his titles. A list drawn up by Hausherr includes, in addition to "spiritual father," "father" or "abba(s)" (with "amma(s)" as its feminine equivalent): *géron*—which is rendered "elder" in the example quoted from Antony—, or *presbyteros*, both of which are appropriate since he would normally be an older person; *didascalos*, used because he would have to instruct; and further terms indicative of training or correction; moreover, in cenobitic communities the father would usually be in some sense a "superior", and in these circumstances *prostatès, épistatès, éphestós* could also be used. Of all the titles, "father", with or without the adjective "spiritual", is the most common and also the only one which expresses everything and emphasises what is essential.[62]

While we shall have to examine later in more detail the qualifications needed by a spiritual father, it is useful here to take note of Rousseau's remarks about the early period.

> A claim to the title of ἀββᾶς, spiritual father, depended on a wide range of qualifications, recognized throughout the desert.

The requirements comprised: belonging to a historical tradition; personal experience; hard work (physical); interior watchfulness; purity of heart; visions; foreknowledge and insight; inspiration and discernment.[63] Many of these we shall be encountering again, but what must be stressed here is that from the outset spiritual fatherhood, though in itself a 'charismatic' rather than an 'official' ministry, has never been effectively exercised by those who lack the necessary qualifications.[64] For this reason, Symeon,

---

[61] Antony, *PG* 65, 88B; Hausherr, '*Penthos*', *O.C.A.*, 132, (1944), p. 83.

[62] Hausherr, *Direction spirituelle*, p. 13.

[63] Rousseau, *Ascetics*, pp. 22–31, *passim*.

[64] By 'charismatic' ministry is meant one which depends on the possession of a personal gift (χάρισμα), which may or should be recognised, and the use made of it supervised, by ecclesiastical authority, but which that authority cannot of itself bestow. The possibility of conflict between 'charismatic' ministries and those of an official nature is obvious, and examples of such conflict can easily be found, but one can also discover instances of harmonious co-operation, v. Barringer, *Penance*, pp. 105, 159f., 178.

as we shall see, felt himself called upon to condemn some of his contemporaries for falsely claiming to be spiritual fathers when in essential matters they were quite unfitted to act as such.

Examples from the pre-Basilian era show, as Rousseau describes them, a variety of types of relationship between a spiritual father and those who had recourse to him.

> Questioners may have come on isolated occasions, to appeal in general terms to the father's spiritual wisdom . . . When communities were expanding in Nitria and Scetis, questioners may have sought for more detailed advice, which would have required a more lengthy revelation of their state of soul and longer acquaintance and deeper knowledge on the part of the father. Finally, once a young man had found a mentor suited to his taste, he would stay in his company, and in that of his fellow disciples for a considerable time, even until death.[65]

Dissatisfied though he was with eremitical forms of monasticism, St. Basil the Great was very far from wishing to do away with spiritual fatherhood which had by his time become something of an institution. Both Lowther Clarke and de Mendieta agree in translating a rather obscure sentence of Basil's in a way which brings out the idea that one should expect to find one's spiritual director in a monastery:

> Such a guide it is difficult to find in solitude, unless one has already formed a link with him in community life.[66]

Whatever the exact meaning of Basil's statement, he certainly had no intention of undervaluing spiritual fatherhood, for in the very same context he writes of the cure of sin being undertaken with understanding by one who genuinely loves. Moreover he elsewhere insists that being a spiritual father to his monks is the first duty of a monastic superior.[67] This is doubtless an admirable ideal in theory, but as will become clear in connection with Symeon, it could and did lead to difficulties in practice: a hegumen might be immersed in matters related to the temporalities of his monastery, and might indeed have been chosen more on account of his ability in this respect than because of his qualities as a spiritual guide; on the other hand, a monk might be convinced that the true good of his soul required him to have not the hegumen but some other person as his father.

---

[65] Rousseau, *Ascetics*, p. 36.

[66] W.K. Lowther Clarke, *St. Basil the Great*, Cambridge, 1913, p. 163; E.A. de Mendieta, *L'ascèse monastique de S. Basile*, Maredsous, 1949, p. 121, n. 6; Basil, *Regulae fusius tractatae*, VII, PG 31, 929A.

[67] cf. K. Baus, 'Early Christian Monasticism', *History of the Church*, (edd. H. Jedin and J. Dolan), London, 1980, II, 368f., referring to Basil, *ibid.*, *XXIV–LIV*, PG 31, 984C–1044B.

Problems of this kind resulting from Basil's requirement led to the state of affairs described by Hausherr as a result of his study of monastic *typika*,

> a continual oscillation between two positions: a single spiritual father who is at the same time also hegumen, and a freedom to choose accorded more or less sparingly to individuals.[68]

Nevertheless, in spite of difficulties which might arise when there was a rigid insistence on combining spiritual fatherhood with hegumenate, already

> by the time of the Council of Chalcedon, the monastic penitential institutions of confession of λογισμοί, spiritual direction, and the correction of sinners within the sphere of the monastic *ecclesiola* have become normative.[69]

Thus by the tenth century spiritual fatherhood had a long history behind it; it had a special relationship with the monastic life; and the rules governing its exercise in monasteries were liable to give rise to various disagreements.

However, although spiritual fathers were generally monks[70]—not of course necessarily cenobitic monks—and every cenobitic monk in theory at least had a spiritual father, yet it must not be imagined that these facts mean that we can neglect the outside world in our discussion. At all times some people living in the world are found numbered amongst the spiritual children of some fathers, but naturally the relationship in this case cannot be the same as when the disciple is living the specifically 'religious' life of a monk, and may be subject to the authority of his father *qua* hegumen. The secular person not only has responsibilities different from those of the monk, but also is free at any time to cease from submitting himself to his father's spiritual direction, perhaps becoming the disciple of someone else, or perhaps no longer following any guide.

It may be asked why in Byzantium it was to monks rather than to the secular clergy that those living in the world seem regularly to have turned

---

[68] Hausherr, *Direction spirituelle*, p. 114.

[69] Barringer, *Penance*, p. 53.

[70] There is a dearth of information about the secular clergy of the Byzantine world in Symeon's time and earlier, but for the reasons to be given in the next paragraph it appears to have been unusual for someone not a monk to be accepted as a spiritual father. However, the conceited and sinful priest Manos in the *Life* of St. Cyril the Phileote (ed. E. Sargologos, *Subsidia Hagiographica*, Brussels, 1964), who claims to have priests among his spiritual children (p. 158), seems not to have been a monk, for he is introduced (p. 154) simply as τις ἱερεὺς τῆς ἀρχιεπισκοπῆς Δέρκου. In *Ep 1*, pp. 122–124, Symeon argues that because of their worldliness etc., the power to bind and loose has passed from bishops and priests and now belongs to monks, or rather to those monks who are true to their profession. Certainly our sources give the impression that the great majority of spiritual fathers were monks.

when they sought a spiritual father. At first sight one might suppose that
the parish priests would have been better qualified to help those who like
themselves had not withdrawn from the everyday life of ordinary men and
women. However, as a result of the high value ascribed to virginity,
coupled with the fact that celibacy was not imposed on the non-monastic
clergy, the secular priest was seen simply as a cultic figure, and for confession and spiritual direction it was felt preferable to turn to monks who
were believed to be more perfect Christians and to possess the gift of discernment.[71] Of the parish clergy, on the other hand, it has been said:

> The people liked the *papas* and respected them hardly at all, because they
> were like themselves.[72]

In the light of this it is understandable that a man or woman living in the
world and wanting spiritual help would be more likely to seek it from a
monk than from a parish priest, and would probably be drawn to some
monk who had a reputation as a spiritual father. Naturally there might
be shortcomings on either side, and Symeon, as we shall see, was convinced that some people who acquired spiritual fathers did so insincerely,
while at the same time some who wished to be fathers to secular disciples
had no business to undertake this ministry.

Spiritual fathers in Symeon's time, then, although they had disciples or
children both outside and inside the monasteries, can for our purposes be
taken as belonging to the monastic order, but this is far from the same as
saying that they were all ordained priests. The monasteries as a rule had
among their memebers only a few in priests' orders, no more than needed
to officiate in Divine Liturgy and the other services. Moreover, as we have
seen, spiritual fatherhood is essentially a 'charismatic' ministry, whereas
priesthood is in the Christian Church necessarily an 'official' one. The
same man might, of course, be at once a monk, a spiritual father and a
priest, but the fact that he could equally well be the first two of these
without being also the third, was bound to raise the question of whether,
if unordained, he was or could be authorised to absolve those who came
to consult him.

This is a matter which calls for some discussion, for Symeon, though
himself ordained, produced *Ep 1* (*De Confessione*) as a vehement rejoinder
to those who sought to attach the power to absolve simply and exclusively

---

[71] cf. Holl, *Enthusiasmus*, p. 311.

[72] E. Le Barbier, *S. Christodule et la réforme des couvents grecs au XIe siècle*, Paris, 1863,
p. 10, (cited by L. Oeconomos, *La vie religieuse dans l'empire byzantin au temps des Comnénes
et des Anges*, New York, 1972 (reprint of 1918 edition), p. 126; cf., "The priest never
became a curate in the Christian East. There his central task remained the celebration of
the Eucharist ...," I. Illich, *Gender*, London, 1983, p. 152, n. 112.

to the holders of ecclesiastical office as such. He had been asked whether it was lawful to confess to unordained monks, since authority to bind and loose was believed to have been granted to none but priests,[73] and in reply, after writing at some length in favour of his 'charismatic' stance, concluded with what for him was the most important argument of all: his own father, the Studite, had been one "who had no ordination from men."[74]

It must be remembered that although a judicial aspect is always bound to be involved, the Eastern Church has an approach to confession and absolution which is less marked by forensic notions than that of the Church in the West. As has often been remarked, and as will be illustrated in connection with Symeon, an Eastern spiritual father normally views his relationship with the penitent primarily in therapeutic terms. There are also other factors which contribute to making the claim of an unordained father to absolve less startling than it at first sight appears to those who view matters solely on the basis of the theology and practice of Western Catholicism. There the confessor, acting as such, has the responsibility of granting or withholding absolution on a specific occasion, whereas in the East we shall find the spiritual father ideally more concerned to help his child to attain, perhaps after many years, a new and authentic personal relationship with God, one result of which will be an interior assurance of divine forgiveness. Furthermore, for the attainment of this end very great importance is attached to the father's intercession, and, regardless of his 'official' position in the Church, the greater his sanctity, the more effective his prayers are held to be—convictions which in the last chapter we saw were shared by Symeon. Finally it must be noted that although, in spite of Symeon and others, the Eastern Orthodox Church has in practice reserved to bishops and priests the authority to absolve, the formula used is precatory, and not the Western "I absolve thee."[75] In consequence, the distinction between sacramental absolution and intercession by the father for his disciple may well appear less sharp in the East than in the West.[76]

It is, then, not difficult to understand how unordained spiritual fathers could find themselves at the centre of controversy. Ordination was certainly not needed for much of what they did, such as interceding or giving counsel and direction, and it is not surprising if occasionally, perhaps in

---

[73] Symeon, *Ep 1*, p. 110, 1–5.

[74] Symeon, *ibid.*, p. 127, 6f.

[75] Since Symeon's time, however, some Orthodox Churches have adopted the Western form as a result of Latin influence.

[76] It should be noted that, as will be observed in a later chapter, there is also a possibility of confusion between absolution and giving permission to communicate.

response to pressure from men or women very conscious of having sinned, they claimed the right to grant sacramental absolution.[77] There is in fact evidence that although strictly speaking unordained monks were not supposed to hear confessions, their doing so might be unofficially or even semi-officially tolerated.[78] From the other side, of course, there would always be on the part of the 'official' element in the Church a natural desire to ensure that this 'charismatic' ministry of spiritual fatherhood was exercised under proper control. Barringer in his intensive study of the matter concludes that confession to unordained monks was a temporary phenomenon, for when it became more than a pastoral supplement, "it provoked a firm, measured reaction on the part of the canonists."[79] At all events, it is an inevitable part of the background which must be taken into account when Symeon is under consideration.

Monasticism

Something, it is clear, must be included concerning the monastic heritage into which Symeon entered. While it would be out of the question to attempt at this point to write a history of Eastern monasticism up to the tenth century, some of its features need to be mentioned briefly because of their relevance to our study. Thus, in spite of Symeon's having had there only a short and stormy sojourn, we begin with the Studios monastery.

As Holl observed, Nicetas regarded Symeon as a true exponent of the tradition of St. Theodore the Studite: in his address to the monks and to his disciple and successor Arsenius, at the time of his resigning the hegumenate of St. Mamas', words are placed on Symeon's lips which state this quite definitely.[80] There is no reason for doubting Nicetas' general accuracy here, for not only were Theodore's "reforms widely disseminated by

[77] cf. Hausherr, *Life*, p. LXXVII, "the power to bind and loose is only one part of the spiritual father's role, and perhaps not the main part."

[78] cf. P. Gautier, 'Le Chartophylax Nicéphore,' *R.E.B.* 27, (1969), pp. 170–172, 182–184, where two letters written c. 1100 A.D. imply that some monks, unordained and perhaps "inexperienced and unlearned," were doing this; the *typikon* of St. Mamas', compiled after its rebuilding in the 12th century, orders all the monks to have the hegumen as spiritual father, "even if he is not a priest, because he has authority from the ecumenical patriarch ...," Hausherr, *Direction spirituelle*, p. 114.

[79] Barringer, *Penance*, p. 194. Krivochéine, *Lumière*, pp. 146f., insists that the Orthodox Church has never officially pronounced on the question from the theological point of view, although as a matter of practical discipline it has allowed only bishops and priests to give absolution; K. Ware, 'Tradition and Personal Experience in Later Byzantine Theology,' *Eastern Churches Review*, III, 2, (1970), p. 137, inc. n. 25, writes in similar terms.

[80] Holl, *Enthusiasmus*, p. 13, n. 1; Nicetas, *Life*, 63, 15–17 (cf. also *ibid.*, 44, 14f., 61, 20–23).

his writings, his will, the *hypotyposis*, and his Catechisms,''[81] but Symeon must have absorbed many of the characteristics of Studios as a result of the influence of his spiritual father who remained there until his death.

When Patriarch Sergius II reluctantly expressed his admiration for Symeon's refusal to compromise in the words, "You are genuinely a Studite ...,"[82] we have already remarked that he had in mind "that policy of uncompromising opposition [which] their master Theodore handed on to the Studites."[83] However, Sergius' words are true in respect of more than Symeon's resolute refusal to moderate his publicly expressed devotion to the memory of his spiritual father. Krivochéine noticed a resemblance between *Cats XI, XII* and *XII* (on the themes of Lent and Easter) and some of the *Catecheses* of Theodore, the opening of *Cat XIII* particularly resembling *Parva Catechesis* 1, 1–5 and 2, 1–2.[84] Bouyer and Völker also, though the latter with some qualification, both agree that the influence of Studios played an important part in Symeon's development.[85]

Nevertheless there was one matter about which neither the Studite nor Symeon conformed to the intentions of Theodore, of whom Leroy wrote:

> The goal which he establishes for monasticism is not the acquiring of contemplation, but the realising of the old Christian ideal. The monastery is a kind of village on the Christian pattern, and nothing more.[86]

This accounts for the importance ascribed to work in the Studite tradition, a feature which also Leroy notes. However, as often happens after the death of a great founder or reformer, by the tenth century there had been a decline in the quality of the community's monastic life, resulting in what we have already found occasion to mention in a wider context, "the formal cenobitism which developed at Studios under Theodore's successors."[87] It was in reaction to this that Symeon's spiritual father (and probably some others in Studios) came to look upon contemplation as being in fact the proper goal at which a monk should aim, and to teach

---

[81] H. Delehaye, 'Byzantine Monasticism,' *Byzantium*, (edd. N.H. Baynes and H.St.L.B. Moss), p. 150, quoted chapter III, n. 74.

[82] Nicetas, *Life*, 108, 2.

[83] H. Delehaye, *op. cit.*, p. 162.

[84] Krivochéine, *SC* 104, pp. 152f., n. 1, *ibid.*, p. 191, n. 2.

[85] L. Bouyer, *A History of Christian Spirituality*, London, 1968, II, 572; Völker, *Praxis*, p. 86.

[86] J. Leroy, 'La réforme studite,' *O.C.A.* 153, (1958), p. 195.

[87] Krivochéine, *Cats SC* 96, intr. p. 41, quoted at end of chapter III; H-G. Beck, 'The Greek Church in the Epoch of Iconoclasm,' *History of the Church*, (edd. H. Jedin and J. Dolan), London, 1980, III, 53, remarks that Theodore's efforts did not meet with a success which endured.

that for its attainment ἡσυχία should be cultivated rather than work or involvement in the common life.[88] Symeon, indeed, unlike Theodore, seems to consider work to be of no intrinsic value, but merely a means for combating the temptations which may attack a novice who sits idly in his cell.[89]

What is to be understood by ἡσυχία in the context of monasticism? Away from cities it had for a long time been accepted that a monk, who felt called to a life of contemplation and was judged to be of sufficient maturity, might with his hegumen's blessing withdraw to some kind of cell, outside, but fairly close to the monastery.[90] This was clearly not always practicable in the case of an urban monastery, but it might still be possible to cultivate solitude and freedom from the pressures of community life, and thus although still living in the monastery to enjoy ἡσυχία. According to Meyendorff,

> Symeon taught the practice thereof in the very centre of Constantinople, at the monastery of Studios.[91]

In this strange statement the practice of withdrawal within the monastery is ascribed to the teaching of the New Theologian, who certainly did teach it, but could not conceivably have done so during the short time he was at Studios. In fact the practice goes back at least to Symeon's spiritual father—perhaps his being a Studite is the cause of the confusion—, for in an earlier section we have already met with his assertion that the monk should be in his monastery as one who is and is not and does not appear, or rather does not even make his existence known. Although the actual word ἡσυχία does not occur here, it is obvious that what is being advocated is a life of withdrawal to the fullest extent possible within the monastery.[92]

Symeon's monastic background was thus far from being purely cenobitic, in spite of the influence that Studios exerted upon him. It is, then, readily comprehensible that he is found making use of the verb ἡσυχάζω

---

[88] On ἡσυχία, v. Glossary. No one English word adequately represents its technical meaning, and therefore it has been left in the original Greek.

[89] *Cat XXVI*, 71–75.

[90] cf. M. Jugie, *Dictionnaire de Théologie Catholique*, II (ii), Paris, 1932, col. 1750f., and D. Obolensky, *The Byzantine Commonwealth*, New York, 1982, (1st edit. London, 1971), p. 387.

[91] J. Meyendorff (tr. C. Lawrence), *A Study of Gregory Palamas*, Leighton Buzzard, 1974, p. 18.

[92] *Cat VI*, 172–174. It was not only in Constantinople and other large cities that this practice obtained, for there are also instances of solitude being sought by means of enclosure within a cenobitic community not situated in urban surroundings, e.g. Barsanuphius and John at Thavatha, v. D.J. Chitty, *The Desert a City*, Oxford, 1966, p. 132, and L. Regnault and J. de Préville, *Dorotheus SC* 92, intr. p. 15.

when in his description of the training of a monastic spiritual child he reaches the stage where the father bids him quietly await the revelation of the Holy Spirit.[93] Whatever the full explanation for Symeon's resignation from the hegumenate, Nicetas is quite justified in writing in this context of his love for ἡσυχία.[94] Symeon then was in touch with the old tradition of withdrawal from community life into solitude, a tradition which had been adapted to fit the conditions of urban monasteries, and which greatly attracted both his spiritual father and himself.

The Personality of the Studite

We must now as it were bring together spiritual fatherhood and monasticism, two of the aspects of Symeon's background, by considering one particular monk, Symeon the Studite, who as his spiritual father exercised such a massive influence upon him. Unfortunately, we are hampered by the lack of evidence: apart from a small amount of the Studite's own writing, there is only what we can learn from his disciple, Symeon, and from Nicetas, the latter's biographer, neither of whom can be claimed to be impartial witnesses.

On the basis of what can be inferred from Nicetas' *Life*, taken in conjunction with a remark of Symeon's in *Cat XVI*, it appears that the Studite was born in 918 or thereabouts, became a monk in Studios in 942 and died at approximately the age of seventy in 986 or 987.[95] In that he was never ordained to the priesthood, he followed the practice of the majority of Orthodox monks. Nicetas and Symeon both insist that he was uneducated, a *topos* frequently found in writings of a hagiographical tendency and not to be too readily accepted.[96] In fact his writings show him capable of expressing himself in the kind of Greek which by the tenth century could only come from the pen of one who had had at least an elementary education, something which has already been spoken of in connection with Symeon himself.

Furthermore, the Studios *hypotyposis*[97] prescribed that on days when they were not engaged in manual works, monks were to obtain a book from the library and read it, so that we may presume him to have had

---

[93] *Cat XX*, 162.

[94] Nicetas, *Life*, 59, 8–10, in which is found the expression φίλη ἡσυχία that is also used by Nicolas of Ancyra with reference to the resignation of Gregory of Nazianzus from his bishopric (J. Darrouzès, *Documents inédits d'ecclésiologie byzantine*, Paris, 1966, p. 258) cf. as evidence for Symeon's own feelings, *Hymn XLIII*, 11–14.

[95] For the Studite's dates, *Cat XVI*, 38, v. Hausherr, *Life*, p. XC, (cf. Nicetas, *Life*, 72, 10–12) and Krivochéine, *SC 96*, pp. 313f., n. 4).

[96] Nicetas, *Life*, 72, 13—ἀγράμματος; Symeon, *Cat VI*, 195—μαθήσεως γραμμάτων ὑπάρχων ἀμύητος.

[97] Studios *hypotyposis*, *PG 99*, 1713AB.

some acquaintancce with Christian literature. Besides what he learnt from books belonging to the monastery, the Studite must have been familiar with at least one book which he owned himself, and which he judged suitable for lending to the young Symeon at an early stage in their relationship.[98] The very fact that the loan was possible indicates that this book was the Studite's property and did not belong to the monastery. His disdain for book-learning—"Gain God, and you will have no need of a book"— was thus not as absolute as one might at first be inclined to suppose.[99]

Nicetas credits the Studite with possessing gifts of healing and miraculous powers,[100] and it may be conjectured that it was these, as well as his reputation for sanctity, which gained him spiritual children in Constantinople. From Symeon we learn that they were numerous, and that he used to go and visit them.[101] At the same time it appears that he was not always or universally accepted as saintly, but the fact that some viewed him in an unfavourable light was probably what he desired and intended, strange though this may seem. There is, however, strong evidence, which must now be examined, that in order not to be reputed pious he deliberately acted as a holy fool (σαλός).

According to Mango, the deliberate feigning of madness is first found in the fourth century in a cenobitic context, the motive being a wish to add to one's humiliations for the sake of gaining a greater heavenly reward, though another motive, that of evangelization, can be seen in the case of the most famous holy fool, St. Symeon of Emesa.[102] Symeon and some others sought in this way to reach the most despised elements in society, who were impervious to the type of approach made to them by respectable Christians. These two motives exactly correspond with what Nicetas says about the Studite's

> wishing to conceal the treasure of his dispassion—for he fled from the praise of men and the honours they bestow as if from a serpent that bites the heel—, and doing this also in order that, by means of this bait, he might unobserved haul up from the pit of destruction some of those lying there, indeed all of them if possible . . .[103]

---

[98] The reference is to the work(s) of St. Mark the Hermit described in n. 50, *Cat XXII*, 34f., cf. Nicetas, *Life*, 4, 16, where Diadochus is added, apparently by mistake, v. Hausherr's note *ad loc.*.

[99] The Studite's maxim was perhaps something of a *topos*, cf. Climacus, *Sc. Par.* 5, 780D–781A, *ad Pastorem*, 1165C.

[100] Nicetas, *Life*, 72, 12.

[101] Symeon, *Cat XVI*, 31–34.

[102] Mango, *Byzantium*, p. 112 (cf. *St. Matthew*, 6. 1ff.). For an example of humiliations being sought by a nun who feigned madness, v. Palladius' account, *PG* 34, 1106A–1107C; the motive of evangelism is evident in Symeon of Emesa's words to his companion in the desert, "Let us depart and save others also," *PG* 39, 1704A.

[103] Nicetas, *Life*, 81, 6–10.

In spite of the absence of the actual word σαλός, we cannot miss seeing here the two motives depicted by Mango, even though we are not informed what social class the Studite hoped to evangelize.

Although none of our sources applies the word σαλός to the Studite, Rydén is justified in speaking of him as "a part-time holy fool," meaning thereby that for some part of his life he lived as such.[104] In the same context there is a suggestion of what may well be the reason why Nicetas and Symeon avoid the term σαλός, namely that it was not seldom brought into disrepute by "holy fools of a more doubtful sincerity," impostors who adopted this mode of life in its external features but were in reality far from being saints. Rydén quotes a telling passage in which Symeon himself utters a warning against such people.[105] Clearly there might often be uncertainty about the genuineness of individuals of this kind, and it is of interest in this connection that Holl observed that the charges brought by Stephen the syncellus against Symeon are more concerned with his "canonising" an unworthy person than with his lacking authority to "canonise".[106] In fact Symeon does depict his spiritual father in a way which by the standards of contemporary monasticism would have appeared bizarre, to say the least:

> Symeon, the holy, the devout (εὐλαβής), the Studite, was not afflicted by shame regarding any man's limbs and organs, neither if he saw others naked, nor if he himself was seen naked . . .[107]

Furthermore, as Hausherr argued, the appellation εὐλαβής could originally have been intended sarcastically, "because his enemies accused him of a serious lack of modesty."[108] It is very possible, then, that the syncellus had indeed learnt about the Studite's strange behaviour, and that Nicetas is substantially correct when he represents him as declaring to the synod:

> [Symeon's] spiritual father was a sinner, but he is lauding him as a saint [enrolled] among the saints.[109]

---

[104] L. Rydén, 'The Holy Fool,' *The Byzantine Saint*, London, 1981, p. 111, citing I. Rosenthal-Kamarinea, 'Symeon Studites, ein heiliger Narr,' *Akten des XI internationale Byzantinisten Kongresses*, (1958), pp. 515–519.

[105] Symeon, *Cat XXVIII*, 365–386. It may be added that in *Cat VI*, 300f., Symeon indignantly asks whether his hearers think the Studite μῶρος, a word meaning 'fool', but which does not have the specialised meaning of σαλός.

[106] Holl, *Enthusiasmus*, pp. 20f.

[107] Symeon, *Hymn XV*, 205–208—εὐλαβής, rendered 'devout' in most English versions, is used to describe a Biblical Symeon in *St. Luke* 2. 25.

[108] Hausherr, *Life*, p. LXXIX.

[109] Nicetas, *Life*, 81, 13f., and cf. Symeon, *Cats VI*, 304–308, *XXXVI*, 99–125, and most significantly *XX*, 80–87, where we may detect an autobiographical touch in the final

The evidence thus all fits very well together and strongly supports the view that the Studite at times conducted himself in ways that were characteristic of a holy fool.

Further confirmation that this is true is to be found by comparing what Nicetas says about the Studite's dispassion and its results, with incidents and sayings in the *Lives* of the two most famous holy fools, St. Symeon of Emesa and St. Andrew the fool. According to Nicetas, the Studite

> was totally mortified as to his flesh in consequence of dispassion of the highest order . . . and as for any bodies coming near to him, his perception of them was like that which a corpse might have of another corpse.[110]

Symeon of Emesa, as an act of deliberate folly, on one occasion made his way into the women's section of the public baths, and said of himself afterwards, "I remained like a piece of wood among other pieces of wood."[111] In the *Life* of Andrew, the two images of "corpse" and "wood" are combined, and a third is added, for he was once in the company of some prostitutes who tried unsuccessfully to arouse his sexual appetite, and one of whom finally remarked:

> This fellow is a corpse, or a piece of wood that cannot feel, or else a stone that never moves.[112]

The similarity of *motif* in these three cases strongly suggests that Nicetas, even though for good reasons he avoided the actual word, nevertheless wished to indicate that the Studite should have been respected as a saintly σαλός.

Symeon's responsiveness to the Studite's teaching has already been noted in this chapter, and we now turn to his writings in order to see if direct evidence can take us further in our attempt to assess him. Hausherr, Darrouzès and Krivochéine all accept the Studite as the author of forty *Chapters* which are in several manuscripts not differentiated from those of the Symeon the New Theologian, but in *Patmiacus* 427 are designated as the work of "Symeon the devout (εὐλαβής)."[113] Thirty-three of

---

words of the injunction not to be scandalized at the sight of one's spiritual father eating μετὰ πορνῶν καὶ τελωνῶν καὶ ἁμαρτωλῶν . . . ἀλλὰ μηδὲ τοῖς ὀφθαλμοῖς βλέπων, τούτοις πιστεύσῃς τὸ σύνολον· πλανῶνται γὰρ καὶ οὗτοι, ὡς ἔργῳ μεμάθηκα—had Symeon once been scandalized through seeing the Studite in such company?

[110] Nicetas, *Life*, 81, 3–5.

[111] Symeon of Emesa, *PG* 99, 1713C.

[112] Andrew the Fool, *PG* 111, 653A; cf. also Symeon the New Theologian's insistence on the possibility of one who has God within him remaining unharmed even if γυμνός τῷ σώματι γυμνοῖς αὐτοῖς ἐνωθήσεται (*Tr Eth VI*, 209f.).

[113] Hausherr, *Life*, pp. XLIV–XLVII, presents the full arguments on the basis of the manuscripts and of citations in *Cats IV*, 11f. and *VI*, 271–273; Darrouzès concurs,

these appear in Migne,[114] again not differentiated and thus wrongly ascribed, and Hausherr adds another in translation.[115] For the most part, they are short paragraphs intended to provide advice for a novice, or for a monk who is beginning to make a serious effort to advance in the spiritual life.

It is unfortunate, however, that we cannot from these *Chapters* gain a great deal of information about their author. They indicate that he lived in a cenobitic monastery, and reveal him as a person with a practical approach to the opportunities for spiritual progress afforded by the sometimes untoward circumstances encountered in such an environment. One of the themes later taken up by his disciple Symeon, the necessity of keeping so far as possible aloof from one's fellow-monks, reinforces what we observed about the Studite's belief in the importance of ἡσυχία, and may also be evidence that the general tone of his monastery gave him concern on account of its lack of spiritual earnestness. This would accord with what we have already discovered about the contemporary condition of Studios.

An attractive glimpse of the writer's character is provided by the manner in which he qualifies his advice about keeping aloof:

> [Cultivate] single-mindedness and spiritual exile from all (ξενιτεία), but visit the sick and encourage the afflicted. Do not turn away from any who ask your help on the pretext that you yourself should be holding converse with God, for charity (ἀγαπή) is better than prayer.[116]

If it has to be admitted that a study of the *Chapters* penned by the Studite adds little to our knowledge of his career, there is certainly nothing in them which contradicts what can be learnt from Symeon and Nicetas concerning his personality. What unfortunately they do not provide is any definite clue to help us understand the reason why he was able to exercise the profound influence on Symeon of which we have already been made aware. To explain this we can do no more than suggest that his temperament, his methods as a spiritual father and the skills which he possessed were closely attuned to Symeon's needs.

Chs SC 51, intr. p. 13 and p. 27, inc. n. 2; cf. Krivochéine, *SC* 96, p. 315, n. 1, and for details of *Patmiacus* 427, *ibid.*, intr. pp. 102f.

[114] Migne, *PG* 20, 668C–685C, numbered 120–152, in a collection of *Chapters* printed among the works of Symeon the New Theologian—they total 33, in spite of Hausherr's remark on p. XLV that Migne reproduced 32.

[115] Hausherr, *Life*, pp. XLIXf.

[116] *PG* 120, 680BC, the concluding words being closely similar to Climacus' μείζων ἀγαπὴ προσευχῆς, *Sc. Par.* 26, *PG* 1028B; ξενιτεία will be discussed in a later chapter.

Heretical Movements

It would be wrong to conclude this chapter without raising the question of whether Symeon was at all influenced by the teachings of some of the dualistic heretical movements which flourished in his time. Deppe, for example, expressed astonishment that Symeon was never accused of Messalianism;[117] Holl likewise conjectured that one factor which contributed to Symeon's name's being virtually forgotten for a considerable period after his death, was the suspicion aroused on account of the Bogomils by anything which savoured of *enthusiasmus*.[118] It is true that one can easily recognise points at which Symeon's teaching resembles that of such sects, yet even if, perhaps unconsciously, he may have been to some extent influenced by their heresies, there are important respects in which he can be shown to have held beliefs very different from those of the dualists.

One can only speculate as to how Symeon might have come into contact with heretics of these kinds, if indeed he ever directly did so. But it is possible that already in his time some of them, having assumed the monastic habit, were penetrating into monasteries in Constantinople and there disseminating their doctrines. Obolensky, referring it is true to a later period, writes that

> both Anna [Comnena] and Zigabenus explicitly state that the Bogomils dressed as monks and led the monastic life,

and also that

> they recruited many adherents in the monasteries, which were also the centres of Hesychasm.[119]

However in the light of the relationship which Obolensky elsewhere shows to have existed between monasticism in Constantinople and in Bulgaria in the ninth century, we may find some significance for Symeon's time in his statement that

> by the middle of the tenth century, if not earlier, heretical proselytism had been active and often successful in the monastic circles in Bulgaria.[120]

---

[117] Klaus Deppe, *Der wahre Christ. Eine Untersuchung zum Frömmigkeitsverständnis Symeons des Neuen Theologen und zugleich ein Beitrag zum Verständnis des Messalianismus und Hesychasmus*, (dissertation), Göttingen, 1971, p. 37, cited by Krivochéine, *Lumière*, pp. 62f., n. 74.

[118] Holl, *Enthusiasmus*, p. 214.

[119] D. Obolensky, *The Bogomils; A Study in Balkan Neo-Manichaeism*, Cambridge, 1948, pp. 254, 219.

[120] D. Obolensky, *ibid.*, p. 105, on the basis of Cosmas, *Traité*; in *The Byzantine Commonwealth*, New York, 1982, (1st edit. London, 1971), p. 129, he writes of young Bulgarians being sent to Constantinople for training in the monastic life, citing Photius, *PG* 102, 904–905.

An obvious partial parallel between Symeon's teaching and that of the Bogomils is found in connection with confession. These heretics, according to Cosmas, rejected the Church's provision for absolution by its priests, and insisted that one must look for forgiveness through confession to those who were truly spiritual, those, that is, who had been initiated as Bogomils.[121] Symeon, we have already seen, maintained that the essential qualification for reconciling the penitent was to be a truly spiritual man, whether one had been ordained priest or not, and in this respect his position resembled that of the heretics. Nevertheless being himself both monk and priest, he was not so much concerned to deny that ordination confers the right to absolve, as to demand high standards among the priesthood and to warn any unspiritual cleric:

> Do not presume to give absolution without having received in your heart Him that taketh away the sin of the world.[122]

Doubtless Symeon and the Bogomils were far from being in total agreement about confession and absolution, but they did at least concur in asserting that if one wished to be really qualified as a minister of reconciliation it was not enough to rely simply upon ordination.

As far as the sacraments of Baptism and the Eucharist are concerned, the Bogomils would participate in the latter in order to avoid being detected and persecuted, while for the Messalians "it was simply meaningless."[123] On the other hand in Symeon's case one can cite instance after instance which reveals the sincerity of his devotion to the Eucharist.[124] However, by insisting that "not all who are baptized receive Christ through Baptism,"[125] he might be taken as going some way towards the Bogomils' position: they maintained that it was completely useless to be baptized and that in place of Baptism another initiation ceremony of their own was required, in preparation for which converts must submit themselves to a long course of instruction.[126] Symeon certainly stresses the importance of repentance as a "second purification," which he considers essential for those who have sinned after being baptized in infancy, in order that they may fully receive the grace of the Spirit. On the other hand, he does not deny that in the sacramental Baptism of infants the Spirit is received for

---

[121] D. Obolensky, *The Bogomils*, pp. 133, 135, cf. Cosmas, *Traité*, p. 249.

[122] Symeon, *Tr Eth VI*, 419–421, cf. *Cat XXVIII*, 262–290.

[123] Bogomils, Obolensky, *op. cit.*, p. 196; Messalians, Vööbus, *Early Monasticism*, p. 137.

[124] Symeon, e.g. *Hymn LV*, 145–157; his high Eucharistic doctrine will be discussed in chapter VII.

[125] Symeon, *Tr Eth X*, 324f.

[126] Bogomils, Cosmas, *Traité*, p. 257.

the remission of original sin. In spite of all his emphasis on the need for repentance, he never implies that it can be regarded as a substitute for Baptism, but only as an additional necessity.[127]

Another point at which it appears that Symeon may show some contact with ideas prevalent in heretical quarters leads us into an examination of the actual words he used. The Messalians, according to Theodoret, taught amongst other things that

> the Holy Spirit manifests his presence in a way that is perceptible and visible (αἰσθητῶς καὶ ὁρατῶς).[128]

Gouillard presents an example of this belief in a debased form: a disciple of Eleutherus of Paphlagonia is reported to have said to a bishop whom he was attempting to win over.

> Open your mouth so that I may spit into it, and with your own eyes you will see the Spirit descend upon you.[129]

Symeon also was prepared to speak of "perceptibly" beholding God or Christ, and it appears that copyists or editors felt that he was here treading on dangerous ground, for Krivochéine has observed that at two places αἰσθητῶς is in some manuscripts replaced by the variant εὐαισθητῶς. In fact there is little real difference between the two words, but the preference for the latter

> is explained by the editors' wish to avoid an expression which, completely orthodox though it was in Symeon's usage, ... could be a cause of scandal on account of the unpleasant Messalian resonances which it evoked.[130]

These examples demonstrate that Symeon was not isolated from the ideas and sentiments in vogue among adherents of heretical sects such as the Messalians and the Bogomils. Accordingly, it is not surprising that works ascribed to him were chosen after his death as suitable for interpolation by someone who wished to propagate under acceptable auspices the heretical teachings of Constantine Chrysomallos, whose writings came, as we have already seen, to be condemned by the Synod as a mixture of enthusiasm, Messalianism and Bogomilism. At the same time it is instructive to reflect on the irony of the fact, also mentioned earlier, that Symeon's

---

[127] Symeon, *Hymn LV*, 28–51 (33, δέδωκας τὴν μετάνοιαν εἰς κάθαρσιν δευτέραν); Krivochéine, *Lumière*, pp. 150f.

[128] Theodoret, *Hist. Eccles.* IV, 11, *PG* 82, 1145A, quoted by Krivochéine, *SC* 96, intr. p. 152, who also cites, as a later authority to the same effect, St. John of Damascus, *De haeresibus*, *PG* 95, 732B.

[129] J. Gouillard, 'Quatre procès de mystiques à Byzance (vers 960–1143),' *R.E.B.*, 36, (1978), p. 50, and cf. p. 16, where he connects this incident with Symeon's aspirations.

[130] Krivochéine, *SC* 96, intr. pp. 151f., referring to *Cats II*, 423 and *XXIV*, 64.

own *Ep 1* must have been felt by some to need support from an authority more conspicuously orthodox than its real author, and so was boldly attributed to St. John of Damascus. (In reality what Symeon propounds in this letter is very little different from his teaching in *Tr Eth VI* and *Cat XXVIII*.) The truth is that by whatever paths Symeon came to hold and express, at times in very forceful language, certain views apparently not far distant from those of the heretics, he arrived at his conclusions essentially as a result of vivid personal experience. Deep feelings did indeed inspire him to put forth in striking words teaching which could appear to have a leaning towards heresy, and it is not impossible that, had he lacked the support of highly-placed spiritual children such as those who helped him at the time of his exile, he might have incurred further troubles by being charged with Messalianism.[131]

Conclusion

The intention of this survey has been to introduce the major factors composing the heritage into which Symeon entered or which contributed to his "formation". It might be objected that the Orthodox Church, with its whole range of doctrine, worship, sacraments and personal piety, ought to have been described, and not merely mentioned in connection with monasticism, spiritual fatherhood and some of the heresies which assailed it. It seemed best, however, not to attempt what could not be adequately accomplished in much more than the space available, and therefore the Church as a whole was deliberately omitted from this chapter. But it must not be forgotten that Symeon, though in some respects he may seem to have had affinities with heretics, and critical though he undoubtedly was of certain features of the Church of his day, still maintained the importance of "thinking in an orthodox way."[132] One must, therefore, never lose sight of his roots which are to be found firmly planted within the tradition of Orthodoxy.

---

[131] I have written more fully about this subject in 'St. Symeon the New Theologian and Dualist Heresies—Comparisons and Contrasts', *St. Vladimir's Theological Quarterly*, Vol. 32, No. 4/1988, pp. 359–366.

[132] *Hymn L*, 202.

CHAPTER FIVE

SPIRITUAL FATHERHOOD: SECURING A FATHER

Having surveyed the background in relation to Symeon, we can now proceed to investigate his contribution to our understanding of the meaning of spiritual fatherhood. The natural starting-point for this enterprise is the beginning of the relationship between disciple or client and father, or rather the search for the latter undertaken by the former. We have considered the reasons which impelled Symeon to try to find a spiritual father, and have seen how he was led to attach himself to the Studite. How far was his a typical experience, and what did he learn from it? What teaching did he give about this subject, and how was it related to that of earlier authorities? In this chapter these and similar questions will be our concern.

The Basic Motive

> The people came with their religious needs—writes Vööbus—to the huts of anchorites and to the monasteries of monks and nuns, making their peace of heart dependent upon the blessings and intercessory prayers available in these places. Here they laid down their problems of the inner life and their restless thoughts before men to whom they supposed all the secrets of heart and thought were known.[1]

A longing of this nature for spiritual help in a general sense would of course operate as a motive leading people to search out someone who could give them guidance either on a specific occasion or at more or less regular intervals. Some men and women, however, and amongst them especially those prepared to forsake the world, were driven by an urge that can be more sharply defined, the desire to be assured of salvation. So, in the words of Dörries,

> the basic question with which every person who entered the monastic life addressed himself to the elder: πῶς σωθῶ; was a confessional question. It expresses the need of a distressed conscience . . .[2]

---

[1] Vööbus, *Early Monasticism*, p. 318.
[2] H. Dörries, 'Confession', *T.U.*, 80 (1962), p. 298; cf. Hausherr's statement that monks are *"par antonomase ceux qui veulent être sauvés,"* *Direction spirituelle*, p. 298; and, for modern times, "I became a monk so as to make certain of my eternal salvation," described as the usual answer given when Athonite monks were asked why they had entered a monastery (E. Amand de Mendieta, *Mount Athos, the Garden of Panaghia*, Berlin, 1972, p. 217).

In such cases recourse to a spiritual father is explicitly felt to be a step on the road leading to salvation for all eternity.

This, the tradition of early monasticism, is that in which Climacus was nurtured and which he transmitted to later generations:

> As a ship which has a good helmsman reaches harbour safely, with God's help, in the same way a soul which has a good pastor easily climbs up to heaven, in spite of a great deal of earlier wrong-doing. As one who has no guide easily loses his way in spite of being very intelligent, so someone who is self-directed as he travels on the monastic road may easily perish, in spite of possessing all the wisdom of the world.[3]

In this passage Climacus made use both of positive imagery—reaching heaven—, and of negative—not missing one's way—, and each of the two could equally well provide a motive for discovering and relying on a spiritual father.

Such was the tradition, well represented by Climacus, and thus something with which Symeon was familiar. But the latter's insistence on the need for a spiritual father clearly owes much not only to his faithfulness to the heritage of the past,[4] but also to his own personal experience. Thus, in the course of his thanksgiving to God, he remarks that while still living in the world he had

> longed to see one of thy saints in the belief that through him I should find mercy from thee.

Shortly afterwards he amplifies this in the words:

> Mindful of my sins, I sought only for forgiveness of them and desired ... to find a mediator and ambassador, in order that through his intercession and my service of him, I might, at least in time to come, find pardon for my many faults.[5]

Here there is a plain statement of Symeon's motive: ''in time to come (ἐν τῷ μέλλοντι)'' indicates that when he began looking for a spiritual father, the object he had in view was the securing of eventual salvation, and, as we saw, this defective understanding of spiritual fatherhood probably contributed to his falling away in the period after his first vision. However, he was aware that others with similarly distressed consciences, though perhaps with truer ideas of a father's work, would likewise look for help in the same direction.

---

[3] *Sc. Par.* 26, 1089B. This is something of a *topos*, cf. Dorotheus, *Doctrinae* V, 61, 8f. and *passim*.

[4] Symeon's connection with Studios may have meant that he knew St. Theodore's letter in which he asks, τί γὰρ πατρὸς ἀληθινοῦ ποθεινότερον καὶ τοῦτο ἐπὶ θεοῦ λαμβανόμενον; *PG* 99, 909B.

[5] *Cat XXXV*, 19–21, 73–78; cf. also chapter III, Additional Note B.

> The man who as a result of sin has become enslaved to the devil ... and become the devil's child instead of God's—what will he do for himself in order to regain the past state from which he has fallen? He will most certainly seek a mediator, one who is a friend of God, and able to restore him to what he was before, and to reconcile him to his God and Father.[6]

The motive so far encountered has apparently been the acquiring of peace of mind as a result of gaining an assurance of salvation through the mediation of a spiritual father, although in the last passage quoted we find some idea of restoration in the present and not simply the thought that forgiveness may not be secured until the age to come. But it is necessary to look into the matter more deeply, and it must not be assumed that traditionally either spiritual fathers or their disciples thought of salvation in the limited way that the immature Symeon understood it. On the contrary,

> When men such as Antony, Macarius and their disciples repeated their eternal request: Speak a word to me: How may I be saved? εἰπέ μοι ῥῆμα πῶς σωθῶ; what they wanted was not simply to escape hell and the mortal sin which leads to it, but a radical healing of every disease of the soul together with fulness of life for the soul in God. Their spiritual fathers understood the request precisely in this way, and in reply offered them prescriptions embodying the great laws of sanctity and the most effective methods of attaining it.[7]

This attitude was no doubt never that of all spiritual children, but good fathers, on finding that any of their clients were moved by nothing more than a concern to escape damnation, would naturally have always tried to help such people to progress towards less limited aspirations. Symeon as a young man was, on his own confession, not consciously motivated by any desire for fulness of life, for as he later said to Christ,

> How could I ever have conceived the thought that thou, O Master, Creator of all that exists, dost unite thyself to men whom thou thyself didst fashion ... so that in consequence I might have come to long for such benefits and to seek them from thee? How could I have known, O Lord, that I have such a God, such a Master, Protector, Father, Brother and King as thou who didst become poor and take upon thee the form of a servant, for my sake?[8]

These words provide an explicit repudiation by Symeon of his having been capable of anticipating any positive spiritual experience in the present, at the time when he was starting on the quest which was to lead him to the Studite.

---

[6] *Ep 1*, p. 115, 1–11. (Both in this extract and in the previous one, 'mediator' translates μεσίτης.)

[7] I Hausherr, 'Vocation chrétienne et vocation monastique selon les Pères,' *Études de spiritualité orientale*, O.C.A., 183, Rome, 1969, p. 405.

[8] *Cat XXXV*, 38–45, with reminiscences of *II Corinthians* 8. 9, and *Philippians* 2. 7.

We may therefore assert that in spite of the fact that traditionally there had been deeper motives than that of simply ensuring one's future salvation which led people to attach themselves to a spiritual father, such motives came to influence Symeon only as a result of his becoming a disciple. His outlook was transformed by what he learnt from the Studite, as well as by his own direct mystical experiences. Further motives which might have influenced him, if in his early life he had been more familiar with the whole tradition of ascetical theology, will come to light when we proceed to consider the benefits to be expected from securing a spiritual father.

Before this, however, it is necessary to summarise a fairly long section of *Ep 3*, which shows Symeon's awareness of the existence of some who, unlike himself, were apparently complacent about their present condition and their prospects of future salvation. Opposing them, Symeon insisted that without self-knowledge it is truly impossible to understand the necessity of having a spiritual father in order to be assisted in keeping God's commandments and in escaping from the snares of the devil. Anyone who ignorantly thinks that he needs no instruction or help from others is conceited, and also unaware of the fact that he knows nothing. His blindness is caused by his love for this present world. In order to avoid being like this, the man to whom the letter was written is bidden to pray that his eyes may be opened, a prayer which God will by no means reject, and as a result of which he will come to know himself and to appreciate the truth of what Symeon has told him.[9]

The above represents Symeon's reaction to a complacency which feels no need for a spiritual father, since it believes itself capable of keeping the commandments and overcoming the devil. The cure for this condition is prayer, which as we shall see holds a most important place in Symeon's teaching, but as regards motive, his basic position in unchanged: a spiritual father is to be sought in order to enable one to escape from the devil's clutches. This Symeon never denied, although he came in due course to understand that there is a great deal more that a father can do for his disciples. We have already had a hint as to the nature of these further benefits which the relationship can afford.

A Good Father—the Benefits

Symeon then began by thinking of a spiritual father as the human means

---

[9] *Ep 3*, 215v–216r, cf. also the introduction to the prayer for finding a spiritual father in *Tr Eth VII*, 435f., "Do not desire to justify yourself, but humble yourself before God," the command to be humble here standing in contrast to the attitude castigated in *Ep 3*.

by which he would be enabled to gain the assurance of future salvation, but as a disciple of the Studite he found that he was receiving much more than this. If therefore, generalising from his own experience and being realistic in his estimate of his contemporaries, he could write as though motives similar to his own would be what first impelled most of those who did so to seek for a father, he was equally concerned to teach that discipleship ought to bring with it real benefits in the present as well as the promise of escaping damnation at the last.

Something of the way by which Symeon reached this understanding is made clear to us by a passage in which, speaking of himself, he says to Christ

> Set free from care, I followed [the Studite] and I rejoiced, O Word, with joy unspeakable as I beheld him following in thy footsteps and often holding converse with thee. But when I saw thee, our good Master, present with my guide, my father, the love and the longing I had were inexpressible. I passed beyond faith and hope, and I was wont to say, 'Lo, I see things to come, and the Kingdom of heaven is here, and before my eyes I behold those good things which eye has not seen nor ear heard. Since I possess these, what more can I hope for, or in what else show that I have faith? Beyond this there will be nothing greater.'[10]

This implies that in the course of his discipleship Symeon came both to perceive, and also somehow to share in, the Studite's mystical experiences. It shows him gaining an understanding of salvation as not simply a prize to be enjoyed after death, but also a participation in eternal life in the present, for both of which blessings, humanly speaking, he was indebted to his spiritual father.

Apart from the mystical dimension involved, there is nothing extraordinary in the situation so disclosed: a good spiritual father, who himself enjoys a real and living experience of God, will naturally help his disciples to reach the same condition. Conversely, the traditional wisdom of direction insisted that "only he who has himself become πνευματικός can be πνευματικὸς πατήρ to others."[11] It became accepted as axiomatic that it was through the agency of such a father that one might attain to a real experience of God while still on earth. Thus, to quote Climacus,

> If, when [your director] continually reproves you, you acquire greater faith and love towards him, you should know that the Holy Spirit has come

---

[10] *Hymn XXXVII*, 29–43, cf. *Cat XVI*, 9–12, and *Cat XXXVI*, 247–250, where Symeon speaks of the blessings he is now receiving as being all that he would want even after death, and is reproached by Christ as μικρόψυχος.

[11] R. Reitzenstein, *Historia Monachorum und Historia Lausiaca*, Göttingen, 1916, p. 195, cited by Hausherr, *Direction spirituelle*, p. 195.

invisibly to dwell in your soul, and the power of the Most High has over-shadowed you.[12]

Symeon also came himself to give teaching along the same lines,[13] but since in the passage cited in the last section he maintained that before he had had the Studite as his father he knew nothing about the possibility of experiences of this kind, it may justifiably be concluded that the main reason why he so taught was that *his discipleship* had made all this real to him.

If we summarise two passages and lay out the results in parallel, we shall see further evidence that it was not so much what he had read as what he had lived through that shaped Symeon's teaching about the benefits to be expected in the present from finding a good spiritual father. The column on the left is drawn from what is itself a summary, which follows the autobiographical thanksgiving that forms the bulk of *Cat XXXV* and seems to have been added for the purpose of adapting this as a *Catechesis*; the right-hand column is an abstract of the opening of a straightforward *Catechesis*, dealing with spiritual progress. In both cases Symeon is tracing the steps by which, with a father's guidance, a penitent attains to maturity in Christ.

Cat XXXV, 247–267 (*Autobiographical Summary*)	*Cat XIV*, 5–23. (*Straightforward Address*)
Symeon, in darkness, was stirred by his conscience to seek forgiveness, and to this end to look for a mediator.	A man who abandons the world cannot by himself learn true μετάνοια.
He found a mediator, pastor and ambassador, designated as such by a vision.	Therefore he goes to someone who is τεχνίτης and ἔμπειρος.
But there followed a time of relapse, until the pastor recovered him.	
Symeon showed obedience, trust, humility, and submission to the pastor.	He submits to him, receives his teaching as God's, regarding obedience to it as a matter of life or death.

---

[12] Sc. *Par.* 4, 725D, the language being reminiscent of *St. Luke* 1. 35 (the Annunciation).

[13] *Cat XX*, 161–180, speaking of conscious reception of the Holy Spirit by the disciple of a good and genuine spiritual father, and drawing on the language of *Acts* 1. 8 and 2. 1–4 (Pentecost).

His progress in knowledge and contemplation led to his complete transformation.	His progress leads to his becoming a full-grown man in Christ.[14]

The similarity between these two summaries demonstrates how Symeon's teaching was based not only on the tradition he had received but also on the experience through which he had passed. That there are benefits in this present life as a result of having a good spiritual father, this was indeed a part of his teaching, but it was teaching he gave because he had been the Studite's disciple. Although Symeon was familiar with Climacus, in this instance what he learnt from the latter was important as confirming his experience and not *vice versa*.[15]

The same cannot be said, however, with regard to some other matters about which we can see Climacus and Symeon in agreement when they speak of the benefits which may be conferred by a spiritual father. Thus when both of them are found decidedly opposing all attempts to live "without direction (ἰδιορρυθμῶς),"[16] there seems no reason to doubt Symeon's dependence on Climacus. Again, when in a long autobiographical passage Symeon recounts how, by means of the Studite, his "Moses", he was set free from "Pharaoh" and his "countless folk," the forces of evil,[17] it appears likely that his imagery was drawn from the passage near the beginning of the *Scala Paradisi* in which Climacus, speaking of the need of sinners for a spiritual father, pictures them as requiring "a Moses", so that "they may cross the sea and rout the Amalek of the passions."[18]

However, Symeon was far from being a mere plagiarist entirely dependent on the images to be found in Climacus, for he was capable of using one which is absent both from the *Scala Paradisi* and the *Liber ad Pastorem*. This is the parallel between physical and spiritual begetting, on which he based his insistence that if spiritual birth (or re-birth) is to take place, a spiritual father is an absolute necessity.

As children born according to the flesh are neither begotten nor born without a father, so to be born from above is impossible for anyone who does not have

---

[14] "A time of relapse" naturally has no equivalent in *Cat XIV*, where Symeon is describing what ought to be the normal course of development; τεχνίτης and ἔμπειρος are discussed in the next chapter.

[15] cf. Darrouzès' remark about Symeon's use of the Bible and of the Fathers, quoted p. 43.

[16] Symeon, *Cat XX*, 52–54, cf. *Hymn XLIV*, 190; Climacus, *Sc. Par.* 4, 680C, *ibid.*, 26, 1024B, *ibid.*, 27, 1105A—v. Glossary for further details about the implications of ἰδιορρυθμῶς.

[17] *Hymn XVIII*, 124–224, "Moses", *ibid.*, 164, 197, 209, 219; "Pharaoh", *ibid.*, 212f.

[18] *Sc. Par.* 1, 633D–636A, cf. *ad Pastorem*, 1201C–1208A.

the Spirit from those who themselves have been born from above. And as the fleshly father causes fleshly children to be born, so a spiritual man renders spiritual those who want to become his true spiritual sons.

Accordingly,

> If then the disciple is his teacher's spiritual child, a person who is seeking a father ought by all means to seek one who himself has had a spiritual birth, who consciously knows his God and Father, in order that by such a one he may himself also be brought to spiritual birth and be distinctly designated a son of God.[19]

Symeon's language is, it must be admitted, somewhat confused, because in these extracts he is combining two ideas, that of becoming the spiritual child of one's director, and that of becoming through the director a child of God. There is certainly nothing very original in the imagery for one who is accustomed to call the spiritual director a ''father'', but Symeon's confused metaphors provide an interesting example of his ability to elaborate on one of the potential benefits to the disciple without having to depend on Climacus.

We thus have a good deal of evidence which testifies to the advance of Symeon, through experience, through increasing knowledge of traditional teaching and through his own reflection, to an understanding of the benefits conveyed by a spiritual father, which was less limited than that with which he began. Although he did not abandon, either for himself or as a motive deserving the attention of others, the belief that finding a saintly father was the way to make sure of one's own salvation, he yet came to realise that much more was involved in being such a man's disciple than he had at first suspected. A demonstration of his development is provided in *Cat XVII*, where he recounts how he was given assurance (πληροφορία) of the forgiveness of his sins, was raised to the heights of contemplation, and how there was bestowed on him an eternal kingdom which cannot be shaken.[20] The context here, it is true, is a description of visionary experience rather than anything directly pertaining to spiritual fatherhood, but it must be remembered that, as has already been adumbrated and will be more fully discussed later, the responsibility of the father definitely includes helping and guiding his disciple along the path of progress in contemplation. Increasing maturity thus resulted in Symeon's not only realising that his first expectations of what would be gained from finding a spiritual father had been too restricted, but also in his coming to

---

[19] *Ep 4*, 121–126 and 158–161—''from above'' translates ἄνωθεν, for which here (as in *St. John* 3. 3, which Symeon had in mind) ''from above'' or ''again'' are equally possible as renderings.

[20] *Cat XVII*, 61–70, with the last words reminiscent of *Hebrews* 12. 28.

emphasise to others the benefits which should be looked for in this present life, as well as those to be expected after death. And, finally, it must never be forgotten that the decisive cause of this change in Symeon was what we found him acknowledging himself, his experience as a spiritual child of the Studite.

A Bad Father—the Dangers

It must not be supposed that either Symeon or his predecessors imagined that the benefits, at which we have been looking, would be automatically received in consequence of attaching oneself to any spiritual father, whatever his character or abilities. On the contrary, there were very definite statements made to the effect that everything is dependent on the father's being a man of the right type, and that it is absolutely disastrous to become the client or disciple of someone unworthy to undertake this office. Moreover, in the opinion of many writers, bad fathers were by no means few in number.

We shall look in the next chapter at the qualifications regarded as necessary for spiritual fathers, but before doing so it is appropriate at this stage to notice some of the warnings given about the dangers which would follow from attachment to a father of the wrong type. From the earliest period, commonsense will have led to the utterance of such warnings, since the spiritual father is invested with immense authority, and a disciple is instructed that once he has attached himself to a chosen guide he must thenceforth never presume to judge or criticise him. It is, incidentally, reasonable to suggest that the damage they anticipated would be caused by an unworthy father may in part account for the castigation by Symeon and Nicetas of worldly and unspiritual hegumens,[21] for the hegumen, as already noted, was *ex officio* his monks' spiritual father, according to the *typika* of many monasteries.

By the sixth century, then, there was already an abundance of material intended to warn those seeking a spiritual father about the possible dangers involved. Thus a story about two of the Desert Fathers and their different ways of treating the same penitent concludes:

> I have related this so that we may know what danger there is in manifestation, whether of thoughts or of sins, to those who do not have discernment.[22]

Similarly Cassian included among the teaching he had received from the Abbot Moses a sombre reflection:

---

[21] Symeon, *Cat XVIII*, 479–495, Nicetas, *Life*, 42.
[22] Ward, *Desert Fathers*, p. 28, translating original in *PL* 73, 928C.

There are some, and indeed, sad to say, they comprise the larger number, who having become tepid in youth grow old in the same disposition and in slothfulness, and thus gain authority for themselves not by reason of maturity of character but simply by reason of age ... Our most cunning adversary utilises their grey hairs for the purpose of deceiving young men ..., leading them to hurtful tepidity or to deadly despair through the teachings and habits of these men.[23]

Climacus puts the matter very clearly when, speaking from the point of view of the would-be disciple, he gives the following advice:

Before we enter upon [our discipleship], if we have any cunning or prudence about us, let us examine, scrutinise and, so to speak, put our director to the test, as a precaution against taking one who is a sailor for a helmsman, a sick man for a physician, one who is swayed by passions for a dispassionate being, or the open sea for the harbour, with spiritual shipwreck as a result. But once we have entered upon the race of pious and submissive living, let us from then on totally refrain from examining our noble president of the games ...[24]

In this clear distinction between the client's duties before and after he has acquired a spiritual father, Climacus is plainly far from recommending a hasty and unconsidered submission either to a possibly inexperienced person or to one who might prove completely unqualified to be a spiritual father. The consequence of an unfortunate choice could well be "shipwreck", since it is normally necessary to have "a good helmsman" if a ship is to "reach harbour safely." Furthermore it is obvious that should a wrong choice have been made through inadequate scrutiny at the outset, the possibility of disaster is enhanced by the very fact that once "entered upon the race," the disciple is under an obligation to obey his "president of the games" unhesitatingly and uncritically.

As one who had entered into a long heritage of ascetical theology, Symeon not surprisingly uttered similar cautions. Using an image different from those employed by Climacus but no less indicative of the likelihood of disaster, he warned the imaginary aspirant addressed in *Cat XX*, to be careful not to "follow the wolf as though he were a shepherd."[25] He had shortly before this remarked on the scarcity of genuine directors in comparison with the large number of those qualified in outward appearance only.

Those who understand how to be good pastors and physicians to rational souls are in truth but few, especially nowadays. There are in all likelihood

[23] Cassian, *Conlationes*, II, 13, *C.S.E.L.*, XIII, Vienna, 1886, p. 53, cf. very similarly Pseudo-Basil, *De renuntiatione saeculi*, *PG* 31, 632C.

[24] *Sc. Par.* 4, 680CD—"director" and "helmsman" both translate κυβερνήτης.

[25] *Cat XX*, 216f.

many with pretensions as to fasting, keeping vigils and observing a form of devotion, or for whom indeed these things may be realities; even more find no difficulty in reciting much material they have learnt by heart, and in teaching by means of words; very few, however, can be found who eradicate passions by weeping and acquire for good and all those virtues which include all the others.[26]

It is interesting to observe how in this passage Symeon's suspicion of a mere book-knowledge of spirituality comes to the fore, and it is reasonable to see this as another example of his being influenced by his experience as a disciple of the Studite, whose teaching we have already discovered included the maxim that those who had gained a genuine knowledge of God had no need of book-learning. Moreover, when Symeon insisted that "the wolf" could be distinguished from "the shepherd" by the fact that the latter would have "eradicated the passions by weeping," he was touching on a subject, the importance of tears, to which he himself frequently reverted, and which was also prominent in the teaching given by his spiritual father.[27] At the same time, the very fact of Symeon's uttering these words is indirect testimony to his conviction that, in the Studite, he had himself met with a father who had attained complete dispassion and had by no means possessed only "the externals of devotion."

Using not quite the same imagery, Symeon elsewhere writes about the danger of resorting to a spiritual father who is not himself mature.

One who is of this kind [sc. mature and spiritually experienced] is able also to lead Christ's flock in the way of God's commandments; but as for him who . . . is not like this, it is evident that he does not keep his soul's faculties in an enlightened and healthy condition, and it will be much better for him to be guided himself, rather than guide others with all the risks therein involved.[28]

In *Ep 1* we find the potential spiritual child being warned in outspoken language:

---

[26] *ibid.*, 197–204. The first sentence quoted is also put into the mouth of St. Cyril the Phileote by his biographer (*Life*, ed. E. Sargologos, *Subsidia Hagiographica*, 39, (1964), p. 99), and might be thus suspected of being a mere *topos*. While it is likely that good spiritual fathers will never be numerous and that this will always be lamented, little importance need be attached to the appearance of these words in the *Life* of Cyril, since the writer was a wholesale borrower, who drew material from Symeon amongst others, v. Darrouzès, *R.E.B.*, 25, (1967), p. 256, cf. *SC* 122, intr. p. 72. (Similarly, the rarity of good directors is noted by N. Grou, *Meditations on the Love of God*, originally published 1796, London, 1960, p. 106.)

[27] *Cat XXIX*, 225–230 is a significant passage, because Symeon here speaks vehemently on the subject and cites the authority of the Studite; cf. Hausherr, *Life*, p. XLVIII for the prominence of tears in the latter's *Chapters*.

[28] *Ch* I, 54, 24–29.

Do not find one who is a flatterer or the slave of his belly, and strive to make him your counsellor and confederate. If you do, he may comply with your self-will and teach you what you will welcome but not what God loves, and thus you will remain an enemy [of God], unreconciled to him. And [do not choose] an inexperienced physician, lest he either plunge you into the depths of despair through excessive severity and inopportune surgery and cauterisation [of the soul], or else through overmuch tenderness leave you in your sickness but thinking you are healthy—most terrible of fates—, resulting in his being the means of delivering you up to eternal punishment, a fate very different from your expectations.[29]

The seriousness of the matter for Symeon is implied also in *Cat XXVIII*, a work which has much in common with *Ep 1*, and in which there is a sentence denying that the power to bind and loose, to act as priests and to teach, has been given to men who are not really spiritual and whose authority is based simply on their having been ordained.[30] As the quotation from *Ep 1* shows, Symeon was profoundly conscious of the danger inherent in the fact that any who attached themselves to such persons, instead of to genuine and mature spiritual men, might be relying on those who were incapable of reconciling them to God, and thus while in reality still sick might be deceived into imagining that their souls had been healed.

There seems to have been not a little discussion in monasteries and elsewhere about the merits and demerits of different fathers, and it is interesting that Symeon, who found it necessary to issue warnings to others, had earlier himself been warned of the folly of continuing to be a disciple of the Studite. It was doubtless during his short time in the Studios monastery that he was reproached by some who advised him to have recourse to a spiritual father whose standards and demands were less exacting and more in accordance with the conventions of the age.

Why act foolishly and labour to no purpose?—they would say—Why follow this impostor and deceiver in the vain and futile expectation of recovering your [spiritual] sight? Such a thing is impossible nowadays. Why follow him, when it hurts your feet and makes them bleed? . . . Alas for you! You will forfeit the kind treatment that would be given you by sympathetic men who love Christ and also love their brethren, and you will endure the afflictions and tribulations to which, inspired by vain hopes, you submit yourself, but you will never really obtain what this cheat and deceiver is promising you.[31]

---

[29] *Ep 1*, p. 117, 6–13. The concept of the father as spiritual physician will discussed in the next chapter.

[30] *Cat XXVIII*, 291–296.

[31] *Cat XXXVI*, 102–116, cf. Nicetas, *Life*, 17; "deceiver (πλάνος)" occurs elsewhere, notably in *Hymn XXXII*, 1–4, where Symeon complains that the term is applied to him on account of his claim to have received the Holy Spirit because of the Studite's prayers, and in *Cat XXVII*, 52f., and *Ch* I, 49, 24f., where πλάνοι are significantly coupled with ψευδοδιδάσκαλοι.

This passage strongly suggests that Symeon was not simply repeating traditional wisdom when he gave warnings about the dangers resulting from the very existence of spiritual fathers of the wrong kind: here again his experience was decisive, for having personal knowledge of the attempts of others to persuade him to transfer from a conscientious to a lax father, he had the best of reasons for doing all in his power to put potential spiritual children on their guard.

Although Symeon did refer in *Ep 1* to the possibility of harm being caused by "excessive severity" on the part of the spiritual physician, it is evident that he was more commonly concerned about the dangers to be feared in consequence of the choice of a father who, for whatever reason, had not attained dispassion and who therefore inevitably fell short of enjoying the full experience of God. Thus in the *Chapters*, we find a strongly-worded warning about the disaster that will ensue if a wrong choice is made.

> If you desire to renounce the world and to be instructed in the Gospel way of living, do not give yourself into the hands of an inexperienced (ἄπειρος) teacher or one who is dominated by passions (ἐμπαθής), lest you should be instructed in the devil's way of life and not that of the Gospels; good lessons come from good teachers and bad from bad, and rotten seeds will assuredly produce rotten crops.[32]

Here experience is mentioned, but the emphasis seems to be laid on the moral state of the potential director, whereas elsewhere Symeon shows himself very anxious lest anyone should be misled by a guide who lacks Christian wisdom.

> He remains in ignorance ... He imagines himself to be a leader, though he is no leader but travels along a road of which he has no knowledge, or rather he misses the road and precipitates himself and his followers down into the eternal fire. Again, he imagines himself to be a teacher though he is no teacher of others but a liar and deceiver, for he does not possess in himself the true wisdom, which is our Lord Jesus Christ.[33]

What impelled Symeon to write in this way was his conviction that nothing less than the eternal salvation of souls was at stake, and that while a good spiritual father would ensure that those who in sincerity attached themselves to him were saved, one who was immature, lax, inexperienced or ignorant would inevitably lead any who became his children towards damnation.

In all this work of cautioning the unwary about the dangers to be anticipated from bad fathers, Symeon was far from merely reproducing

---

[32] *Ch* I, 48.
[33] *Tr Eth XV*, 182–189, cf. *Cat XXVIII*, 201–218.

conventional wisdom, even though from his reading he must have been aware of it. But he was equally, and perhaps more vividly, aware of the existence of contemporaries whom he felt to be endangering others by their failure to possess the qualifications needed for spiritual fatherhood while anxious to be accepted in this role.[34] Those with a vocation to the monastic life, who would be likely to have their hegumen as their spiritual father, needed to find a community led by someone of the right kind, not a man addicted to self-indulgence and luxury, and not one who would be frequently leaving the monastery and parading here and there with a large escort mounted on expensive-looking mules.[35] As for those living in the world and seeking a spiritual father, we shall see later that Symeon was very conscious of their being surrounded by unworthy persons who wanted to recruit spiritual children from self-interested motives, and that competition from such men was one of the difficulties with which a genuine father had to contend. It was against such a background that he not only gave warnings about the dangers resulting from a bad choice, but also instructions about how to find the right person to be one's spiritual father.

The Need for Prayer, Divine Help and Prudence

For those who believed, as many did, that eternal salvation might be gained or lost through the right or wrong choice of a spiritual father, that choice was obviously a momentous matter. It is not therefore surprising that Climacus enjoined the greatest prudence, and to the passage from his writings already quoted one might add the following, in which the need for self-knowledge on the part of the intending disciple is stressed.

> Let us decide to whom to submit ourselves in the light of the nature of our passions, and so make a suitable choice [of a spiritual father]. If you lack self-control and are inclined to lust, let him be a trainer of [spiritual] athletes, an ascetic, and one who is inflexible with regard to diet, but not a wonder-worker, ready to welcome and entertain all and sundry; if you are arrogant, let him be quick-tempered and difficult to placate, but not gentle and kindly. Let us not be on the look-out for men endowed with foreknowledge or with second-sight, but principally for those who are really humble, and whose conduct and abode are what our diseased self requires.[36]

The useful guidelines in this passage require that a person wanting to find a spiritual father should possess not only self-knowledge but also an ability to sum up the characters of those whom he might encounter in his search.

---

[34] cf. *Tr Eth VI*, 383–401, quoted in chapter IX, p. 232.
[35] Hegumens of this type are castigated in *Cat XVIII*, 476–483.
[36] *Sc. Par.* 4, 725CD.

It does not, however, in spite of what Völker in his comment on it implies, state that prayer enters into the question.[37] Climacus indeed never directly mentions prayer as a necessary preliminary to the search.

With Symeon the case is far different. *Cat XX* is devoted to the subject of spiritual fatherhood, and in the introductory part Symeon is found affirming that anyone who is doing his own will, even in the smallest degree, will never be enabled to obey Christ's command to leave father and mother, and take up his cross and follow him. Having then explained that he proposed to proceed as though he were addressing a single individual, Symeon continued:

> Brother, call earnestly upon God, that he may show you a man capable of shepherding you well . . .[38]

Thus, unlike Climacus, Symeon emphatically prescribed that in the search for the right spiritual father, prayer must precede everything else. A few lines further on, without mentioning prudence or judgement, Symeon apparently envisaged the neophyte as already having some relationship with a director, so that he would now experience one of two things: either through grace his confidence in his existing father would be strengthened, and thus he would continue with him, or the Holy Spirit might send him to someone else. If the latter should happen, he need not hesitate to obey this leading, but ought then to attach himself to the man who would be designated to him either by direct revelation from God, or else "by means of his servant."[39] (There are obvious parallels here with Symeon's personal experiences, described in chapter III.)

The same theme is found also in one of the *Epistles*:

> We need great earnestness, much vigil and many prayers, so that we may not fall into the hands of a deceiver, a cheat, a false apostle and false Christ, but instead meet with a teacher who is genuine, a lover of God and one who bears Christ within himself . . .[40]

Here, at the very point at which he both assumed the existence of men who

---

[37] Völker, *Praxis*, p. 116.

[38] *Cat XX*, 30–46; cf. the prayer suggested in *Tr Eth VII*, 437–445. It is because prayer has been enjoined at the start, that in *Cat XX*, at 196f., caution can be recommended.

[39] *Cat XX*, 50–60. The identity of God's "servant" is uncertain: it seems unlikely that he is the spiritual father who is being abandoned, and so perhaps he is envisaged as one of a group of senior monks or favoured disciples of the new father, who might act as an intermediary between the holy man and the public—cf. chapter VI, pp. 93f., and also the way in which, after the death of his spiritual father, Gregory asked the advice of a certain John, who suggested that he should approach St. Basil the Younger, *Acta Sanctorum*, March III, Paris, 1865, p. *25, 26DE.

[40] *Ep 3*, 210v–211r, cf. also *Ch I*, 49, 16f.

were far from possessing the qualities which ought to mark a spiritual father, and also implied that there was a real danger of the unwary falling into their hands, Symeon proposed "many prayers" as one of the safeguards to protect a would-be disciple. Climacus, on the other hand, in the passage quoted in the last section had spoken of reliance on one's own judgement and even on "cunning (πονηρία)." This is in sharp contrast to the warning which Symeon gave to the person he addressed in *Ep 3*, who was told not to imagine that he would be able by means of his own prudence to recognise a true and holy spiritual father.[41]

In this respect, then, the difference between the two writers appears quite striking, and we can do no more than conjecture possible reasons for it. Symeon, for instance, normally gives his teaching in a direct and straightforward manner, whereas Climacus

is often intentionally enigmatic . . . [He] avoids spelling out his conclusions too plainly.[42]

If this is the case, the difference perhaps is more apparent than real, for in so important a matter—and of its importance for him there can be no doubt—, Climacus might take it for granted that any serious disciple ought not to need telling that prayer is essential. Furthermore, although he must surely have had other readers in mind, formally at least Climacus wrote the *Scala Paradisi* for John of Raithu, the hegumen of a monastery and a man for whose spiritual maturity he clearly had great respect;[43] Symeon, on the oither hand, was addressing himself in *Cat XX* to those whose position was that of actual or potential spiritual children. Hence an injunction to pray would be appropriate in their case, but unsuitable in the *Scala* in view of the status of the person for whom it was nominally being written.

Nevertheless, here also it would be unwise to dismiss the possibility that in this respect also Symeon's teaching was shaped by his own experience. We must refer again to the passage in *Cat XXXV* which was mentioned earlier. Here, in the course of his address to God, he said:

I longed to see one of thy saints in the belief that through him I should find mercy from thee.[44]

Symeon, however, was told by everybody that there were no saints living

---

[41] *Ep 3*, 213r.
[42] Ware, *Climacus*, p. 9.
[43] cf. *ad Pastorem*, 1201C – 1208A, and also the introduction to *Sc. Par.* according to which John must "supply what is lacking" (628AB).
[44] *Cat XXXV*, 19–21.

on earth at that time, but he refused to acquiesce in such a view of the situation.

> None the less I never believed what they said, but I had an answer for such people, as thou knowest, O Christ my Master. I used to say, 'My Lord, have mercy! And has the devil become so much more powerful than God our Master that he draws all men to himself and enrols them in his party, so that not one is left to take God's part?' It is for this reason, I think, that thou, O King who lovest mankind, didst cause thy holy light to shine on me who sat in the darkness of this life and in the midst of evils, and in that light didst reveal to me thy saint. [45]

It is tempting to describe as a prayer the words which Symeon says he uttered, but formally considered they are perhaps no more than simply an answer to those who had caused him disappointment, an answer preceded by a few words apostrophizing the Lord. They are introduced, it will be noted, by ''I used to say,'' not by any formula indicating the offering of a prayer to God. All the same, as is shown by the last sentence of the passage quoted, Symeon did feel that in his distress he was thrown back on God, and that God then came to his help. We may reasonably infer that this experience was, in part at least, the reason for his later discouraging others from depending on their own judgement when they came to the point of choosing a spiritual father.

> Do not suppose that you will discover him by relying on yourself and your own prudence, for this is impossible. [46]

Remembering his instruction to the would-be disciple to begin by praying to be shown a good spiritual father, we cannot deny that the tone of Symeon's advice appears different from that of Climacus. The difference may then reasonably be ascribed to the effect on him of his experience, and it does not seem fanciful to suppose that the answer, ''My Lord, have mercy! . . . ,'' was one which Symeon himself felt to have had in it something of the quality of a prayer.

If, however, someone follows Symeon's advice and starts by earnestly praying for guidance, there remains the question of how to recognise the divinely chosen spiritual father. He himself, of course, was in no doubt that he had been guided to the Studite, for he said to Christ,

---

[45] *ibid.*, 78–90; ''draw all men'' parodies the words of Christ in *St. John* 12. 32.

[46] *Ep 3*, 213r. It is noteworthy that ''prudence (φρόνησις)'' is precisely what Climacus does recommend in conjunction with ''cunning (πονηρία)'' in the passage from *Sc. Par.* 4, 680CD, quoted in the last section—contrast however *ibid.*, 24, 984D, πάλαιε πλανᾶν σου τὴν φρόνησιν.

Thou leddest me to the man who was to become my father on earth—such was thy good pleasure.[47]

God's provision for Symeon was confirmed by the vision he was granted:

Thou didst count me worthy to see him … standing near thy divine glory, yet thou hadst not decked him with a crown or with shining raiment—no! his appearance was unaltered, and thou didst show him to me in heaven just as he was wont to appear in our company, and as he was seen day by day on earth. What was thy purpose? It was that I should not reckon him who was with us as a different being from him whom I saw there, and so—lost sheep that I was—be deceived and wander away from the good shepherd.[48]

This type of revelation Symeon did not regard as a privilege so rare that others had no reason to expect that God would indicate to them directly the right man to be their spiritual father. On the contrary, as we have already seen, he envisaged that a disciple might be sent by the Holy Spirit to a father whom God would make known to him "by revelation (μυστικῶς)."[49] In providing for this, just as in enjoining prayer, Symeon struck a different note from Climacus, who apparently never took into account the possibility or likelihood of direct divine intervention at this point.

But in spite of his own experience Symeon did not of course claim that there was no other way by which a person could recognise the right spiritual father. We have met one alternative in the same sentence from *Cat XX*, a human adviser, "[God's] servant," who might make his future father known to the neophyte. Besides this, although he warned someone looking for a spiritual father not to rely on mere human prudence, he by no means ruled out the total use of one's natural faculties. Such use is implied in his assumption that the beginner would go to a man who is "proficient and experienced (τεχνίτης καὶ ἔμπειρος),"[50] and still more in his saying that one ought to seek for a man "who himself has had spiritual birth, who consciously knows his God and Father."[51] These are all matters which could only be verified by some personal investigation, even though a person in search of a spiritual guide would very likely first hear of them from the mouths of others, when—as Symeon had done—he began to ask people of his acquaintance to help him in his quest.

Moreover in the same letter in which he insisted that relying on one's own prudence could not lead to a successful outcome, Symeon had included

[47] *Hymn LVI*, 13f., one of many similar expressions.
[48] *Cat XXXV*, 106–113, cf. *Cat XXXVI*, 77.
[49] *Cat XX*, 59.
[50] *Cat XIV*, 9.
[51] *Ep 4*, 158–161.

a description of the qualities of a holy and good pastor and of one of the
opposite type. To this he added the significant words:

> When therefore you see someone engaged in any of all these [wicked prac-
> tices], seeking the glory that comes from men, and in order to please men
> relaxing the commandments of God, you must recognise him as a deceiver
> and not a true [father].[52]

The implication is that since a disciple in search of a spiritual father
is here supposed to be capable of recognising the unworthiness of one
man through his conduct, he would equally be able on the same basis to
acknowledge the goodness of another. Again, in *Ep 1* there is a long
passage setting out the criteria for recognising those genuinely entitled to
be accepted as spiritual fathers. This contains a loose quotation from
I Corinthians 12. 8 – 11 and other New Testament texts, and also makes it
clear that those who are really qualified can be known by their Christlike
behaviour.[53]

The evidence thus demonstrates that while, whatever his reason,
Climacus never mentioned it, prayer was for Symeon a necessary prerequisite in the search for a spiritual father, and that he thought it impossible to succeed by relying on one's own prudence. In other words,
Symeon was very conscious of the need to depend on divine assistance,
and he strove to inculcate this attitude in those to whom he gave instruction. On the subject of actual recognition, however, he closely resembled
Climacus, since both of them required a would-be disciple to take notice
of the life and conduct of any man whom he was considering as a possible
father.[54] Indeed, with regard to the criteria by which assessment should
be made, Symeon's guidance was more detailed than that of Climacus.

A final point which must be briefly mentioned concerns the interior
disposition of the spiritual child. There is an affirmation by Symeon in
Ep 3 to the effect that

> those who hide themselves beneath the darkness of their own passions, lusts
> and wills, and walk therein as in the depth of night, find teachers of their
> own kind.

On the other hand, a little earlier he had cited *Acts* 10 to prove that God

---

[52] *Ep 3*, 213v – 214v, cf. *St. John* 5, 44, and 12, 43, *St. Matthew* 5. 19, *Galatians* 1. 10.

[53] *Ep 1*, p. 124, 22 – p. 127, 2.

[54] *Tr Eth VII*, 400 – 405, including μηδὲ ἐρεύνα τοὺς βίους αὐτῶν is not really an exception, for here Symeon is addressing someone seeking to make progress in the spiritual life,
and warning him against the temptation to gad around seeking out and conversing with
monks who enjoy a considerable reputation and whose manner of life appears very impres-
sive. If by God's grace he already has a spiritual father, he is to speak about his concerns
to him alone, but if he has no father he must look to Christ.

will always provide the earnest and sincere seeker with a genuine spiritual father, just as St. Peter was sent to Cornelius, the devout Roman centurion.[55] In addition, then, to his need of prayer and prudence, the would-be disciple was warned that he must be truly attempting to live the Christian life. Such a person, in Symeon's view, could confidently expect to discover a good father.[56]

The Recipients of Symeon's Warnings

Before we leave the subject of securing a spiritual father, there is one further question which we must discuss: for whom did Symeon intend the advice and warnings which have occupied our attention in the two preceding sections?

The obvious answer could be that he was addressing pious Christians, living in the world, who were concerned about their souls and who had not as yet found, and committed themselves to, a spiritual father. This on the whole would accord well with the situation as portrayed in *Ep 3*, from which several quotations have been made. A difficulty, however, arises in that the title prefixed to this letter in *Vaticanus graecus* 1782 states that it was addressed "to one of his disciples ...," while Symeon towards the end both repeats his exhortation to the recipient to secure a spiritual father, and also addresses him as "my beloved and spiritual child."[57] One may assume that whoever composed the title based himself on Symeon's terminology, but was not troubled by any sense of incongruity when styling the recipient "a disciple," even though the latter seems as yet not to have entrusted himself either to Symeon or to any other spiritual father. This is true not only of the person who wrote the title, but the letter itself shows that Symeon also could apparently regard this correspondent as his "spiritual child," without thereby implying that the relationship between them was that of father and committed disciple. Symeon, in other words, was prepared to act as father to this person on this one occasion, without its necessarily following that their relationship would become permanent.[58] It must also be reckoned a possibility that while addressing a single individual Symeon was aware that his letter would be circulated to others as well, and that therefore in his advice he had a wider constituency in mind,

---

[55] *Ep 3*, 211v–212v.

[56] cf. also *Cat XXVIII*, 335–388, where it is maintained that a spiritual-minded disciple will recognise a father of the same kind—on the circular nature of this advice, v. Hausherr, *Direction spirituelle*, p. 183. V.C. Christophorides, *op. cit.*, p. 117, also draws attention to this passage in *Cat XXVIII*.

[57] *Ep 3*, 221r.

[58] cf. the quotation from Rousseau, *Ascetics*, given in chapter IV, p. 54.

while perhaps being fairly certain that the recipient of *Ep 3* was in fact likely to proceed further and become his "spiritual child."

A person such as this devout secular might, of course, either continue to live in the world as a committed disciple of a carefully chosen father, or might intend sooner or later to become a monk. In the latter case, since he would probably be expected to have the hegumen of his monastery as his spiritual father, the warnings to be careful about whom he chose would really amount to advice to exercise care in selecting which community to join.

With *Cat XX*, with which also we have been concerned and which is of course ostensibly addressed to monks, the problem arises in another form: why should the intending disciple be instructed to pray to be shown the right spiritual father, when as a member of a monastery he was in all probability supposed already to have as such the hegumen, or at least someone designated by him? Indeed, since the *Catechesis* was intended for Symeon's own monks, was he not himself the spiritual father of all those to whom it was addressed? The difficulty here, however, is more apparent than real, since although found amongst the *Catecheses* and classed as one of them, this work, almost at its beginning, is stated to have been in reality a letter.[59] Symeon, then, was here concerned with others besides his monks, and it would seem probable that we have to do with a kind of circular letter, designed primarily for earnest Christians living in the world, men of a type not unlike the recipient of *Ep 3*. Since in it he dealt not only with the choice of a spiritual father but also with the disciple's subsequent duties and rewards, Symeon could well have considered that much of what he had written would edify his monks, who had apparently asked him for a "profitable discourse (λόγος ὠφελείας)."[60] If he then made his letter available to them after adding an introduction, this would account for its position among the *Catecheses*.

We conclude, therefore, that when Symeon gave advice and warnings about the selection of the right spiritual father, he had in mind not the monks over whom he presided, but Christians living in the world, conscious of their need, yet requiring both to be encouraged to seek a guide for the right reasons and to be cautioned against falling into the hands of the wrong kind of person.

---

[59] *Cat XX*, 14f.
[60] *ibid.*, 10–15.

CHAPTER SIX

THE SPIRITUAL FATHER'S QUALIFICATIONS

The Meaning of "Qualification"

I. Hausherr, in his *Direction spirituelle en Orient autrefois* devotes a chapter to the *"qualités requises pour être père spirituel."* He classifies them under the headings "moral" and "intellectual", and then has a section dealing with questions of Church order involved in hierarchical qualifications.[1] In a study which is focused upon Symeon, however, a somewhat different approach is suggested by some words found in his *Life* and by a phrase from his own writings: Nicetas says that Symeon was esteemed by one of his spiritual children, the patrician Genesios, as one who had the ability "to be pastor and physician of souls,"[2] while he himself, as was indicated in our summary of the opening of *Cat XIV*, assumed that a penitent would have recourse to someone who was τεχνίτης and ἔμπειρος.[3]

τεχνίτης is a word which implies some kind of professional training: it means, according to Lampe, "artificer, craftsman, artist" and is used "of skilled workers, including makers of perfumes, hairdressers, cooks, astrologers, copyists of scriptures, church architects."[4] It could fittingly be used also of a person who had been taught how to function effectively as a spiritual pastor and physician, and it is worth noticing that the cognate word τέχνη was employed by Dorotheus of Gaza to denote the skill of a father in persuading a disciple, who was unwilling to do so, to reveal his thoughts (λογισμοί).[5] The word τεχνίτης implies, moreover, that the skills in question could be systematically imparted and more or less definitely recognised—in the realm of spirituality no less than in areas such as cookery, astrology or architecture, and we shall later see some examples which substantiate and illustrate this point.

But Symeon could never be content that any Christian, and far less any spiritual father, should possess merely a theoretical or academic knowledge of the subjects which he needed to know. Hence to τεχνίτης he added ἔμπειρος, which makes the point that the guide to whom a client resorts

---

[1] Hausherr, *op. cit.*, Ch III, pp. 56–123.
[2] Nicetas, *Life*, 55, 2f., cf. Symeon, *Cat XX*, 198f.
[3] Symeon, *Cat XIV*, 9.
[4] Lampe, *Lexicon*, p. 1392, τεχνίτης.
[5] Dorotheus, *Doctrinae*, V, 65, 24.

must not only have received the necessary training as it were academical-
ly, but must also have assimilated it in his actual life and experience
(πεῖρα).[6] If indeed we not infrequently get the impression that Symeon
felt compelled to lay more stress on πεῖρα than on τέχνη,[7] we must not
allow ourselves to suppose that he in any way undervalued the latter, for
this would have been impossible for one who was the heir to a long tradition and who in particular was conscious of the training he had received
from his father the Studite.

Obviously, when we speak of qualifications for spiritual fatherhood, we
do not have in mind any system of formal examinations and certificates.
Instead, the model is one of apprenticeship, and it is significant that
Lemerle could state that something similar to this was the normal way of
qualifying as a member of one of the learned professions in Byzantium.

> How does one become a doctor, an engineer, a judge or an official in the
> imperial offices? There are certainly plenty of examples which demonstrate
> that knowledge is often gained by means of working alongside someone who
> has mastered the subject.[8]

In much the same way, one who was to become a spiritual father would
in part be trained simply by being the disciple of an existing father. No
doubt he might also receive suggestions as to what books to study, but the
more important factor will always have been the influence exercised on the
"apprentice" by his father as a living person, one who "guides and forms
others, not primarily by words of advice, but by his companionship."[9]

The way then in which the qualifications necessary for spiritual fatherhood were gained, both before, during and after the time of Symeon, will
have been somewhat as follows: a recognised father would attract disciples, or perhaps even in a sense recruit them, as is implied in the statement
that Cassian

> considered that [fathers] should not seek for pupils among the virtuous or
> perceptive only, but rather among those who are weighed down with sorrow
> and grief, repenting of their former misdeeds.[10]

---

[6] An interesting juxtaposition of the two words is found in Diadochus of Photice, who
speaks of God's providence in creating remedies which could be used at some future time,
as a result of the skill which physicians would gain through experience: ἔμελλεν ὑπὸ τῆς
ἀνθρωπίνης πείρας ποτὲ συλλέγεσθαι ἡ τέχνη, Ch LIII, 2f. (SC 5, 2nd edit., 1955).

[7] cf. Darrouzès' description of Tr Th I and Trs Eth I, IV, V and VI as "des antirrhé-
tiques, contre les faux savants qui n'ont pas la véritable expérience", SC 129, p. 121, n. 1.

[8] Lemerle, Premier humanisme, p. 261, cf. also, ibid., p. 150.

[9] K. Ware, 'The Spiritual Father in Orthodox Christianity', Cross Currents, XXIV,
(1974), p. 300.

[10] Cassian, Conlationes, XIV, 17, C.S.E.L., XIII, Vienna, 1886, p. 422 (apud
Rousseau, Ascetics, p. 204); cf. the training of Dositheus by Dorotheus, while himself a
disciple of Barsanuphius, SC 92, p. 128, 1–17, and the significant, καὶ ἔτι μαθητὴς ὤν,

Amongst his disciples he would find one or two who were specially receptive, and to the training of these he would devote particular care, with a view to their eventually being able to succeed him as spiritual guides. Such men might at some stage be entrusted with a part of their father's work, more or less under his supervision, while he was still living and could superintend them. At length, by the time he died, they would have become qualified, as men both τεχνῖται and ἔμπειροι, to be spiritual fathers in their own right.

For the middle of the eleventh century this procedure is illustrated by the career of Nicon, who had been tonsured by, and became the favourite disciple of Luke, the founder of a monastery on the Black Mountain, to the North of Antioch in Syria.

> Luke taught him and gave him the commandments of the Lord in writing, also narrating the entire story of his own [i.e. Luke's] life . . . He was chosen by Luke to assist in the correction of the brethren.

Nicon, however, although he did duly become a spiritual father, did not succeed peacefully to Luke's position in the monastery. Presumably he became unpopular in the first place through his efforts to help Luke, and then through his exercise of the function of instructing and correcting monks throughout the patriarchate of Antioch, another duty which was entrusted to him. At any rate, he was forced to flee, but his correspondence reveals that he again in his turn had a favourite disciple, Gerasimos, who became a monk in the monastery of St. Sabas, and to whom he wrote in an intimate style.[11]

In Symeon's life much the same pattern can be traced: from early days the Studite probably regarded him as his eventual successor, for he once said to Symeon while he was still "a young man,"

> I have confidence in God, who has richly bestowed his grace upon me, that he will bestow a double portion of it upon you, simply because of the faith you have in him and in me, humble as I am.[12]

The "double portion" is an obvious reference to the story of Elijah and his being succeeded as a prophet by Elisha, as indeed Symeon shortly afterwards renders explicit.[13] Moreover it is to be observed that on the very day when this prediction was made by him, the Studite had been

---

p. 144, 5f., and also the reference by A. Gardner in *Theodore of Studium: His Life and Times*, London, 1905, p. 175, to Theodore's "'son' Naucratius, afterwards his successor at Studium, and probably already selected as such by [him]."

[11] I. Doens, 'Nicon de la montagne noire,' *Byzantion*, XXIV, (1954), pp. 131–140.
[12] *Cat XVI*, 7, 67–70.
[13] *ibid.*, 71f.; v. *II Kings* 2. 9, and cf. *I Kings* 19. 16.

visiting various of his spiritual children in the city and had taken Symeon with him while doing this.[14] To accompany his father in this way was no doubt part of Symeon's training as an apprentice, and while we do not know if he was present at interviews between the Studite and any or all of these secular disciples, it would seem that what he observed on occasions such as this confirmed him in his belief that he had found a living saint. "[The Studite] benefited many simply by allowing them to see him," was the comment Symeon interjected, presumably because he felt that here was more evidence of his father's sanctity, for as Brown puts it, "merely to see a holy man stirred East Romans deeply."[15] Furthermore, we learn from Nicetas that after Symeon had had to move to St. Mamas', the Studite both visited him frequently and after two years began to consider

> placing him as a lamp now burning upon the lampstand of the Church of the faithful, that on all those therein he might cause to shine that light of knowledge by which he himself had been illuminated.[16]

Even after Symeon had become hegumen of the monastery of St. Mamas, and so *ex officio* the spiritual father of his monks, we find him refusing to function independently of the Studite on a particularly solemn occasion, namely when one of the monks was on his deathbed. After recording the words which the dying man spoke to him, Symeon in his account of the event continues: "Then he conversed privately with our holy father."[17] One would like to press the plural "our" as proof that Symeon regarded the Studite as equally with himself the spiritual father of the monastery, but to do so would be illegitimate, since in the same sentence he can be found speaking of himself in the first person plural, as indeed he often does elsewhere. But the required confirmation is available in the words which, so he reports, were addressed *to* him by the dying monk and which include the phrase, "with confidence in God and in the prayer of our holy father."[18] This shows that Symeon at that time regarded the Studite, and taught his community to regard him, as in a real sense the spiritual father of them all. Putting this in other words, we may say that though hegumen, Symeon had not as yet completely left behind the role of apprentice.

Later, Symeon himself trained one of his disciples, Arsenius, with particular care. It is true that Nicetas does not say that this man was from

---

[14] *Cat XVI*, 31–35.
[15] *Cat XVI*, 34; P. Brown, 'The Rise and Function of the Holy Man in Late Antiquity,' *J.R.S.* LXI, (1971), p. 97.
[16] Nicetas, *Life*, 24, 1f. and 29, 8–10.
[17] *Cat XXI*, 21–30, 39f.
[18] *ibid.*, 26f.

early days thought of as a potential successor, but we are surely intended to regard it as significant that his training is described in considerable detail.[19] Other disciples of Symeon, by contrast, are merely mentioned by name,[20] apart from one, a bishop from the West, who had come to Constantinople to do penance for having accidentally killed his own nephew, and who would never have wished again to undertake a position of responsibility.[21] It comes consequently as no surprise when Nicetas states that Symeon, on deciding to retire from the hegumenate, arranged for Arsenius to become the new hegumen, being satisfied that he was now mature enough to succeed to this responsible office.[22] It is noteworthy that even so Arsenius in his turn may not have thought himself, or been thought by Symeon, to be qualified for totally independent exercise of the spiritual side of the office, since while he

> was to lead the flock, [Symeon] was to support the leader by prayer, to observe the secret impulses of the other brethren and to direct them to what was better and more perfect.[23]

Hausherr, in his note on these words, interprets them as meaning that "even after his resignation Symeon remained the monks' spiritual director."[24] This interpretation, however, to the extent that it suggests that Symeon continued as the sole director, is not borne out by the charge which he is represented as delivering to Arsenius, in which the latter is reminded of the need for "great care in examining the λογισμοί of each [monk]."[25] We shall find that such a task is a principal responsibility of a spiritual father, so that Hausherr's comment goes too far in implying that Symeon continued to be, while Arsenius in no sense became, the monks' director. Nevertheless, without going so far as this, we may reasonably maintain that at the time of his resignation, Symeon although satisfied with Arsenius' progress and willing that he should become hegumen, still did not regard the apprenticeship as altogether at an end.

This is in fact where the model of apprenticeship has to some extent to be corrected, valuable though it is as a help towards understanding how the qualifications needed by a spiritual father were acquired. The apprentice, at the end of a stated period, regards himself and is regarded by

---

[19] Nicetas, (*Life*, 45–51) devotes seven chapters to Arsenius.

[20] Nicetas mentions six by name in a single chapter, *Life*, 58.

[21] The reason for the bishop's coming to St. Mamas' has to be explained and his penitential behaviour described, and therefore Nicetas devotes six chapters to him (*Life*, 52–57).

[22] Nicetas, *Life*, 59, 12–15.

[23] *ibid.*, 59, 20–23.

[24] Hausherr, *ibid.*, p. 81, n. 1.

[25] Nicetas, *Life*, 63, 1f. In the next chapter we discuss the meaning of λογισμοί in a context such as this.

others as qualified to work as an independent craftsman; a spiritual father's disciple, on the contrary, however much special training he may have received, will, if his progress in πεῖρα has been real, have been continually becoming more humble, and therefore, so long as he has access to his father, he will not think himself qualified to function in total independence.

What the Qualifications Involve

Before examining the images and actual language employed by Symeon and others, it will make for clarity if we sketch in outline, with the use where necessary of modern terms, something of what is involved in the qualifications needed by a spiritual father in order to fulfil his obligatons to his children. Of the four subjects to be touched on, three call mainly for τέχνη and one for πεῖρα.

Discernment

The spiritual father is required to listen to his disciples disclosing to him their λογισμοί, and he then needs skill so as to be able to evaluate what they tell him and interpret to them its significance. To do this effectively presupposes a knowledge of what we might call practical psychology, as is suggested in the words of St. Theodore the Studite addressed to Plato, his uncle and spiritual father, "You are my light, an ever-shining lamp for the dark λογισμοί of my soul."[26] Discernment (διάκρισις) is the term used for this skill, and it is something which plays a great part in attracting clients to any father who has a reputation for possessing it. Thus, of the father of St. Cyril the Phileote it is stated that besides being nobly born,

> he was adorned with all virtue and surpassed many in discernment, for which reason many would resort to him to their profit, not only people living in the world, but also the more devout hegumens.[27]

Discernment is not much dwelt on by Symeon, but he naturally assumed that a properly-qualified spiritual father would possess this skill, and he refers to it in a significant context, just after lamenting the rarity of good directors who have acquired "those virtues which include all the others."[28] One of these virtues, he continues, is "charity (ἀγάπη)," which in its turn is "the source of perfect discernment."[29]

---

[26] Theodore, *PG* 99, 909B.
[27] Cyril, *Life*, (ed. E. Sargologos), *Subsidia Hagiographica*, 39, (1964), p. 99.
[28] *Cat XX*, 197–204, quoted in chapter V, p. 80.
[29] *ibid.*, 206–209.

Although from the point of view of spiritual fatherhood discernment must spring from a religious understanding of human nature and be directed towards a religious end, it is obvious that in order to possess it one needs to know something of what would now be called psychology.[30]

Support

Not only ought the father to be able to help his disciple by discernment, but also he should know how to assist him in his conflict with sins and vices, and with the temptations which may lead to them. A spiritual child will have made a good start by the very act of disclosing his λογισμοί, since

> in the struggle for the soul it is Satan's concern to prevent confession and that of the counselling holy man to break down the barrier of silence.[31]

At this stage, a conscience which has begun to be more sensitive is likely to require both the assurance that forgiveness is available for sins committed in the past, and also assistance in overcoming temptations in the future. Furnishing the needed support may make heavy demands on the father, as the following example illustrates.

> [A] brother was attacked by lust. He got up at night, went to an old man and told him his thoughts. The old man comforted him and he returned to his cell strengthened. But the struggle began again in him. Again he went to the old man. And he did this many times. The old man did not reproach him but spoke to him of what might help him, saying to him, 'Do not give way, but rather come every time the demon wars against you.'[32]

Demands of this nature may have been in Symeon's mind when in his charge to a hegumen he said

> Nights no less than days you will spend in anxious care for the souls entrusted to you, lest any single one of them should become a prey to wild beasts, be devoured by the bear of covetousness, swallowed up by the dragon of anger, or torn in pieces by the vultures of proud thoughts (λογισμοί) . . .[33]

---

[30] There is a valuable discussion of διάκρισις in K. Ware, 'The Spiritual Father in Orthodox Christianity,' *Cross Currents* XXIV, (1974), pp. 301–304.

[31] Dörries, 'Confession', p. 289, citing *PG* 65, 345D, ''In none does the Enemy rejoice so much as in those who do not articulate their thoughts (λογισμοί).''

[32] Ward, *Desert Fathers*, pp. 7f., no. 32; cf. in Hausherr, *Direction spirituelle*, p. 141, the title of one of the sections on the spiritual father's duties: *Porter une part de leur fardeau.*

[33] *Cat XVIII*, 433–438. *Cat XVIII*, after a long and lively description of the choice of a new hegumen, concludes with a charge instructing him in duties of his office. Some of this, but not the passage quoted, is reproduced by Nicetas in the charge which he records Symeon as giving at the installation of Arsenius, his successor.

The spiritual father thus requires knowledge of how best, in each individual case, support may be given to the tempted in their struggles, but as
well as this knowledge he is expected to have the patient willingness to continue providing support for as long as it is needed.

Ability to Train

Because the disciple must accomplish more than the negative feat of overcoming temptations to the various vices, that is, because he must be
helped positively to acquire virtues, the spiritual father has also to be well
versed in what is called 'ascetical theology.' This involves giving practical
advice concerning the nature of the virtues and the appropriate methods
of cultivating them. Much of the *Scala Paradisi*, as well as much in the
writings of many other fathers, including Symeon, is devoted to such
matters, albeit in general terms, for in specific details such teaching can
only be given individually to each disciple in accordance with his needs
at the time. A good example, illustrating Symeon's ability in this sphere,
is found in his *Ep 2*, written to a disciple living in the world, and providing
guidance in respect of such things as attendance at church, private prayer
and fasting. The practices are enjoined, Symeon writes, in order to keep
his correspondent mindful of the sins he has committed, and thus, we may
add, by implication to help him advance in the virtue of penitence. As a
master of ascetical theology, Symeon in this letter prescribes in considerable detail what we might term 'a rule of life.'[34]

Spiritual Experience

While the three so far mentioned all come under the heading of τέχνη, the
fourth field in which a spiritual father ought to be qualified is evidently
to be classed as πεῖρα. Symeon, we have seen, came to understand that
a conscious experience of God, in a mystical yet personal relationship,
is the truest benefit received in this life through a spiritual father. But
in order to give effective guidance in this area and to safeguard his disciples against the dangers of self-deception, the father must himself be
one who has at least some first-hand acquaintance with this level of prayer.
An excellent example of what is involved can be found in the description
which Symeon gives of a disciple, who has had a mystical experience,
consulting his spiritual father about it and receiving the reassurance,
"My child, that is He [sc. Christ]."[35] Clearly only from one who is

---

[34] *Ep 2*, 205v–208r; in the next chapter we shall discuss the contents of this letter in
more detail.
[35] *Tr Eth V*, 294–316; in the next chapter this passage, which is in fact autobiographical,

himself ἔμπειρος can such an endorsement of a vision be safely received.

In the above we have given an outline description of four fields in which a good spiritual father needs to be qualified. An attempt has been made to portray them so far as possible in contemporary Western terms, which, it is hoped, will serve as useful landmarks as we proceed to examine the terms employed by Symeon as well as by some of his predecessors.

The Physician of the Soul

In the language used by Symeon to depict the qualifications necessary for spiritual fatherhood two images are especially prominent, those of the physician and of the shepherd.[36] In this section we shall consider the former, beginning our treatment of the subject with what Barringer writes concerning the period 330–451 A.D.,

> the clear intent of all penitential language is to heal the wounds of sin as these touch both the individual Christian and the whole community. This medicinal understanding of penance certainly dates from the earliest Christian ages ...

He gives various examples which show how this understanding was characteristic of the thought of the Eastern Church,[37] and it is not then surprising that in later writers, amongst them Climacus and Symeon, we find the spiritual father described unequivocally as one who needs to be qualified as a physician of souls.

In the first chapter of his *Scala Paradisi* Climacus succinctly remarks:

> Because of the suppurating condition of our wounds, we need someone who is very much a τεχνίτης, and also a physician.[38]

What it means to be such a skilful and highly qualified physician of the soul, he spells out in detail in the second chapter of his *Liber ad Pastorem*. Here he translates into what he considers as their spiritual equivalents the means of treatment employed in ordinary medical practice. Thus, to cite just three items from a lengthy catalogue,

---

will receive further consideration. It is noteworthy that Fraigneau-Julien, summing up Symeon's mystical teaching, writes: "Tandis que les autres auteurs vont de la doctrine à l'expérience, Syméon va de l'expérience à la doctrine." (*op. cit.*, p. 202)—cf. the last section of the present chapter.

[36] cf. *Cat XX*, 198f., οἱ καλῶς ποιμαίνειν καὶ ἰατρεύειν ψυχὰς λογικὰς ἐπιστάμενοι.

[37] Barringer, *Penance*, pp. 32f., 34f., 110, 160. Amongst these examples we may note the striking: οὐκ εὐθύνας ἀπαιτῶ ἁμαρτημάτων, ἀλλὰ τοῖς ἀσθενοῦσι φάρμακα κατασκευάζω, John Chrysostom, *Vita Phocae*, 1, PG 50, 699.

[38] *Sc. Par.* 1, 636AB.

a plaster is the healing of the passions which can be seen, that is those of the body; a dose is the healing of passions which are internal, and the expulsion of unseen filth; a desiccative is humiliation that stings and heals the suppuration of self-conceit.[39]

This device used by Climacus clearly demonstrates how the τέχνη of a spiritual ἰατρός was held to include a wide range of skills needed to deal with the different diseases of the soul, and it may be added that it was the acquisition of these skills which entitled him to claim to be a τεχνίτης. On this basis, to be effective as a healer, a spiritual father ought to be qualified to function as a psychologist, a sympathetic supporter and an ascetical theologian, to use the terminology employed in the last section.

It is surprising that, although Symeon himself was, as we shall see, very much aware of the need for spiritual fathers to be well qualified as physicians of the soul, he never appears to claim this qualification for his own father, the Studite. The reason for this omission can only be conjectured, but it may be suggested as a not unlikely explanation that he took this qualification for granted and saw no need to mention it, whereas he frequently found it necessary to concern himself with vindicating the Studite's sanctity in opposition to those who regarded him as a charlatan. Symeon's nearest approach to the use of a medical image when speaking of his spiritual father is to be found in the passage in which he recalls what he heard from the mouths of those trying to persuade him to abandon the Studite. He was reproached for his "vain and futile expectation of recovering ... [spiritual] sight" through "this impostor and deceiver," and the hardships he suffered in consequence were contrasted with "the treatment that would be given" by those attempting to win him over.[40]

A passage in which Symeon acknowledges his own need of a spiritual physician occurs in *Hymn XII*, which must be assigned to a period when all was going well for him, since he admitted that he had succumbed to the temptation to consider himself "rightly held in honour by all men, and also praised because worthy of their praises." He then continued, using language reminiscent of that employed by Climacus, but, it is interesting, without any mention of the Studite,

---

[39] *ad Pastorem*, 1168D–1169C, cf. also *Sc. Par.* 8, 833CD, and for the difference between the skilful and the unskilful physician, *ibid.*, 26, 1020BC. It is interesting to find that Dorotheus of Gaza prefers to restrict the role of spiritual physician to Christ himself, *Doctrinae*, XI, 113, 22ff., while Symeon, without so restricting it, does also apply the title to Christ, *Hymn XLVI*, 8.

[40] *Cat XXXVI*, 102–104 and 111, from the passage more fully cited in last chapter; the Greek has ἀναβλέψαι, an obviously medical term, which in the context has to be rendered "recover [spiritual] sight," while "treatment" translates θεραπεία (the verb θεραπεύω occurs four lines earlier), which may, but need not necessarily, connote medical treatment.

How is it that I do not . . . perceive my stripes, that I am not grieved and do not weep? [How is it that] I do not lie down in some hospital and seek for healing, call for physicians and show them my wounds, laying bare my hidden passions, so that they may apply desiccatives, plasters and cauteries . . . ?

It is possible that Symeon here is not really so much thinking of himself as of a certain Oporopoulos, for according to the scholiast it is he whose manner of life is being lamented inasmuch as

being totally devoted to the glory that comes from men, he dared without the Spirit to theologize about the things of the Spirit.[41]

Whether the scholiast is correct or not, one would in any case not have been surprised, indeed one might have expected, to be confronted here with a reference to Symeon's spiritual father as the person most qualified to bring him healing. It is true that the Studite might have been no longer living when *Hymn XII* was written, but in that case one might have expected to find an expression of Symeon's sorrow that this great physician of the soul could not now come to his help. There can, however, be no doubt that if challenged on the matter he would have vehemently insisted that the Studite possessed every one of the qualifications needed by a father, including that of knowing how to act as a spiritual physician.

Another passage in which Symeon made use of this same image of the physician was quoted in part in the last chapter. If we look at it again, concentrating now on what may be gathered from it that bears upon the question of qualifications, we shall notice the emphasis placed upon the ability to diagnose accurately and to prescribe appropriate treatment, and the fact that to do this πεῖρα as well as τέχνη is required.

[Do not choose] an inexperienced (ἄπειρος) physician, lest he either plunge you into the depths of despair through excessive severity and inopportune surgery and cauterisation [of the soul], or else through overmuch tenderness leave you in your sickness . . .[42]

A page or two earlier, Symeon had implied that knowledge of the right treatment, when translated into spiritual terms, was in part at least a matter of understanding what penances were needed to heal the diseased soul.

Let us run to the spiritual physician, and by means of confession vomit out the poison of sin, spitting out its venom. As an antidote let us eagerly accept from him the penances (ἐπιτίμια) given in response to our repentance.[43]

---

[41] *Hymn XII*, 63–120, first quotation 91f., second 105–110, scholiast's reference to 69.
[42] *Ep 1*, p. 117, 9–12.
[43] *ibid.*, p. 115, 26—p. 116, 3; an ἐπιτίμιον was usually something much more severe than the very light penances normally imposed to-day by Western confessors, but Dörries,

These extracts from *Ep 1* demonstrate an awareness that the spiritual physician must be skilful both in diagnosing the true condition of a soul and in choosing the penances which will be most effective in promoting the healing of the sinful conditions revealed in confession. Translating this statement into the terms used in the previous section, we may say that what is required is a knowledge both of practical psychology and of ascetical theology.

The need for psychological understanding, coupled with tact and skill in dealing with others, comes very much to the fore in a passage found in *Tr Eth VI*, and it is worthwhile quoting at some length from the imaginary case-history which Symeon there presented.

> To demonstrate [the spiritual physician's] skilful treatment (ἔντεχνος ἰατρεία) through what I say, I shall speak as though describing an actual happening. The spiritual physician is approached by a sick man, who is so stupefied by his disorder and has a mind so entirely disturbed, that he asks for what would harm rather than heal him, that is to say what would worsen his disease and result before long in death. The kindly and sympathetic physician, on seeing his brother, understands his infirmity and the inflamed nature of his disorder and its distention. He observes the invalid to be virtually at death's door . . . When then a wise spiritual physician sees his brother in a state such as we have described, he neither shouts at him, nor puts him off, nor tells him, 'You are demanding what would be bad for you, indeed fatal; I will not give you that kind of help.' [He refrains from saying this] lest the other on hearing it should make his escape and go to someone selse without experience (ἄπειρος) of disorders of this kind, and so die straight away. No! What he does is to welcome him, keep him by him, encourage him, show him every token of love and liberality, in order to convince him that he will use the medicines he has asked for to work his cure, and that he will satisfy his desire . . . The experienced (ἔμπειρος) physician does not immediately refuse the sick man what he asks for, but promises to satisfy all his requests; the sick man is enthusiastic about the pleasing things he tells him, accounting them good; the physician conceals the ways in which he is helping him.[44]

This extract hints at what will be examined later, the shallowness of some clients, particularly seculars, and their habit of deserting one spiritual father for another, if they felt the first to be insufficiently complaisant. This being the case, Symeon recognised that if those who consulted a father were not to run off and suffer spiritual death at the hands of an inexperienced practitioner, it was necessary for the physician of the soul to be skilled not only in diagnosing the true condition of penitents, but also

---

'Confession', p. 291, observes that long periods of penance were rejected by the Desert Fathers.

[44] *Tr Eth VI*, 276–311 (excerpts); cf. Gregory of Nazianzus, *Oration XXXI*, *PG* 36, 161AB.

in making use of innocent subterfuges so that they might be retained and their treatment begun. To be qualified in these ways, the future spiritual father needed teaching such as is given in this passage, but as the words "experienced" and "without experience" suggest, it would be necessary for him to get not only theoretical knowledge but also actual practice in real life. And since Symeon was very conscious that what was at stake was nothing less than the fate of a human soul, one must suppose that he would always have wished to ensure that disciples selected for special training would gain this practical experience by at first working in consultation with their own highly-qualified spiritual father. Such supervised activity would in fact be a part of their apprenticeship.[45]

Before ending our consideration of the spiritual father's need to be qualified as a physician of the soul, we must allude to the subject of dispassion (ἀπάθεια). Although this will be further discussed both in a later section of this chapter and also when the training of disciples is investigated, it must be mentioned here as a prerequisite for the work of the spiritual physician. Christophorides[46] has rightly drawn attention to Symeon's awareness that a father would himself suffer spiritual injury, if he sought to heal the souls of others without himself having become dispassionate. Thus in *Tr Eth VI*, which is largely devoted to the subject of dispassion, the following significant passage is found shortly before the long excerpt previously quoted:

> The understanding of holy men remains unstained, even if they look into filthy and shameful passions, for their mind is devoid of, and a stranger to, all passionate (ἐμπαθής) desire. If ever it determines to enter upon an investigation of such things, it does so for no reason other than a wish to observe and understand the passionate movements of the passions and their workings, and [to know] what causes them and what remedies dispel them, just as we hear that physicians do [with regard to the body] ...[47]

Thus the attainment of dispassion, which is one of the accompaniments of holiness, must be regarded also as an indispensable qualification if the father, as spiritual physician, is to be able to diagnose sins and bring healing to sinners without endangering himself in the process.

To sum up this section, we may say that Symeon was following a well-established tradition in his use of medical imagery when referring to spiritual fatherhood and the qualifications needed by those who undertake

---

[45] cf. Dorotheus of Gaza who consulted Barsanuphius about problems in connection with the directing of his fellow-monks (Regnault and de Préville, *SC* 92, intr. p. 23, citing *Letters of Barsanuphius and John*, 331, 332 and 333—re-edited by S.N. Schoinas, Volos, 1960).

[46] *op. cit.*, p. 80.

[47] *Tr Eth VI*, 262–270.

it. The tradition understood healing as a basic requirement of the sinner's soul, and Symeon accepted and was confirmed in this understanding through his own experience as a disciple and as a spiritual father. Moreover, he observed the sad consequences which resulted from people attaching themselves to men who claimed to be physicians of the soul but lacked skill, experience, or both of these, and he was thereby convinced that fathers must be properly qualified if their work was to be properly accomplished.

The Pastor

When attempting to write about the qualifications needed by the spiritual father in his role of pastor, one is confronted at the outset by two difficulties. The first has to do with language: Greek has the single word, ποιμήν, 'shepherd', which can be used either literally or metaphorically; English, except when speaking of God or Christ, prefers to substitute for 'shepherd' in the metaphorical sense the Latin 'pastor', which—unlike 'shepherd'—conveniently possesses a cognate adjective, 'pastoral'. But while Greek has the verb ποιμαίνω, 'to shepherd' or 'to look after [a flock],' a word which can be used either literally or metaphorically, English has no verb corresponding to the noun 'pastor'. It will therefore at times be necessary to resort to the cumbrous device or inserting ποιμαίνω in brackets, in order to make it clear that the original contains this verb, used metaphorically, and here translated by some periphrasis.

The second difficulty lies in the fact that as compared with "medical" qualifications, those classified as "pastoral" are bound to appear somewhat vague. The reason for this is that although τέχνη is involved here also, it is chiefly his moral and religious qualities that make someone a good Christian pastor, and such qualities do not usually get assessed in terms of technical skill. Of the categories proposed in the second section of this chapter, we can anticipate that the most important for the pastor will be found to be the fourth, spiritual experience, together with the second, support for the tempted and erring. This will include the knowledge of how best to help them, together with a willingness to continue doing so, however troublesome it may prove.

For Christians the origin of the shepherd/pastor image is of course to be sought in the Bible, and particularly in the New Testament where it is used of Christ. In the *Fourth Gospel* he is represented as claiming himself to be the Good Shepherd (ὁ ποιμὴν ὁ καλός), who knows his sheep and lays down his life for them;[48] in *I Peter* he is styled the Chief Shepherd

---

[48] *St. John* 10. 11–15, cf. the parable of the shepherd and the lost sheep, *St. Matthew* 18. 12f., *St. Luke* 15. 3–7.

(ἀρχιποίμην), and the elders of the Church are exhorted to work under him as the shepherds of (ποιμαίνω) God's flock.[49] Such an injunction will have led to its seeming very natural to employ pastoral terminology in connection with spiritual fatherhood, since the hegumen of a monastery normally undertook this latter duty *ex officio*, while being at the same time the pastor, under Christ, of his monks. It is also noteworthy that in *Ephesians* 4. 11, the only place in the New Testament where the noun ποιμήν is used in its metaphorical sense of persons other than Christ, it is coupled with διδάσκαλος, and we have seen that teaching is one of the tasks expected of the spiritual father, and "teacher" one of the names which he may be given.

Symeon linked medical and pastoral qualifications in his phrase, "those who understand how to be good pastors and physicians to rational souls," but he was not the first to do so. This is shown by the presence in Climacus of a sentence which, when compared with Symeon's words, strikes the reader as more vividly reminiscent of the New Testament:

> A good shepherd (καλὸς ποιμήν) will give life to (ζωοποιήσει) and will heal his spiritual (νοερός) sheep.[50]

It is not hard to discover in his *Liber ad Pastorem* the various qualifications which Climacus considers that the pastor requires: they include guilelessness, zeal, prayer, vigilance and—above all—love, which "marks out a true shepherd, since the Shepherd was crucified because of [his] love."[51] What such requirements amounted to in practice is well brought out by Dörries.

> The gentleness with which [some fathers] sought after those who had isolated themselves out of fear or obstinacy touches the reader all the more for its not being the expression of soft yielding but often being combined with an actually inflexible severity of demand.[52]

Whatever the reasons why Symeon did not speak of the Studite as a spiritual physician and never referred to his qualifications in that area, we find that he had no reluctance about describing him as a pastor. When Nicetas styles him "the good shepherd," in an account of his care for Symeon,[53] this may be an instance of dependence on the latter who

---

[49] *I Peter* 5. 1–4; cf. Christ's words to St. Peter, ποίμαινε τὰ πρόβατά μου, *St. John* 21. 16.

[50] Climacus, *ad Pastorem*, 1168A (ζωοποιέω is used by Christ of himself as Son of God in *St. John* 5. 21); cf. Symeon's charge to a hegumen, ὡς δὲ ἰατρὸς ... ὡς δὲ ποιμὴν ..., *Cat XVIII*, 469f.

[51] *ad Pastorem*, 1165B, 1168A, 1177B.

[52] Dörries, 'Confession', p. 288.

[53] Nicetas, *Life*, 24, 1.

himself uses the same expression with reference to his father.[54] Besides this, Symeon more than once employs language which testifies to his recognition of the pastoral ability possessed by the Studite. Thus, remembering the occasion when although he had been favoured with a visionary experience he had shortly afterwards become a "lost sheep," Symeon says to Christ, "thou didst convert (ἐπέστρεψας) me through him, that saintly man."[55] The pastoral reference is evident in view of the LXX version of *Psalm* 22 (23), sometimes called the "Shepherd Psalm," in which occur the words τὴν ψυχῆν μου ἐπέστρεψεν. In *James* 5. 19f., where the verb ἐπιστρέψω also occurs, there is equally a pastoral undertone since the subject-matter is the conversion of "any among you [who] wanders from the truth," and it is possible that these verses too were in Symeon's mind. At all events in terms of *I Peter* 5. 1 – 4, he had experienced the Studite as an effective and well-qualified pastor who, acting under the direction of Christ the Chief Shepherd, was the agent who effected his conversion.

But in connection with this topic we must revert to the fuller description in *Cat XXII* of the period of Symeon's life touched on in those words from *Cat XXXV*. Usually the image of the shepherd would suggest that we are dealing with one who takes initiatives, such as, for example, going out to search for a lost sheep. An initiative of this kind might be thought to be implied in "thou didst convert me through him," the phrase which we have just examined. It would, however, be wrong to insist that being a pastor must mean undertaking at all times an active role of this kind, and this is borne out by the actual course of events narrated in *Cat XXII*. Here, in what ostensibly is the second part of the young man George's story, Symeon confesses that

> Little by little I became oblivious of all that I have just recounted [sc. the vision] and reached the point of being in total darkness ... I even looked upon that saint as a mere ordinary man ... In spite of my unworthiness, I did not entirely keep away from him, but used to confess to him the events of my life (τὰ γινόμενα ἐξηγόρευον), and even though, being deaf to my conscience, I did not obey his injunctions, I would frequently go to his cell when I chanced to be in the city.[56]

In these words there is well brought out the patience of the pastor, ready to remain available but in the background, watching over a member of his flock who has wandered away, without intervening until an appropriate occasion presents itself. By implication also the reader is given a glimpse of the attractiveness of the Studite's personality, which could

---

[54] Symeon, *Cat XXXV*, 113 (καλὸς ποιμήν), *ibid.*, 256, 262 (ποιμήν alone).
[55] *ibid.*, 118.
[56] *Cat XXII*, 285 – 308 (extracts).

make Symeon feel that he was a welcome visitor, even at a time when he might have seemed to be likely to prove, from the spiritual point of view, a total disappointment. In fact, when dealing not with a sheep but with a human being, the wise pastor knows that waiting patiently and keeping in touch so far as possible is often the most effective method of proceeding, until there comes an opportune moment for taking an initiative.[57] As Symeon put it,

> after many years had passed, God who loves mankind, had mercy on me in response to the prayers of [the Studite], and by means of him rescued and delivered me from much error and from an abyss of evils.[58]

Such was Symeon's experience as a recipient of pastoral care which for a long period was unobtrusive, but unfortunately we shall discover that, when a pastor himself, he apparently lacked the Studite's capacity for being patient with the erring.

As to his teaching about the qualifications for pastoral work which ought to be found in a spiritual father, we must notice first that Symeon insisted that freedom from earthly concerns was of great importance. Because of his stress on this, he appears to have been unhappy about the results of the practice of combining in one person, the hegumen, both spiritual and administrative responsibilities. Thus he writes:

> He who wishes to care for (ποιμαίνω) Christ's flock ... can he at the same time manifest anxiety over fields and be concerned about possessions, taking legal action to protect these things and to repel those who would harm or threaten them, now having to go before the courts, and now to withstand accusations and lies, sometimes even incurring responsibility for oaths and for perjury?[59]

It is indeed easy to see how his necessary concern for the temporalities of his monastery might prevent a hegumen from paying much attention to his own personal and spiritual development, a less tangible matter, but in reality essential for any one aspiring to be, in the true sense, a successful pastor. St. Stephen the Younger, for example, was probably conscious that he needed to protect himself against distractions of the kind

---

57 cf. Archdeacon Cunningham's opinion that "a clergyman ... should aim to retain a hold as a friend on those who could no longer regard him as a teacher" (A. Cunningham, *William Cunningham—Teacher and Priest*, London, 1950, p. 90).

58 *Cat XXII*, 301–304.

59 *Tr Eth XI*, 649–657; cf. *Cat XVIII*, 483–488, where the body of monks is termed a "flock (ποίμνη)," and the hegumen is bidden to delegate administration so far as possible, and not to go out of the monastery on business more than once a month, and *Hymn XLIII*, 11–19, where Symeon laments that he has to choose between "being anxious about the affairs of the monastery, giving thought unreservedly to temporal needs," or on the other hand "cultivating ἡσυχία" and "gently teaching others."

mentioned by Symeon, for we learn that after the number of his monks had increased to twenty, he handed over the administration of the monastery to his disciple Marinus, and withdrew to a small cell so that he might lead a more ascetic life. His withdrawal, however, by no means resulted in his ceasing to act as a spiritual father; on the contrary, we are told by his biographer that many resorted to him "in order to be profited."[60]

On the positive side, Symeon held that the hegumen as spiritual father must be available and attend to everything involved in "being at the head of a flock (ποίμνη) and caring for the salvation of his neighbours."[61] This would mean that he ought to have the knowledge and ability necessary for instructing them, since

> care for a flock (τὸ ποιμαίνειν) means nothing other than paying attention, by means of preaching and teaching, to those being cared for (οἱ ποιμαινόμενοι).[62]

In much the same way, in words which he believed were addressed to him by the Lord, Symeon was reminded that his own duty as hegumen was to lead his "sheep" to "the pastures of [Christ's] commandments."[63] But in this context it is made clear that more than purely intellectual or moral qualifications are needed for such teaching, since the flock must also be led to "the spiritual (νοερός) mountains of mystical contemplations."[64] With the introduction of this concept we are once again moving into the realm of πεῖρα, since a pastor who himself has no experience of "mystical contemplations" would find it hard to guide his spiritual children to those "mountains". A qualification of the same type, but more basic in what it explicitly prescribes, can be observed in Symeon's warning:

> Do not attempt to function as a [spiritual] shepherd (ποιμαίνω) until you have gained the Good Shepherd as your true friend.[65]

Similarly, and here again linking pastoral and medical imagery, he wrote:

> You, who still sit in darkness and have not acquired the eye which sees the true light, are you not afraid to be the pastor (ποιμαίνω) of your brethren? When you yourself are sick, and unable even to recognise your own

---

[60] *Life*, written by Stephen the Deacon, *PG* 100, 1104D–1108A, cited by J. Leroy, 'La réforme studite,' *O.C.A.*, 153, (1958), p. 53.

[61] *Tr Eth XI*, 399–401; cf. also the injunction that the hegumen shall make himself available twice a day to hear confessions, "having laid aside every other work of whatever kind . . . ," 'Le *typikon* de la *Théotokos Évergétis*' (ed. P. Gautier), *R.E.B.*, 40, (1982), p. 29.

[62] *Tr Eth XI*, 496f., with a reminiscence of *I Timothy* 5. 17.

[63] *Hymn XLIII*, 70–73; cf. *Tr Eth XI*, 542f., *Ch* I, 54, 25f.

[64] *Hymn XLIII*, 72f.

[65] *Tr Eth VI*, 413f.

wounds, are you not ashamed to act the physician (ἰατρεύω) to others?[66]

From the foregoing examples, it is evident that Symeon, no less than earlier writers, expected a spiritual father both to manifest certain definite qualities in himself and also to be leading a life free from unsuitable distractions, if he wished to be thought fit for the pastoral side of his work, as one who must care for his disciples, clients or spiritual children. Moreover, since the Biblical image of the shepherd/pastor comes to full expression in Christ, who is both the Good Shepherd and the Chief Shepherd, it is not surprising that when anyone is to act as ''under-shepherd'', the qualifications he requires are sometimes expressed in most demanding terms. These qualifications are demanded because, as Symeon put it, his task is to

> preserve [the] flock for Christ our God, the Chief Shepherd, keeping it safe and with its size increasing . . .[67]

The implication is that to the extent that a spiritual father is deficient in any or all of the qualifications needed by a pastor, he is liable to cause injury to souls which are not his but belong to Christ himself.

Further Requirements

As well as all that is conveyed by the images of spiritual physician and of pastor, there are some further respects in which Symeon considered that a spiritual father ought to be qualified. These must now be briefly discussed.

Teaching

We begin with the ability to teach, which is in fact frequently coupled with, or implied in, the activity of a pastor. What knowledge should the father, as teacher, be qualified to impart? For Symeon, devoted as he was to the Bible, the first answer to be given was obvious: ''the divinely-inspired and useful teaching of the Word,'' or—as he represents Christ as saying—''the life-giving food of my commandments.''[68]

This last phrase suggests the use of the Scriptures for the purpose of

---

[66] *ibid.*, 397–401; cf. *Cat XXVIII*, 209–218, where Symeon insists that unless a man lives as he ought to live, he is not qualified to ''care for (ποιμαίνω) [the flock] in accordance with the will of the Chief Shepherd.''

[67] *Cat XVIII*, 439f.; cf. *ibid.*, 576, where the hegumen is again addressed as ποιμὴν τῶν προβάτων Χριστοῦ.

[68] *Ep 1*, p. 125, 1f., a reminiscence of *II Timothy* 3. 16; *Tr Eth XI*, 542f.

instructing disciples about the way in which Christians ought to live, but Symeon also expected that a spiritual father would know how to teach others to draw from them material for use in their private devotions: he advised a novice, "Let there be psalms fixed by your spiritual father for you [to recite] . . . ," and when giving instruction to one of his own children about his evening prayers, told him to say *Psalm* 6.[69]

Symeon is also found bidding a hegumen to

> apply [himself] carefully to the reading of the ordinances and canons [of those who were] eye-witnesses and disciples of the Word.[70]

This is presumably a reference to the *Apostolic Canons*, mentioned a little earlier in the same *Catechesis*. A spiritual father might not need to teach such material directly, but he would find in it background information on which to draw when giving instruction to his disciples about their ecclesiastical duties.

Bearing Burdens

We shall refer again in the next chapter to "*Porter une part de leur fardeau*", one of the headings under which Hausherr classifies the duties of a spiritual father in regard to his disciples, and we have already mentioned the need for him to be qualified to undertake a supportive role. Although there is no one Greek word which expresses this aspect of the father's qualifications, the concept none the less can distinctly be discerned. Accompanying it there very frequently occurs a reminiscence of St. Paul's words, "Bear one another's burdens . . . ," shortly after which, paradoxically, he utters the warning: "Each man will have to bear his own load." The original here has φορτίον for 'load' and βάρος for 'burden',[71] but by a strange and presumably unconscious reversal of the apostle's terms, Climacus offered the advice that

> he who is able and willing to toil with you on the φορτίον of your sins should be your father.[72]

Similarly he could write elsewhere that

> a simple monk is a rational animal, is obedient and lays his φορτίον entirely on the one who leads him.[73]

---

[69] *Cat XXVI*, 282f.; *Ep 2*, 207v.
[70] *Cat XVIII*, 551–553. Krivochéine (*SC* 104, pp. 306f., n. 1) has a note about the origins and history of the *Apostolic Canons*, which were not in truth composed by the Apostles, the "eye-witnesses" of Christ.
[71] *Galatians* 6. 2 & 5; cf. *Romans* 15. 1.
[72] *Sc. Par.* 3, 665D.
[73] *ibid.*, 24, 984C.

The Pauline vocabulary, however, was correctly employed by Symeon when he recommended a hegumen to find colleagues who would assist him by, amongst other things, "taking on the burdens (βάρη) of the brethren."[74] Somewhat later in the same *Catechesis*, but also in connection with this subject, he again came very close to St. Paul's language when enunciating the principle that the hegumen, "as one who is strong, must bear the infirmities of the weak."[75] This might leave us with the impression that, in Symeon's understanding, the spiritual father's qualification as a "burden-bearer" consists merely in his being willing and able to give effective support to those whose pastor he is, when they are faced with the need to struggle against infirmities and temptations. However, something more than this is suggested by the word, translated "taking on," which Symeon used in connection with "the burdens of the brethren." This verb, ἀναδέχομαι, and its cognate noun ἀνάδοχος can, as we shall discover, signify an acceptance of responsibility by the father for the sins of his spiritual children. Without anticipating our subsequent discussion of this perhaps startling concept, it is necessary to point out here that, because of it, the image we have been looking at implies a much deeper and more costing type of qualification than it superficially suggests.

Love

Although not the kind of qualification which can be assessed by prescribed standards, love or charity (ἀγάπη) is manifestly essential as a motive if a spiritual father is to undertake the bearing of his children's burdens, particularly when this somehow involves him in responsibility for their sins. Christophorides emphasises the importance of love as one of the qualities he ought to possess,[76] and we observed that according to Climacus it is inseparable from genuine pastoral work, since "love marks out a true shepherd . . . ."

Symeon was no less convinced than Climacus about the necessity of love, and his sentiments are strikingly revealed in *Cat I*. In this, addressing his community on the day of his installation as hegumen, he apostrophized ἀγάπη in a long and lyrical passage in the course of which he engaged himself, in imitation of the apostles and martyrs whom love inspired in former years, to suffer and endure everything in order to edify and benefit his monks.[77]

---

74 *Cat XVIII*, 429.
75 ibid., 468f., cf. *Romans* 15. 1.
76 *op. cit.*, pp. 105–109.
77 *Cat I*, 70–134.

It must not be assumed that the love thus spoken of is no more than a matter of the relationships between one human being and his fellows; though directed towards other human beings, it is to be understood rather as a means of expressing one's love for God.[78] This is well brought out in pseudo-Basil's *De renuntiatione saeculi*, where prominent among the qualifications to be looked for in a spiritual father there is found the requirement of "love for God (ἡ πρὸς Θεὸν ἀγάπη) attested by his works."[79] In the same way Symeon in his inaugural *Catechesis* spoke of ἀγάπη as

> kindling in me a boundless love (πόθος) for God and for my brethren and fathers.[80]

On the basis of this qualification, he can be seen in these and the words about to follow, even though he tactfully called the older monks his "fathers", indirectly justifying his right as hegumen to claim to be *ex officio* spiritual father of St. Mamas': it was ἀγάπη that installed him in this ministry.[81] It cannot be doubted that he held the same love to be indispensable for everyone called to minister as a spiritual father.

Discipleship

To conclude this section, we must mention Symeon's insistence that the qualifications for spiritual fatherhood cannot possibly be acquired unless one has had a spiritual father of one's own and been obedient to him. (Here in a sense we return to the model of apprenticeship which was considered earlier.) In *Ep 4*, writing to one whom he addressed as "spiritual father," but whom he evidently suspected of not being genuinely qualified, Symeon enjoined him:

> You must first become a disciple of Christ and moreover be well instructed by him in his mysteries, and only so attempt to instruct others in them. You must follow a spiritual father, and without turning back travel along the way which leads to Christ . . .[82]

This insistence is exactly what one might expect if the normal mode of becoming a spiritual father was through apprenticeship to someone already established as a practitioner of this demanding ministry. All apprentices

---

[78] According to Christian theology, this love for God is itself an acceptance of, and a response to, his love—*I John* 4. 19, "We love, because he first loved us."

[79] Pseudo-Basil, *PG* 31, 632B.

[80] *Cat I*, 129f.

[81] *ibid.*, 133f.

[82] *Ep 4*, 326–329.

were necessarily disciples, and Symeon was maintaining that a genuine father needed to stand in a succession of predecessors, each in turn having received a true spiritual formation.

Symeon's Emphasis on Experience

While examining the qualifications required for spiritual fatherhood, we have referred more than once to Symeon's evident concern with experience (πεῖρα).[83] Before concluding the chapter, we must now underline his emphasis on this aspect of the matter, and discuss some of his statements which illustrate different manifestations of it.

Part of a passage already quoted for a different purpose shows Symeon's reaction to what he observed of the depth and reality of the Studite's spiritual life.

> I rejoiced . . . as I beheld him following in thy footsteps and often holding converse with thee . . . I saw thee, our good Master, present with my guide, my father . . .[84]

In these words he reveals something of the impression made on him when he found that prayer, for the Studite, was quite clearly nothing less than a real meeting and conversation with Christ. Indeed, if it is legitimate to press the words "I saw thee," we might understand him to be saying that he was somehow able to share in a vision or visions which his father was permitted to behold. Certainly in *Hymn XVIII* some kind of shared visionary experience seems to be implied in the description of the Studite standing in the midst of a fire, calling Symeon to him and then embracing him.[85] Possibly, however, "I saw thee" should not be interpreted as denoting more than a deep-seated feeling on the part of Symeon that when the Studite was at prayer, Christ's presence could be almost physically perceived. In either case, the important point, so far as we are now concerned, is that Symeon was convinced that as a disciple he had had a spiritual father of whose experience in the realm of mystical prayer he could be absolutely certain.

Furthermore, Symeon is tireless in claiming that the Studite was truly and totally dispassionate (ἀπαθής), and we have seen that acquiring the personal quality of dispassion is essential if a spiritual father is to function safely as a physician of souls. Some of Symeon's ardour in making this claim is doubtless to be understood as his response to those who challenged

---

[83] cf. Völker, *Praxis*, p. 114.
[84] *Hymn XXXVII*, 30–34.
[85] *Hymn XVIII*, 143–160.

it as part of their campaign to deny the Studite's sanctity, but in the following passage the claim is obviously made in connection with an assertion that his father was qualified to be a true spiritual teacher.

> He came to equal many of the most illlustrious martyrs. That is why he was glorified by God, and became dispassionate and was a saint, having received within himself the Paraclete in, so to speak, his entirety. Then, just as a father freely gives an inheritance to his son, so he filled me, his unworthy servant, with the Holy Spirit, without any toil or any payment on my part.[86]

When we remember that, after the ending of the persecutions, the life of a monk began to be considered as the equivalent of literally dying for one's Christian faith,[87] we shall recognise that here there is a very illuminating sequence: the Studite's progress in the monastic life was accepted by God as no less valuable than the martyrs' sacrifice; it was therefore rewarded by the gifts of dispassion and sanctity, and as a result he was enabled to receive the Holy Spirit in full measure and personally—"within himself;" thus he was qualified thereafter, as a spiritual father, to be the agent through whom the Spirit was passed on to Symeon, his disciple and spiritual child.

The qualifications of the Studite from the point of view of τέχνη are of course taken for granted in claims such as this, where all the emphasis is put on the interior life. This is typical of Symeon's stress on the primacy of personal experience and of his assumption that it was superfluous to dwell on his father's skill as a pastor. Symeon made no mention of this skill, for example, when describing his own time as a backslider, in spite of the fact that, as we saw, it must have been the Studite's great pastoral expertise which enabled him to retain some hold upon one who had "ceased to observe his injunctions," and regarded him as "a mere ordinary man."[88]

If we turn to the teaching given by Symeon, recalling what was adduced under the various headings, we can find in it further evidence of the way in which he laid stress on experience. He held that the father, as spiritual physician, needed not simply theoretical knowledge, but the practical ability which comes from being ἔμπειρος;[89] as pastor, the father must have personally experienced the friendship of Christ, the Good Shepherd;[90] and how could he to guide others as they climbed to "the spiritual

---

[86] *Cat VI*, 261–267; cf. for claims that the Studite was totally dispassionate, *Hymn XV*, 205–214, and Nicetas, *Life*, 81, 3–5.

[87] For the monk's life as equivalent to martyrdom, cf. Symeon's disquisition on this subject in *Tr Eth X*, 566–611.

[88] v. pp. 106f.

[89] *Tr Eth VI*, 308.

[90] *ibid.*, 413f.

mountains of mystical contemplations,''[91] if he were not himself familiar with that terrain?

Furthermore, it can be shown that Symeon could see a connection between πεῖρα, as growth in love personally experienced, and the gaining of discernment. To demonstrate this, we quote a passage that includes words cited in an earlier section of this chapter and follows immediately some lines reproduced in chapter V, with a few of which we must start.

> By virtues which include all the others, we mean humility ... and charity (ἀγάπη) which ... is itself the source of perfect discernment. This in its turn does not go astray when guiding both itself and those who follow it, but brings them safely across the spiritual (νοητός) sea.[92]

Here, when indicating the importance of discernment Symeon affirmed that it is acquired not by attaining some proficiency which might be, as it were, an external matter, but rather through a person's possessing or being possessed by love/charity, an experience which is essentially internal.

In the same context, he spoke also of humility, "which annihilates the passions and procures heavenly, angelic dispassion." Humility too, if genuine, is an inward state of soul, and by mentioning it here Symeon in effect contrasted it with what he had just referred to rather slightingly, the more overt pious and ascetic practices of many would-be spiritual fathers. Over against such people are the few who, doubtless without neglecting those practices, sincerely try to acquire the two "virtues which include all the others,''[93] and which are rooted in a person's internal disposition. Humility and charity, since they cannot be gained simply by τέχνη, thus illustrate very well the importance which Symeon in his teaching assigned to this type of experience.

Passing to a different area, we must take note of a long section in another *Catechesis*[94] in which Symeon is at pains to oppose the claim to have the power to "bind and loose," when it is made by those whose qualifications are only external and based on "human appointment and ordination.''[95] Such priests he contrasts with those who can justly claim the power because they "offer themselves to the Lord, and as a perfect, holy and acceptable sacrifice manifest their pure worship internally and in a spiritual fashion, in the temple of their body ...''[96] Here once

---

[91] *Hymn XLIII*, 72f.

[92] *Cat XX*, 204–211.

[93] *ibid.*, 205f., 199–204.

[94] *Cat XXVIII*, 190–296, to which H. Graef drew attention (v. 'Spiritual Director,' pp. 612f.).

[95] *ibid.*, 291–293.

[96] *ibid.*, 265–268, containing a wealth of Biblical allusions.

again, although the actual word πεῖρα does not appear, the type of character being described is closely related to it: all the emphasis falls on the need for inner, spiritual experience, so that we have yet another instance of Symeon's insistence that this is an indispensable qualification for spiritual fatherhood.

Finally, something should be said about Symeon's own practice as a father. From Nicetas we gain the impression that he regarded his personal mystical experiences as revelations to be conveyed to his spiritual children, provided they were worthy to receive them. In a passage in the *Preface to the Hymns*, where the language is reminiscent of pseudo-Dionysius, we are informed about Symeon's method.

> The divine visions which in sacredness he had contemplated, he revealed to his disciples as though in payment of a debt. He did so as a person of the highest rank, [sharing] ungrudgingly, but yet in proportion to their capacities, with those who ranked second and were subordinate to him. He communicated sacred things to those who with understanding and entire devotion had shared in the sacred initiation, and he did this in proportion to their worthiness. He kept such matters from the laughter and mockery of the uninitiated, or rather he kept those [scoffers], if he found any such, from coming into conflict with God, because he did not divulge these [mysteries] to all and sundry while he was himself still to be seen among the living.[97]

When Nicetas here speaks of Symeon's taking care not to expose scoffers to the risk of "coming into conflict with God (θεομαχία)," he gives us a glimpse of the farthest reach to which πεῖρα can extend; this is nothing less than the higher levels of contemplation. A spiritual father may need to be familiar with such states of prayer, in order to be capable of bringing others "to spiritual birth,"[98] but if this birth is understood as mystical experience, there is here a possible source of danger, should he attempt prematurely to share what he has received in contemplation with those as yet unable to profit by it. Presumably Symeon regarded all his monks as worthy to hear descriptions of visions and other teaching of a mystical character of the kind which survives in his *Catecheses*, while reserving for the more mature among them detailed instruction of a more esoteric nature. At all events he made no secret of his desire to assure all his monastic hearers that what he taught them was grounded in what he had experienced.

---

[97] Nicetas' *Preface* is printed in *SC* 156, pp. 106–135, and the quotation is taken from lines 215–223; "sacred initiation" represents the Greek ἱερατικὴ τελείωσις, which Paramelle translates as "initation sacerdotale." As this might seem to imply that Symeon spoke of his visions only to disciples who had been ordained priest, which is somewhat unlikely, a less specific rendering appears preferable.

[98] *Ep 4*, 158–161.

Humble though I am, poor, destitute of [all] good and servant of all you holy [brethren], yet I have had experience (πεῖρα) of God's love for men and his compassion, having drawn near to him by repentance and the mediation of holy Symeon, my father and your father . . .[99]

These words form part of an appeal by Symeon to his community to accept what he longed to share with them, the treasure of conscious fellowship with God. In spite of being nothing in himself, he knew that he was qualified by πεῖρα to make this offer, for he could genuinely claim personal knowledge of God's love for men, while at the same time—a significant point—he had, in his approach to God, been dependent on the mediation of his spiritual father.

From the foregoing, it will have become clear that for Symeon a very great deal was involved in becoming qualified to act as a spiritual father. If his assessment of the requirements is accepted, not only must the insincere be excluded, but also any well-meaning amateurs who have not through an ''apprenticeship'' learned the necessary skills. This conclusion will be even more definitely established when after considering qualifications we proceed to examine, in the next chapter, the actual duties which Symeon held that the spiritual father ought to undertake.

---

[99] *Cat XXXIV*, 44–48; cf. "Experience is the school of the Holy Spirit who speaks to the heart words of life, and all that we say to others should come from this source," J.-P. de Causade, S.J., (1675–1751) *Self-Abandonment to Divine Providence*, (trans. A. Thorold, revised by J. Joyce, S.J.), Fontana Library of Theology and Philosophy, 1971, p. 66.

CHAPTER SEVEN

THE SPIRITUAL FATHER AT WORK

i) Preliminary

Because of the amount and the variety of the material to be looked at in our investigation of what a father actually does or should do for his spiritual children, this chapter is divided into three parts. But even before entering upon the first of these, some preliminary observations are needed.

It is inevitable that classifying the spiritual father's work under separate headings will introduce an element of artificiality, since nothing that he does can really be isolated from its context in a personal relationship. However, for the sake of order and clarity some suitable way of handling the material by dividing it into sections is inevitable, and different writers have employed different schemes.

Hausherr devoted a chapter to the spiritual father and his duties and divided it into sections headed: 1. *En accepter les fonctions?* 2. *Prier pour ses enfants spirituels.* 3. *Porter une part de leur fardeau.* 4. *Aimer ses enfants spirituels.*[1] Christophorides has a rather similar chapter, the six sections of which deal in turn with acceptance of spiritual fatherhood, instruction, prayer, correction, love and severity.[2] Ware, writing of the gifts which "distinguish the spiritual father" and of the way in which they are utilised, mentions "insight and discernment," which are needed when he receives the disciple's disclosure of thoughts (λογισμοί); "the ability to love and to make others' sufferings his own," which must be expressed in a genuinely caring relationship; and "the power to transform the human environment," which is exercised in various ways including that of helping

> disciples to perceive the world as God created it and as God desires it once more to be.[3]

For our purposes, none of the above is completely satisfactory, in view of the large quantity of material to be found in Symeon's writings from which information about training can be gained. What we can learn from

---

[1] Hausherr, *Direction spirituelle*, chapter IV; we have in fact already discussed some of Hausherr's requirements in our last chapter.

[2] Christophorides, *op. cit.*, chapter IV.

[3] Ware, 'The Spiritual Father in Orthodox Christianity,' *Cross Currents*, XXIV, (1974), pp. 301–304.

him concerning this subject is indeed a good reason for including Symeon in any attempt to study spiritual fatherhood, and this chapter has therefore been arranged in such a way as to give full scope for illustrating what he actually expected would be done. Accordingly, after a few more preliminary remarks, there will be an investigation of the part played by a spiritual father in trying to ensure his client's salvation; next, we shall proceed to discuss and illustrate what is involved in training, and this very long section will be sub-divided in order to take account separately of different facets of the process; finally, we shall consider the closer fellowship with God into which training is intended to lead the disciple. On the basis of this method of classification, intercessory prayer by the father does not get mentioned in a section by itself, although it will feature quite prominently as a means towards ensuring salvation for the spiritual child. Nevertheless, both prayer and also a truly caring relationship, which again is not treated separately, are presupposed throughout.

It should be remembered, as we approach the subject of the spiritual father at work, that we shall not be examining something of a uniform nature, but rather a relationship of "extreme flexibility," for

> some may see their spiritual father daily or even hourly ... others may see him only once a month or once a year.[4]

Symeon, for example, must obviously have modified very considerably his style of direction according to whether he was concerned with one of his monks at St. Mamas', with a spiritual child living in the world or with a disciple in the little group which surrounded him at the oratory of St. Marina. It is true that, as has already been remarked, there is little information available concerning the spiritual guidance of seculars, and inevitably therefore most of our investigation will focus upon a father's work in relation to those who, at least in theory, were dedicated to the quest for their own salvation, isolated from the world and under the care of one who had assumed a large measure of responsibility for their eternal happiness. But even given this practical limitation, the concept of flexibility is still important, for as Symeon's writings clearly testify, his monks themselves were of varying temperaments, and as spiritual children might be either zealous or recalcitrant. Symeon, therefore, and other writers on the subject, can on some occasions be found describing the ideal, but at other times can be seen struggling against a variety of obstacles encountered in their efforts to help their disciples reach it.

What flexibility means will be most clearly shown in the section which deals with training, for training has of course to be adapted to the needs

---

[4] Ware, *ibid.*, p. 310.

and circumstances of those who receive it; one might also expect that there would be evidence of spiritual fathers showing flexibility because of a concern that each of their disciples should experience fellowship with God as something in the deepest sense natural to himself, yet Symeon, perhaps because of some temperamental defect, actually shows very little sign of thinking along these lines; still less, in the area which we are to examine first does the idea of flexibility loom large, but this is not surprising, for whether with a smaller or greater degree of understanding, all clients of spiritual fathers are likely to have one and the same goal, salvation.

ii) Ensuring the Disciple's Salvation

It is by his prayers more than by anything else that a spiritual father is expected to secure eternal happiness for his children. When we recall that one of the alternative titles for a hegumen is "superior (προεστώς)," and that spiritual fatherhood was held to be one of a hegumen's responsibilities, we can see that some words of Climacus are significant, and provide us with a suitable introduction to this section.

> As a helmet of salvation they have the protection given by the superior through his prayer.[5]

This sentence links the assurance of salvation both with the person of the spiritual father and with the work of prayer which he undertakes on behalf of his disciples. Similarly, Ware writes:

> The spiritual father helps his children by interceding for them. This is clearly seen in *The Sayings of the Desert Fathers*: what you say when you visit your *abba* is 'Pray for me.'[6]

What is the reason for holding that the father has a duty to engage in prayer in order to ensure that his spiritual child will be saved? It lies in the belief that the intercession of a holy man cannot fail to be efficacious. A Scriptural basis for this belief can be found in the text, "The prayer of a righteous man has great power in its effects,"[7] which, it should be noted, comes in a section where confession of sins and forgiveness are mentioned. It would be wrong, however, to suppose that the Bible encourages superstitious reliance on intercession to save each and every sinner, for there is another text:

> If any one sees his brother committing what is not a mortal sin, he will ask, and God will give him life for those whose sin is not mortal.

---

[5] Climacus, *Sc. Par.* 4, 677D, with allusion to *Ephesians* 6. 17.
[6] Ware, *Climacus*, p. 40; cf. Rousseau, *Ascetics*, p. 36.
[7] *James* 5. 16.

Here "any one" is regarded as capable of effectively interceding, but with the important proviso that the sinner must not have placed himself beyond the scope of prayer, since according to the next words,

> There is sin which is mortal; I do not say that one is to pray for that.[8]

In fact, the boundary between faith and superstition in this area is difficult to define, and we have already observed the youthful Symeon under the influence of ideas which appear superstitious, when he was utterly determined to find a living saint to have as his spiritual father.

Whether based on superstition or on faith, the importance attached to the prayers of a spiritual father is well illustrated by some words of Climacus:

> Do not be astounded at what I am going to say . . . It is better to sin against God than against our father, because if God be angry with us, he can be reconciled to us by our guide, whereas if we incur the latter's wrath, we shall be left with no one to make atonement for us.[9]

Although this is consciously paradoxical, as Climacus makes plain by his "Do not be astounded . . . ," it remains a striking testimony to belief in the value of prayer by a spiritual father as the means of reconciling his children with God. The passage, Ware points out, illustrates the way in which the father works as mediator (μεσίτης), an allied concept, the meaning of which is seen in some lines in the *Liber ad Pastorem*. These, without actually styling the hegumen μεσίτης, speak of him as "the friend of the Great King, who can plead on our behalf with boldness in the royal presence."[10]

In all the above, we are of course reminded of Symeon and his early hope of obtaining salvation by finding a "saint", who would be his μεσίτης and through "intercession" secure "pardon" for him.[11] We did indeed observe that Symeon's actual experience as a disciple led him to perceive that a spiritual father's work comprises much more than this, but this never led to his abandoning the conviction that humanly speaking it was through what the Studite had done for him, and was continuing to do, that he would be saved. This conviction, moreover, extended to a firm belief in the power of his father's prayers, for "I was confident that whatever he wanted he could have from [Christ]."[12] There are some interesting lines in which Symeon can be seen refining, though still not

---

[8] *I John* 5. 16.
[9] Climacus, *Sc. Par.* 4, 725D–728A.
[10] Ware, *Climacus*, p. 40; Climacus, *ad Pastorem*, 1172D.
[11] *Cat XXXV*, 19–22, 74–78.
[12] *Cat XXXVI*, 164f.

abandoning his early and rather crude expectation of gaining happiness in the world to come.

> Who drew and guided me towards these good things? Who raised me up from the depth of this world's deceit? ... Who showed me the way of repentance and of sorrow [for sin], by means of which I found the day that has no end? [He who did this] was an angel, not a man, yet one who is a man ...[13]

Here, "day" stands for the life of the redeemed in heaven, of which Symeon had already begun to enjoy a foretaste as a result of his fuller understanding of Christianity, but which he could enjoy completely only in the next world, since it "has no end." He could never forget that he owed this salvation to the Studite, "an angel, ... yet ... a man."

Some attention has already been given to Symeon's statement about a sinner's need for a μεσίτης "to reconcile him to his God and Father."[14] We must now notice how, as a mature spiritual father, he was aware of the danger of a person's superstitiously relying on help from outside without assimilating it internally. Symeon would not allow it to be supposed that a father, through his intercession, could "reconcile" a client who was, and remained, a stranger to personal religious experience.

> He who has not received Christ and his Father and the Holy Spirit, so as to know the One God living and walking within his heart ... Who will be a mediator (μεσιτεύω) for such a one, or reconcile him to God ...?[15]

It is evident from such words that Symeon, though he insisted on the need to secure a spiritual father, was far from teaching that once this had been done, salvation would be an automatic consequence. Reconciliation with God was out of the question for those who hardened their hearts, even if they were to find some one prepared to act as their mediator.

As for the spiritual father, it was made clear in the preceding chapter, that it is essential that he should be ἔμπειρος if he is to do everything necessary for the welfare of his children. In our present concern with the father's work as a mediator, we should notice this as an area in which Symeon was very conscious of the need to have gained experience for oneself before trying to function on behalf of others. He portrayed God as condemning those who

> do not even have any knowledge of My grace, but yet undertake to act as mediators (μεσιτεύω) for others, while themselves being guilty of countless faults.[16]

---

[13] *Hymn XVIII*, 124–130.
[14] *Ep 1*, p. 115, 9–11, referred to in chapter V, p. 72.
[15] *Hymn LVIII*, 205–212.
[16] *ibid.*, 115–117.

It was not only with other fathers in mind that he expressed the need for would-be mediators to be persons of experience, but he could also be troubled by doubts as to his own worthiness to undertake this work.

> How am I to act as mediator for others—he asked Christ—, when I do not have love and freedom of access (παρρησία) to thee, through faith and good works?[17]

In his teaching Symeon thus remained close to what he had found in Climacus concerning the spiritual father's task of ensuring the salvation of his disciples, particularly through his work of intercession as their μεσίτης. Nevertheless, here as elsewhere, he manifested his characteristic emphasis on the need for personal experience, and he can be seen stressing it as required by father and client alike.

We must next consider an extension of the concept of the father as mediator, namely that of the ἀνάδοχος, another term used in connection with the work of ensuring the disciple's salvation. When applied to a spiritual father, ἀνάδοχος signifies "one who takes responsibility for another," being ready to "assume responsibility for his disciple's sins."[18] Barringer remarks that although the idea is found in Pachomius, with the use of the cognate verb ἀναδέχομαι, it is there not necessarily linked to concern for salvation at the Last Day: in one instance it denotes acceptance before the hegumen of spiritual responsibility for the future conduct of a penitent sinner. Barringer, however, also points out that the thought of a father's making himself responsible for the eternal well-being of his spiritual children is an established *topos*.[19] It is thus only to be expected that there can be found in Climacus, as well as the actual word, a plain statement of the consequences of the theory underlying it.

> If someone has obtained a completely clear conscience as regards obedience to his spiritual father, from then on he day by day awaits death as if it were a sleep, or rather as if it were life. This is because he knows definitely that when he departs, it will not be he, but his director, who will be called to account.[20]

Because of his desire to stress the need for conscious personal experience, Symeon is not surprisingly more reticent than Climacus about this aspect

---

[17] *Hymn XX*, 76–78.

[18] Ware, *Climacus*, p. 41.

[19] Barringer, *Penance*, p. 42 and p. 232, n. 138. It is interesting to note in connection with this word that "St. Catherine of Siena used to say to sinners who came to her: 'Have no fear, I will take the burden of your sins.'" (E. Underhill, *The Spiritual Life*, London, 1937, p. 99.)

[20] Climacus, *Sc. Par.* 4, 705B, cf. letters of Barsanuphius to Dorotheus quoted by Regnault and de Préville, *Dorotheus*, SC 92, intr. p. 25.

of a spiritual father's work. The *Sources Chrétiennes* indices record him as using the verb ἀναδέχομαι no more than three times, in each of which it denotes the receiving of a disclosure of λογισμοί.[21] Symeon has the noun once in the context of repentance, purification and reception of the Spirit, when writing of the need to gain "complete remission of sins from one's father and ἀνάδοχος."[22] In *Ep 1* he unequivocally employs it to represent one who accepts responsibility for another's sins, but significantly in the following lines speaks of the sinner as needing "sincere and painful repentance."[23] Thus we can observe here once again Symeon's reluctance to allow the work of a spiritual father to be understood as something automatic. The same reluctance is found in a passage where without using the word Symeon comes close to accepting the role of ἀνάδοχος for himself, but where he emphatically states at the same time that the penitent must not have "any hesitation in his heart or be double-minded."[24]

The theology underlying the concept of an ἀνάδοχος will strike many as extremely questionable in terms of Christian doctrine, but the motive which led to its use should be understood as having originated in, or been inspired by, a real love for souls and a wish to afford pastoral support to the spiritually distressed. St. Paul himself, after all, could use somewhat similar language to express his longing for the conversion of his fellow-Jews,

> I could wish that I myself were accursed and cut off from Christ for the sake of my brethren, my kinsmen by race.[25]

Expressions such as this should be recalled by those who seek to justify the use of ἀνάδοχος or other similar expressions to be found in writers on the subject of spiritual fatherhood.

Our discussion, however, must now concern itself with more general ways in which a father is expected to care for and protect his disciples, as a part of his work undertaken to ensure their salvation. This largely involves what we to-day would call 'pastoral care,' although Climacus, as we have seen, makes use of the image of the helmsman as well as of that

---

[21] *Tr Th I*, 292, *Tr Eth V*, 524, *Tr Eth VI*, 395. Unfortunately the *Catecheses* have no index that would include such terms, but there is one for all the other works of Symeon so far published by *Sources Chrétiennes*.

[22] *Ch III*, 46, 24–26. Darrouzès in a note of *ad loc.* explains the word in monastic terms as "*un parrain de profession*," but in the light of the Symeon's usage in *Ep 1* there seems no reason for assigning it any other than the ordinary meaning.

[23] *Ep 1*, p. 116, 8–17.

[24] *Cat XXX*, 221–227, in the course of which Symeon styles himself τοῦ εὐσπλάγχνου ἐγγυητής, ... τοῦ φιλανθρώπου ... ἀντιφωνητής and protests, "If [God] forsakes you, may I be cast into the eternal fire in your stead."

[25] *Romans* 9. 3; cf. Moses, in *Exodus* 32. 32.

of the shepherd. At the very beginning of the *Liber ad Pastorem* he speaks of the hegumen as shepherd, helmsman, physician and teacher, and significantly describes the helmsman as one

> who is able to deliver the ship not merely from a great wave but from the mighty deep itself.[26]

Although the nautical metaphor may seem somewhat strange to those who are more inclined to restrict themselves to pastoral imagery when speaking of the care of souls, we have here a telling picture of the work of the spiritual father in steering his disciple away from danger and into the harbour of salvation.

This protective care could most easily be undertaken as the two met in daily life. An excellent example of this can be seen in the *Life* of St. Dositheus who as a young soldier, very ignorant but earnestly desiring to escape damnation, arrived at a Palestinian monastery and was entrusted by the hegumen to the care of St. Dorotheus. Dorotheus was reluctant to undertake this charge, but in the end complied after receiving from the μέγας γέρων, St. Barsanuphius, the command: "Receive him, for it is through you that God will save him."[27] The narrative continues with accounts of Dorotheus' methods of training and of how Dositheus reacted to them, and it remains clear throughout that the training is continually being reviewed in the light of the father's concern for his young disciple's salvation. Thus, when the latter began to gain some understanding of the Scriptures, Dorotheus reacted swiftly out of a conviction that it was more important "that he should be kept safe through humility" than that he should become a Biblical scholar.[28] Whether we think in terms of a pastor or of a helmsman in charge of the soul, we can understand that the close supervision needed by Dositheus was made possible by the fact that Dorotheus, who was in charge of the infirmary, had arranged for him to be his assistant.[29]

It is clear, however, that there are many circumstances in which daily contact of this kind is impossible, and we had an instance of contact reduced temporarily to a minimum in the life of Symeon himself: while he was still pursuing a secular career, and was moreover a backslider, the Studite could do no more than pray for him and welcome him on the occasions of his visits. During the short time that Symeon spent in the Studios monastery, he could be closely supervised by his father, in the same way

---

[26] *ad Pastorem*, 1165B.
[27] Dositheus, *Life*, 4, 1–19.
[28] *ibid.*, 12, 4.
[29] *ibid.*, 1, 18–20 and 6, 2.

as Dositheus had been by Dorotheus. After his move to St. Mamas', this cannot have been possible to the same extent, although in Nicetas' words "the good shepherd (pastor) watched ceaselessly over his disciple."[30] This remark significantly alludes to Christ's claim to be the Good Shepherd, who knows his sheep, gives them eternal life and ensures that they will never perish.[31] In the same way, the pastoral work of the Studite, Christ's "under-shepherd" and Symeon's spiritual father, was undertaken in order to ensure that his child should not fail to attain salvation.

Symeon's own teaching shows how well he understood the purpose of this kind of care. In the course of the address to a hegumen from which we quoted in the last chapter, he told him:

> Thus you will save many, bringing them to perfection in [their performance of] works that are perfect . . . [32]

What is involved in training spiritual children "in their performance of works" we shall investigate in the next section, but the object of the hegumen's efforts is here plainly stated: he is to ensure the salvation of many. The spiritual father thus bears a tremendous responsibility for his clients, who for their part and in order to find him, ought to have been praying earnestly to

> reach quickly the haven of a good father . . ., for the sea of life contains much which is dangerous and might lead to perdition at the last.[33]

Symeon is here using language which echoes Climacus' nautical metaphor,[34] instead of the "shepherd" imagery employed in *Cat XVIII*, but the purport is in both cases the same. He can be shown to have held the traditional view of the spiritual father as one whose task it is to ensure his children's salvation, both by intercession (even going so far as to accept responsibility for them before God), and also by pastoral care to the extent that personal contact makes such care possible. This understanding of spiritual fatherhood was undoubtedly traditional, but for Symeon as the Studite's disciple, it was above all what he believed had been, was being, and would be confirmed in his own experience.

---

[30] *Life*, 24, 1f., with which cf. Symeon, *Cat XXII*, 311, "the merciful Lord . . . deemed me worthy to be constantly with him, unworthy though in truth I am." (This must refer to Symeon in St. Mamas', since he states that he had by now been a monk for two or three years, *ibid.*, 270f.)

[31] *St. John* 10. 11, 14, 28.

[32] *Cat XVIII*, 443f.

[33] *Ch* I, 17, 24–29.

[34] *Sc. Par.* 26, 1089B.

iii) Training

This section will inevitably cover a wide field, for we must consider training in relation to the body, thoughts (λογισμοί), moral character, spiritual life and dispassion (ἀπάθεια). While looking in some detail at each of these in turn, it is important that we do not lose sight either of the totality of the spiritual father's work or of his qualifications for it. This reminder is necessary in view of the fact that the training a father gives is not an end in itself, but is intended to contribute towards fitting his disciple for the enjoyment of eternal life, and therefore it is of the utmost importance that he who aspires to train others should be qualified, particularly as a spiritual physician and a pastor, since it is only by means of his skill in prescribing treatment that success can be expected. Furthermore, although Climacus could write approvingly of the deliberate sending of one particular novice to a cantankerous spiritual father,[35] the system of training, as we shall discover, normally demands of the father a genuine, but unsentimental, love for his spiritual children. Accordingly, Symeon was grateful that Christ had granted him "to be loved by" the Studite,[36] and he avowed to his monks,

> I came to have a dispassionate passion (προσπαθεῖν ἀπαθῶς) for you more than for all others, and I confess that although commanded to love all men equally, [for you] I have come to have a greater love.[37]

The rigorous discipline entailed in the training we shall be considering must be seen as grounded in "the sharp compassion of the healer's art."[38]

The Body

Vööbus has detected a marked difference in attitude towards physical asceticism as between Egyptian and Greek monks on the one hand and monks in Syria on the other. There was "a certain passion toward pain and affliction in Syrian asceticism," whereas in Egypt and in Hellenized circles the clearly-stated aim was to kill, not the body, but its dangerous desires.[39] But whatever his background, any spiritual father was expected to give directions to his disciples about the kinds of food and the amounts they should eat. Thus we read that Dorotheus, after undertaking to look

---

[35] *Sc. Par.* 4, 724B.
[36] *Cat XXXV*, 23f.
[37] *Cat XIX*, 40–42.
[38] T.S. Eliot, *Four Quartets—East Coker*, IV.
[39] Vööbus, *Early Asceticism*, pp. 293ff., the words quoted being found on p. 299.

after Dositheus, began by training him to manage with less and less food. When a meal-time came, he told him: "Eat as much as you like, but tell me how much you eat." Gradually Dorotheus reduced the quantity, until at last the young Dositheus was eating only one ninth of the amount of bread which he had originally taken.[40]

Dositheus died after only some five years in the monastery, and it may well have been that the consumption which killed him was caused, or at least aggravated, by this training in limiting the quantity of food he ate. But the *Life* in no way suggests that Dorotheus was intentionally hard or unnecessarily strict; on the contrary, after Dositheus' death some of the monks grumbled on hearing that Barsanuphius, the μέγας γέρων, had sent a message to him as he lay dying and therein virtually assured him that he would go to heaven. In their eyes Dositheus had not been conspicuous for asceticism and did not deserve this mark of esteem.[41]

Naturally, in a work such as that of Climacus there are no detailed regulations about food and fasting addressed to individual spiritual children, but the subject of one chapter of the *Scala Paradisi* is gluttony and its evil consequences. Amongst other things, Climacus teaches that "being satiated with food engenders fornication, but afflicting one's belly leads to purity."[42] At the same time, he reveals elsewhere his understanding of the danger of relying too much on one's ascetic achievements, for he warns his readers:

> Do not be too certain that you will avoid falling because you are master of your body; it was a being who never eats who was cast out of heaven.[43]

Climacus in fact was well aware of the ambivalent feelings which the body inspires. He could personify it as "ally and enemy, assistant and opponent, helper and betrayer . . . ," adding, "at one and the same time I both turn from him and embrace him."[44] Aware of his own ambivalence towards it, Climacus was insistent that the body must not be ignored when a monk's training was under consideration, since

> we who live in communities are to struggle every hour against all the passions, but perhaps especially against these two: gluttony and irritability.[45]

Climacus may be taken as a representative of the general background

---

[40] *Life*, 5, 1–22 (in Regnault and de Préville, *Dorotheus*, *SC* 92).
[41] *ibid.*, 10, 15–22, and 11, 1–19; cf. also Hausherr's reference to Dositheus, *Direction spirituelle*, pp. 81f.
[42] *Sc. Par.* 14, 864C.
[43] *ibid.*, 15, 881D.
[44] *ibid.*, 15, 901D–904A.
[45] *ibid.*, 4, 725B.

influences which affected Symeon, but can we trace in the latter's teaching about disciplining the body any particular emphases derived from his own spiritual father? If compared with the practice of some ascetics, the Studite's *Chapters* do not give the impression of being excessively harsh in the demands which they make, and in this they stand in the tradition of St. Theodore of Studios, who "deprecated over-strenuous fasts."[46] Thus, while one of the *Chapters* lays down that the three Lents are to be observed by fasting, which is to be more rigorous in Great Lent than in the other two, it prescribes a single meal a day all the rest of the year. On Saturdays, Sundays and festivals, however, more than one meal is apparently permitted, though satiety must be avoided.[47] By way of advice about the kinds of food he should take, the cenobite is told by the Studite:

> Eat what is set before you, whatever it may be, and similarly drink wine in moderation and without complaining. If you are by yourself, because you are ill, eat raw vegetables with oil. If one of the brethren sends you food, receives it like a guest, thankfully and humbly, and partake of some, whatever it is. Then send what remains to some other brother who is poor and devout.[48]

Furthermore,

> If you go to a meal with some devout brethren, partake of what is before you, whatever may be there, without making any distinction [between foods of different kinds]. But suppose someone has ordered you not to partake of fish or of some other foodstuff, and that is served, go and persuade the person who gave you the order to give you leave to partake, should he be close at hand. But should he not be, or should you even know that he will not grant it, but yet are unwilling to offend [your brethren], tell him about it after the meal and ask for forgiveness. If you do not wish to pursue either of these courses, you had better not go to the brethren.[49]

Although, as in the case of Climacus, our examples have had to be taken from general teaching which the Studite gave, the robust common-sense of the advice in this last quotation leaves us with the impression that its author knew a great deal about actual monks, the dietary restrictions imposed on them by their spiritual fathers, and the resulting problems which they might have to face.

---

[46] J.M. Hussey, 'Byzantine Monasticism,' *Cambridge Medieval History*, Cambridge, 1967, IV (ii), 176.

[47] *Ch* 142, 680B; Great Lent is the period leading up to Easter, and of the other two Lents one falls in Advent, and the other after Pentecost; to eat a single meal daily is less rigorous than the practice of those monks who ate only every other day, as for instance did some who criticised Dositheus (*Life*, 11, 4f.).

[48] *Ch* 145, 681B.

[49] *Ch* 148, 684A.

Concerning the Studite's actual training of Symeon, there is some direct evidence in *Cat XVI* which corroborates what is suggested by the *Chapters*, that is to say that, judged by the standards of his time, he would not have been thought to be imposing on his spiritual children an excep-tionally rigorous programme of bodily asceticism. Symeon says that his own ardour was in fact restrained by his father, who "speaking impera-tively ... would give me an order, and so I used, unwillingly, to eat."[50] This remark incidentally reminds us that a father needs to have acquired the τέχνη necessary to enable him to assess correctly the physical and spiritual state of his disciples: some novices, such as Dositheus in Dorotheus' estimation, must be taught to moderate their appetite for food, while others, who are too enthusiastic, have to be restrained from inordinate fasting.

The Studite also regarded it as important that a disciple should be taught not to over-value asceticism. Thus one evening, after an active day when Symeon had accompanied him on visits to spiritual children in the city, he gave the order,

> Eat, my child, and drink, and henceforth do not be sad, for had not God willed to have mercy upon you, it would not have been his good pleasure that you should come to us.

Then, after their meal at which they ate and drank "more than [they] actually needed," the Studite said:

> Know, my child, that it is not fasting, keeping vigil, bodily toil or any other praiseworthy activities which cause God to rejoice and to reveal himself—[not these,] but a heart and soul humble, truly simple and good.[51]

The insistence on a spiritual child's eating instead of fasting may be linked with a realisation that he needs to eradicate his self-will, a topic to be exa-mined in the next chapter, but in recounting this incident Symeon shows that his father was aware that an over-enthusiastic beginner must at times be held back and taught that there are more important objectives than physical asceticism.[52] The Studite's words were not, of course, meant as a repudiation of all ascetic practices, but were intended to put them, and all other good works, in their proper context in the Christian scheme of

---

[50] *Cat XVI*, 22f., where μετ' ἐπιτιμίου is the Greek rendered 'imperatively', but which it would be more usual to take as meaning 'with a penance,' although this would not suit the sense—perhaps the difficulty of the expression is the reason for the variant μετ' ἐπιστήμης found in one manuscript.

[51] *Cat XVI*, 31–57 (extracts); that internal disposition is of more value than exterior mortification is something of a *topos*, cf. Basil, *Reg. fus. tract.* 128, *PG* 31, 1168D.

[52] Nicetas, however, in the use he makes of *Cat XVI* for his narrative, puts all the emphasis on eradicating self-will, v. *Life*, 12, 2–17 and 18, 11–20.

things: in this they will be valued, not for themselves, but as outward expressions of, or as helps towards attaining, the right inward dispositions.

Since he was a spiritual father but not a hegumen, the Studite was untroubled by that concern for monastic discipline which was evidently a matter of anxiety to Symeon in his official position at St. Mamas'. Therefore it is not surprising that at times Symeon can be found showing a tendency to be less mild and more rigorous than his father. From the *Catecheses*, as well from Nicetas' narrative, we gather that many members of his community were lax in their behaviour, and this no doubt is one of the reasons why Symeon as hegumen reacted strongly in the opposite direction, even though this led him to adopt an attitude different from that of the Studite. Nevertheless, he did at times have to moderate the inordinate zeal for asceticism displayed by an enthusiastic monk, as Nicetas makes clear in his section devoted to the training of Arsenius.

On one occasion, while still at the beginning of his monastic life, this disciple undertook a total fast throughout the first week of Great Lent, in spite of Symeon's attempt to dissuade him. The result was what, because of his τέχνη, Symeon had anticipated: during the vigil in church on the fourth night Arsenius fainted and fell to the ground. He was revived with the wine and bread which Symeon had foreseen might be needed and which he had arranged should be in readiness. Nicetas stresses the fact that Arsenius had not yet received sufficient training in asceticism to be able to endure so absolute a fast; it was thought right that he and other beginners should have some food after the ninth hour, whereas Symeon himself, whom Arsenius wished to imitate, had through practice become capable of undertaking a total fast without succumbing physically. In somewhat the same way, then, as Dorotheus had trained Dositheus to manage with less and less food, Symeon, we may suppose, had planned gradually to introduce Arsenius to more and more rigorous fasting. Moreover, as from Symeon's obedience the Studite drew a lesson about the relative value of asceticism and goodness, so Nicetas records that Symeon drew a different kind of lesson from the unwillingness of Arsenius to allow his zeal to be moderated:

> Since it was through your soul's presumption and refractoriness that you were eager prematurely to win a greater [reward] and carry off a first prize by surpassing the others, you have missed a lesser prize and got what you deserve.[53]

---

[53] Nicetas, *Life*, 47, 12–21 and 48, 1–25. It is interesting that St. Benedict insisted that any voluntary abstinence undertaken by a monk in Lent must be approved by the abbot, "*quia quod sine permissione patris spiritualis fit, praesumptioni deputabitur et vanae*

Cat XXVI, in which Symeon addressed an imaginary typical novice and in which he claimed to be passing on the tradition that he had received "from our fathers," enables us to see where he agreed with, and where he differed from, his spiritual father in matters concerned with training about food and eating. They both gave a warning against "satiety" (κόρος), but Symeon's demand was the more exacting of the two, since when he came to repeat his warning, he also told his novice to restrict his eating to much less than his needs, and to do this to the limit of his ability to endure.[54] On the other hand, whereas the Studite had assumed that ordinarily only one meal a day would be eaten, Symeon, though also recommending this, both permitted those who really needed it to take a biscuit, with a cup of water, after Vespers, and also implicitly allowed the sick to have more food.[55] Symeon agreed with the Studite in saying that one should eat what was set before one, though his concern for the mortification of desire led him to add that one should deliberately abstain from anything which might appear specially attractive. But it is important to observe the reason for this additional demand, namely the necessity for obedience in regard to such minor details lest a monk should lapse "little by little into greater and hurtful desires."[56] In fact, for Symeon, as for his father, self-discipline with regard to food was not an end in itself but, as he said on another occasion, "fasting is the beginning and foundation of all spiritual activity."[57]

A significant point concerning which there is a difference between the two directors is their attitude to hospitality: the Studite, we saw, permitted the acceptance of an invitation by "devout brethren," but Symeon would forbid anything of this nature. Such strictness, it was suggested, is explicable when we remember that he was the hegumen of a monastery which contained not a few monks who were very different from Arsenius. In *Cat IV* Symeon in fact drew a lifelike picture of undisciplined and self-indulgent brethren seeking invitations and looking for excuses to eat and drink, especially after Compline,[58] and it was doubtless with men of that sort in mind that in *Cat XXVI* he totally prohibited the practice.[59]

---

gloriae ...," *The Rule of St. Benedict in Latin and English*, (ed. and trans. J. McCann), London, 1952, XLIX, p. 114.

[54] Studite, *Ch* 142, 680B; Symeon, *Cat XXVI*, 149 and 184f.

[55] Studite, *loc. cit.*; Symeon, *op. cit.*, 260–267, where the Divine Liturgy (Eucharist) is followed immediately by the meal (121f.), but cf. *Cat XXX*, 107f., where a penitent should take no food until evening.

[56] Studite, *Ch* 145, 681B; Symeon, *Cat XXVI*, 190–194 (cf. *I Corinthians* 10. 27), and *ibid.*, 201f. (cf. *I Timothy* 6. 9)

[57] *Cat XI*, 85.

[58] *Cat IV*, 247–315.

[59] *Cat XXVI*, 211–221.

The importance that Symeon attached to training in abstemiousness is manifested by the fact that when in *Cat XXVI* he described how a novice ought to spend his day, he devoted well over one third of his remarks to behaviour in the refectory.[60] That in this respect he tended towards exaggeration, as compared with the Studite, can fairly be concluded from such words as:

> Set your will to observe these things, beloved brother, even if this of necessity entails your death, for in no other way will you be enabled to escape the demon of gluttony.[61]

Similarly, the whole of *Cat XI* is a panegyric on the benefits of fasting, in which Symeon can be seen labouring to persuade his monastic spiritual children not to relax their efforts after the first week of Great Lent has ended.

Such examples reveal something of the work of a spiritual father in fostering asceticism; in *Ch* I, 26, we can see another aspect of the great responsibility which rested upon him if he had his disciples beside him: according to Symeon, however much one of them might suffer from thirst, he ought not to ask for permission to drink but to wait for his father to be inspired to give it.[62] This prohibition serves to strengthen the impression we have gained that in general, and probably because of his experiences in trying to re-establish discipline in St. Mamas', Symeon was more demanding than the Studite in the manner in which he wished to train monastic disciples in asceticism with regard to eating and drinking.

Outside the monastery as well as inside, spiritual children need to be helped to discipline their bodies. In *Ep 2* we fortunately possess an example of the training given by Symeon to a disciple living in the world. In the section of the letter which deals with food and fasting,[63] this man was bidden to abstain on Wednesdays and Fridays from meat, cheese, eggs, wine and fish, but was told that if he found it too taxing to do without all of these, he might partake moderately of fish and wine. Even though stricter abstinence was required of him during the Lents, this letter makes it clear that Symeon was realistic, and content to demand less from seculars than from monks. This section of *Ep 2* is important because it provides definite evidence that Symeon believed himself responsible for training all his disciples, secular as well as monastic, not only in spiritual matters, but also in bodily asceticism—there could be no other reason for his entering into details of the kinds and amounts of food and drink they should consume.

---

[60] *Cat XXVI*, has in all 319 lines, and the refectory is the subject of lines 121 to 249.
[61] *ibid.*, 222–224.
[62] *Ch* I, 26, 8–15.
[63] *Ep 2*, 207r.

Although he spoke or wrote mostly about fasting, Symeon did not neglect other matters in which the body needs ascetic training. It is interesting to notice how he realised that man is a psychosomatic entity and thus affected, not only by diseases and by what he consumes, but also by the climate and by sleep or the lack of it.[64] Sleep indeed Symeon spoke about on one more than one occasion: in *Cat XXVI* he gave the novice instructions about the times at which he should go to rest and get up again in order to have an opportunity for private prayer before joining in the community's worship.[65] He permitted a short siesta, but only in summer, and remarked that this was less likely to be prolonged if the disciple was moderate in his eating and confined himself to bread, vegetables or pulse, and a limited quantity of water.[66] By way of contrast, we can take note of Symeon's satirical description in *Cat IV* of the gluttonous monk, who does not pray in the evening before going to sleep because his stomach is too full, and then on waking says to himself that it is still early and, having fallen asleep again, discovers when he finally wakes that he has no time for prayer before going to church for the service of *Orthros*.[67]

It would be fair to say that Symeon's general principle was that, subject always to the higher duty of obedience to one's spiritual father, any suggestion of mitigating bodily asceticism should be reckoned a temptation and as such should be resisted. This is exemplified in connection with bathing, which in Byzantine monasteries was considered to be a way of indulging the flesh and thus something to be strictly controlled.[68] Symeon's ruling was:

> If urged by [your spiritual father] or by your fellow-ascetics to have recourse to baths, foods or bodily comforts by way of relaxation, do not consent, but be always ready for fasting, hardship and the utmost self-control. [Be like this,] so that if it is indeed your father in the Lord who urges you to resort to some creature comfort, you may be found obedient to him; but if he does not do so, you will joyfully endure what you have voluntarily chosen to undertake, and so your soul will be profited.[69]

This is not altogether clear, but it seems that Symeon envisaged that other

---

[64] *Cat XXV*, 122–155, cf. *Ch* I, 73, 4–11.
[65] *Cat XXVI*, 293–297.
[66] *ibid.*, 249–254.
[67] *Cat IV*, 299–315; concerning *Orthros* v. n. 156, below.
[68] "Monastic *typika* of the eleventh and twelfth centuries varied between washing twice a month to three times a year, but the most usual frequency was once a month," A. Kazhdan and G. Constable, *People and Power in Byzantium*, Dumbarton Oaks, 1982, p. 69; cf. St. Augustine, who in *Ep 2* 11, 13, instructed female religious to keep to the custom of bathing once a month (*C.S.E.L.*, LVII, p. 367, 10–16); Symeon apparently expected a penitent to renounce baths altogether, *Cat XXX*, 63.
[69] *Ch* I, 21, 17–26.

monks, or even a too kindly spiritual father, might on occasion suggest to a disciple that he should bathe or indulge himself a little in some other way. Such suggestions, according to Symeon, should most certainly be resisted if made by fellow-monks, and should not even be followed if they came from the spiritual father, unless made a matter of obedience. In that case the disciple would have to mortify his will rather than his body, as Symeon himself had done when bidden by the Studite to eat and drink.

If then we are to summarise Symeon's teaching, we must say that he maintained that the spiritual child ought to have a bias towards the more austere ascetical practices, though always being ready to obey a definite order; the father, on the other hand, was responsible as a trainer for adapting his injunctions so that they corresponded with the physical, moral and spiritual capacities of his children at the different stages of their development. If, as in the case of Arsenius, a father who could watch over the consequences saw fit to allow a disciple to attempt something excessive and doomed to end in failure, this would be for the purpose of teaching a spiritual lesson. In spite of his rigorous disposition, however, Symeon could state explicitly that one's physical asceticism is of benefit neither to God nor to one's neighbour, but that it is profitable to oneself, provided always that it is undertaken with humility and spiritual understanding.[70] This unexpected admission may do something to alter the unfavourable impression produced on many modern readers by the ascetic teaching of Symeon and others like him. Symeon himself would certainly have denied that he was unduly harsh, and would have concurred with the Desert Father who asserted, "We were taught to be killers of our passions, not killers of our bodies."[71] Even if he appears by to-day's standards to be excessively rigorous, his intentions were basically the same as those of Vonier, a twentieth-century Bendictine abbot, according to whom, "The aim of asceticism is to strengthen virtue . . ."[72]

Thoughts (λογισμοί)

What is undertaken in connection with the thoughts arising in a client's mind cannot perhaps strictly be described as training, but it is convenient to discuss it at this point when we are leaving the physical and preparing to pass to a consideration of the moral and spiritual aspects of the father's

---

[70] *Tr Eth VII*, 117–124.
[71] Poemen, *Apophthegmata Patrum*, PG 65, 368A.
[72] A. Vonier, *The Human Soul and its Relations with Other Spirits*, London, 1913, p. 127, cf. F.W. Faber, *Growth in Holiness*, London, 3rd edit., 1859 (reprinted 1928), p. 138: "To be spiritual, bodily mortification is indispensable."

work as a trainer. The work involved does not have for its starting-point the prescribing of certain actions, but rather the encouraging of a disciple to disclose, so far as possible, every thought that has occurred to him, particularly those which are perplexing. The spiritual father listens carefully, for he has the task first of interpreting to his child the significance and origin of these thoughts, and then of helping him understand what lessons he should learn from them with regard to his conduct in the future.

It is important at the outset that we appreciate the fact that, while in speaking of the disclosure of thoughts language may be used which suggests to Western ears what Anglicans and Roman Catholics understand by 'confession', in reality something quite different is being discussed, even though it may on occasion be combined with 'sacramental confession.' The spiritual father, who as already stated is not necessarily in holy orders, invites the disclosure of *all* thoughts which come into his child's mind, whereas the confessor, as such, requires merely to be told about those which are sinful.[73] It is obvious that listening to complete disclosures of this kind may make heavy demands upon the father's patience as well as upon his insight, but nevertheless it will readily be understood that this can be a very practical method of gaining a true knowledge of each individual's inner development, as a result of which effective guidance can be given. As Climacus sees it, the work of encouraging and responding to the disclosure of thoughts is included among the activities of the father in his role of spiritual physician, and he will be "unable to heal the patient," unless the latter "with complete trust reveals his wound."[74]

Complete openness was and is the ideal,[75] but there is evidence that by no means all spiritual children found it easy at all times to disclose their thoughts to their fathers. This reluctance was indeed sometimes particularly noticeable in the case of monks, in spite of the fact that the practice was supposed to be a regular feature of their life. Thus, the frankness of Dositheus was evidently thought worth recording as an example, for his biographer writes that

he was so outspoken and eager to declare his thoughts that often when he

---

[73] It is interesting that in *Tr Th I*, 291–293, Symeon differentiates confession of sins from disclosure of λογισμοί.

[74] *ad Pastorem*, 1184AB; cf. Moschus, *Pratum Spirituale*, PG 87, 2933A, εἰ θέλεις ἰατρείας τυχεῖν, εἰπέ μοι εἰς ἀλήθειαν τὰς πράξεις σου, ὅπως κἀγὼ ταύταις ἀρμόζοντα προσάγω ἐπιτίμια.

[75] This is stressed by both Eastern and Western writers, eg. Faber, *op. cit.*, pp. 311f., "Our sins and imperfections, the working of our passions, our inward disorderly inclinations, our temptations and the secret suggestions of evil which haunt us, the style of architecture of our castles in the air ... must all be open to [our spiritual director]."

was taking great care over making a bed [in the infirmary], he would see [Dorotheus] coming by and say to him, 'Sir, sir! My thought is telling me, You are a good bed-maker.' [76]

In the last chapter we noticed that "the counselling holy man" was frequently faced by the need "to break down the barrier of silence," and Symeon's older contemporary, Patriarch Antony III, who had been a Studite monk, found it necessary to appeal for the revival of the practice of confession (ἐξαγόρευσις) of thoughts.[77] It seems likely that some of the reluctance on the part of monks to reveal their thoughts sprang from the more or less successful attempts to compel them to have the hegumen and none other as their spiritual father. Apart from the fact that a hegumen, while perhaps very capable as an administrator, might not necessarily inspire confidence as a spiritual guide, some monks could very well have feared that too full a disclosure might lead to disciplinary action but not to healing for a troubled spirit. An appreciation of such fears probably lies behind the Studite's opinion that

> it would be right for all to go to the hegumen for confession [of thoughts], but since some are unwilling to reveal their thoughts to the hegumen on account of their great frailty and their lack of trust in him,

these should choose, and remain faithful to, some other brother.[78] This reminder of an antecedent difficulty is an essential preface to our survey of some of the material which bears on this part of a spiritual father's work.

It is unnecessary to spend much time illustrating the importance which the tradition concerning spiritual guidance attaches to the disclosure of thoughts,[79] but since we have seen that it may be difficult sometimes to persuade the client to reveal all that has come into his mind, it is relevant to summarise from the *Apophthegmata Patrum* an anecdote about Macarius. This is an excellent example both of a spiritual father's way of eliciting disclosure, and of the counsel given after thoughts have been confessed.[80]

---

[76] *Life*, 7, 1–5.

[77] Hausherr, *Direction spirituelle*, pp. 159f., citing A. Papadopolous-Kerameus, 'Αντώνιος Στουδίτης καί τινα σύμμικτα, Jersualem, 1905, pp. 5–12; Zosima, a 19th century Russian *staretz* (spiritual father) appears to have encountered similar reluctance on the part of monks, v. S. Bolshakoff, *Russian Mystics*, Kalamazoo/London, 1977, pp. 172f.

[78] *Ch* 36, *Life*, pp. XLIXf.

[79] cf. "The man who will not reveal his thoughts finds them marshalled against him; but the man who speaks out with confidence before his fathers puts those thoughts to flight, and wins himself peace," Esaias of Scetis (*Asceticon*, XV, 76), quoted by Rousseau, *Ascetics*, p. 20.

[80] Dörries, 'Confession', p. 288, cited from *PG* 65, 261A–264B—the popularity of this narrative for hortatory purposes is evidenced by its being used by Dorotheus, *Doctrinae* V, 65 and 66.

Learning from a vision that Theopemptos was being tempted by the devil, Macarius went to visit him, but found him too ashamed to admit the truth when asked, "Are your thoughts warring against you?" Macarius thereupon acknowledged that even after many years of asceticism he was himself still beset by thoughts of sexual impurity; thus encouraged, Theopemptos was enabled to confess to being similarly assaulted. Macarius then questioned him about other vices and repeated the same process. Finally he enquired about the extent of his fasting, and Theopemptos replied that he was accustomed to fast until the ninth hour. Macarius recommended him to prolong his fast till evening, to learn by heart and recite the Gospel and other Scriptures, and "if the thought comes, never look down, but up, and the Lord will help you." After this, Macarius departed, and a later vision assured him that Theopemptos was now victorious over Satan.

Although Symeon must time and again have disclosed his λογισμοί to his father, we have no actual references to his doing so. That this should be the case is not really remarkable, for the practice was taken for granted, and we can be sure that Symeon was not exempted from it, especially since in the Studite's *Chapters* there can be found the bidding:

Every day you are to confess every thought to your spiritual father.[81]

It is reasonable also to conjecture that what Symeon taught provides indirect evidence as to what he himself was actually accustomed to do, and two passages from his writings are therefore selected for quotation and comment. First, in one of his Hymns, which is entitled "An Instruction to Monks who have recently renounced the World, and to Men living in the World ...," he gave each and every reader the unequivocal order:

Tell [your father] your thoughts, including any temptation, as if you were speaking to God, and do not hide anything.[82]

Theopemptos, as we saw, was inhibited by shame from entering upon the process of disclosure, but until he could be prevailed upon to confess his thoughts, Satan retained power over him. Probably this or some story of the same kind was known to Symeon, but having discovered how greatly his teaching was influenced by his own experience, we may conjecture that as well as finding the necessity for openness emphasised in traditional teaching, he had himself learnt the lesson, willingly or unwillingly, as a spiritual child of the Studite.

Secondly, in *Cat XXVI* there occurs the very demanding admonition:

---

[81] *Ch* 122, 669C.
[82] *Hymn IV*, 27f.

"Every hour, if possible, confess the thoughts of your heart to your spiritual father."[83] Now Symeon, as we know from Nicetas, was lodged in his father's cell when first admitted at Studios, and it may therefore be surmised that at that period he really could and did disclose his thoughts every hour, since in the circumstances this would have been a real possibility. (Dositheus, in much the same way, could at more or less any time tell Dorotheus about his thoughts when the two were together in the infirmary.) If Symeon had been trained to confess at frequent intervals, this might well have constituted an additional reason for his reluctance to abandon the Studite and accept as his spiritual father the hegumen,[84] who with many other matters requiring his attention would have been unable to afford him the requisite amount of time. There was indeed a regulation in the Studios *typikon* to the effect that each day the hegumen, at a certain point in the course of the office of *Orthros*, was to go aside and receive any monks who wished to come to him for the healing of their spiritual diseases, but in so large a monastery there could not have been much time to allot to each individual.[85] Symeon, therefore, quite apart from his personal loyalty to the Studite, would have been very liable to sense that the kind of spiritual fatherhood offered by the hegumen was bound to prove an inadequate substitute for the attention he was currently receiving, and thus he would have been strengthened in his determination not to abandon the one for the other.

His "Every hour, if possible, ..." suggests that even Symeon, when he became hegumen of the much smaller monastery of St. Mamas, probably found that with increasing numbers he was unable literally to make himself available every hour to listen to every monk disclosing his thoughts. That, however, remained his ideal, and the basis for it may plausibly be ascribed to his experience as spiritual child of the Studite. It is noteworthy also that in spite of having himself stubbornly refused to accept the hegumen as his spiritual father, and in spite of the Studite's specifically permitting a monk to disclose his thoughts to one of his brethren in whom he felt able to have confidence, there is no evidence that Symeon allowed the community in St. Mamas' any choice in the matter. This apparent inconsistency is explicable when we remember the poor condition

---

[83] *Cat XXVI*, 299f.

[84] Nicetas, *Life*, 11, 4–11, and 21, 5–12. Even when Symeon came to have a separate cell (*Cat XVI*, 75ff.), the Studite, holding no official position and not being a priest, could have frequently listened to Symeon's disclosures of his thoughts.

[85] Studios *typikon*, *PG* 99, 1712B, and for the perfunctory nature of the hegumen's ministrations, cf. J. Leroy, 'La vie quotidienne du moine studite,' *Irénikon*, XXVII, (1954), p. 33; v. also 'Le *typikon* du sébaste Grégoire Pakourianos,' (ed. P. Gautier), *R.E.B.*, 42, (1984), p. 75.

in which he found the monastery. There was very likely no one whom he could regard as qualified to receive permission to undertake this work in addition to himself, and he at first relied to some extent on the Studite.[86] In these circumstances, although his ideal remained the very frequent disclosure of thoughts to which he had been accustomed as a disciple, we may understand why when recommending that this be done hourly, he was realistic enough to add "if possible," and not to insist on more than a daily confession.[87]

In following this line of thought we have already come to see something of the great importance which Symeon in his teaching attributed to the obligation to reveal one's thoughts.[88] From many parts of his writings examples could be quoted which would reinforce this impression. One such is selected for comment, because it shows Symeon's awareness of the demands which this practice must make on the spiritual father, not merely in terms of willingness to devote time to his disciples and to be patient in listening to them, but also as regards the skill needed in order to evaluate what he hears. In his charge to a hegumen, Symeon said:

> Take great care [in your dealings] with all [the monks] and in examining the thoughts of each [of them], so that you may know who amongst them all ought to be admitted to join with others in prayer and communion, and who ought to be excluded and made to join the penitents, giving themselves to repentance with tears. [You must take this great care], lest either through ignorance or through partiality, you make the church of God no holy temple but a den of robbers or a resort of harlots, in which case you will not escape the fearful judgement of the wrath of God.[89]

According to this, the thoughts disclosed to a father provide him with the raw material on which to base his decision not only about the spiritual condition of the monk who has described them, but also about the treatment

---

[86] In the last chapter we saw that Symeon expected his monks to accept the Studite, while still living, as their spiritual father, with himself as a kind of apprentice; *Cat XIX*, 82–84, "If you truly love me, reveal to me the purposes of your hearts," suggests that after the Studite's death he regarded himself as their sole father. In theory he perhaps made an exception in the case of potential hegumens, for in *Cat XVIII*, 311ff. he stated that on the death of a hegumen a possible successor should consult his spiritual father and only agree to be appointed if the latter gave permission.

[87] *Cat XXVI*, 299–303.

[88] As well as the references already given, v. *Cat IV*, 388–396 (on which cf. Völker, *Praxis*, p. 123, who remarks that it is precisely the bad monk who is unwilling to disclose his thoughts), *Ch I*, 58, 13–25, and *Tr Eth VI*, 75f., an explicit command to reveal each and every thought; in *Cat III*, 267–271, Symeon enjoined the discerning of one's own thoughts.

[89] *Cat XVIII*, 541–549. If it be asked what hegumens were to do about their λογισμοί, the answer may be suggested by a passage in the *Life of St. Euthymius*, hegumen of Psamathia, where it is stated that he and Arcadius, hegumen of Studios, disclosed their thoughts to one another (*Life*, ed. P. Karlin-Hayter, *Byzantion*, XXV, (1955), p. 62, 17f.).

which should be prescribed by way of an appropriate ἐπιτίμιον. To reach the right decision requires psychological understanding as well as a knowledge of what is laid down in the Church canons mentioned by Symeon a few lines earlier. It is true that, perhaps somewhat typically, he here stressed the enormity of a lax decision and the guilt which a hegumen would incur as a result of it, although we should not forget that elsewhere he accepted the possibility that despair might be caused through excessive severity.[90] But at the same time, however skilful and experienced the hegumen might be as an assessor of thoughts, in the type of case envisaged it would very likely be difficult for monks to perceive and accept his decisions not as disciplinary measures imposed by their monastic superior but as treatment prescribed by their spiritual father—further justification for the Studite's conceding that monks might resort to someone other than the hegumen.

In Symeon's words quoted above there was a distinct note of sternness, both in the admonition to the spiritual father and also in the way in which he was advised to treat his children. There was nothing to remind us of Macarius' gentle and persuasive method of dealing with Theopemptos. What evidence is there that Symeon could behave in such a fashion? It must be admitted that if direct evidence is demanded, it cannot be produced. We have, however, cited an instance which displays his understanding of the danger of too much severity, and we noted in the last chapter the approval with which he described the methods of a "kindly and sympathetic [spiritual] physician."[91] Besides this, in the *Catecheses* as well as elsewhere, Symeon from time to time accused himself of many shortcomings and sins. In the *Hymns*, in which for the most part he was addressing God, these confessions may be understood simply as what they purport to be; in the *Catecheses*, it is possible that, although he did not combine these admissions with a direct appeal for the disclosure of thoughts, he hoped by acknowledging his own faults that he, like Macarius, would thus encourage his monks to have confidence to approach him as a sympathetic listener.[92] Last, but by no means least, it must be insisted that the devotion which Symeon inspired in many disciples, both monastic and secular, is further indirect evidence that in his dealings with those who were responsive he proved in practice to be gentle and understanding as well as stern.

In the nature of the case we could hardly expect to have any written records of Symeon's conversations with those who came to him to disclose

---

[90] *Ep 1*, p. 117, 10f., quoted in chapter VI, p. 101.
[91] *Tr Eth VI*, 283.
[92] cf. *Cat V*, 87f., *Cat XII*, 6–13, 241f., *Cat XXX*, 255–259.

their thoughts. Fortunately, however, there does exist a narrative which, although describing a vision, appears to reproduce with reasonable accuracy the kind of encounter that actually took place.[93] In his section devoted to miracles, Nicetas, who in his youth had been Symeon's disciple, recounts an experience of his own, referring to himself in the third person in accordance with Byzantine custom. One Lent, being by now a mature monk, he was practising his usual austerities, but was plagued by an evil spirit of sexual immorality (πορνεία). Even after self-examination he could not understand the reason for the onset of these impure thoughts, and in great distress at being unable to find a remedy for his "passion" (πάθος), he prayed fervently to God and the saint, that is to Symeon, who by this time was dead. One day while Nicetas was lying on his pallet, Symeon came to him in a waking vision (καθ' ὕπαρ), addressed him by name and said:

> My child, do you not know the origin and cause of these passionate thoughts (ἐμπαθεῖς λογισμοί)?

Nicetas replied that he had examined himself thoroughly, but could find no reason for them.

> I have come—said Symeon—to reveal this to you, and you must pay heed to my words. Know, my child, that it is the result of arrogance and conceit persisting in the thinking portion (λογιστικὸν μέρος) of your soul. Humble your mind by measuring yourself and your achievements by the standard of Christ's commandments, and [the trouble] will soon vanish.

With that the vision ended, and Nicetas on obeying his father's order found a speedy cure for his spiritual disease.

> He humbled his mind and measured his own good deeds against one part of Christ's sufferings, his being spat upon, and was immediately freed from being vexed by thoughts and passion.

Although all the details in this episode might be explained away as the working of Nicetas' subconscious mind, it is clear that the visionary experience could never have been convincing to him, had it not been one which generally speaking was in harmony with his memory of the occasions when he had disclosed his thoughts to Symeon. In artistic terms we may claim that this account, while not a photograph, is yet a true—if perhaps idealised—portrait of Symeon and his method of dealing with a disciple who came to disclose his thoughts.

The sequence of events presents no unexpected features, and is instructive as being typical, one may suppose, of many similar cases in which

---

[93] Nicetas, *Life*, 149, summarised in the text.

Symeon in his life-time was involved. A temptation makes itself felt through unclean or "passionate thoughts;" thereupon an attempt is made by the disciple to understand the cause of this temptation, and failure leads to the decision to reveal the matter to the spiritual father, this stage being represented by Nicetas' prayer to God *and the saint*; the saint's answer to the prayer is to manifest himself, thereby showing that as spiritual father he has listened to the disclosure of his disciple's thoughts; because he has the gift of discernment, he has understood the root cause of Nicetas' trouble, and he therefore explains it as being the consequence of self-satisfaction and conceit, two interior faults; then he prescribes a remedy of the kind needed to heal the spiritual sickness which he had diagnosed, not the perhaps anticipated extra dose of physical asceticism, but a remedy which strikes at the root of the disease. There follows, naturally enough, a testimony to the efficacy of Symeon's prescription with which of course Nicetas faithfully complied.

There is a final point deserving mention in this narrative, which emerges in what are almost its last words: these speak of Nicetas' growth in trustful love for his spiritual father, and so bring home to us the fact that willingness to disclose thoughts, and the consequent frequency with which they are disclosed, will increase in proportion as disciples find themselves benefited by so doing. A spiritual father who succeeds in helping those who come to him with their disclosures, will inevitably find that more and more demands are made upon him.

Conduct and Character

Whatever its merits as a true portrayal of Symeon, the account which we have been considering demonstrates clearly that the disclosure of thoughts is not an end in itself, but is undertaken by a spiritual child in order to gain help in his efforts to lead the Christian life more perfectly. Sometimes the emphasis will fall on the overcoming of temptations, and sometimes on the acquiring of virtues.[94] These objectives must be understood as concurrent, not consecutive, since the possibility of being tempted will always remain, at least until a disciple has undergone the "transformation" (ἀλλοίωσις), which results in complete dispassion—something which will be discussed later. Thus Nicetas, at the time when he was troubled by "passionate thoughts," was obviously far from being a novice, since he was permitted to live apart in an underground cell.[95] If we

---

[94] cf. P. De Meester, *De Monachico Statu juxta Disciplinam Byzantinam*, Vatican, 1942, p. 364, "Aliquando Pater Spiritualis, ὁ πνευματικὸς πατήρ, non solum ad confessiones audiendas eligitur, verum etiam ad discipulos in vias sanctae asceseos dirigendos."

[95] Nicetas, *Life*, 149, 18.

observe the order in which Climacus arranges his 'steps', it is noticeable that he places some virtues to be cultivated, for example obedience and sorrow (πένθος), before vices such as anger and despondency (ἀκηδία, accidie) which of course are to be fought. Then the non-physical disorder, despondency, is followed by the extremely physical one of gluttony, and the virtue of humility does not appear until fairly close to the summit of the ladder. In effect,

> while placed in ordered sequence, the different steps are not to be regarded as consecutive stages, the one terminating before the next commences.[96]

When writing about virtues and vices Climacus is, in general, mostly concerned to provide an analysis of their origins, to describe their manifestations, and to exhort his readers to appropriate behaviour. He also includes a number of illustrative anecdotes, by means of which we are given from time to time a picture of some spiritual father engaged in the work of teaching his disciples to overcome the vices and acquire the virtues. It is in the *Liber ad Pastorem* that Climacus gives direct instructions about training, for example:

> Train them not to injure one another in any way, yourself setting an example.[97]

Although his works are of a quite different nature, Symeon shows his familiarity with the tradition as it reached him through Climacus by the manner in which he deals with many of the same matters.[98] Yet as with much else, so here with regard to training in conduct, we shall be unable to escape the conclusion that nothing influenced him so profoundly as his personal experience of discipleship to the Studite.

Nicetas includes some details of how Symeon was trained, and for these he must have depended either on information given to him orally or else on the written materials which he inherited. In view of his hagiographical interest it is possible that he has also added some items or comments of the type which he felt were demanded by the conventions of this style of composition. There is, for example, a conventional air about the his statement that Symeon, at the start of his monastic life, was told by the Studite to "meditate (φιλοσοφῶ) on the narrow way" and to "keep in mind [his] sins and reckon up the punishments" which were their due.[99] There is,

---

[96] cf. Ware, *Climacus*, pp. 12–16 (quotation from p. 16).

[97] *ad Pastorem*, 1189D.

[98] Symeon's knowledge of Climacus was discussed in chapter IV; a good example can be found in *Cat IV*, 540–542, where he refers to him by name and quotes from *Sc. Par.* 6, 796B.

[99] Nicetas, *Life*, 11, 9f., 17f.

of course, no reason why what seems to conform to pious expectations may not actually have been said or done, and this could certainly be true in the case of some other words found in the same context:

> Concern yourself with no one other than yourself . . . Be a stranger (ξένος) to all, and avoid familiarity.[100]

There are grounds for surmising that such orders, conventional though they may appear, were really given to Symeon, for they reflect an emphasis in the Studite's teaching which his disciple remembered and subsequently transmitted.

> [The Studite] who lived among a large body of monks once said: 'The monk should be in his monastery as one who is and is not and does not appear, or rather does not even make his existence known.' This he explained by saying, 'as one who is there bodily, but not there spiritually; appearing only to those who are pure in heart through the action of the Holy Spirit; not making his existence known, because he has nothing to do with anybody.' O blessed words . . . by means of which he revealed how we ought to walk with God, when he said that we should have nothing to do with anybody.[101]

Although there is no verbal identity, the two passages are so alike in outlook that they suggest that Nicetas was not simply influenced by his knowledge of conventional expectations when he gave his readers to understand that the Studite, while training Symeon, did indeed stress the importance of keeping aloof from fellow-monks. (We shall see later that Symeon himself gave instructions of the same kind.) There could be many reasons for discouraging novices from conversing with fellow-novices or with other monks, but it must not be overlooked that Climacus had castigated talkativeness (πολυλογία) as a vice, "the chair of vainglory . . . annihilator of compunction . . . darkener of prayer." Silence, on the other hand, he had extolled as a virtue, and insisted that

> he who has known the fragrance of supernal fire flees from the company of men as a bee flees from smoke, for just as smoke drives the bee away, so does such a man find company abhorrent.[102]

Symeon himself has unfortunately left no detailed record of the training in conduct given him by his father. It would seem that much of what he learnt he derived not from verbal instruction but from simply being in the Studite's company. This is suggested by his saying to Christ,

---

[100] *ibid.*, 11, 14–17; cf. the Studite, *Ch* 126, 672B, "you must be a stranger (ξένος) to every brother in the monastery," ξενιτεία being one of the marks of the perfect monk, cf. p. 152.
[101] Symeon, *Cat VI*, 171–182.
[102] *Sc. Par.* 11, 852AB, 852D.

> Thou gavest me a guide to lead me towards thy commandments. Set free
> from care, I followed him, and I rejoiced, O Word, with joy unspeakable,
> as I beheld him following in thy footsteps . . . [103]

Here what is conveyed to us is the importance of the father's whole conduct as a model for his disciple, but perhaps something different is implied
when Symeon relates how he was, as he believed, addressed by Christ in
words which included the following:

> I gave you into the hands of a tutor (παιδαγωγός)—you know whom I
> mean—and he took good care of you as a little child, growing up hour by
> hour, and he brought you up well.[104]

In this at first sight the emphasis seems to be on instruction, even though
no indication of the content is afforded, but it must be remembered that
a παιδαγωγός was originally not an instructor but a slave who accompanied a boy from home to school or to his teacher's house. However, some
thought of teaching may be discernible in the words, "brought you up
well," and the παιδαγωγός in any case had to supervise the conduct of his
charges. At all events, from these two passages taken together we may
conclude that, as Symeon saw it, his training in virtue had been imparted
to him both by precept and example, the latter being furnished by the
Studite consciously and unconsciously through his behaviour day by day.

These passages, though disappointingly meagre, are straightforward;
we must now quote a longer, but more cryptic, description of how Symeon
was reformed while under the tutelage of the Studite. In this he refers to
progressive liberation from sins and purification from the defilement
resulting from them, but he cannot be said to provide a clear account of
how he was trained. When he looked back on this period of his life, it
seems that Symeon was chiefly conscious of the slowness of the process by
which he gained, or regained, his spiritual sight.

> When I was all filthy and had my eyes, my ears and my mouth encrusted
> with mud—he said to Christ—thou didst commit me to thy servant and dis-
> ciple . . . saying to me, 'Hold fast to this man, cleave to him and follow him,
> for he it is who will lead you away and wash you clean' . . . I followed him
> without turning back, as with much labour he led me to fountains and
> springs . . . Had he not held my hand, stood me by the spring, and guided
> my spiritual hands (χεῖρες τοῦ νοός), I should have been unable to find

---

[103] *Hymn XXXVII*, 27–31; cf. D.J. Chitty, *The Desert a City*, Oxford, 1966, pp. 70f.,
for leaders who preferred to show the way by example rather than by precept, and add
Poemen to the instances he cites (Dorotheus, *Doctrinae*, IV, 52, 7–11), and cf. also Ware,
Climacus, p. 37, for the importance of "the personal example which the father sets in daily
life."

[104] *Hymn XLI*, 56–58, a passage which will be further discussed later in this chapter.

where the fountain of water was. And even when he showed me and often permitted me to wash myself, I would take up in my hands not only the pure water but also the clay and mud which was to be found beside the spring, and thus make my face dirty. Often as I felt around to find the fountain of water, I actually pushed earth into it and stirred up mud. Then in my utter blindness I would dirty my face with mud, mistaking it for water and imagining that I was making myself perfectly clean.[105]

After this Symeon went on to describe the ineffectual attempts to detach him from the Studite, and then spoke of the continuance of his pilgrimage and of mystical experiences in which he was conscious of Christ himself bathing him in the waters.[106] By this time the sphere of moral training has been left behind, but in the earlier passages dealing with his purification under the guidance of the Studite, the symbolism of washing away mud must be taken to refer to the process by which Symeon was cleansed from the filth of the sins in which he had indulged in his early life, and in speaking of which he elsewhere used the image of mud.[107] His father "with much labour" led him by the hand to the springs of water, which in his blindness he befouled even while washing in them, and it seems reasonable to interpret this as a picture of the laborious training needed to free him from evil habits and temptations, and of his frequent failures to profit by this training. Symeon's image of himself as blind or partially blind harmonizes with this interpretation, in view of the Biblical tendency to speak of sin in terms of blindness.[108] Unfortunately, however, although this passage is interesting because of its suggestion that Symeon needed, and was patiently given, a long and arduous training, it does not provide any further information about the actual way in which the Studite helped him overcome vices and acquire habits of virtue.

It is understandable that Symeon, as he continued with his thanksgiving, allowed the moral implications of blindness to give way to the conception of it as a state awaiting the mystical illumination which he felt was finally bestowed on him by Christ. This development is precisely what ought to be expected, since the training in regard to conduct and character undertaken by a spiritual father is intended as no more than a necessary prelude to the task of introducing his disciple to a deeper personal relationship with God, a matter which we shall speak of later.

---

[105] *Cat XXXVI*, 68–98 (extracts).

[106] *ibid.*, 102ff., (quoted in chapter V), and 126–155, where towards the end the image of water merges into that of light.

[107] e.g. *ibid.*, 30, 59, *Hymn XXX*, 223, *Tr Eth VI*, 263 (βορβορώδη πάθη); cf. "*sordens omni genere vitiorum, iacui diu in luto faecis,*" St. Bernard, *Sermones super Cantica Canticorum*, II, 3 (*Opera*, edd. J. Leclercq, C.H. Talbot, H.M. Rochais, Rome, 1957, pp. 15f.).

[108] cf. *II Corinthians* 4, 4, *I John* 2, 11.

Proceeding to a consideration of Symeon's own work as a father with the responsibility of training his spiritual children, we find in Nicetas some generalities, such as the following:

> Even if tested by him in a multitude of ways which appeared grievous and trying, they had a faith in [Symeon] and a love for him which remained steadfast—the exception being any [monk] who revealed himself as a depraved child, corrupted by evil habits.[109]

The most interesting feature in this is the suggestion that there were those for whom Symeon's methods proved to be too exacting, and this is in harmony with indications in the *Catecheses* that he did meet with resistance from some of his community.[110] Indeed the rebellion, of which an account is given in Nicetas' *Life*, testifies to the fact that Symeon did not succeed in making his training acceptable to the less devout at St. Mamas'.[111]

When we seek to discover how Symeon attempted to train individual disciples, we are bound to concentrate on the section which Nicetas devotes to Arsenius, for he is the only one about whom details of this kind are available. Concerning Arsenius we are told that before being given the habit, he was tested to see if he could endure various kinds of hard service and suffering. Having proved his submissiveness, displayed his desire to struggle for virtue and performed the most menial types of service, he was tonsured. Subsequently Nicetas records that Symeon trained him in the struggle for virtue, found him eager to obey and again made him undertake various degrading duties.[112]

There follows the story, which we have already looked at, of how Arsenius was permitted to have his own way and attempt to fast more rigorously than at that stage in his training he was capable of doing. The result of his failure was actually a great growth in his humility, and Nicetas next gives two examples of how Symeon found ways to increase this still further. Thus, once when Arsenius had killed some crows which were eating the monastery's store of corn, he came and proudly reported to Symeon what he had done. The sight of the dead birds, victims of a "senseless fury," saddened Symeon, and he ordered them to be fastened to a cord and hung round Arsenius' neck. Arsenius was then led round the premises and exposed to the derision of the other monks, all of which

---

[109] Nicetas, *Life*, 57, 16–19.

[110] cf. *Cat XII*, 252–262, *Cat XIX*, 132–173, *Cat XXXIV*, 169–213, for examples of how Symeon pleaded and expostulated, and *Hymn II*, 54–56, for a complaint about what he had to suffer because of "the jealousy of demons" and because of "the weak among these my brethren."

[111] *Life*, 38, 1–19, and 39, 1–22, discussed in chapter III.

[112] *ibid.*, 45, 9–20, and 47, 4–9.

he endured so readily that he shed torrents of tears and accused himself of being a murderer.[113]

Nicetas then recounts a final incident concerning the training of Arsenius, which again reveals Symeon's ability to seize an opportunity for teaching presented by the circumstances of life in a monastery. In this case he was able to impress on his disciple the need

> to keep his attention fixed on himself alone, and at the same time not to consider anything eaten as *per se* a source of defilement ... He wished also to demonstrate to those sitting at table how extremely humble [Arsenius] was.

A guest who was sick was being entertained, and on Symeon's orders was served with young pigeons. Symeon noticed that Arsenius, seated at the same table, was watching this with a gloomy expression on his face. He therefore rebuked him, and after quoting two New Testament texts, said:

> Eat some of them yourself, and understand that you have incurred more defilement from your thoughts than from devouring pigeons.

With these words, he flung a pigeon at Arsenius, who obediently, but with tears, began to eat. When Symeon saw him actually chewing it, he stopped him before he could swallow and bade him spit it out,

> for if you once start eating, glutton that you are, the entire dovecot will prove insufficient for you.

Once again, Arsenius obeyed his spiritual father without hesitation.[114]

The excessive harshness of such methods of training a disciple may produce on us a disagreeable impression, but in so far as Arsenius was treated with abnormal severity it will have been because he had early been singled out by Symeon as a likely successor to himself. Seridos, who became hegumen of his monastery at Thavatha, was trained with similar harshness by St. Barsanuphius, "in order that he might emerge from his hands like gold from the furnace."[115] No doubt Symeon, who knew how much fasting Arsenius could stand, was equally aware of the extent to which he could endure treatment of the kind which Nicetas describes and be benefited and not harmed by it.

Nicetas' anecdotes illustrate an important feature of this kind of training in virtue, namely that for its effectiveness it depends to a large extent on

---

[113] *ibid.*, 49, 5–26.

[114] *ibid.*, 50 and 51. The texts used by Symeon were *St. Matthew* 15. 11 and 19 (quoted loosely), and *Romans* 14. 3; cf. Dorotheus, *Doctrinae*, XV, 162, 19–24, for a warning not to look on critically when others for some special reason are served special food.

[115] *Letters of Barsanuphius and John*, Volos, 2nd edit. 1960, pp. 268–270, cited in *Dorotheus, SC* 92, intr. p. 16.

the spiritual father's knowing how to use the events of daily life as opportunities for inculcating obedience, humility and so on. Neither of the incidents just described was the result of premeditation, but neither occasion found Symeon unprepared, and accordingly he was able to make both of them contribute to the training of Arsenius. It must be added that if he had not been hegumen and thus the person to preside at the meal, he could scarcely have behaved as he did while at table in the monastery. In any event, training of this nature clearly depends on the disciple and his father being for long periods in each other's company, something which is unlikely in the case of most of the monks in a large monastery of which the hegumen is the sole spiritual father, and impossible when a monk has spiritual children who are living in the world.

This being so, we may legitimately surmise that when the numbers at St. Mamas' rose, Symeon perhaps felt that he could no longer exercise close supervision over each monk, and therefore concentrated especially on a small group of the more responsive, including Arsenius and any others who appeared capable in due course of becoming spiritual fathers. The six names given by Nicetas as Symeon's "chosen disciples" testify to the existence of such a group.[116] No doubt, too, in the latter years of his life, when surrounded by a small community of like-minded disciples at St. Marina, he rejoiced at being able to draw from day-to-day occurrences material to assist him in the training of each one of them. Nicetas as a youth knew him at this time,[117] a fact which justifies us in believing in the essential accuracy of the picture of Symeon as a trainer of disciples which is presented in the *Life*.

Even when there is no suggestion of a person's having been singled out as likely in the future to become a spiritual father, it is possible to cite numerous examples of disciples being trained by harsh methods like those which, as Nicetas reports, Symeon employed in the case of Arsenius. Climacus, for instance, tells how the hegumen of the monastery he visited near Alexandria commanded one of his monks, Isidore, to stand at the gate, bend the knee to all who entered or left, and say: "Pray for me, father, for I am an epileptic." This treatment, which lasted no less than seven years, was prescribed for the vices which the hegumen had observed in Isidore.[118] On one occasion, when he had himself heard the same hegumen berate a monk and order him to leave the church, Climacus

---

[116] From *Life*, 38. 10 and 39. 8, we learn that there were more than thirty monks at the time of the rebellion; the "chosen disciples" are named *ibid.*, 58, 4–6, and in chapter VI we saw that potential successors might be selected and trained specially.

[117] *Life*, 133, 1f.

[118] *Sc. Par.* 4, 689A–C.

asked the reason for his being treated in this way, since he happened to know that the man had not committed the offence for which he was ostensibly being punished. The hegumen replied that he too was aware of this, but added:

> A superior injures himself and also the ascetic if he does not every hour make it possible for him to win the crowns of endurance of which he [the superior] knows him capable, whether through being insulted, dishonoured, despised or ridiculed.[119]

From his own writings, which thus provide support for Nicetas' narratives about him, we can gain direct evidence that Symeon could use much the same methods of training as those depicted by Climacus. Thus when invoking the monk Antony, who had lived and recently died in the most exemplary fashion but had not apparently been singled out as a "chosen disciple," Symeon made an admission which is surely significant.

> Now at all events you know my disposition towards you, and how I rebuked you and used every method to keep you safe through my admonitions, never hating you or loathing you, but greatly loving you and unceasingly afire with affection for you.[120]

Again, it is instructive to observe one of the reasons why Symeon held that a disciple ought to love his spiritual father: "Love your teacher who knows well how to secure greater rewards for you by means of humiliations."[121]

The written works of Symeon do not include anything which in scope or arrangement resembles the *Scala Paradisi*. Nevertheless it can be shown that most of the virtues which Climacus discusses Symeon also inculcated, something by no means strange since he was a person steeped in tradition and determined to revivify it in his own day.[122] Climacus placed charity or love (ἀγάπη) at the top of his ladder, with dispassion (ἀπάθεια) coming one step below it; Symeon did not differ much from this pattern when he spoke of humility and love as "virtues which include all the others," the former being that "which procures ... dispassion,"[123] and elsewhere

---

[119] *ibid.*, 692C – 693C.

[120] *Cat XXI*, 140 – 144; "to keep you safe" reminds us of the work of securing a spiritual child's salvation, discussed in the previous section.

[121] *Cat XX*, 108f.

[122] The only virtues in the headings of the various "steps" of *Sc. Par.* not appearing in the indices of Symeon's *Chs* and *Trs Th / Eth* are διάκρισις, πραότης, ἀκακία and ἁπλότης, but the adjective ἁπλοῦς occurs in *Ch* II, 17, 25 and III, 64, 30, while διάκρισις is found in *Cat XX*, 209; a good example of Symeon's concern for a renewal of tradition in his own day is his antipathy to those who maintained the impossibility of reaching the levels of sanctity attained in the past, *Cat VI*, 251 – 258, *Cat XXIX*, 137ff.

[123] *Cat XX*, 204 – 206, cf. *Tr Eth IV*, 371f., where "faith and holy humility" are called "a firm and secure basis."

insisted that perseverance in fasting would help each monk to overcome his vices and gain the virtues he lacked, and thus to reach "the harbour of dispassion."[124]

There are some interesting points which should be noticed in *Cat XXVI*[125] in connection with spiritual exile (ξενιτεία)[126] and silence, virtues which Symeon wished to impress upon the imaginary novice to whom he purported to be speaking for the benefit of all his monks. In the first place, he fitted his injunctions into the framework of the monastic day, warning the novice that when he left the church after *Orthros*, he should not chatter but go to his cell and pray privately. Then he must undertake some work and not wander around the monastery but "maintain silence and that separation from others which is spiritual exile." The novice was also forbidden to enter another monk's cell, unless directly ordered to do so, and if while going about his work he came upon others talking he was ordered not to join them. Renewing the command to maintain silence and spiritual exile, Symeon instructed him to ask himself:

> What could I have to say that is good, I who am nothing but mud, a fool, yes and an exile (ξένος) too, and unworthy to speak or to listen or even to be numbered amongst men?

Then the novice was given a longer passage to say to himself concerning ξενιτεία, beginning:

> Who am I, an outcaste and a worthless individual, base and beggarly—who am I to enter anyone's cell? When he sees me, will he not turn away from me as from some loathsome object . . . ?

A second interesting feature has to do with these expressions which the novice was advised to use in addressing himself: Symeon reveals that he was conscious that they would be liable to seem artificial, and therefore added that they should be repeated while

> keeping your sins before your eyes. You are to say the words as though they issued from your very soul, not merely from your lips. And even if to begin with you are unable to say them as from your soul, still you will attain to that by degrees, as grace assists you.

Here there is evidence of Symeon's psychological realism and his understanding of a genuine difficulty which might be felt by a sincere novice.[127]

---

[124] *Cat XI*, 46–74, while Climacus commends fasting in *Sc. Par*. 14, 864C–872B.

[125] *Cat XXVI*, 67–113, summarised and with extracts quoted.

[126] Climacus treated of ξενιτεία in *Sc. Par*. 3, 664B–669A, and dealt mainly with the monk's separation from the outside world and from his family, whereas Symeon was ever conscious of the danger that "the world" might invade the monastery.

[127] The Studite, when he made a similar demand in his *Ch* 123, 669CD, apparently

(In one of his letters also he showed an awareness of the fact that a humble estimate of oneself does not come naturally, for he exhorted his correspondent to pray that his eyes might be opened, and to seek eagerly for this humility.[128])

The section of *Cat XXVI* which we are considering closes with Symeon's fervent appeal to the novice:

> Only listen to me, lowly as I am, only lay this foundation, brother, only start doing, practising and saying these things, and God will not forsake you. He loves you greatly and desires that you should come to the knowledge of the truth and be saved.[129]

The whole passage, with this conclusion, thus illustrates how Symeon's training was bound up with his own religious fervour, as well as being carried out both with genuine psychological awareness and with an understanding of the realities of life in a monastery such as St. Mamas'.

Another passage in a different *Catechesis*[130] reinforces what the last quotation suggested, that is to say that Symeon's high ideals as a spiritual father had their true basis in his personal religious life and his relationship with Christ. On this occasion he started by quoting—not quite accurately—from the Gospel, "Inasmuch as you did it to each one of these, you did it to Me."[131] He then went on to expound these words by saying that Christ spoke them not only with reference to those who suffer from physical hunger,

> but also concerning all our other brethren who are wasting away, not through a famine of bread and water, but through idleness and through a famine of obedience to the commandments of the Lord.[132]

After a parenthesis, Symeon then continued:

> I think it is with reference to this [famine] rather [than the other] that the Lord says, 'I was hungry and you gave me nothing to eat, I was thirsty and you gave me nothing to drink' ...[133]

The conclusion drawn from this interpretation is that Christ

> truly thirsts and hungers for the salvation of each one of us, and our salvation

---

lacked this awareness. He too forbade the novice to enter another monk's cell (*Chs* 120 and 124, 668D, 672A), a prohibition which goes back to the Pachomian rule (H. Chadwick, 'Pachomios and the Idea of Sanctity,' *The Byzantine Saint*, London, 1981, p. 20.).

[128] *Ep 3*, 216r, 216v.
[129] The final words are reminiscent of *I Timothy* 2. 4.
[130] *Cat IX*, 33–51.
[131] *St. Matthew* 25. 40.
[132] An echo of *Amos* 8. 11.
[133] *St. Matthew* 25. 42.

consists in abstaining from all sin. But it is impossible for abstention from all sin to become a reality, if one does not practise the virtues and fulfil all the commandments. Thus our Master, who is God and Lord of all, is accustomed to be fed by us through our fulfilling the commandments.

It is true that here Symeon was not directly dealing with the work of a spiritual father,[134] but in spite of this the passage is very relevant to this subject, because a father is bound to be concerned with training his disciples to overcome vices and acquire and practise virtues. Symeon, we can now see, understood this aspect of the work as something undertaken not only for the sake of those being trained, but also, and in a sense primarily, for the sake of Christ himself, whose hunger and thirst for the salvation of human souls would be assuaged when men were rendered capable of keeping the commandments. Symeon's consciousness of the idiosyncratic nature of this exegesis can be detected in his, "I *think* it is with reference to this ..."

This genuine devotion, joined to a naturally enthusiastic temperament, should be seen as the background from which arose the excessive idealism that Symeon manifested in his capacity of spiritual father to his monks. But he can be shown to have been strongly influenced also by his intense belief that the climate of contemporary opinion was seriously at fault in acquiescing in low standards, as though these were inevitable in the Byzantium of the day. Thus he launched an attack on latter-day "heretics" in *Cat XXIX*, the title of which begins,

That one should not assert that it is impossible nowadays, for anyone who wishes, to reach the summit of virtue and emulate the saints of old ...

He explained that

those of whom I am speaking, and whom I call heretics, are they who insist that there is nobody in our time and amongst us capable of keeping the commandments of the Gospel and of becoming like the holy fathers.[135]

Those who held these opinions were in Symeon's eyes guilty of a most odious form of "heresy", inasmuch as by denying the possibility of "becoming like the holy fathers," they denied by implication the sanctity of the Studite. Conversely, the—for Symeon—indisputable fact that his spiritual father had equalled or surpassed the great saints of old,[136] necessarily carried with it the corollary that, in spite of any impediments which

---

[134] However, in the lines immediately preceding Symeon had spoken of the conduct of "the great" towards "the small," who resemble "true children."

[135] *Cat XXIX*, 137–140.

[136] cf. *Cat VI*, 163–166, extolling the sanctity of the Studite, who lived "in our own generation ... in the famous monastery of Studios."

life in a cenobitic community might be thought to involve, it ought to be possible to train monks to reach the same level of perfection. This conviction, as well as the religious motive previously described, lay behind the idealistic fervour which Symeon manifested and which led him to castigate the worldliness infecting the monasticism of the period.[137]

> In my opinion—Symeon told the members of his community—you rely for the salvation of your souls merely on your cloak, your cowl and your *analabos*—and some of you even on a long and majestic beard ...[138]

Having reminded them of the certainty of the Last Judgment, he continued:

> Where then will be the robe which covers and adorns our bodies? Where then will be our splendid *analaboi*? ... Where will be our luxurious dinners and our lengthy meals with their unseasonable conversations? Where will be these great reputations then? Where the sanctity, which we are now believed to possess or believe ourselves to have? ... Where will be the splendour that belongs to people living in the world and in positions of power, people who come to visit us and because of whom I, wretch that I am, am the first to think and esteem myself more splendid than others? ...[139]

These extracts provide us with a good illustration both of Symeon's ardour and of his resolute opposition to the contemporary climate of opinion. This he believed to be responsible not only for the prevalence of worldly ambitions in the monastery, but also for the diffusion of the false gospel that the standards of the past were no longer attainable. Such considerations should be borne in mind when we look at his efforts to train his monks at St. Mamas'. But it may still be felt that tirades of the type of *Cat XXIX* were probably unlikely to win general support for his ideals, even though in the last sentence quoted Symeon did once again explicitly class himself with those whom he was criticising.

When we come later to consider the difficulties of a spiritual father, we shall have to take account of the disappointments which Symeon encountered as hegumen. Here it is sufficient to say that since, without a struggle, it is impossible either to overcome vices or to acquire virtues, a spiritual father cannot hope for success in training related to conduct and character unless he has disciples who have begun ardently to desire sanctity. If they

---

[137] cf. similar accusations made by Symeon's contemporary Cosmas in Bulgaria, *Traité*, pp. 100f. (A. Vaillant, *op. cit.*, p. 24, reckons the date of the *Traité* as a little after 972.)

[138] *Cat XXIX*, 262–265; the ἀνάλαβος looks something like a scapular and represents symbolically the cross which the monk takes up (ἀναλαμβάνω) each day, thus providing a good target for Symeon's irony; as a eunuch, Symeon perhaps felt that some might regard his own beardless condition as a mark of inferiority.

[139] *Cat XXIX*, 271–297 (extracts).

lack that desire, all his efforts are doomed to failure. Symeon found a longing for holiness in Arsenius and others like him, and this he was able to
foster. But many of those who, as monks, were supposed to be his spiritual
children, were men of a very different type and so did not respond to his
enthusiasm. A father may know that humility and love are "virtues which
include all the others," and he may be able to devise suitable methods for
fostering them, but the basic difficulty remains: how is he initially to plant
in the unresponsive a desire to become loving and humble?

Spiritual Life

The guidance given by a spiritual father would be lacking in some of its
most essential elements if it failed to include training in private prayer,
instruction about how to participate in liturgical worship and teaching
about receiving Holy Communion. The evidence concerning such guidance is often either anecdotal or unspecific, but Symeon has fortunately
left a reasonable amount of material which can be used to exhibit his
methods of training spiritual children in these matters.

Dositheus, whom we have more than once had occasion to mention,
and who lived in the sixth century, is said to have had God always in
remembrance, because he had been taught by Dorotheus to repeat un-
ceasingly, "Lord Jesus Christ, have mercy on me," and at intervals,
"Son of God, help me." However, when he lay dying, Dorotheus

> said to him, 'How goes it with your prayer, Dositheus?' When he replied,
> 'Forgive me, sir, I have not the strength any longer to maintain it,'
> [Dorotheus] said to him, 'Then give up your prayer; simply keep God in
> mind and think of him as present with you.'[140]

This vivid narrative presupposes the recital of private prayer aloud or at
least in a whisper, and distinguishes it from the interior act of keeping God
in mind. It also shows how one disciple of an exceptional kind was dealt
with by Dorotheus, whose *Doctrinae*, addresses not unlike Symeon's
Catecheses, and like them also delivered to monks, "contain no theoretical
and systematic instruction on prayer." Notwithstanding this absence of
formal teaching, the *Doctrinae* do include many scattered references to the
subject.[141]

Somewhat similar was Climacus' approach, as it has been described by
Ware:

> He gives no description of the liturgical offices, no advice about preparation

---

[140] Dositheus, *Life*, 10, 1–14.
[141] L. Regnault and J. de Préville, *SC* 92, p. 72 (quotation), and pp. 72–75.

for Holy Communion, and its frequency, no specific instructions about methods of private prayer, about formulae, bodily postures, breathing exercises and the like. These omissions are surely ... deliberate ... What he offers is not techniques and formulae but a way of life, not regulations but a path of initiation.[142]

Dorotheus and Climacus, however, in dealing with individuals probably did follow some definite plan of training in prayer, adapted as necessary to the needs of each person, and in his letters Dorotheus shows himself willing sometimes to give quite specific guidance.[143]

The teaching of the Studite, as found in his *Chapters*, is of a fairly general nature, but it calls for some attention on our part in view of the influence which it must have exerted on Symeon. It is interesting, first, to notice a minor agreement between *Ch* 124 and an actual piece of direction given by the Studite as Symeon recorded it in *Cat XVI*, when describing the occasion when he was compelled by his father to eat and drink and was taught about the comparative values of asceticism and humility. When he had been thus instructed, and after some further conversation had taken place, Symeon went to his cell for the night, and on departing was bidden "only to say the *Trisagion* and [then] go to sleep."[144] In the Studite's *Ch* 124 the principle is laid down that

one *Trisagion* [said] with attention before sleeping is more valuable than a four hours' vigil [spent] in unprofitable conversations.[145]

It must be admitted that, to quote Krivochéine,

as well as in the Eucharistic Liturgy, the *Trisagion* is continually recited in other Church services, and also in private prayers,

and therefore too much must not be made of the parallel. Nevertheless, we can at least claim that in the particular instance recounted in *Cat XVI* the Studite is revealed as acting in conformity with his general commendation of the practice of saying the *Trisagion* before going to sleep.

One might have expected to discover in the Studite's *Chapters* not a few examples of devotional teaching which his spiritual child, who was so devoted to him, would later repeat in his own writings. This, however, is not the case, for while a general similarity of tone is discernible, there

---

[142] Ware, *Climacus*, p. 9.

[143] e.g. "Unite prayer to meditation," Dorotheus, *Ep 4*, 189, 7.

[144] *Cat XVI*, 76f. The words of the *Trisagion* are ἅγιος ὁ θεός, ἅγιος ἰσχυρός, ἅγιος ἀθάνατος, ἐλέησον ἡμᾶς, and Krivochéine *ad loc*. has a long note on the prayer, from which the sentence quoted in the text has been taken.

[145] *Ch* 124, 672A; Symeon (*Cat XXX*, 147f.) recommended other prayers after the *Trisagion* and before sleep.

are at the same time some striking instances in which Symeon manifests independence. Such a state of affairs is not after all surprising when it is remembered that the Studite's surviving work consists solely of a series of *Chapters*, intended for a novice in a monastery, whereas Symeon has left a large amount of variegated material, some of it directed towards others besides monks.[146]

With this in mind we may proceed to examine some actual examples. The Studite seems never to have tired of insisting on the importance of tears, compunction (κατάνυξις) and sorrow for sin (πένθος).[147] In this he was, of course, heir to a long tradition, his predecessors including writers such as Ephraem Syrus, Evagrius Ponticus and Climacus, while he in his turn was faithfully followed by his disciple Symeon, who took as a kind of text for one of his *Catecheses* the injunction never to communicate without shedding tears.[148] On the other hand, the Studite's surviving writings nowhere mention as a necessary condition for receiving Holy Communion Symeon's requirement, which may be rendered, "if you are worthy and have received the necessary absolution."[149] Here the original, εἰ εἶ ἄξιος καὶ ἀπελύθης εἰς τοῦτο, . . . is of uncertain meaning, and I have, but with some hesitation, followed Paramelle who translates it as, "*Si tu es digne et as reçu l'absolution necessaire, ...*" This suggests sacramental confession as an essential preliminary to Communion, with absolution presumably being given by the spiritual father. But while ἀπολύω can certainly mean 'absolve', it can also have other meanings, including that of 'allow', and if this is how it ought to be translated here, what Symeon insisted upon was not absolution, but only the obtaining of permission to communicate.

In whatever way we render the sentence under discussion, the spiritual father must certainly be understood as being involved, even though he is not actually named. Since in *Ep 1* Symeon vehemently asserted the right

---

[146] In *Chs* 120, 668C, and 123, 669D, the Studite indicated that he was addressing a novice; Symeon wrote *Ep 2* to a spiritual child living in the world, the *Trs* were intended for both monastic and non-monastic readers, and the *Cats* were spoken to the whole community at St. Mamas', not merely to the novices.

[147] *Chs* 121, 123, 126, 136, 140, 142, 144, 151, 152.

[148] *Ch* 144, 681B, cited by Symeon, *Cat IV*, 11f.; Ephraem Syrus, quoted by Vööbus, *Early Monasticism*, p. 284; Evagrius Ponticus, *De Oratione*, V–VII, *PG* 79, 1168D–1169A (wrongly ascribed to Nilus in Migne); Climacus, *Sc. Par.* 7, 804AB; Symeon, *Ch* I, 35 and 36, *Cats passim*.

[149] *Cat XXVI*, 119; Krivochéine in his note *ad loc.* refers to "*une permission (absolution)*," and assumes that this is bestowed by the spiritual father, as indeed the context clearly indicates; Hausherr, (*Direction spirituelle*, p. 117) quotes from a *typikon* which orders the disclosure of λογισμοί to the spiritual father alone, on the grounds that his is the responsibility for allowing a monk to communicate—cf. *Cat XVIII*, 541–549, quoted and discussed pp. 140f.

of monks, whether ordained or not, to hear confessions and absolve their spiritual children, there is no difficulty in supposing that in the *Catechesis* in which the requirement in question is found, Symeon's meaning was that every father must give sacramental absolution to his disciples before the latter received Communion. If, however, he had in mind no more than permission to communicate, this also is certainly something which according to Symeon it was the father's responsibility to give or to refuse, and, as we shall see, he himself did temporarily withhold such permission from the secular disciple to whom he wrote *Ep 2*. Thus, on either interpretation, the words we have discussed show Symeon extending the role of the spiritual father to include a matter not mentioned in the Studite's extant writings.

With regard to attendance at services, whereas the Studite directed the novice he was addressing to be the first to arrive, and except for some great necessity, the last to leave, Symeon slightly modified this: he confined himself to prohibiting departure before the end of the final prayer, but did not say anything about endeavouring to be the first to arrive.[150]

While in the last example the difference between the two is rather trivial, it is much more noticeable when one examines their instructions about how the time allotted to the novice's vigil at night should be spent. The Studite prescribed two hours for reading, and two for prayer "in compunction and with tears." He suggested certain psalms and prayers, but left a good deal to the choice of the individual.[151] Symeon, on the other hand, was much more explicit: in *Cat XXVI*, he told the monk to shut the door of his cell, take his book and read about three pages. Then,

> stand up to pray, singing quietly and praying to God without being audible to anyone else.

There follow in some detail instructions abut posture and concentration, with tears and groans being demanded. We shall revert to this section for fuller examination hereafter, but one sentence must be quoted now:

> Let there be psalms presribed by your spiritual father for you [to recite], such as will provide you with words [expressing] repentance and compunction, and will suit your capacity and your disposition.[152]

---

[150] Studite, *Ch* 137, 673D–676A; Symeon, *Cat XXVI*, 60–62, while in *Cat XXX*, 188f. he bade the novice whom he purported to be advising to go *with* all the others to *Orthros*. According to Nicetas, (*Life*, 28, 8f.), Symeon at St. Mamas' was the last to leave.

[151] *Ch* 144, 681A.

[152] *Cat XXVI*, 272–285 (extracts); Symeon did not, however, restrict the monk to these psalms, since in the next sentence he suggested that additional ones might be recited. In *Cat XXVI*, 42f., Symeon stated that he would speak (or write, *ibid.* 16) to his whole community in the form of an address to a single monk, and we may assume that the teaching in it is a specimen of what he wished novices (and others) to receive.

Here, in comparison with the Studite's treatment of the subject, the more detailed type of direction, which it is expected will be given, again indicates that Symeon was liable to go beyond his father, while covering much the same ground. Both of them, it should also be noted, elsewhere provided their disciples with special prayers to be used for special purposes.[153]

Hitherto, we have only been looking at material from Symeon in so far as it needed to be introduced in order to be compared or contrasted with what could be found in the *Chapters* written by the Studite. Dependent as we are upon these *Chapters* for all direct information about his methods of training spiritual children in prayer, we cannot rule out the possibility that some of the additional teaching supplied by Symeon may actually have been derived from what he remembered of the oral instruction given him by his father. Certainly, as must repeatedly be emphasised, it was not reading even what the Studite had written but personal experience, including experience as a disciple, which inspired Symeon with his own longing to reach the higher levels of mystical prayer. It could well indeed be the case that, in what can be learnt from him about the training which should be given by the spiritual father, there is more of the Studite's influence than can now be traced. We can at least be sure that Symeon, when training others in prayer or discoursing on the subject, always believed himself to be true to the spirit of the teaching which he had himself received from his father.

In view of his position as hegumen/spiritual father of his monks, anything that Symeon said to them in his *Catecheses* on the subjects of prayer, worship and Holy Communion might be cited to provide examples of his methods of training spiritual children with regard to these matters. But most attention will be directed to *Cat XXVI* and *Cat XXX*, because it is in these that Symeon, in both cases after stating that he would proceed as though addressing an individual, gave detailed and systematic instruction. *Ep 2*, which contains teaching of the same kind, but adapted to the needs of a disciple living in the world, is a useful complement to the *Catecheses* with their—inevitably—monastic orientation.

Cat XXX, which according to some manuscripts was addressed to "those who have recently renounced the world," deals at great length with repentance, and includes directions for both private prayer and behaviour in church. Symeon told the novice to stand during the services as though he were with the angels in heaven, trembling, and considering himself unworthy of a place amongst his brethren.

---

[153] Studite, *Ch* 140, 677A–C; Symeon, *Cat XXX*, 70–97, *Ch* I, 60, 5–19.

Concentrate your attention on yourself, so as not to be looking this way and that way, with a busybody's concern for the brethren and the way each one stands or sings the psalms. Concentrate on yourself alone, and on the psalm-singing and on your sins, and call to mind the prayer you prayed in your cell. During the service speak no idle word whatsoever to anyone, and do not leave before the final prayer. If possible, do not sit down even during the reading, but go to some inconspicuous spot and stand and listen, as if God who is over all were speaking to you through the reader.

After giving directions as to how one should behave if selected to be a reader or a *canonarch*, Symeon concluded this section with a call for self-examination and amendment.

When you leave [the church] after the dismissal remind yourself of how you spent yesterday, and if you committed any fault, amend your behaviour to-day.[154]

The above calls for little comment, but it should be observed that although in the course of it Symeon spoke of the need to feel unworthy, he did not specifically enjoin weeping while in church. In *Cat XXVI*, on the other hand, he advised his readers that, if possible, they should always have wept before the conclusion of the service and the reading, for

while you shed sweet tears, you spend the time in church as if you were in heaven itself, amid the Powers on high.[155]

As in *Cat XXX*, Symeon dealt with the subject of behaviour in church in the course of *Cat XXVI*, and generally speaking there is no great difference between the instructions given in the two *Catecheses*. Nevertheless, *Cat XXVI* shows him laying increased emphasis on some points and expressing his concern about certain additional matters. Thus, in it he named four separate services which the monks should attend in the course of each day, and naturally had most to say about how they ought to behave when he dealt with *Orthros*,[156] the first act of liturgical worship to be mentioned. The novice was told to take part "intelligently and without going

---

[154] *Cat XXX*, 189–220 (summary and extracts); Nicetas (*Life*, 28, 5–7) states that Symeon himself stood throughout the services motionless and weeping; a *canonarch* was a monk who intoned beforehand the words to be sung by the choir, so that only one manuscript was needed—on Mount Athos *canonarchs* are still to be found (Krivochéine, *Cat IV, SC* 96, pp. 334f., n. 1).

[155] *Cat XXVI*, 47f., 57–59.

[156] *Cat XXVI*, 23. *Orthros*, corresponding to the Western Matins and Lauds, is sung after midnight, in the very early hours of the new day (Krivochéine, *SC* 113, pp. 70f., n. 1); the [*Divine*] *Liturgy*, *Cat XXVI*, 114, is the Eucharist; *Lychnikon*, *Cat XXVI*, 258–261, corresponds to the Western Vespers, and is in fact the first office of the liturgical day, sung at dusk (Krivochéine, *op. cit.*, p. 91, n. 1); *Apodeipnon*, *Cat XXVI*, 268 (where it is styled "evening prayers"), corresponds to the Western Compline (Krivochéine, *op. cit.*, pp. 92f., n. 1)—these make up the "four separate services."

to sleep;''[157] weeping during the service was commended, as we have just seen; the body, Symeon enjoined, should be kept absolutely still, and there should be no leaning against a wall or a pillar; and one should not allow oneself to be "distracted by the less zealous, who chatter and whisper to one another."[158] This last remark indicates once again that Symeon, however unwillingly, had to recognise that not all his monks would strive to conform to the ideals which as their spiritual father he consistently set before them, and that therefore the best he could do for obedient disciples was to warn them against being led astray by brethren who were not particularly devout.

Because of the length of the monastic services, it cannot be denied that by making demands such as these Symeon laid a heavy burden both on the bodies and on the minds of his monastic spiritual children. It is not then at all astonishing that several of them disappointed him and that, in another *Catechesis*, he felt obliged to censure the kind of monk who

> slips out of the service during the reading of the divine Scriptures, sits down nearby or far off, and gossips with some others, now he and now they telling idle tales, one saying, 'Have you heard what the hegumen did to such-and-such a brother?,' and someone else [adding], 'Well, what will you say if I tell you what he had done to so-and-so, poor fellow?'[159]

Although, as the *Catecheses* show, Symeon had no illusions about his monks and the temptations by which they were beset, it was perhaps characteristic of him that his method of training them in liturgical worship seems to have consisted largely of telling them that they ought to concentrate on the words of the service and to remember the angelic Powers.[160] Climacus revealed himself as possessing a more practical understanding when he wrote:

> Let your mind be occupied in contemplating the oracles which are being recited, or have a fixed prayer to say as you wait during the singing of the alternate verses.[161]

It may be that an explanation of Symeon's attitude can be discovered in *Cat IV*, from which the description of the gossiping monk has just been quoted, for only a few sentences earlier he had said,

> It is not the result of nature, as some hold, but of deliberate choice, that each

---

[157] *Cat XXVI*, 25.
[158] *ibid.*, 47f., 57–59, and 28–35.
[159] *Cat IV*, 144–151.
[160] *Cat XXVI*, 26–28, *Cat XXX*, 189f.
[161] *Sc. Par.* 19, 937D, the context being antiphonal singing. *Sc. Par.* 19 is very interesting both because of the echoes of it which can be found in Symeon, and in view of what he did not reproduce.

man becomes either humble and given to compunction, or else stubborn of heart, hardened and devoid of compunction.[162]

If the story of Arsenius and his attempt to fast excessively is true—and there would seem to be no reason for Nicetas' having invented it—, Symeon was not lacking in τέχνη when it was a matter of estimating the physical strength of his monks. The emphasis, however, which he laid on the power of choice may well have been one cause of his unrealistic and unsympathetic mode of dealing with those who morally or spiritually were weaker brethren. Some at least of them might have been helped if, like Climacus, Symeon had recommended a short prayer that could be recited mentally while the choir on the opposite side of the church was singing its appointed verses.

We have already seen how Symeon insisted that before Holy Communion was received a person must first be absolved by, or perhaps obtain permission from, his spiritual father. Infrequent reception of the Sacrament, however, is far from what was intended as the consequence of this restriction, for in *Cat XXVI*, in which it occurs, Symeon was describing how the monk ought to conduct himself throughout each day. It may be assumed, therefore, that the *Divine Liturgy* was celebrated daily at St. Mamas', apart from those days on which the Church does not permit a celebration, and that Symeon expected his monks to be present and to communicate if allowed to do so.[163] He was certainly determined that his disciples should never think lightly of the Eucharist, whether they attended it as communicants or simply as worshippers.

> Tremble while you stand [there], as though you were watching the Son of God being sacrificed for you.[164]

This attitude to the Eucharist, based on a vivid sense of the reality of Christ's presence, was deeply rooted in Symeon's own spiritual experience, and in no way a mere piece of conventional piety which he felt obliged to inculcate in others. In one of his prayers to Christ, for instance, he said:

> Where the bread is placed and the wine poured out in token of thy flesh and blood, O Word, there thou thyself art, my God the Word, and by the coming of the Spirit and the power of the Most High these things become in truth thy body and blood, and we are bold to touch God the unapproachable . . .

This was for him part of his experience as a priest, an experience which

---

[162] *Cat IV*, 126–129.
[163] *Cat XXVI*, 119f.; cf. Krivochéine's note *ad loc.*, mentioning *Cat IV*, 612–616, where daily Communion is also referred to.
[164] *Cat XXVI*, 118f.

164 THE SPIRITUAL FATHER AT WORK

in a sense rendered him superior to the angels, inasmuch as while minis-
tering at the altar

> I touch with my hands and consume in my mouth Him before whom they
> stand shuddering in fear.[165]

If angels themselves tremble at the presence of Christ, clearly human worshippers should be no less filled with awe. Here, of course, Symeon was
totally in accord with the spirit of the *Liturgy of St. John Chrysostom*, in
which, at the beginning of the *Anaphora*, the climax of the service, the deacon proclaims: "Let us stand aright; let us stand with fear . . ."[166] For
Symeon this awe was much more than a formal requirement, imposed by
the language of the Liturgy; it was a real part of what he was conscious
of having experienced, and it was something which he was convinced
ought to be experienced by others.

Moreover, as he saw it, while those present at the Divine Liturgy
should be awestruck in the presence of the numinous, they ought not to
remain oblivious of a moral challenge. This challenge can clearly be
recognised in the words which he envisaged Christ at the Last Judgement
addressing to unworthy members of the hierarchy:

> Why were you not afraid to hold and to consume Me who am unspotted and
> undefiled, when your hands were impure and your souls more impure still?
> . . . Why did you lavish what belonged to the poor on your familiar friends
> and on your kinsfolk? . . .[167]

In such a passage Symeon showed himself an authentic heir of the Judaeo-
Christian tradition, which allows of no disjunction between the numinous
and the ethical.

The directions given in the *Catecheses* are inevitably of a general nature,
in spite of Symeon's sometimes adopting the device of addressing a single
imaginary monk or novice; in these writings we cannot really see him
engaged in the work of training an individual disciple. By way of contrast,
in *Ep 2* he can be observed actually giving direction to a non-monastic
spiritual child. This man he temporarily forbade to communicate, for

> you must not share in the divine and awesome gifts, I mean the immaculate
> body and blood of our Master and Lord, Jesus Christ, . . . until you have
> a mind firmly resolved to oppose the wicked deeds of sin, and until you gain
> a will steadfastly inclined to choose the good, and with an utter hatred for
> sin.

---

[165] *Hymn XIV*, 55–74 (summary and extracts).
[166] *Euchologion*, Venice, 6th edit., 1891, p. 61.
[167] *Cat V*, 654–658.

However, Symeon presumably recognised the limitations imposed on him when dealing with someone with whom he was not in daily contact, and he therefore left it to this spiritual child to decide for himself when it would be right to communicate.

> But when you perceive that you have reached such a state, my brother, then approach with unwavering faith and partake, not of mere bread and wine, but of the body and blood of God, of God himself ...

At the same time he felt obliged to utter a warning:

> If, without first becoming someone of this kind you receive Christ, then the demons will see that you have held God in contempt and have drawn near unworthily, and they will return against you violently with greater jealousy ... [168]

Here, then, as spiritual father of a Christian living in the world, Symeon can be seen as no less concerned than when dealing with monks to emphasise the numinous and ethical challenge which confronts the communicant who receives the holy sacrament. The difference between his treatment of his monks and of this correspondent lies in his giving the latter the entire responsibility for deciding when he should communicate, but this presumably was no more than a response to the practical requirements of the situation: the two were living so far apart that letters had largely to take the place of frequent personal meetings, though had these been possible, Symeon would no doubt have thought it his duty to prescribe the right time himself.

Because this man was temporarily to abstain from receiving Holy Communion, Symeon gave him special instructions concerning his attendance at church. After being present during the first part of the Eucharist (Liturgy of the Catechumens),

> you must leave the church while the celebration of the Divine Mystery is being accomplished, when the priest or the deacon says, 'As many as are catechumens, go forth.' Do not, however, go far away, and do not enter into conversation with anybody at that time, but stand in the narthex of the church in front of the doors. Call to mind your faults and mourn over them, and then go back inside after the elevation of the Divine Mysteries. [169]

It would appear that Symeon expected this disciple to return to church later in the day, for the first words of the next sentence of his letter are, "In the evening, after Compline ...." The fact that he omitted any

---

[168] *Ep 2*, 207v.

[169] *Ep 2*, 207r. The dismissal of the catechumens takes place before the Great Entrance, which is itself the prelude to the *Anaphora, Euchologion*, p. 55; the elevation follows the Communion, the deacon saying to the priest, ὕψωσον, Δέπota, *ibid.*, p. 72.

mention of Vespers between the Divine Liturgy and Compline reveals
Symeon's understanding of the difference between what might should be
demanded of monks and what might reasonably be expected of those
living in the world. Again, the fact that he said nothing about demeanour
in church, apart from the caution against talking to others while standing
in the narthex, is evidence of Symeon's recognising that this penitent,
sinner though he had been in the past, now had strong motives for conduct-
ing himself devoutly during the services, and did not need the warnings
about behaviour and distractions which were necessary in St. Mamas'.
There we saw how Symeon realised that some of his monks were not very
devout, and how he feared that contact with them might tempt even the
more spiritual into behaving irreverently.

When dealing with the time after Compline, Symeon in this letter gave
quite detailed instructions to his disciple about the private prayers to be
said, but did not specify any particular bodily posture, apart from order-
ing a number of prostrations (μετάνοια). However, just as in *Cat XXVI*
he envisaged that the spiritual father would lay down the psalms a monk
should recite before sleeping, so here he stated exactly what prayers and
psalms were to be repeated by his secular disciple. They were:

> The *Trisagion*; *Psalm* 50 (51); 'Lord, have mercy,' fifty times; 'Lord, pardon
> me, a sinner,' fifty times; then *Psalm* 6 ('O Lord, rebuke me not in thine
> indignation . . .'), and 'Lord, pardon me whatsoever I have sinned in deed
> and word and by thought,' fifty times.[170]

These extracts from a letter of direction are most interesting, not only as
exhibiting Symeon in the role of spiritual physician prescribing devotional
exercises which he considered appropriate to a penitent disciple, but also
because they help to counteract the impression which we might have
gained from the *Catecheses* that he was prone to make unrealistic demands
on all his children. It would not, in fact, take very many minutes to say
the prayers and psalms listed, and although the numerous repetitions
might strike some Western Christians to-day as very mechanical and
unreal, this is not how they would appear to a person brought up in the
Eastern liturgical tradition.

In *Ep 2*, then, we are afforded a valuable glimpse of Symeon undertaking that part of a spiritual father's work which is concerned with the
training of a client in prayer and devotion, at a level suited to his particular needs and attainments. But there is no mistaking the authoritative tone
which Symeon adopted in his letter, and this was doubtless a reflection of
his personality. It is only to be expected that spiritual guides will differ one

---

[170] *Ep 2*, 207r. It is noteworthy that here again the *Trisagion* is to be used at night.

from another in temperament, and that their styles of direction will reflect these differences. A complete contrast to Symeon's style can be found in a long letter written by Baron von Hügel in the twentieth century. Addressing a spiritual daughter, he began:

> You will not *for one moment* strain or torture yourself to think or do any one of the things here proposed to you. Only in the degree and manner in which . . . they really come to your mind and really appeal to your own heart and conscience, will you quietly accept them . . .[171]

It must not be thought that an approach of this almost diffident kind will be found only in the modern period or in the West, for Barsanuphius, whom we have encountered several times already, could write: "You know that I have never laid any constraint on anyone . . ."[172] It was Symeon's temperament that impelled him to train his disciples by giving them definite orders, whenever he considered that it was reasonable to do so.

We must now revert to Symeon's directions addressed to an imaginary but typical novice, which were glanced at earlier only so far as was necessary in order that we might compare them with those of the Studite. In *Cat XXX*, in which he envisaged a novice who was definitely a penitent, Symeon went into great detail in the instructions he gave about the way in which repentance and sorrow for sin ought to be expressed. After making ready in his cell the mat on which he would later sleep, the man was to stand up to pray as though he were a condemned prisoner.

> First of all recite the *Trisagion*, and then say the *Our Father*, and while so doing call to mind who you are, and who and of what kind is the Father whom you are addressing. When you proceed to say 'Lord, have mercy' and wish to stretch out your hands towards the height of heaven, direct your eyes upwards and keep them fixed on your hands, on which you must concentrate your thoughts. Call to mind your evil deeds and how greatly you sinned with your hands, and the kinds of shameful actions you perhaps engaged in by their means. So be afraid, and say within yourself, 'Woe is me, impure and defiled as I am! It may be that when God sees me shamelessly spreading out my hands before him, he will remember my iniquities, committed by means of these [hands], and will send fire upon me and consume me.'

After this, the penitent was to clasp his hands behind his back, as if he were being led away to execution, and to say, "Have mercy on me a sinner, unworthy to live, but truly deserving every punishment," with other prayers which God's grace might suggest to him. Then he was ordered to

---

[171] J.P. Whelan, *The Spirituality of Friedrich von Hügel*, London, 1971, pp. 226f., quoting the letter which was published in *Dublin Review* (1951).

[172] Barsanuphius, quoted by S. Tugwell, *Ways of Imperfection*, London, 1984, p. 90, from *Barsanuphe et Jean de Gaza: Correspondence*, (trans. L. Regnault, P. Lemaire, B. Outtier), Solesmes, 1972, p. 51.

recall his sins, beat himself unmercifully, clasp his hands together again, and stand in prayer to God. Next he should strike himself on the face and pluck out some of his hairs, asking himself, ''Why have you done such-and-such things?'' After this, when he had done sufficient violence to himself, he was to join his hands in front of him, stand up with joy in his soul, recite two or three psalms and prostrate himself as many times as he thought his strength would permit. Then,

> Stand up again, collect your thoughts and review in your mind what you have said, and it may be that God will grant tears and compunction to come upon you. If so, do not relax until they have passed, but if they fail to come, do not be disquieted, but say to yourself, 'Compunction and tears are for those who are worthy and have prepared themselves for them ... Is it not enough for you that you are alive?' Having said this, give thanks, sign your face, your chest and your whole body with the sign of the precious Cross, and lie down on your mat [to sleep].[173]

The novice, we should note, was not absolutely compelled to follow this rather terrifying set of instructions, for even Symeon did not do more than describe it as ''fatherly advice,'' and propose it as one possible ''method of repenting with genuine fervour.''[174] It is interesting, too, that in this context he specifically invoked the authority of Climacus, for the latter had described in detail the extremely harsh treatment voluntarily accepted by some penitent monks.[175] Nevertheless, the contrast between what we have in *Cat XXX* and the much more moderate tone of *Ep 2* is very striking and demands some comment.

The difference could well be due to the fact that in the *Catechesis* Symeon was addressing monks, from whom it would be natural to expect greater and more painful penances than from secular disciples. But a further reason can also be suggested, namely his understanding of the circumstances of the two types of penitents, monastic and secular. When any of his monks embarked on a penitential programme, Symeon knew that as spiritual father and hegumen, he would be at hand to watch over them. We saw how he took precautions to deal with the consequences of Arsenius' insis-

---

[173] *Cat XXX*, 145–184 (summary and extracts). The ardent desire for tears, and the sense of disappointment at their absence, are very understandable in the light of Climacus' assertion that tears are even superior to baptism, ''though it may be audacious to say so,'' *Sc. Par.* 7, 804AB.

[174] *Cat XXX*, 143, 123f.

[175] *Cat XXX*, 140–142; *Sc. Par.* 5, 764B–781A; cf. Krivochéine, *Lumière*, p. 73, n. 20. It is interesting to compare the way in which Climacus stressed sorrow for sin (πένθος) as the means of purification for all who have sinned after being baptized as infants, *Sc. Par.* 7, 804B (cf. 816D), with what Symeon taught about the necessity of repentance (μετάνοια) for post-baptismal sin, *Tr Eth XIII*, 193–221 (cf. *Tr Eth XI*, 133–139, part of a penitential prayer).

tence on·trying to undertake more than his physical strength permitted, but clearly he could not act thus with regard to a person whom he directed by correspondence. Apart therefore from the possibility that Symeon knew that the man to whom he wrote *Ep 2* was physically or mentally unsuited to the mortifications described in *Cat XXX*, it is not unlikely that he considered it prudent to be somewhat lenient in his injunctions, since he could not personally watch over a spiritual child who lived outside the monastery. Such restraint is in keeping with the quite moderate regulations about fasting which we saw that he prescribed in the same letter; a wise spiritual father, such as Symeon in these respects showed himself to be, will not enjoin or permit rigorous ascetic practices which might prove dangerous, if he knows that he will not be able to modify what he has prescribed should the need arise.[176]

Like *Cat XXX*, *Cat XXVI*, contains instructions relating to the body, but since Symeon did not in this work have in mind a person with special reasons for manifesting penitence, these directions are more in the nature of aids to prayer than methods to induce compunction. However, as the following quotation shows, Symeon could not altogether refrain from mentioning tears.

> Concentrate your thoughts and do not allow them to stray in another direction. Join your hands, put your feet together and keep them still, in one position, and close your eyes to prevent them from looking at other things and distracting your mind. But lift your mind and your whole heart to heaven and to God, and with tears and groanings cry for mercy from on high.

After this Symeon wrote the words discussed earlier about the spiritual father determining what psalms were to be recited, commensurate with the monk's "capacity and ... disposition." He explained this last phrase as follows:

> It is in proportion to your vigour and your manly strength that you should determine the psalms to be sung, the number of genuflexions to be made, and the length of time to stand [in prayer], so that you will not have your conscience reproving you and saying, 'You were capable of standing longer to sing and make confession to God.'[177]

Here Symeon reveals himself as a spiritual father giving practical advice

---

[176] cf. F.P. Harton, *The Elements of the Spiritual Life*, London, 1932, p. 185, "It is quite certain that no voluntary austerities should be practised unless permission has been asked and obtained from one's director."

[177] *Cat XXVI*, 275 – 289 (summary and extracts). The reference to conscience seems an autobiographical touch, cf. *Cat XXII*, 61 – 64, "If then his conscience said to him [George, i.e. Symeon], 'You should certainly accomplish some more prostrations . . .,' he readily obeyed it . . ."

of the sensible kind which acknowledges that it is a mistake for human beings to embark on their religious exercises without taking the body into account. The same impression is given by the conclusion of this section, in which, as in the corresponding passage in *Cat XXX*, the monk is bidden to sign his whole body with the Cross, stretch himself out on his mat and sleep until midnight.[178]

Furthermore, unpleasant as we may find the programme given in *Cat XXX* for inducing repentance, we cannot deny that the combination of physical and mental ingredients shows that Symeon had a good understanding of the interaction of mind and body, whilst it should be admitted that his instructions, if carried out, would in all likelihood be effective in eliciting the compunction and tears which he regarded as so important.[179] And, theologically, it must here be emphasised that Symeon was no Pelagian: he enjoined mortification as a means of disposing oneself for receiving the gift of tears and repentance, but he recognised that God might either bestow or withhold this at his own discretion. Thus, as we saw, he was concerned that the novice should not be too upset if it was not given him to weep.[180]

It would have been extremely interesting if amongst Symeon's surviving works we could have found a treatise dealing specifically with the work of a father in training disciples in the spiritual life. Nevertheless, in the absence of such a work, the material we have examined has enabled us to learn a great deal about the ways in which he himself undertook this duty. In his performance of it, as in much else, his practice can be seen as influenced by tradition, theology, temperament and personal experience.

Dispassion (ἀπάθεια)

The devotional activities which we have just been considering are for the Christian, in one sense, ends in themselves. But when investigating the work of the spiritual father as a trainer of disciples, we may legitimately view them also as steps on the path which leads to the experience of union with God. If they are so regarded, then dispassion may be thought of as a further step beyond them, which is indeed how Climacus understood it, since having assigned prayer to the twenty-eighth rung of his Ladder (*Sc. Par.* 28), he placed dispassion on the twenty-ninth.

What we find here is a description and eulogy of dispassion, with

---

[178] *Cat XXVI*, 295–297.
[179] cf. *Ch* III, 23, 24–27, denying the possibility of genuine repentance before one has obtained πένθος and tears.
[180] *Cat XXX*, 175–181.

exhortations to acquire it. But, significantly, having already accepted as one way of defining dispassion that it is "the perfect but limitless perfection of the perfect," Climacus went on to affirm that it cannot be won in its perfection, "if we neglect a single virtue even of the most pedestrian kind." Furthermore, by adding to the words of the psalmist, he even represented God as claiming it as a title for himself: "Be still and know that I am God and am Dispassion."[181]

Since teaching of this kind formed part of the tradition known to Symeon, we must not conclude our discussion of the work of the spiritual father in training disciples without considering dispassion. It is necessary first to look at the meanings conveyed by the word ἀπάθεια. Lampe in his *Lexicon* gives examples of a variety of uses, noting particularly that in connection with the contemplative life patristic writers employ it in a Christian sense, but with "its Stoic origin still discernible." Bardy remarks that

it has an important place in descriptions of the spiritual life, but not all writers understand it in the same way ... The majority give [it] a deeply Christian meaning. [It] is in fact a gift of God, a grace earned for men by the incarnation of the Word.[182]

Although, as we shall discover, Symeon did speak of dispassion as a gift of God, he would also have agreed with a modern Greek writer who insists that

to become passionless (ἀπαθής) in the patristic and not in the Stoic meaning of the word, requires struggle, time, hardship, fasting, vigils, prayer ...[183]

Dispassion, moreover, is a quality of which holy fools stand in particular need. As Saward puts its:

Their asceticism is of a particular kind—that of an extreme *apatheia*. In them the growth of *apatheia*, which must accompany all spiritual endeavour, helps them to resist the lure of worldly respect and honour ...

Speaking of holy fools who seek to evangelize and to identify themselves with "the mental and moral outcasts," he points out that

in all such 'dangerous' encounters the fool is guarded by his spiritual discipline and *apatheia*, which do not destroy warm and loving relationships but rather protect him against the tyranny of the instincts ...[184]

---

[181] *Sc. Par.* 29, 1148C, 1149D, 1152B, quoting *Psalm* 45. 11 (46. 10).

[182] G. Bardy, *Dictionnaire de Spiritualité*, I, Paris, 1937, col. 727–746 (quotation from col. 738).

[183] Theocletus, *Between Heaven and Earth*, Athens, 1956, pp. 128f., quoted by E. Amand de Mendieta, *Mount Athos, the Garden of the Panaghia*, Berlin, 1972, p. 323, and cf. also Ware, *Climacus*, pp. 32–34, and Koder, *SC* 156, p. 227, n. 2.

[184] J. Saward, *Perfect Fools: Folly for Christ's Sake in Catholic and Orthodox Spirituality*, Oxford, 1980, pp. 29f.

Saward's remarks are very relevant in connection with the Studite, who it was argued in chapter IV ought to be considered a holy fool. To support this contention, some lines from *Hymn XV* were quoted, and we must now notice that in the same context Symeon described how the Studite, if he saw others naked or was seen naked himself, "remained unmoved, unharmed and dispassionate (ἀπαθής) . . ."[185] This suggests an awareness on the part of Symeon that unless his father could be shown to have been truly dispassionate, his conduct would not entitle him to be regarded as a saint. After all, Symeon himself on one occasion thought it needful to warn his hearers against pretenders to sanctity who acted like fools (σαλός), and were all too readily believed to do so out of eagerness "to conceal . . . their virtue and dispassion."[186] When therefore he wrote of the Studite's behaviour in terms which suggested its resemblance to that of holy fools, Symeon took care to stress his true dispassion which protected him "against the tyranny of the instincts." The implications of this phrase are well illustrated by further words from this *Hymn*, addressed to an imaginary critic:

> If *you* happen to be naked and [your] flesh touches [another's] flesh, you become sexually inflamed like an ass or a stallion.[187]

Dispassion is, of course, important for others besides holy fools, and indeed the Eastern Church looks upon it as having close links with sanctity. As Krivochéine remarked, Symeon even taught that

> dispassion is superior to sanctity, or rather is a higher degree of sanctity, itself comprising differing degrees.[188]

Naturally, then, it cannot fail to have its place in a spiritual father's programme for the training of his disciples. However, just as Symeon had to contend against those who asserted that it was impossible to be a saint in contemporary Byzantium, so he found himself forced to contend with those who would not admit

> that even now there are some who are dispassionate and holy and filled with divine light, dwelling in our midst.

In the same sentence, he described these dispassionate persons as

> having so mortified their members which are upon the earth from all impurity

---

[185] *Hymn XV*, 212.
[186] *Cat XXVIII*, 369–375, cited by L. Rydén, 'The Holy Fool,' *The Byzantine Saint*, London, 1981, pp. 111.
[187] *Hymn XV*, 215f.
[188] Krivochéine, *Lumière*, pp. 376f., citing *Tr Eth IV*, 61–63.

and impassioned desire, as not only of themselves never to conceive what is evil or to move towards the doing of it, but also not to undergo any change from the state of dispassion which is theirs, even if others tempt them.[189]

This description, with its reminiscence of St. Paul, clearly implies that for the attainment of dispassion human effort is required if one's members are to be mortified. At the same time, Symeon's words testify to his conviction that there were in his own day some who through their efforts had become truly dispassionate, and accordingly were for ever impervious to the assaults of evil whether from within or from without. Yet Symeon, we shall discover, was not consistent in what he said about these matters, and in fact there are other examples of inconsistency which can be detected in his treatment of this subject.

That the spiritual father is involved in a person's gaining dispassion, is implied in some lines in a *Catechesis*, which warn the hearers that to die without having acquired it would entail their exclusion from the Kingdom of Heaven. It will be remembered that a spiritual father, even when his work is not understood in a crude or mechanical way, is bound to have as his aim the securing of salvation for his disciples, something which can be symbolically represented by the Kingdom of Heaven. The training given must therefore include all that is necessary to help spiritual children become dispassionate. In the passage with which we are concerned, Symeon spoke of the need for

> the understanding to be given wings by repentance and tears and the spiritual humility which results from them, and thus raised to the height of dispassion.

Should this not come to pass, one would in this life constantly be the prey of one passion or another, and after death one would be excluded from the Kingdom and subjected to eternal punishment.[190] In his *Catechesis* Symeon was addressing monks, but it is noteworthy that the lines quoted follow a paragraph in which he had emphasised the importance of struggling against what he called "lesser passions," such as "greediness" and "grumbling", to select two out of his long list. Symeon stressed that faults of this nature needed to be overcome, as well as the "great passions," for example, "thieving" or "sodomy".[191] There is naturally no reason to suppose that he would have exempted people living in the world from the requirement to strive for mastery over the "lesser passions," which could injure them no less than those living under monastic vows.

---

[189] *Ch* III, 87, 9–15; cf. *Colossians* 3. 5 (A.V.), "Mortify . . . your members which are upon the earth."

[190] *Cat V*, 1059–1067.

[191] *ibid.*, 1013–1049.

We must conclude, then, that in Symeon's opinion seculars as well as monks were obliged to struggle to acquire dispassion, if they wished to be saved. This conclusion is supported by the fact that all Christians are called on to repent, and indeed the necessity of repentance received considerable emphasis in the context we have been considering,[192] while, as we noticed in chapter IV, Symeon expected that in order to learn how to repent properly, a person would have recourse to a spiritual father. The father's help in this matter is thus an element in the training of a disciple to become dispassionate, which itself can be described in positive terms as "entering into the supra-sensible realm."[193]

This view of repentance as a precursor of dispassion leads appropriately to our consideration of a passage in *Cat XXX*, in which Symeon urged the novice whom he purported to be addressing to continue as a penitent until his last breath. Through so doing, he would, by God's grace, be granted

> not only a fountain of tears, but also ... liberation from all his passions.

In this way, he would be brought to "purification and dispassion," and made

> a partaker of the Holy Spirit, and the equal of the great Fathers, Antony, Sabas and Euthymius.[194]

Symeon's teaching in this place envisages dispassion as something to be attained at the end of a process. This process includes repentance, and it is one in which a man's own efforts play a prominent and decisive part.

On reading *Cat XX*, however, we receive a different impression. Here Symeon is found asserting that, at the time foreseen by the spiritual father, the disciple undergoes an experience in which the Holy Spirit comes to him as he came to the first disciples at Pentecost, and

> then every passionate thought (ἐμπαθὴς λογισμός) disappears, and every passion in the soul (πάθος ψυχικόν) is driven away.[195]

It is true that the actual word "dispassion" does not occur in these lines, but the language clearly reveals that the dispassionate state is being described. Yet it is represented, not as in *Cat XXX*, as the prelude to receiving the Spirit in a special way, but rather as the consequence, or perhaps the concomitant, of such reception. Furthermore, although effort has been involved in the disciple's attendance upon, and obedience to, his

---

[192] In *Cat V*, 1054–1067, μετάνοια occurs twice and μετανοῶ once.
[193] *Ch* III, 33, 1f., cited by Krivochéine, *Lumière*, p. 374, and found in a *Chapter* dealing with ἀπάθεια.
[194] *Cat XXX*, 253–273 (summary and extracts).
[195] *Cat XX*, 172–174.

spiritual father—these matters have been dwelt on in the preceding paragraphs[196]—, nevertheless at the point where there occurs this reference to
what is in effect dispassion, all thought of effort has receded: the disciple
is to expect the *gift* of the Holy Spirit's presence, and all he can do is to
await it in solitude and quiet.[197] No doubt, if taxed with inconsistency,
Symeon would have denied the accusation, retorting that God's grace and
man's effort are both indispensable, and that the teacher must sometimes
place the emphasis on one and sometimes on the other. In the same way
he would probably have asserted that it is right to understand dispassion
both as a prerequisite for the coming of the Holy Spirit, and also as a consequence of a person's receiving the Spirit in a particular, fully conscious,
way. Be this as it may, it is important to remember that, in spite of the
apparent inconsistency, in these two *Catecheses* we find dispassion connected in one way or another both with the Holy Spirit and also with the
work of the spiritual father.

An inconsistency of somewhat the same kind can be discovered if *Hymn
XLVI* is compared with *Cat XI*. The former is a prayer of confession. In
the course of it Symeon begged that his soul might be cleansed and healed,
and then proceeded to name several virtues, which he asked God to bestow
on him again. The culminating virtue of which he made mention was dispassion, which had implanted in him the desire for union with God. In
the past all these good things had been his, but Symeon confessed that
though he had then been raised above all passion, he had not continued
thus, but through self-reliance had become slack and had fallen victim to
anxieties about earthly matters. Accordingly he concluded his *Hymn* with
a brief prayer to be restored to his former condition and enjoyment of the
divine light.[198] It must be said that this confession of a fall from dispassion appears in itself rather inconsistent with the impression Symeon had
given a little earlier when, making use of nuptial imagery, he stated that
"dispassion lived with me, and never left me."[199] However, in view of
the evident emotion under which he was writing, it would be a mistake
to make too much of this point.

In *Cat XI*, on the other hand, Symeon spoke of dispassion not as the
culmination of a series of divine gifts, but rather as the almost automatic
result of human perseverance in fasting.

Fasting, assisted by the keeping of vigils, makes its way into the heart and

---

[196] *ibid.*, 60–160.
[197] *ibid.*, 161–166; yet a few lines later humility is stated to procure dispassion, *ibid.*,
204–206.
[198] *Hymn XLVI*, 11–49, summarised.
[199] *ibid.*, 29f., cf. 40–45.

softens its hardness, causing springs of compunction to flow in the place where formerly debauchery was to be found. And I beseech you, brethren, let each of us strive earnestly for this to be effected in us. Then, with God's help, we shall easily cross all the sea of the passions, and having passed through the waves of temptations caused by him who cruelly tyrannizes over us, we shall reach the haven of dispassion.[200]

A reason for the difference between the above and *Hymn XLVI* can easily be suggested, and may fairly be claimed as accounting for the apparent inconsistency: the two passages were produced for very dissimilar purposes. In the *Catechesis* Symeon, speaking as hegumen and spiritual father, was exhorting his monks to continue fasting rigorously throughout the whole of Great Lent, and not to follow the common practice of relaxing their efforts after the end of the first week.[201] He therefore wished to stimulate them to further endeavours and to encourage them with the hope of thereby becoming dispassionate. In *Hymn XLVI*, on the other hand, he can be seen probing into his own soul, and being brought to realise that the healing which he needs can never be an automatic result of physical asceticism, but in truth can come to him only as a gift from God. It should be noted, too, that even when in the *Catechesis* he was stressing the benefits of fasting as a means towards the attainment of dispassion, Symeon did not forget to speak of "God's help" in the course of his exhortation to continued effort.

While we are considering this subject, there is an interesting sentence at the beginning of *Cat XX* which ought to be quoted. As so often, Symeon's language is rather imprecise, but it seems that he could visualise a state of partial dispassion as a kind of preliminary stage leading to the complete attainment of this condition. He stated that he proposed to explain

> what is profitable to the soul and assists it in its flight from the world and in [gaining] deliverance from the passions, love for God, and perfect dispassion.[202]

What is the relationship between this programme and the passage, towards the end of the same *Catechesis*, according to which the Pentecostal experience, given by God, would cause or at least coincide with the expulsion of "every passion from the soul?" Although at first sight what is there described might be taken to be the equivalent of "deliverance from the passions" here, this can hardly be Symeon's real meaning, because nothing less than the reception of the Holy Spirit is the climax to which, in this *Catechesis*, all the spiritual father's work is directed.[203] But in the

---

[200] *Cat XI*, 66–74.
[201] *ibid.*, 21–41.
[202] *Cat XX*, 17–20.
[203] *ibid.*, 165–174.

programme just quoted, mention is made not only of "deliverance from the passions" but also, and as a climax, of "perfect dispassion." It seems then reasonable to suppose that Symeon envisaged the novice reaching first a preliminary stage, in which he would be more or less freed from subjection to his passions, and then subsequently by the grace of God receiving an outpouring of the Holy Spirit and the disappearance of "every passionate thought," otherwise described as "perfect dispassion."

Although it must be admitted that he has not expressed himself clearly in the matter, this supposition absolves Symeon to some extent from a charge of inconsistency, and moreover it accords with Krivochéine's remark about "differing degrees" of dispassion, and with a distinction made by Hausherr between a "first" and "second" *apatheia*.[204] It provides an example also of the lack of preciseness which Darrouzès states is not uncommon when dispassion and its division into stages are being discussed.[205] As far as the spiritual father's work is concerned, the significant fact is that this idea of two degrees of dispassion occurs in the very *Catechesis* which includes the advice to begin one's pilgrimage towards God by

call[ing] earnestly upon [him], that he may show you a man capable of shepherding you well.[206]

It is not possible, however, to extract from the whole process of training something that might be described as training in dispassion, in order to illustrate it in isolation by means of examples. This is because what we have been considering is, in its first stage, "the fruit of asceticism, fasting and mortifying the senses,"[207] and in its second, nothing less than a gift conveyed by the Holy Spirit, or received together with him. Nevertheless, in spite of this limitation on what could be attempted, our discussion will have made it clear that dispassion is so important a subject, and so much bound up with the training of disciples, that of necessity it had in some way to be included in this section.

We have now looked at many matters that can be classified either as training, or as closely related to it: discipline of the body; all that is involved in the disclosure of thoughts; regulation of conduct and reformation of character; instruction about how to pray, how to participate in worship, how and when to communicate; and finally encouragement to acquire dispassion. It is by attending to these that the spiritual father can

---

[204] Hausherr, *Life*, pp. XXVIIf.; cf. also B. Fraigneau-Julien, *op. cit.*, pp. 138f., and the reference there given to *Cat XVIII*, 370–375.

[205] Darrouzès, *SC* 51, p. 97, n. 1.

[206] *Cat XX*, 45f.

[207] Hausherr, *Life*, p. XXVII.

help his disciples live a more dedicated and holy life. All these matters had a place in the tradition into which Symeon entered, and we have seen something of the way in which in practice he understood and applied this tradition. The demands made on spiritual fathers who undertake this kind of training programme are very obvious, and those of them who, like Symeon, try to be conscientious, can hope to achieve success only if they draw on all the resources of τέχνη and πεῖρα at their disposal.

iv) The End of the Father's Work

By definition, training is not an end in itself but is a process directed towards an end. However much training he has given, the spiritual father has not fulfilled his obligations until he has brought his children to a stage at which they personally experience an intimate relationship with God. This is, of course, another aspect of the salvation which was Symeon's original objective for himself, but which he came to perceive as something much richer in content than a mere escape from future damnation, and as in some sense capable of being enjoyed even in this present life.

It will inevitably be somewhat difficult to investigate this facet of a father's work, since our subject-matter is a range of experiences which, because of differences of background and temperament, will vary from person to person. Moreover, since we are approaching the frontiers of mysticism, we must expect to encounter descriptions couched in language that is symbolic and pictorial. Thus we must anticipate a lack of precision, both in terminology and with regard to the experiences described and their sequence. As far as language is concerned, a statement made by Climacus is instructive:

> Love (ἀγάπη), dispassion, and adoption as sons, differ in name, but in name only. Think of them as being like light, fire and flame, which co-operate in a single activity.[208]

If writers hold such opinions, whether consciously like Climacus, or perhaps unconsciously in the case of others, we shall not succeed in under-standing them by making use of methods which depend on exact linguistic analysis. Again, with regard to experiences and the order in which they occur, we should not be surprised at being confronted with instances of apparent vagueness and lack of consistency, an example of which we have just had occasion to notice in Symeon's statements about dispassion.[209]

---

[208] *Sc. Par.* 30, 1156B.
[209] cf. *Philippians* 2. 12f., where two consecutive verses of St. Paul's are superficially at variance with one another.

Nevertheless, in spite of these difficulties which must throughout be borne in mind, it is not impossible to try to present some kind of sketch of the goal to which by his labours the spiritual father ought to be leading his children.

> Spiritual fatherhood—so Hausherr wrote—has no *raison d'être* other than that of bringing a person out of slavery into the liberty of the children of God ... This blessed transformation is effected by completely substituting the divine will for the human.[210]

With this it is interesting to compare an account of the monastic ideal in Orthodoxy, a long description of which may be summarised as follows: a complete break with the world; the absolute rejection of all purely human knowledge; the abandoning of the body, the world and family ties; self-renunciation and the surrender of one's own free-will; a ceaseless struggle against all forms of sin; the mortification of the body, the senses and the imagination; watchfulness, sobriety, and obedience to one's spiritual father—the monk who faithfully follows this path becomes open to receive the impulses of the Holy Spirit, and living a life of real contemplation, he in fact attains a new life in Christ, being 'divinised'.[211]

This description taken from a modern writer is in some of its features strikingly similar to the thought of St. Gregory of Nyssa, in which, according to Jaeger,

> God is the inaccessible object of a long process of purification of the soul, through which it approaches the knowledge of 'the absolute good' by degrees ... Christianity is ... the mystery of the separation and liberation of the soul from all material bondage to the senses and its ascent and return to God.[212]

This is followed a few pages later by the statement that for Gregory the process of salvation

> is interpreted as the gradual purification of the soul (καθαρισμός) from the stain (μολυσμός) of the material world and its final liberation (λύτρωσις) from the servitude (δουλεία) of the passions (πάθη) ... This true freedom consists in the complete absence of passion (ἀπάθεια): the free man is ὁ ἀπαθής.[213]

Climacus was following much the same line of thought when he wrote:

> I consider dispassion to be nothing other than a spiritual heaven within the

---

[210] Hausherr, *Direction spirituelle*, p. 165.
[211] E. Amand de Mendieta, *Mount Athos, the Garden of the Panaghia*, Berlin, 1972, p. 214.
[212] W. Jaeger, *Two Rediscovered Works of Ancient Christian Literature: Greogry of Nyssa and Macarius*, Leyden, 1954, pp. 73f.
[213] *ibid.*, p. 79.

heart (ἐγκάρδιος νοὸς οὐρανός) . . . The man who is genuinely dispassionate, and recognised to be such, is one who has rendered his flesh incor-
ruptible, raised his spirit above everything created, and subjected to it all his
senses . . . Others again define dispassion as a resurrection of the soul taking
place before that of the body, while others call it perfect knowledge of God
(ἐπίγνωσις Θεοῦ τελεία), second only to that of the angels.[214]

This last example shows how dispassion might be regarded as an endow-
ment of a positive kind: instead of being understood only as a negative
achievement, laboriously acquired by means of ascetic training, it could
also be thought of as a condition of blessedness and perfection, an antici-
pation of Heaven. Furthermore, in the same section as that in which the
above quotation is found, Climacus expressly writes that the dispassionate
person no longer needs a human guide, since

he has been raised above all human instruction and apprehends the Lord's
will within himself through some illumination.[215]

This is formally at variance with Climacus' other statement, quoted in
chapter V, about the necessity of a spiritual father,[216] but clearly his intention now is to indicate that the need for such a guide no longer exists
once the disciple has been established in a state of dispassion, and so has
attained to a personal knowledge of God and of God's will.

It must not, however, be supposed that the attainment of this condition
was held to preclude the possibility of subsequently falling away. Indeed,
it seems that in one of his *Chapters* the Studite deliberately made provision
for such an occurrence, since he included a prayer to be used by a monk
or novice conscious of having lost his enjoyment of the grace of God. The
condition from which such a person would have fallen, as well as the stages
leading up to it, and one reason for its having been forfeited, are all
described in the lines which precede the prayer:

Keep your spirit (νοῦς) ever directed towards God . . . Esteem yourself more
sinful than everyone else. If you keep this in your remembrance for some
time, your mind is likely to be illuminated, as by a ray of light. And the more
you seek after it . . . , the more clearly it appears; and as it appears, so it is
loved; and as it is loved, so it purifies; and as it purifies, so it renders you
godlike, giving you light and teaching you to distinguish what is good from
what is worse. But, brother, much toil is needed, together with God's help,
for this [illumination] to become perfectly at home in your soul . . . Beware
that you do not suffer harm through excess of joy and of compunction, and
that you do not consider these benefits the result of your own toil rather than

---

[214] *Sc. Par.* 29, 1148BC.
[215] *ibid.*, 1149C.
[216] *Sc. Par.* 26, 1089B.

of God's grace; [if you do,] they will be taken from you, and you will often seek them in your prayer, but will not find them. Then you will understand what a gift you have lost ... But, brother, even if this does occur, stretch out your hands and pray, saying ...[217]

In the above it is true that the Studite does not explicitly admit, as Climacus had done, that after reaching a level at which he is directly illuminated by God, a disciple no longer needs any human teacher. Such an admission is nevertheless implied in the idea of his being able to discern for himself what is good. At the same time, we must not suppose that the Studite was suggesting that at this stage a disciple might deliberately detach himself from his spiritual father, for elsewhere he insisted on the permanence of the relationship.[218] All that may be inferred from the *Chapter* we are examining is the obvious truth that strictly speaking divine illumination renders an earthly guide unnecessary. However, should the disciple fall from this high estate, he will of course again require human assistance, just as Nicetas, at the time of his vision, needed help in order to overcome the "arrogance and conceit" which he had allowed to infect his soul.[219]

The two sayings of the Studite recorded by Symeon in *Cat VI*, can likewise be interpreted as pointing to a condition in which personal knowledge of God makes human guidance, whether oral or written, no longer necessary:

Gain God as a friend for yourself, and you will have no need of the help of man,

and,

Gain God, and you will have no need of a book.[220]

The second of these, in so far as it is not merely conventional, no doubt reveals something of the Studite's suspicion of human cleverness, and the first might be taken as connected with his desire that the novice should isolate himself, so far as possible, from all his brethren. Yet it is not unreasonable to claim, in the light of what we are now discussing, that these two sayings may have borne an additional meaning, and have been intended also to urge the hearers to strive towards reaching a permanent state of conscious fellowship with God.

The attaining of such a state is, in any case, a matter to which writers in the tradition we are examining not infrequently referred, and when

---

217 Studite, *Ch* 140, 676C–677A (extracts).
218 *Ch* 36, *Life*, pp. XLIXf.
219 Nicetas, *Life*, 149, 28—v. p. 142.
220 *Cat VI*, 190–192.

they did so they often remarked upon the change accompanying it. This change they commonly designated ἀλλοίωσις sometimes with the epithet καλή. The same word could also be used for the transformation involved in becoming dispassionate,[221] which is readily understandable in the light of what we have seen concerning the close connection between dispassion and the stage in spiritual progress at which God is experienced personally. Writers might vary with regard to the exact type of change denoted by ἀλλοίωσις, but in spite of such differences many agreed in ascribing it to divine activity, and quoted the LXX version of *Psalm* 76 (77). 11, "This ἀλλοίωσις is from the hand of the Most High." Gregory of Nazianzus cited this text when speaking of a moral transformation,[222] whereas Symeon made use of it in connection with entry upon the spiritual condition with which we are now concerned.[223]

It is noteworthy that Symeon at one time might imply that this change is produced by divine action, and at another that it is the result of human activity, an apparent inconsistency resembling those found in his references to dispassion. Thus he could write that the attainment of virtues leads one to divine knowledge of the mysteries of Christ, and

> when one has reached their level and become habituated to them, he is transformed by the noble transformation (τὴν καλὴν ἀλλοίωσιν ἀλλοιοῦται), and from being a mere man he becomes an angel.

Although here Symeon, following St. Paul, spoke of the virtues which he listed as "the fruit of the Holy Spirit,"[224] they clearly could not be acquired without some human effort, and this he therefore implied by the very fact of mentioning them. In another passage, however, when treating of baptism as a new birth, in spite of a mention of the commandments, Symeon placed his emphasis on the work of deliverance performed by God in making us his children. He quoted from *St. John's Gospel* the words

> who were born not of blood, nor of the will of the flesh, nor of the will of man, but of God,

and continued,

> [the evangelist] here gives the name 'birth' to the spiritual transformation

---

[221] cf. Hausherr, *Life*, p. XXXII; on the different names for this, v. Krivochéine, *Lumière*, p. 418.

[222] Gregory of Nazianzus, *Or. XLIV, PG* 36, 616C.

[223] *Tr Eth IV*, 594f.; cf. *Cat XVIII*, 378f., where there is a reminiscence of *Psalm* 76 (77), but the change is termed μεταποίησις.

[224] *Tr Eth VIII*, 195–209; cf. *Cat XXXV*, 261–267, where a string of virtues lead to ἀλλοίωσις, which itself is necessary if the Holy Spirit is to indwell one.

(πνευματικὴ ἀλλοίωσις) which is effected and made visible in the baptism of the Holy Spirit.[225]

Once again, there is no real inconsistency between these passages, but rather a desire to stress either the divine or the human factor, whichever is demanded by the teaching being given on a particular occasion or in a particular piece of writing. Wherever the emphasis falls, the term 'transformation', it is worth remarking, is one which must have appealed to Symeon as well fitted to express the idea of a conscious spiritual experience which was so important to him.

For himself, Symeon had no doubt that this noble transformation had taken place in him. In the light of our present discussion it is interesting to observe how in *Hymn LI*, in which he was primarily giving thanks for the work of Christ within, after describing his experience of being freed from evils, and ransomed from darkness, temptations, passions (πάθη) and from all thoughts (λογισμοί), he went on to speak of becoming conscious of "the strange transformation" in himself.[226] This experience, however, was for Symeon no once-for-all entry into a state in which he would automatically continue, for this passage is one in which he recounted his restoration after the repeated falls which he had earlier confessed, and as a result of which he had forfeited the privilege of enjoying the light of Christ.[227] This treatment of the matter reminds us of how Symeon's spiritual father, the Studite, had likewise envisaged the possibility that a disciple might attain the light yet later succumb to temptation, thus forfeiting the intimacy with God which he had for a while enjoyed.

In *Hymn LI*, probably because the transformation was in fact his restoration to a state previously attained but then lost, Symeon did not mention the Studite. But there are several other places in which, although he did not use the word ἀλλοίωσις, he did emphasise the part played by his spiritual father in leading him onwards until he could experience a close personal relationship with God. A straightforward statement can be found in *Hymn LVI*, in which Symeon in prayer recalled his past:

> Thou didst bring me to him who in thy good pleasure was to become my father on earth, and didst cast me at his feet and [lay me] in his arms. And he it was who brought me by the Spirit to thy Father, O my Christ, and to thyself—O Trinity, my God—, while I wept like the Prodigal (ἄσωτος) . . . , nor didst thou disdain to call me thy son . . . And we, thy humble servants, according to thy good pleasure, are strong in weakness, rich in poverty and

---

[225] *Tr Eth X*, 430–445 (summary and extract, with quotation from *St. John* 1. 13).
[226] *Hymn LI*, 38–54.
[227] *ibid.*, 18–23.

rejoice in all tribulation, since we are outside the world; we are with thee, O Master, and the world has but our body.[228]

In these lines, in which he speaks of his experience of being brought into fellowship with God, there is no direct description of the part played by the Studite, but the reference to the Prodigal Son suggests that Symeon was helped to repent deeply, and in the light of all we know of the importance which both he and his father attached to repentance accompanied by tears, we may reasonably assume that help towards this is being implied.

If, however, Symeon had been asked to explain in more detail how this relationship with God had been established, he would probably have referred to the Studite's work as spiritual physician, to his prayers and to the example of his life.[229] In some passages where entry into this condition is spoken of in rather different terms, it is unquestionably the prayers of the spiritual father that become prominent. Thus, according to *Cat XVI*, the young Symeon asked his father to pray for him, was assured that he would receive a double portion of divine grace, and was then that very night granted a wonderful vision of divine light and addressed by a voice from on high.[230] A more definite reference to the Studite's prayers on Symeon's behalf, and to their effect, is found in the opening lines of *Hymn XXXII*:

> Have mercy upon me, O Master, who am reviled by the faithful as a deceiver (πλάνος) and utterly self-deceived, because I assert that through thy love for men and through the prayers of my father, I have received the Holy Spirit . . .[231]

This is of great interest, not only because of its explicit statement about prayer, but also because it reveals the reaction of ordinary Christians ("the faithful") to the claims made by Symeon or by others, who like him believed themselves to have had a special experience of the Holy Spirit. Just as formerly the Studite had been called a "deceiver", Symeon now found the same insult being levelled at himself.[232] This, we must note, helps to explain why at the outset Symeon had never hoped for more from a spiritual father than a rather crudely conceived type of salvation in the next world: that, and no more than that, was the commonly held expectation of what this ministry should and would secure. By the time he wrote *Hymn XXXII* Symeon's understanding had been enlarged, and

---

[228] *Hymn LVI*, 13–34 (extracts).
[229] cf. *Hymn XXXVII*, 29–43.
[230] *Cat XVI*, 62–122.
[231] *Hymn XXXII*, 1–5.
[232] In *Ep 4*, 38–45, he again complained of similar attacks made on him because of his teaching.

he therefore, both on behalf of his spiritual father and of himself, made claims which conflicted with the commonly held pessimism concerning what was possible for man in tenth or eleventh century Byzantium.[233]

Again, visionary experiences, of gradually increasing clarity and intensity, are in *Hymn LV* unequivocally described as being granted in answer to the Studite's prayers and tears, although in *Cat XXXV* they appear to be simply the consequence of discipleship, while in *Cat XVI* Symeon merely stated that before his vision he had asked for his father's prayers, leaving his hearers to draw the obvious conclusion.[234] These variations are yet another instance of the way in which Symeon emphasised different aspects of a complex of truths on different occasions.

In *Hymn XLI* there is an important passage which seems to indicate that Symeon understood that he had reached a stage when the work of the Studite on his behalf should in some sense have come to an end. By implication, of course, the same would be true in the case of any other disciple who became equally mature. Christ, Symeon believed, said to him:

> I gave you into the hands of a tutor (παιδαγωγός) . . . and he took good care of you as of a little child growing up hour by hour, and he brought you up properly. You have already approached manhood, indeed become a young man, and you yourself know well that I was always with you, growing up in you and shielding you until you had nobly passed through all the stages of growth. Now, then, have you not come of age? More than that, you are in truth a mature man and already on the way towards old age, so how is it that you now desire to be nursed in my arms like an infant? How is it that you ask to be put back into swaddling clothes and carried about? to be fed on milk and to be under the care of a tutor?[235]

Here there is clearly a sense of being rebuked, for Symeon felt that he could justly be held guilty of entertaining a desire to return to spiritual childhood, although he had in fact become a mature (τέλειος) man. But, in addition, since he was a writer who constantly alluded to the Scriptures, his use of the word παιδαγωγός twice in thirteen lines must be regarded as very significant, when we recall St. Paul's use of the same word:

> Thus the Law was a kind of tutor (παιδαγωγός) in charge of us until Christ should come, when we should be justified through faith; and now that faith has come, the tutor's charge is at an end.[236]

Quite apart from his general familiarity with the Bible, Symeon shows

---

[233] cf. Krivochéine, *Lumière*, pp. 32f., for a discussion of "*l'impression d'insolite produite par l'enseignement de Syméon.*"

[234] *Hymn LV*, 80–87 and 101–107; *Cat XXXV*, 129–139; *Cat XVI*, 62–77.

[235] *Hymn XLI*, 56–68, a passage already referred to on p. 146.

[236] *Galatians* 3, 24f. (N.E.B.).

definite knowledge of these verses when in *Cat XXVIII* he speaks of the Law as παιδαγωγός.[237] In *Hymn XLI*, then, it may be legitimately claimed that Symeon, like St. Paul, was thinking in terms of a definite conclusion to the period during which the pupil or disciple rightly remains under his tutor's care. Spiritual fatherhood, in other words, must not produce spiritual infantilism.

Although in his capacity as hegumen Symeon may at times have displayed too much zeal and enthusiasm and too little wisdom and love, he cannot be charged with hypocrisy. It is therefore only what might be expected when, in the teaching he gave to others, there is found the same understanding that a spiritual child may be so thoroughly transformed as no longer to need the care hitherto bestowed on him by his father. Returning again to *Cat XX*, we discover how Symeon taught that with the coming of the Holy Spirit to the disciple,

> the man is totally transformed (ἀλλοιοῦται) and knows God, and for the first time is known by him.[238]

These words occur at the conclusion of the passage describing, in terms of light-mysticism, the effects of what can be called a personal Pentecost. But the description began with the promise that "upon you also will now come the same power of the All-Holy Spirit [as upon the first disciples]."[239] The implication of Symeon's promise is that just as on the day of Pentecost the Holy Spirit came to supply the place of the Ascended Christ who could no longer be with his disciples in the flesh, so the personal coming of the Spirit to an individual will result in his no longer having to depend on his spiritual father for guidance and direction. This conclusion is all the clearer because in the preceding pages Symeon had depicted the relationship between disciple and spiritual father in terms of that between the disciples and Christ during his earthly life.

A similar inference about the goal at which the novice should aim can be drawn from other *Catecheses*. For example,

> If, brother, you thus accustom yourself to performing this task you will make progress in a short time and will speedily become a mature (τέλειος) man, measured by the stature of the fulness of Christ.[240]

The language here is closely akin to that in *Ephesians* ("mature manhood, ... the measure of the stature of the fulness of Christ"); elsewhere,

---

[237] *Cat XXVIII*, 71–82, where life under the direction of the Holy Spirit is for those who have passed beyond the tutelage of the Law.

[238] *Cat XX*, 181f.; cf. *Galatians* 4. 9.

[239] *ibid.*, 165f.

[240] *Cat XXVI*, 49–51; cf. *Ephesians* 4. 13.

Symeon used some of the same phraseology in his description of how a novice who becomes the disciple of a father who is τεχνίτης and ἔμπειρος, "increases in spiritual stature, and becomes a mature (τέλειος) man in Christ our God." The meaning of these last words he spelt out later as follows:

> Every day he increases in spiritual stature, ridding himself of what belongs to an infantile way of thinking, and advancing towards the mature state of a man. For this reason he is transformed (ἀλλοιοῦται) as regards the powers and activities of his soul, in accordance with the measure of his stature . . . [241]

In view of the reminiscence of *Ephesians*, Symeon must be understood as having wished to convey that a disciple on becoming mature enjoys a deep interior relationship with Christ. He proceeded indeed to assert that "when he has become such, at once God dwells within [the spiritual child]."[242] When thus speaking to his monks Symeon did not directly teach that a spiritual father is superfluous, once a disciple has reached maturity and provided that he continues in this state. There can be no doubt, however, that such is the logical consequence of the words we have quoted.[243]

Symeon also employed other language in his attempts to portray the goal to which a spiritual father ought to lead his disciples. Thus the passage in *Cat XX* in which he spoke of the coming of the Holy Spirit concludes with a remark about the condition of the person who is granted this experience: he is made

> a friend of God and son of the Most High and himself a god, in so far as this is possible for men.[244]

Becoming a "son of the Most High" is in fact the reward which we found that Symeon in *Ep 4* promised to those who had recourse to the right kind of spiritual father: such a father would be able to effect the rebirth of his clients as children of God.[245] The third expression, "himself a god," even though it is immediately qualified, may astonish some readers when they first encounter it. In fact, however, it does not really go beyond the well-known statement of St. Athanasius that Christ "became human in order that we might be made divine."[246]

---

[241] *Cat XIV*, 23, 111–115.

[242] *ibid.*, 142f.

[243] cf. *Cat X*, 26–38, for the insistence that not only did the Studite reach perfection, but that others still do so.

[244] *Cat XX*, 185f. (Krivochéine adopts the harder reading, Θεῷ, though noting in the *apparatus* that some manuscripts have Θεοῦ, but in any case "of" must be the rendering in English); cf. *Wisdom* 7. 27.

[245] *Ep 4*, 121–126; cf. chapter V, pp. 76f.

[246] Athanasius, *De Incarnatione*, PG 25, 192B.

Symeon was not afraid to speak of human beings becoming gods, and in *Tr Eth IV* there is another interesting example, where again he qualified the word, and where also in the same context he referred to ἀλλοίωσις, and quoted *Psalm* 76 (77). 11.

> Those then who have been counted worthy to be united with [Christ] and to have him for their Head ... also become themselves gods by adoption, and like the Son of God ... The Father puts on them the best robe, the Lord's cloak, with which he was clothed before the foundation of the world. 'For as many of you as were baptized into Christ, did put on Christ,' as it is said, referring clearly to the Holy Spirit who transforms them in their entirety, in such a manner as befits God, by a strange, ineffable and divine transformation (ἀλλοίωσις), concerning which David says: 'This transformation is from the hand of the Most High' ...247

Here "gods" is significantly qualified by the addition of "by adoption," and the whole phrase is itself expanded by the use of Scriptural terminology, and followed by a text from *Galatians* about "putting on Christ," which is somewhat forcibly interpreted as referring to the work of the Holy Spirit. Whatever judgment one might feel inclined to make concerning Symeon's exegesis, it must be admitted that he desired to affirm only what could claim Biblical support, even though he wished also to go to the utmost limits of language in order to portray the destiny of faithful disciples. It is noteworthy that in the same context Symeon expounded another text in such a way as to make it clear that the transformation of which he spoke was one which began in the present world and would be completed in some future existence. After quoting David, the psalmist, he continued his sentence as follows:

> and the disciple who lay on Christ's breast says, 'Brethren, we are now children [of God], but it has not yet been revealed'—this clearly means to those who are in the world—'what we shall be.'

Continuing his quotation, Symeon conflated with the verse he was using some words from a later verse in the same chapter. He desired to emphasise the difference between two classes of people: whereas the worldlings, as he had just said, remain in ignorance about the glory awaiting true disciples, the latter, possessing the Spirit, know what will be their reward.

> 'But we know,' because of the Spirit whom he has given us, 'that when [Christ] is revealed, we shall be like him.'248

---

247 *Tr Eth IV*, 586–595, with reminiscences of *St. Luke* 15. 22 (the Prodigal Son) and *St. John* 17. 24 (Christ's prayer in the Upper Room), and quotation of *Galatians* 3. 27.

248 *Tr Eth IV*, 595–599; for "the disciple who lay on Christ's breast," v. *St. John* 13. 23, this disciple being traditionally identified with St. John; the quotation (not quite exact) is of *I John* 3. 2, with which 24 is in part conflated.

Symeon, it can thus be seen, held that a spiritual father's work for his disciple ought to culminate in nothing less than the latter's being spiritually transformed and having some experience of the reality of God. But the mystical tradition was well aware of the possibility of a person's being deceived, and of the consequent need to be on one's guard against the devil, who might impersonate an angel, or perhaps even Christ.[249] A director, therefore, was regarded as having the responsibility for pronouncing on the validity or otherwise of his spiritual child's early visionary experiences, and this is what might be considered to be his final obligation. Amongst Symeon's writings can be found the record of a conversation, which was begun by a disciple saying to his father, "I have seen." On being asked, "What have you seen, my child?", he replied by telling of a vision of light, which was so sweet that he could not find words to describe it, but the effects of which on him included a lasting sensation of unspeakable joy, accompanied by rivers of tears. Hearing this description, the spiritual father uttered the simple words of reassurance, "My child, that is He." While apparently still with his father, the disciple was then enabled to behold the vision again. He questioned it, "Is it thou, my God?" and received the answer,

> Yes, I am God, who for your sake became man. And, as you see, I have made, and will make, you god.[250]

This passage is specially interesting because from a parallel in *Cat XXXVI*, as well as from a note in the margin of some manuscripts,[251] we are justified in deducing that Symeon was in fact narrating his own experience: he was the disciple, and the Studite the spiritual father. Here, therefore, we have yet another instance of an event in Symeon's life providing the basis of, or at least support for, some of his teaching. At the same time, this important account supplies illustrations of a father assessing the genuineness of a vision, of a disciple becoming convinced that he has really been brought into contact with Christ, and of deification being promised both in the future and as a present reality.

From all that has been touched on in this chapter, it will have become clear how exacting and demanding was the work of a conscientious spiritual father, according to the tradition into which Symeon entered and which

---

[249] cf. Ward, *Desert Fathers*, p. 50, nos. 178 and 180.

[250] *Tr Eth V*, 294–316.

[251] cf. *Cat XXXVI*, 218–233 (a variant account of the vision, in the first person), and marginal note in three manuscripts at *Tr Eth V*, 301; the incident was briefly mentioned in chapter VI, p. 98.

he himself developed. No doubt, as he and others were aware, many spiritual fathers were incapable of fulfilling all their obligations, even if they sincerely wished to do so. At the same time, skilled, experienced and devoted as a father might be, he could do little or nothing when a disciple was recalcitrant and prepared to travel only a limited distance along the path towards holiness. We must now therefore investigate the expectations which Symeon entertained with regard to spiritual children and the obligations which he believed were theirs. Moreover, we shall need to bear in mind that everything he will be found demanding of disciples, he demanded in the context of all the manifold work which he held to be incumbent on a father.

CHAPTER EIGHT

THE DUTY OF A DISCIPLE

Basis: the Father as 'Icon'

> The old men used to say, 'If someone has faith in another, and hands himself over to him in complete submission, he does not need to pay attention to God's commands but he can entrust his whole will to his father. He will suffer no reproach from God, for God looks for nothing from beginners so much as renunciation through obedience.[1]

The tradition regarding spiritual fatherhood is well represented in this statement, uncompromising in its absoluteness yet holding out the prospect of freedom from anxiety. Nevertheless in the Christian scheme of things such a demand for "complete submission" can properly be made only by God, or at least by one who is accepted as invested with divine authority in the fullest sense. It is thus not surprising that we frequently encounter insistence on total obedience to the spiritual father accompanied by the injunction that, in Symeon's words, the disciple is to render such obedience "as to God himself," something which becomes possible as a consequence of the disciple's "regarding his teacher and guide as God."[2]

We may thus claim that underlying all the demands for obedience on the part of the spiritual child is the concept of his duty to view his father as an icon of Christ, the Incarnate Word of God. Now in Eastern Orthodox theology icons have what may be called a sacramental function: they are not visual aids, but actual means whereby the worshipper is brought into the presence of, and into fellowship with, heavenly realities. Climacus provides an excellent example of the transference of this principle from the realm of iconography to that of living human beings. In one of his anecdotes he describes how he interrogated an aged monk whom the hegumen had kept standing in silence beside the table while others were eating. On enquiring of him what his thoughts were at that time, Climacus received the answer:

> Since I have mentally clothed our pastor with the features of the icon of

---

[1] Ward, *Desert Fathers*, p. 45, no. 158; cf. Rousseau, *Ascetics*, p. 52, "the belief that by submitting to the guidance of the father one could guarantee fulfilment of God's will."

[2] *Cat XX*, 47 and *Ch* I, 55, 1f., where it was possible to translate the verb ἀτενίζω literally—cf. also *Ch* I, 28, 24f.

> Christ, I have never reckoned at all that orders came to me from him, but
> from God. Hence, father John, I stood in prayer to God, not as in front of
> a table at which men were eating, but as in front of God's altar . . .

Here we have evidence of a conscious and deliberate intention to regard
as an "icon of Christ" the hegumen, who was also the monk's spiritual
father and pastor. The effect this had on the relationship is made clear in
the next words of the reply: "I conceived no evil thought at all against the
pastor, because of my faith in him and my love for him."[3] Once a disciple has come to look on his father in this way, it is natural for him to welcome every command as coming from God and to obey it gladly as a
means of expressing faith and love.

When thus formulated, the concept of the spiritual father as an icon
may appear particularly characteristic of the theology of the Orthodox
Church, but ideas closely akin to it are found elsewhere. For instance, it
has been remarked that in Judaism

> the father has a godlike status in reference to the son, and the honour paid
> to parents is a form of the honour paid to God . . . When a professional class
> of teachers comes into existence we find them assuming this divine father-
> son relationship as the basis of their teaching.[4]

In the Western Church it is easy to find expressions not very different in
meaning from those of Climacus' monk, although the word "icon" is
absent from them. Cardinal Manning described how,

> [St. Charles Borromeo's] confessor was with him in retreat; and as he passed
> through his chamber, while he was yet sleeping, he would make a reverence
> to him, in honour of our Lord, whom he regarded in his person.[5]

Fénelon could write to a spiritual child: "Look upon me as the humble
instrument of God, seeing in me but Him alone,"[6] while Grou insisted
that having once made choice of a director, we must "regard him always
in a spirit of faith, as representing Jesus Christ to us."[7]

In the light of these examples, it is strange that Graef, in her assessment
of Symeon's understanding of spiritual direction, should have criticised
him for exaggerating the respect due to the father. She noted that

---

[3] *Sc. Par.* 4, 692B, and cf. *ibid.*, 709A.

[4] P. Carrington, *The Primitive Christian Catechism*, Cambridge, 1940, p. 4 (footnotes 2
and 6 provide examples); cf. also G.A.F. Knight, *A Christian Theology of the Old Testament*,
London, 1959, p. 70 for Biblical instances of the idea of God's presence in human persons.

[5] H.E. Manning, *Sermons on Ecclesiastical Subjects*, I, 331, Dublin, 1863.

[6] F. Fénelon, letter of 21 April 1707, *Correspondance de Fénelon*, Louvain, 1828, IV, 662.

[7] N. Grou, *Meditations on the Love of God*, originally published 1796, London, 1960,
p. 107.

Symeon elaborates this identification of the spiritual director with Christ at great length in catechesis 20.

While she did indeed admit that ''most spiritual writers recommend a religious to see Christ in his superior,'' she maintained this to be ''mostly no more than a matter of obedience,'' whereas

> in the view—and the life—of Symeon the spiritual father occupies a very different place from that of the lawful superior: he is the personal choice of the monk and receives his absolute devotion . . . But . . . if [absolute devotion] is given to a personally chosen director, the mortal man may only too easily be identified with Christ in a way that can even be detrimental to the spiritual life.[8]

It would be interesting to know whether Graef would also have levelled the same kind of criticism at St. Charles Borromeo, Fénelon and Grou, but in any case, so far as Symeon is concerned, it is based on a misunderstanding. Ware explains that

> an icon is in no sense identical with that which it depicts . . . It is the function of an icon to make present a spiritual reality which surpasses it, but of which it acts as the sign.[9]

This is very far from the crude identification to which Graef was rightly opposed, but which she unfairly imputed to Symeon, because his words must be understood in the light of the theology of icons, which was part of the tradition in which he lived, thought, wrote and acted.

Clearly, if there is to be an effective relationship between a spiritual father and his clients, the latter must be willing to be obedient. But the motive for obedience is immeasurably strengthened if the father is looked upon as being an ''icon of Christ,'' for then one can be certain that by obeying him one can ''guarantee the fulfilment of God's will.'' Obedience can then become a joy under all circumstances, since, like Climacus' monk, one will never conceive any ''evil thought at all against [one's] pastor.'' In exhortations to obedience directed towards disciples, the words ''as to God''[10] or ''as to Christ'' are common, and the conception underlying this terminology must be taken into account. If the father is regarded as an icon, he is not being considered as the representative of an absent

---

[8] H. Graef, 'Spiritual Director,' p. 610.

[9] K. Ware, 'Man, Woman, and the Priesthood of Christ,' *Man, Woman, and Priesthood*, (ed. P. Moore), London, 1978, pp. 80f.

[10] e.g. *Cat III*, 216f., *Cat XX*, 47, and *Tr Eth IV*, 153f. which reappears at *Ch* I, 61, 23f. Strictly speaking, only Christ can be an icon of God (*Colossians* 1. 15), but he, in virtue of the incarnation, may be portrayed in icons. Thus in these examples one should perhaps say that obedience is demanded to the father, the icon of Christ, who is himself the icon of God.

Christ, and he is definitely not being personally identified with Christ, but he is understood to be the means whereby Christ, who is of course entitled to demand obedience, is effectively made present to a spiritual child.

It would be too much to claim that wherever there are found appeals to obey a spiritual father as the mouthpiece of God or of Christ, this iconic conception must always underlie what is said. Nevertheless, there can be found amongst Symeon's writings an interesting passage which suggests that he had, more or less unconsciously, adopted the idea as an established background presupposition, by the time he came to compose some at any rate of his works. Apart from unimportant minor variations, the same words occur in two places:

> Men who, in fear and trembling, have laid the good foundation of faith and hope on a rock of obedience to their spiritual fathers, and who then, never doubting, build on this foundation of submission whatever their fathers enjoin them, as though it issued from the mouth of God—these are they who straightway succeed in denying themselves.[11]

This sentence is full of the Biblical echoes with which Symeon's writings abound, and of these we must concern ourselves at present with the image of the foundation being laid upon the rock. The well-known words addressed by Christ to St. Peter[12] do not seem to have influenced Symeon here, but "rocks" and "foundations" also make their appearance elsewhere in the New Testament. Thus in what is called the Sermon on the Plain in *St. Luke's Gospel*, anyone who both hears and performs the words of Jesus is said to resemble a man building a house who "dug deep and laid a foundation on the rock."[13] Here is what was evidently in the background of Symeon's consciousness when he penned the words we have quoted, and the significance of this emerges as we consider his use of the Gospel image. Christ, as teacher, had used the rock as an illustration of the right place for a good foundation, in order to encourage his hearers to build their lives on the basis of obedience to his own words; according to Symeon, the foundation was to be laid "on a rock of obedience" to the spiritual father, an icon, as it were, of Christ, who himself is several times in Scripture[14] referred to as a rock. The extent to which the concept of the spiritual father as an "icon of Christ" had penetrated Symeon's thinking is shown by his transferring, without explanation or

---

[11] *Tr Eth IV*, 151–156, *Ch* I, 61, 20–28.
[12] *St. Matthew* 16. 18.
[13] *St. Luke* 6. 47f.—ἔθηκε θεμέλιον ἐπὶ τὴν πέτραν (the parallel passage in *St. Matthew* 7. 24 does not mention the laying of a foundation).
[14] *I Corinthians*, 10. 4 is a good instance.

apology, the image of the rock from one context to the other. Because in his eyes the spiritual father represented Christ and this had become for him an unquestioned presupposition, he felt no need to justify his novel use of the image.

Compared with the lengthy and explicit identification of which Graef complained in *Cat XX*, the passage we have now examined reveals an even deeper appropriation by Symeon of the notion that a spiritual child ought to regard his father as an icon. Though he is shy of using the actual word, it is a concept which enables us properly to understand many of his expressions.[15] Furthermore, in the light of what we know about Symeon's devotion to the Studite, we can justifiably maintain that herein once more we have an example of how facets of his thought and teaching are to be seen as springing not only from his acceptance of tradition, but also from his personal experience as an obedient disciple.

Obedience, Submission and Elimination of the Will

In one of the homilies of Antiochus the Monk, who died at a date subsequent to 619 A.D., there is a sentence which may be freely translated as follows:

> Obedience (ὑπακοή) is entire submission (ὑποταγή), when one no longer has any will of one's own, and is moved solely by the bidding of one's superior calmly to undertake any activity, whatever he commands.[16]

The attitude here portrayed is the natural consequence of regarding one's spiritual father as an icon of Christ, the topic we have just discussed. The sentence thus serves as a link, since it is a useful introduction to the present section, bringing in the two key terms ὑπακοή and ὑποταγή, and mentioning the abandonment of one's own will, a theme with which they are closely connected and which is also to be looked at here.

Obedience and Submission

Numerous anecdotes illustrate the quality of the obedience which was demanded from their disciples. A good example is provided by Chitty, who recounts an incident concerning Silvanus and his disciple Mark.

---

[15] e.g. ὡς αὐτὸν τὸν Χριστὸν καὶ λαλῶν, οὕτω σεβάσθητι αὐτὸν [sc. your spiritual father] ..., *Cat XX*, 60f. Völker, *Praxis*, pp. 117–122, notes Symeon's emphasis on viewing the father as Christ, referring, like Graef, to *Cat XX*, and citing also *Ch* I, 28, where there is a description of the disciple's joy in seeing and conversing with his fahter, once he has acquired true faith in him so that "when he sees him, he reckons that he is seeing Christ."

[16] Antiochus, *PG* 89, 1556B—for date, v. Lampe, *Lexicon*, p. XIII.

Silvanus, in order to justify to some visitors the favour he showed Mark, summoned all his disciples by knocking on the doors of their cells. Mark was the only one to respond without even a moment's delay, and he was then sent off on some errand. In his absence, Silvanus and those with him entered the cell and could observe that Mark, a calligrapher, had obeyed his father's summons so promptly that he had not even completed the *omega* he had been in the act of writing.[17] The story indeed implies that such immediate obedience was exceptional, but as an ideal it can readily be understood to be the natural consequence of the spiritual child's in a real sense regarding his father as invested with all the authority of Christ.

When the scene is shifted to more formally established cenobitic types of monastic life, obedience naturally acquires certain disciplinary overtones as far as the superior is concerned, but from the point of view of the monk as spiritual child, it never ceases to be an important personal obligation. Thus, in Völker's words, "with Basil there are manifested the outlines of a life controlled and shaped by ὑπακοή."[18] Dorotheus of Gaza at first sight may appear somewhat different, for

> the word ὑπακοή is found some ten times in his *Doctrinae*, but most frequently with reference either to God's commandments or in a mere passing mention.

Despite this,

> it is easy to ascertain from [Dorotheus'] teaching the interest he has in it. This is shown as much by his treating the elimination of one's own will as something essential, as by the primary importance attached to humility. Humility produces obedience, and Dorotheus holds these two virtues to be inseparable.[19]

Climacus devotes to obedience the whole of the very lengthy *Sc. Par.* 4, and emphasises its importance for those living in community, where indeed he implies that it is most likely to be learnt.[20]

As we approach the background of Symeon and his spiritual father, it is worth remarking that Theodore the Studite, who was greatly influenced by Dorotheus,[21] followed him in associating obedience with humility. As Hussey puts it,

> he ... emphasized absolute obedience in the common life, stressing the

---

[17] D.J. Chitty, *The Desert a City*, Oxford, 1966, pp. 71f., referring to *PG* 65, 293D–296A.

[18] W. Völker, *Scala Paradisi: Eine Studie zu Johannes Climacus und zugleich eine Vorstudie zu Symeon dem Neuen Theologen*, Wiesbaden, 1968, p. 28.

[19] Regnault and de Préville, *SC* 92, intr. p. 69, inc. n. 1.

[20] *Sc. Par.* 4, 677C–728C; v. 728B for reference to community life.

[21] Regnault and de Préville, *op. cit.*, intr. pp. 91f. and p. 69.

responsibilities of the abbot both in administration and in spiritual direction.[22]

This was true of Theodore, but we have already discovered that the common life was much less significant in the eyes both of the Studite and of Symeon his disciple; moreover while they were in no doubt as to the necessity for entire obedience on the part of a spiritual child, the one in his teaching, and the other at least through his own actual behaviour, made it plain that for monks the father in question might sometimes be a person other than the hegumen. Furthermore, it may justifiably be asserted that both Symeon and the Studite were concerned that the father should be obeyed because of the spiritual authority belonging to him, rather than because he actually held some official ecclesiastical position. What Darrouzès has stated with regard to Symeon holds true also as regards his spiritual father,

> a true master is one who has received the illumination of the Spirit . . . and not simply one who is hierarchically a superior.[23]

As one might expect, Symeon himself is attested as having been obedient and submissive to the Studite. Nicetas, though without using these precise words, amply conveys their meaning in his portrayal of his hero's early days in the monastery. After recounting the Studite's injunctions he continues,

> Symeon listened to these words as if they were proceeding from the mouth of God, and he followed them to the letter . . . Having once and for all made himself a slave to the elder, he did everything with eagerness, . . . for even if ordered to cast himself into a furnace of fire or into the depths of the sea, he was prepared to do so joyfully and eagerly.[24]

For himself Symeon claimed that the account he had given of his relations with the Studite demonstrated *inter alia* his "obedience" and "submission",[25] and on another occasion he explained how, when bidden to do so, he would eat albeit unwillingly, "for I was afraid of being judged disobedient." This explanation comes a few lines after the statement that his father observed him unhesitatingly accomplishing his orders and nothing but them.[26] Thus, even though Nicetas' language was more extravagant, what he wrote with regard to Symeon's obedience and submission was in

---

[22] J.M. Hussey, *The Byzantine World*, London, 1st edit. 1957, pp. 117f.

[23] Darrouzès, *SC* 51, p. 67, n. 3, but cf. what will be said in the next chapter about Symeon's practice as hegumen.

[24] Nicetas, *Life*, 12, 1–7 (extracts).

[25] *Cat XXXV*, 262f.

[26] *Cat XVI*, 18–23.

essence no different from the claims which Symeon made for himself. At the same time, it is noteworthy that while in Nicetas' record we find the concept of the father's orders being accepted as coming from God, somewhat surprisingly there appears to be no instance in Symeon's own writings of an explicit statement that this was the ground of his obedience. There is, however, but in a different context, an approximation to the idea, when the Studite is said to have received "in himself the totality, so to speak, of the Paraclete," a gift which he then transmitted to his disciple, Symeon.[27]

As one might expect, the obedience and submission which tradition demanded of spiritual children was inculcated in his teaching by Symeon, who himself had so eagerly obeyed and submitted to the Studite. In one *Catechesis* he reminded his monks that in the vows which they made on receiving the habit, they had promised "to submit themselves to their spiritual father as to God." This is interesting in that according to the Rite the promise does not actually contain the phrase, "as to God,"[28] so that its inclusion is perhaps an unconscious but revealing slip on the part of Symeon. Moreover, since it is to the hegumen as spiritual father that the promise is made, his appeal to this vow is a further piece of evidence that Symeon did regard the hegumen as normally occupying this position vis-à-vis a monk, in spite of his own refusal to act accordingly when in Studios.

Symeon's realism manifested itself in an awareness that at times obedience might seem distasteful and could involve a person in acting contrary to his own apparent interests. Thus, he firmly advised the novice, whom he purported to be addressing, that having found the right spiritual father,

> you ought to obey him as if he were God himself, and unhesitatingly accomplish what he tells you, even if in your opinion the things he orders appear contrary to your interests and injurious to you.[29]

The implication here is that, unpleasant though his father's orders may seem, a disciple will be able to fulfil them if reminded that they originate from one who for him occupies the place of God. Elsewhere Symeon added to this thought a reminder of the obedience which Christ himself displayed, and so supplied spiritual children with an additional motive for obeying. For example after *Ch* I, 61, in which he equated obedience to the

---

[27] *Cat VI*, 263–267.

[28] *Cat III*, 216f., cf. *Euchologion*, ed. Zerbos, Venice, 1891, pp. 191 and 207 (in *Cat III*, 143–157, Symeon's quotations show that the Rite he knew was almost word for word the same as in Zerbos' edition).

[29] *Cat XX*, 46–50; cf. for very similar teaching, Climacus, *Sc. Par.* 4, 717B.

spiritual father with obedience to God, he wrote in the next *Chapter* of a
disciple who is refractory and of one who humbles himself, and described
the latter as

> becoming like the Son of God who was utterly obedient to his Father,
> accepting even death, death on a cross.[30]

Incidentally, this reminiscence of *Philippians* 2. 8 recurs in Nicetas' *Centuries*, and were it not a rather obvious text to cite in this connection, it
would be tempting to suggest that in using it he was consciously indebted
to Symeon.[31]

Not only, in accordance with Symeon's teaching, was a spiritual child
expected to obey whatever orders his father might give him, but he was
also instructed not to take any initiative without being bidden.

> Do not ask [your spiritual father] to allow you to keep anything, either small
> or great, [out of your wordly possessions], but let him of his own accord
> decide either to tell you to take something or else give you it with his own
> hand.[32]

Similarly,

> unless you have your father in God's permission, do not give alms of the
> money you have brought with you . . . It is the mark of a pure faith to let
> everything be decided by the spiritual father, as though leaving it in the
> hands of God.[33]

On the same basis, a disciple was not to ask to be allowed to eat or drink;
he was enjoined to wait until the father was inspired to give permission,
however much suffering this endurance might entail.[34]

Now in the last chapter we found that a stage ought to be reached at
which the spiritual child progresses from the tutelage of his director to an
immediate relationship with God, but it must here be observed that even
the total dependence on one's father, which Symeon clearly inculcated,
was itself for him a mark of maturity. In *Tr Eth IV*, as Völker pointed out,
he spoke of "conscious submission (ὑποταγὴ μετὰ γνώσεως)," which he
insisted was an essential component of the "measure of the stature of the
fulness of Christ."[35] In this sense, however it worked out in practice,
even the entire surrender of one's own will was for Symeon a significant

---

[30] *Ch* I, 62—the last two lines being quoted in full.
[31] Nicetas, *Centuries*, II, 54, *PG* 120, 925BC.
[32] *Ch* I, 24, 25–27.
[33] *ibid.*, I, 25, 1–7; cf. Basil's teaching that "true and perfect obedience" includes
"not even doing what is good unless [the superior] so decides," *Ascetica*, *PG* 31, 884BC.
[34] *ibid.*, I, 26, 8–15, and 27, 16–22.
[35] Völker, *Praxis*, p. 118; v. *Tr Eth IV*, 369–375, with its allusion to *Ephesians* 4. 13.

token of Christian adulthood. It was the logical consequence not only of regarding the spiritual father as the icon of Christ, but also of coming to believe—as Symeon had done—that through him one could be initiated, while still on earth, into a personal and living relationship with God.

There is a further matter connected with this absolute obedience which must be mentioned before we leave the subject: in Symeon's estimation it played a most important part in providing for a continual succession of spiritual fathers.

> If [your father] says to you, 'Come into the land of obedience which I will show you,' then put forth all your strength, my brother, and run. Do not give sleep to your eyes, and do not bend your knee or faint through sluggishness or slackness. It may be indeed that there God will reveal himself to you, God who intends to proclaim you the father of many spiritual children, and to give you the promised land which none but the righteous shall inherit.[36]

These lines with their Biblical echoes, echoes above all of the story of Abraham, are quite explicit: it is the disciple who is quick to learn obedience who may expect in due course to become himself the father of future spiritual children. We have noticed that there is evidence to suggest that spiritual fathers would pick out one or more of their disciples as potential successors,[37] and this passage suggests that promptness in learning the lesson of obedience was one of the criteria in accordance with which the selection was made. At the same time, the image of "the promised land" is one more reminder that swift and total obedience was required not as an end in itself, but as a necessary means for attaining a deeper personal experience of fellowship with God.

Elimination of the Will

It is appropriate to discuss this subject here, since references to it are very frequently found in close conjunction with the theme of obedience. A good example occurs in some lines in the *Life* of St. Romylus, which are very apposite, even though coming from a period much later than the time of Symeon.

> If another elder's disciple, overpowered perhaps by [the temptation] to contradict or disobey or by some other [disordered] passion, had been sent to him to be corrected, [Romylus] would speak to him in words such as these, 'My beloved brother, the way along which you are travelling is that of the apostles. Thus, the same reverence which they had for Jesus Christ our Lord and God, each of us ought to have for his [spiritual] father, renouncing his own will once and for all, as the Lord himself taught us ...'

---

[36] *Cat XX*, 65–71; for the reference to Abraham, cf. *Genesis* 12. 1, and 17. 4f.
[37] v. chapter VI, pp. 93–95.

A little later in the same address which he used to deliver to the erring, Romylus would speak of "consciously enduring the elimination of one's own will (τὴν ἐκκοπὴν τοῦ οἰκείου θελήματος μετὰ γνώσεως ὑπομένων)."[38] Here the will and its renunciation appear in the context of the obedience due to a spiritual father, with once again the implied suggestion that he is in some way to be looked upon as Christ. It is also noteworthy that while Symeon wished submission to be "conscious"—and thus mature—, the same demand was made by Romylus with regard to the elimination of the will.

The importance of eliminating one's own will had been recognised long before the time of Symeon, as was demonstrated by the reference to it in the preceding sub-section when we mentioned Dorotheus of Gaza. But Dorotheus himself relied on earlier authority, for he quoted Poemen, the Desert Father.[39]

Dorotheus in one place suggested a method of self-help, "if . . . we wish to be completely set free and liberated . . . :" a person who notices something and begins to think of fixing his attention on it, should say to himself, "Indeed, I will not do so."[40] But although he recommended this method, in the address in which he cited Poemen Dorotheus remarked that

> the soul is in a state of safety when it reveals everything [that occurs to it] and is told by someone who possesses knowledge, 'Do this; do not do that.'[41]

Here, although indirectly expressed, what he enjoined on the disciple amounted to obedience together with the disclosure of thoughts, while a little earlier he had laid down the principle that

> when a person renounces his own will, it is then that he beholds the way of God which is undefiled.[42]

Doubtless Dorotheus was right in teaching that the elimination of one's own will is something that can be assisted by self-help, but for the goal really to be attained, it seems reasonable to hold that there will be a need for assistance from a spiritual father to whom absolute obedience has been promised.

---

[38] F. Halkin, 'The Greek Life of St. Romylus,' *Byzantion*, 31, (1961), pp. 139f. (Romylus belongs to the 14th century); on ἐκκοπὴ θελήματος, v. Glossary; for its connection with submission, cf. Theodore of Studios, οὗ κοπὴ θελήματος, ἐκεῖ ὑποταγῆς τελείωσις, *PG* 99, 836B.

[39] *Doctrinae*, V, 62, 16–21, 63, 1f., referring to Poemen, *PG* 65, 333D–336A; Ward, *Desert Fathers*, pp. 43f., nos. 152 and 156, gives other examples from the epoch.

[40] *Doctrinae*, I, 20–33.

[41] *ibid.*, V, 64, 14–16.

[42] *ibid.*, V, 63, 8f.

There are also several references to ἐκκοπὴ θελήματος in Climacus, and from the point of view of the link between it and obedience we should particularly notice how he encouraged the disciple to:

Take up your cross, carrying it by means of obedience, and firmly enduring the weight of the elimination of your will.[43]

When, therefore, Symeon gave teaching along the same lines, he was in no sense innovating. Moreover, when he spoke of "complete mortification (ἀπονέκρωσις) of one's own will," it is interesting to note that he cited a sentence written by the Studite, in which the subject is connected, not with obedience but with "complete withdrawal from the world."[44] The little that survives and is readily available out of the writings of Symeon's spiritual father does not, in fact, include any further direct references to eliminating or mortifying the will.

Whether or not this was a matter on which the Studite laid much stress, Symeon had both learnt about it from the general ascetical tradition, and had also gained personal experience of the benefits of the practice. He himself related how, when he had been restored after the period in which he had been a backslider, he began again to be granted some vision of the divine light, albeit nothing so wonderful as that which he had originally experienced. Yet even this, he affirmed, was won only by "much toil, many tears . . . and perfect obedience and complete elimination of my own will."[45] Thus although Symeon had certainly met with passages in Climacus, and probably elsewhere, in which obedience was placed beside the elimination of the will, it was with the authority which springs from personal experience that he came to associate the two in his teaching. It might be objected that his claim to have been entirely obedient can be neither proved nor disproved, and was perhaps made in any case primarily in order to edify his monastic hearers, but the reference to "much toil, many tears" has about it a flavour of authenticity which makes it reasonable to hold that his choice of words was based on something more than a desire faithfully to reproduce inherited tradition. This need not invalidate what was said in chapter II about the possibility that out of a concern to keep his monks from belittling the seriousness of a failure to respond appropriately to the grace of God, he said that his efforts had been rewarded by nothing more than his being allowed to "see in some obscure fashion a small and scanty ray of that most sweet divine light."[46]

---

[43] *Sc. Par.* 27, 1100D–1101A; cf. als *ibid.*, 2, 657A, and 4, 704D.
[44] *Ch* 127, *PG* 120, 672C, quoted *Cat VI*, 271–273.
[45] *Cat XXII*, 312–314.
[46] *ibid.*, 316–318; cf. p. 11.

Nicetas provides further support for the view that Symeon, besides becoming familiar with traditional beliefs concerning the importance of eliminating one's own will, had himself undergone this discipline in the course of his training. In the *Life*, at the point where some details are about to be given of the Studite's methods, we read that "the elder wished to eliminate his will . . ."[47] A spiritual father would in any case certainly have entertained such a purpose, and so there is no need to suspect Nicetas' words. But since, though trustworthy in many respects, he was after all writing hagiography, it is fortunate that on this question his evidence need be introduced as no more than additional confirmation of the testimony of Symeon himself.

Some lines near the beginning of *Cat XX* indicate something of the meaning Symeon gave to this concept in his teaching, while they also reveal the importance he ascribed to it. Having spoken of the physical martyrdoms which many in earlier generations had had to endure, he continued:

> But now, since by the grace of Christ we are in a season of profound and perfect peace, we can be assured that crucifixion and death mean nothing other than complete mortification of one's own will—for he who, in however small a degree, fulfils his own will, will never be enabled to observe the ordinate of our Saviour Christ.[48]

Positively, therefore, ἐκκοπὴ θελήματος was in Symeon's eyes the equivalent of the sufferings which the martyrs had had to endure, and by means of which they had been privileged to share in some way in the passion of Christ himself; negatively, as he put it a few lines further on, it was to be reckoned a way of escaping from "living by self-direction (ἰδιορρύθμως) and gathering in the worthless fruits of one's own will."[49] Hence he portrayed the spiritual father as calling to his child:

> Come out from the land of your own will and from the kindred of your own way of thinking.[50]

In this way Symeon made it clear that he wished his disciples to look on the elimination of their own wills, painful though the process would be, as essentially liberation rather than bondage, its purpose being to make it possible for the Christian to devote himself without reserve to obeying God, "whose service is perfect freedom."[51]

---

[47] *Life*, 12, 10 (ὁ δὲ γέρων ἐκκόπτειν θέλων τὸ ἐκείνου θέλημα . . .).
[48] *Cat XX*, 39–43.
[49] *ibid.*, 53f.
[50] *ibid.*, 62–64.
[51] v. second collect at Matins, Book of Common Prayer; cf. Symeon's phrase, εὐπρόθυμος δουλεία, *Tr Eth IV*, 375. 52. *Hymn XXX*, 557–567.

The importance he attached to this area of the spiritual child's obligations is further shown by the fact that Symeon in one of his *Hymns* made
the elimination of the will the climax of a long series of good practices
which he commended—perfect obedience, it is significant, immediately
preceding it.[52] He was, however, far from attempting to hide the far-
reaching and costly nature of what was demanded by such self-surrender.

> A man must, if he is in earnest, renounce his own soul, and this is effected
> by mortification of his will. I am speaking here not only of external matters,
> such as not eating, not drinking, not undertaking anything on an impulse,
> not sleeping, not doing anything that may seem good without being ordered,
> but I also include [mortification] of the interior movement of the heart, such
> as not gazing at anything in a passionate manner . . .[53]

Here we have returned, in a sense, to Dorotheus' suggested ways of self-
help, since although a father, by the orders he gives to an obedient disciple, can promote the elimination of the will so far as external actions are
concerned, the inner sphere of the heart and mind can be controlled only
by each person for himself, with the help of God.

We have remarked how Symeon seems at times to have expected more
from his monks than was realistic in the light of an objective assessment
of the background and temperament of many of them. But he does appear
to have recognised, no doubt regretfully, that genuine ἐκκοπὴ θελήματος
would always be somewhat rare, for

> many renounce this life and its affairs, but only a few renounce their own
> wills.

This state of affairs he saw as a fulfilment of the text, "Many are called,
but few are chosen."[54] Nevertheless, as the examples given have demonstrated, Symeon had no doubt that a disciple *ought* to offer his spiritual
father total obedience and submission of a kind which was bound to result
in the elimination of his own will.

This again, however, he did not reckon to be an end in itself, for in
accordance with tradition Symeon held that his monastic disciples, by
being perfectly obedient to himself, their hegumen and spiritual father,
would most certainly be fulfilling the will of Christ. Thus, when in one
of his *Hymns* he wrote of how he was comforted by Christ in the troubles
and difficulties he had to face in his relationships with some of his monks,
the words which he believed that the Lord addressed to him included:

---

[52] *Hymn XXX*, 557–567.
[53] *Tr Eth VI*, 63–69 (Darrouzès in a note *ad loc.* explains that ψυχή, "*l'âme dont il s'agit
ici . . . désigne surtout la volonté et les sentiments de l'individu*").
[54] *Ch I*, 31, 25–28; *St. Matthew* 22. 14.

> If they do not become dead to their own wills and live in this present life in accordance with your will, fulfilling my will through yours, still you will not lose your reward . . .[55]

With the concept in these lines that it is the will of Christ which is mediated by a spiritual father to his children, we have returned very nearly to the idea of the father as an icon. When the disciple, after the elimination of his own will, replaces it by that of his father, it is to Christ that he must be understood as surrendering himself, and all Christians would, theoretically at least, acknowledge self-surrender to Christ as being a duty to which they have pledged themselves. According to the tradition into which Symeon entered and which he strove to uphold, one way of implementing this pledge is by submitting unreservedly to a spiritual father, and thus "fulfilling [Christ's] will through [his]."

Further Obligations

The duties we have been investigating clearly presuppose that the disciple will have a deep reverence for his spiritual father and an unswerving trust in him. These attitudes, and certain consequences which follow from them, must next be considered.

Trust/Faith/Confidence

Conscious and willing submission is scarcely possible unless one has what may variously be called trust, faith or confidence in the person to whom one is submitting. Rousseau, having referred to Cassian's account of the obedience displayed by John of Lycopolis when "the most daunting tasks [were] imposed upon him" by his spiritual father, commented that

> such confidence could be based only on an intimate knowledge of a spiritual director.[56]

Although doubtless such intimate knowledge will frequently be found, it should not really be reckoned as essential. In fact, the trusting attitude which leads to entire obedience may well depend upon a belief that one has been guided by God to one's spiritual father, who must in consequence be regarded as invested with divine authority and so unquestioningly obeyed. Cassian's own words are instructive: he represents John's father as testing him in order to discover whether his obedience

---

[55] *Hymn XLI*, 157–159; cf. Symeon's appeal in *Cat XII*, 254–259.
[56] Rousseau, *Ascetics*, p. 195.

came from true faith and deep simplicity of heart, or whether it was feigned
and somehow forced, and manifested only when it could be seen by the person who gave him an order.[57]

What is essential as the prerequisite of obedience is the kind of trust or
confidence, which is both genuine and also rooted in a theological understanding of the relationship between a disciple and his spiritual father.

There is no need to pause for comment on Climacus, who enjoined faith
in one's father, coupling it with love (ἀγάπη).[58] With the Studite on the
other hand we must spend longer, since we may profitably cite his vivid
portrayal of the relationship we are studying. After insisting that every
thought (λογισμός) should be revealed to the spiritual father, he proceeded to give the following orders and advice:

> Receive with complete trustfulness (πληροφορία) what [your father] says
> to you, as though it proceeded from a divine mouth. Do not divulge it to
> anyone else by saying, for example, 'When I asked my father such-and-such
> a question, this is what he said to me.' And do not add, 'Did he set it
> forth well, or not?' and 'What then ought I to do to obtain healing [for my
> spirit]?' Such remarks are filled to overflowing with distrust (ἀπιστία) of
> one's father, and inflict injuries on the soul, something which often occurs
> with novices.[59]

Here we are given what is almost a little sketch of an inexperienced and
indiscreet novice, as he returns from a conference with his spiritual father
and encounters another monk. There is no difficulty in supposing that
anyone who, like the Studite, lived in a cenobitic monastery might more
than once have happened to witness an encounter of this nature. At first,
perhaps, the novice wishes simply to talk about the interview, but gradually he seems to sense that his report of his father's words is engendering
certain doubts in the mind of the man to whom he is speaking. Thereupon
his own confidence begins to wane, and he is led to ask two questions typical of a doubter. One can well appreciate that a novice, by yielding to the
temptation to frame such questions, might unconsciously decrease his
own faith in his father. As confidence is essential to the relationship, the
Studite therefore felt it necessary to set down for his readers this warning
against what would undermine it, the thoughtless repeating to others of
words that should be received with unquestioning faith, as if coming from
the mouth of God.

Nicetas, who was concerned amongst other things to portray the relationship Symeon and the Studite as a model of that which should obtain

---

[57] Cassian, *Institutes*, IV, 24, *C.S.E.L.*, XVII, p. 63.
[58] *Sc. Par.* 4, 705A.
[59] *Ch* 122, 669C.

between spiritual father and child, naturally praised the trust or faith which his hero manifested.[60] But although this might be suspected as being merely what was required by the conventions of hagiography, the fact is that Symeon himself had no hesitation in more than once putting forward such a claim on his own behalf. In the light of the controversy in which he was involved because of his cult of the Studite, a sentence in *Tr Eth IX* is particularly significant.

> Our trust in him was confirmed by the revelation of the Spirit within him, and we maintain it in the face of all objections.[61]

However, the conflict with Stephen of Nicomedia was not the only occasion when Symeon was involved in controversy in connection with his spiritual father, for it will be remembered that during his time in the Studios monastery great efforts were made to induce him to abandon the Studite. When in *Cat XXXVI* he described this earlier time of trouble and the criticisms he had had to face, he made it clear by implication that he had continued loyal because of his great trust in his father.[62]

In the light of all this, it is not unreasonable to suggest that, once more, we can see Symeon's personal experience colouring his teaching when we meet with an exhortation such as the following:

> Even if the whole world reviles and abuses [your spiritual father], you must have a faith in him which does not waver ...[63]

Again, in *Cat XX*, in the course of the passage in which he described the relationship in terms of that between Christ and his disciples as recounted in the Gospels,[64] Symeon envisaged the possibility that threats to the father might lead a spiritual child to behave like Peter and deny him; in the same context, indeed, we find the exaggerated suggestion that a disciple might witness his spiritual father being crucified, in which case:

> If you can, die with him; but if you cannot, do not join with the wicked and so become both wicked and a traitor, and do not be a partner of theirs in [shedding] innocent blood. By being a coward and a fainthart you will for a while have deserted your pastor, but still you must retain your faith in him.[65]

---

[60] *Life*, 12, 19 (ἡ πρὸς τὸν πατέρα πίστις).

[61] *Tr Eth IX*, 251–253 (Darrouzès in a note *ad loc.* assigns this work to "the period of the controversies, about 1005"); cf. also *Cat XXXVI*, 75 and *Hymn LV*, 96.

[62] *Cat XXXVI*, 99–125, in which the actual word πίστις refers to faith in God, although the passage as a whole is a description of the failure of attempts to persuade Symeon to give up being a disciple of the Studite.

[63] *Cat XXVI*, 303f.

[64] *Cat XX*, 78–160.

[65] *ibid.*, 145–149.

This is very interesting in that it reveals Symeon's realistic awareness that a disciple may temporarily fail to be loyal, without this resulting in an inevitable loss of confidence in his father. Such a lapse could somehow be tolerated since it would be the result of weakness and thus less heinous than deliberate and permanent disloyalty, but of course what ought really to be manifested is a "sincere and unwavering trust"[66] in one's father. It is this that he wished to be cultivated, since it would be proof against any temptations which might assail one when rebuked, for Symeon was clear-sighted in his perception of the risk of a spiritual child's succumbing to "distrust (ἀπιστία)," a potentially dangerous condition, as a result of being reproved.[67] The mention of the possibility of this happening in consequence of a rebuke leads us to consider the next requirement.

A Right Attitude when Rebuked

Symeon, as has just been mentioned, understood that it might be necessary to warn disciples not to cease from trusting spiritual fathers who reproved them. The need to give such warnings arises from the fact that when a father trains spiritual children along the lines set forth in the last chapter, there will almost inevitably be more or less frequent occasions on which he will have to rebuke them. When reproved, by no means all disciples will find it easy to react in the proper spirit, as exemplified by Arsenius in the account given by Nicetas.[68] It is therefore prudent to ensure that at least all are aware of the evil consequences which may follow upon wrong reactions.

Dorotheus showed considerable psychological insight in one of his remarks:

> If one is disquieted when reproved or corrected with regard to some passion, that is a sign that one was engaged in it of one's own free will; accepting reproof or correction concerning it without any disquiet is a sign that when engaged in it one was carried away, or ignorant of what was taking place.[69]

Here we have an implicit invitation to self-understanding, but no explicit guidance or statement of what is required of one when rebuked. The latter is supplied by Climacus:

> When our superior bestows on us honourable dishonour, reproof and punishment, let us call to mind the dread sentence of the Judge, and in this

---

[66] *Ep 3*, 213r.
[67] *Ch* I, 59, 26–33.
[68] Nicetas, *Life*, 47–51; cf. chapter VII, p. 142.
[69] Dorotheus, *Sententiae* 202, 18, 60–65.

way, making use of the two-edged sword of gentleness and endurance, we shall kill the unreasonable grief and bitterness which will certainly be sown in us.[70]

Climacus' words suggest that the spiritual child who is corrected will be tempted more to indulge in negative internal emotions than to display signs of open rebellion, although "bitterness" might eventually lead to this. In the same way, the "distrust" to which we found Symeon referring at the end of the last sub-section is also, in its initial stages, an internal matter.

Symeon, however, in the passage cited,[71] which is concerned with the dangerous temptations confronting the disciple whom his spiritual father has to admonish or reprove, actually put "contradicting" in front of "distrust".[72] If one contradicts, this is clearly a matter of one's outward behaviour, a failure to keep to the respectful manner of address which ought to characterize a spiritual child who has the right basic attitude towards his father. Although he does not specifically say this, it may well be that in placing "contradicting" first, Symeon pictured the disciple, irritated by a rebuke, immediately answering back in an unseemly fashion, and then later, in the course of his reflection on the incident, justifying himself by deciding that he had lost faith in his father.

Certainly, the dangers involved in behaviour of this kind were very real to Symeon. A little earlier he had written:

Nobody who believed that his life and death lay in his pastor's hand would ever contradict. Ignorance of this [truth] is what leads to contradiction, which itself causes spiritual (νοητός) and eternal death.[73]

Not only then did Symeon regard it as a grave fault to contradict or answer back, but he also considered such conduct to be symptomatic of a failure really to appreciate the ultimate purpose of attaching oneself to a spiritual father, namely the securing of one's salvation. In any case,

he who regards his teacher and guide as God, cannot contradict him. If he thinks and says that he is able to maintain the two [opposed attitudes], let him be well assured that he is mistaken, for he knows nothing of the attitude towards God manifested by those who belong to God.[74]

The outcome of the wrong attitude Symeon described when he wrote of the fate of a person guilty of contradicting or distrusting his spiritual father:

---

[70] Climacus, Sc. Par. 7, 805B.
[71] Ch I, 59, 26–33.
[72] τῇ ἀντιλογίᾳ καὶ ἀπιστίᾳ τῇ πρὸς τὸν πνευματικὸν πατέρα αὐτοῦ καὶ διδάσκαλον . . .
[73] ibid., I, 56, 4–7.
[74] ibid., I, 55, 1–4.

> He is miserably thrust down, while still alive, into the snare and pit of Hades, and becomes the dwelling-place of Satan and of all his unclean power, since he is a son of disobedience and perdition.[75]

We have already referred to, but must now quote in full, Symeon's succinct statement contrasting the right and wrong attitudes and their consequences:

> While the demons rejoice over anyone who contradicts his father, the angels marvel at anyone who humbles himself unto death, for such a one works the work of God, becoming like the Son of God who was utterly obedient to his Father, accepting even death, death on a cross.[76]

Willingness to receive rebukes humbly is a virtue one would expect to find in those who, whether monks or seculars, have sincerely and deliberately resolved to submit themselves to a spiritual father. However, since in his *Chapters*, which were composed primarily for monks, Symeon so emphatically castigated the tendency to answer back, it seems likely that he was aware of there being many in the monasteries who were guilty of offending in this way. This suggestion is confirmed by a passage in *Cat III*:

> If, . . . to put you to the test, the hegumen causes you some slight sorrow, you repudiate your very habit, saying, as I have heard many say, 'Did I come here to be somebody's slave? Am I here to be insulted?'[77]

Although in this case we have no explicit mention of a rebuke, there is every likelihood that monks of the type depicted would, when corrected, have given vent to their feelings in the sort of language they are here represented as using. Such monks caused Symeon a great deal of disappointment, for he felt that they had entered the monastery solely in order to gain material advantages.

> Your only motive in receiving the tonsure was to become a brother and get your share of goods and possessions which probably would never have been yours, had you remained in the world.[78]

It is reasonable to suppose that monks from such a background were men who would need many reminders about the proper attitude to adopt when rebuked, while they might well be persons of the very kind whose conduct would make them most liable to be reprimanded. Whether or not this is a correct supposition, it is certainly probable that Symeon wrote the

---

[75] *ibid.*, I, 59, 30–34, the last phrase having reminiscences of *Ephesians* 2. 2 and *St. John* 17. 12.

[76] *ibid.*, I, 62, 1–5, with reminiscences of *St. John* 6. 29 and *Philippians* 2. 8.

[77] *Cat III*, 124–128, "I have heard . . ." perhaps suggesting Symeon's experience before he became hegumen.

[78] *ibid.*, 105–107.

passages we have quoted from the *Chapters* in the light of his own experience as hegumen and spiritual father.[79]

Even when they are uttered by the best and most skilful of spiritual fathers, there is an inevitable paradox connected with reproofs: those who least require them will be most likely to accept them in the right spirit, while those who most need them will be liable to be resentful and answer back or contradict.

Refraining from Judging

A disciple, however, ought not to be satisfied with himself just because he never speaks to his spiritual father in an unbecoming way, tempted though he may be to answer back when reprimanded: he should not even entertain in his mind thoughts critical of his father, whatever may have provoked them.

We observed how Climacus advocated cunning and prudence in the choice of a spiritual father, but insisted that once chosen, he must not be subject to any further scrutiny by a disciple. In the same context he elaborated this prohibition as follows:

> When the thought of examining or condemning your guide comes upon you, recoil from it as from fornication, and give that serpent no leave to speak, no place, no entry, no starting-point. Say to the serpent, 'You deceiver, I have not been given the right to judge him who rules me, but it is his right to judge me; I have not been appointed his judge, but he has been appointed mine.[80]

The ban on judging is not to be understood as if Climacus wished to pretend that all spiritual fathers are in themselves perfect; what he saw to be at issue was the inner attitude of the spiritual child, since

> the Lord makes the blind eyes of the obedient quick to see the virtues of their teacher, while leaving his defects in darkness.[81]

Such blindness might indeed, Climacus implied, have at times to be deliberately cultivated by the disciple himself. Thus he recounted with approval an answer of John the Sabbaite, who on being asked what one ought to do if one's father were somewhat remiss, replied robustly:

> Even if you see him committing fornication, do not leave him, but address

---

[79] v. Darrouzès, *SC* 51, p. 49, n. 1, and p. 53, n. 1, for other instances of the *Chapters'* being coloured by Symeon's experience as hegumen.

[80] *Sc. Par.* 4, 681A.

[81] *ibid.*, 716D.

> to yourself the words, 'Friend, why are you here?' Then you will find boast-
> fulness vanishing from you, and the fire of lust being put out.[82]

Thus, if a spiritual child ever found himself in such an extreme situation,
Climacus, on the authority of "the great John," would prohibit him from
judging his father. This, though not stated explicitly, necessarily follows
from what is enjoined, for in the absence of a judgment on what he had
seen, the disciple could not decide to "leave him." The example is, in
fact, something of a *topos*, which Ware has traced back to the Desert
Fathers,[83] and which reappears in the Studite.[84] Given their preoccupation with physical chastity, it is not suprising that the writers with whom
we are concerned, when wishing to inculcate the lesson that one must
never presume to judge one's spiritual father, should have made use of a
hypothetical instance which involved his being detected in an act of sexual
misconduct.

Equally, it is not surprising that this same example was utilised by
Symeon to reinforce the same requirement, nor, in view of his devotion
to Scripture, is it remarkable that he quoted an obvious supporting text:

> If you yourself, with your own eyes, see [your spiritual father] committing
> fornication, do not be scandalized and do not let your faith in him be
> diminished. Act in obedience to the One who said, 'Judge not, and you will
> not be judged.'[85]

Nevertheless, although he followed tradition and included amongst the
demands made on a spiritual child this prohibition against judging,
Symeon was more concerned to stress the duty of faithfulness or loyalty
to one's father, the next obligation which we shall discuss.

Faithfulness/Loyalty

In practice there will inevitably be some blurring of the boundaries
between having and maintaining faith or confidence in a spiritual father,
refraining from judging him, and continuing loyal or faithful to him. This
blurring is well illustrated by the fact that the final quotation in the last
sub-section follows, as part of the same sentence, the injunction to hold

---

[82] *ibid.*, 724B, with 'Friend, . . .' quoted from *St. Matthew* 26. 50.

[83] K. Ware, 'The Spiritual Father in Orthodox Christianity,' *Cross Currents* XXIV,
(1974), p. 306.

[84] *Ch* 36, *Life*, p. L.

[85] *Cat XXVI*, 304–307, quoting *St. Luke* 6. 37; Symeon also used the same example in
Cat XVIII, 132–137, when forbidding a monk to set himself against the father who had
tonsured him. Graef, 'Spiritual Director,' p. 609, made far too much of the passage in
Cat XXVI, because she failed to realise that Symeon was simply employing a *topos*.

to one's "faith". This sentence, which includes the words, "even if the whole world reviles and abuses [your spiritual father]," thereby provides an example of Symeon's use of "faith" in the sense of "faithfulness".[86]

It would be natural to expect loyalty on the part of anyone who had once for all subjected himself to a spiritual father, and was resolved to regard him as an icon of Christ and to resist any temptation to judge him. In practice, however, faithfulness was not always in evidence, as may be deduced from a warning given by the Studite.

> You must not abandon one [spiritual father] for another through paying heed to the Enemy's suggestions that . . . you should go to someone else, for if we continue going to the first, we shall gain greater confidence in him . . . If we go to another spiritual [father]—something which indeed is not permissible—, should he belong to our own monastery, all our brethren will accuse us of having lost the confidence we once had in our former [father] . . . and even he to whom we [then] go will suspect that the same may happen with regard to him. We shall acquire the habit of transferring from one to another, and shall be ever seeking to make the acquaintance of stylites, anchorites or hesychasts in order to go and confess to them. Then, having lost confidence in them all, we shall end up making no progress and, worst of all, bringing a curse upon ourselves.[87]

Symeon did not literally follow this absolute and total prohibition of changing from one spiritual father to another, for he could envisage the possibility that, after praying for guidance, a disciple at an early stage might be sent by the Holy Spirit to a new director.[88] Nevertheless, when he enjoined loyalty and spoke of maintaining "your faith in [your spiritual father] . . . even if the whole world reviles and abuses him."[89] what he had in mind was this temptation to be unfaithful. Like his father, Symeon was concerned that spiritual children should resist it and overcome it, and his language suggests that he recalled how he himself had been tempted when having to listen to the critical comments which the Studite's behaviour excited.[90] Furthermore, in a paragraph in *Cat XX* which begins, "If [your spiritual father] bids you follow him, go boldly about the cities with him . . .," we find that Symeon gave the following advice to the disciple:

> If you see him eating with harlots and tax-collectors and sinners, think no passion-filled or merely human thought; rather let your mind think only of

---

[86] *Cat XXVI*, 303f., cf. p. 207.

[87] *Ch 36*, *Life*, p. L ("hesychasts", of course, does not here have its later 'technical' sense); cf. also Climacus, *Sc. Par.* 4, 709D–712A, "Do not flee away from the hands of him who brought you to the Lord."

[88] *Cat XX*, 54f.

[89] *Cat XXVI*, 303f.

[90] cf. *Cat XXXVI*, 99–125.

what is dispassionate and holy and of the words, 'I became all things to all men, that I might win all,' when you see him condescending to human passions. Indeed, do not trust your eyes at all, even as regards what you see with them, for they can be deceived, as I have learnt by experience.[91]

Here it is natural to see an affinity both with the words in *Cat XVI*, in which Symeon spoke of accompanying his father on visits to spiritual children in the city,[92] and also with what Nicetas recorded about the manner of life adopted by the Studite for evangelistic purposes, behaviour which it was argued in chapter IV entitled us to reckon him a holy fool.[93] If Nicetas depended for his description on what Symeon had written in some such passage as this in *Cat XX*, there is no reason to suppose that he misinterpreted what he read. In any case, Symeon's insistence on the duty of remaining loyal to one's spiritual father, even though he is reviled and abused, is certainly linked with his own experience and his determination to continue faithful in spite of the reproaches levelled at the Studite because of his activities as a holy fool.

A slightly different interpretation might be called for in the light of a few lines from another *Catechesis*.

> They called [Christ] . . . demon-possessed, a deceiver, a glutton and a winebibber . . . and our blessed father, I mean the holy Symeon, had that said of him for our sake, or rather, on our account (ὑπὲρ ἡμῶν μᾶλλον δὲ δι' ἡμᾶς).[94]

While from this no doubts arise concerning the Studite and the comments made about his manner of life, it is not possible to be certain exactly what Symeon meant to imply. Earlier in the same work Symeon had spoken of "my holy father" in the singular,[96] but he had also, in an undoubted reference to himself, employed the plural form as well.[96] It could well be the case, therefore, that Symeon in the lines quoted was making a personal rather than a general statement, using "our" in the sense of "my". In that case, he was perhaps indicating that his own conversion had been due, in part at least, to the Studite's willingness to become a holy fool in order to engage in evangelistic work, or alternatively he might have been obliquely letting his hearers know that he was himself aware of the temptation to be disloyal to a father whose conduct excited unfavourable

---

[91] *Cat XX*, 78–87, where there are reminiscences of *St. Matthew* 9. 35, *ibid.*, 9. 11, *St. Mark* 2. 16, *St. Luke* 15. 2, and a loose quotation of *I Corinthians* 9. 19 and 22.

[92] *Cat XVI*, 31–35.

[93] Nicetas, *Life*, 81, 8–10, and cf. chapter IV, pp. 62–64.

[94] *Cat VI*, 303–308.

[95] *ibid.*, 244.

[96] *ibid.*, 231f.

comments. Anyhow, there can be no doubt that he well knew that a
spiritual child might be tempted to desert a father who incurred criticism
as a holy fool, and he therefore felt bound to teach the obligation to remain
faithful in those circumstances.

Outward Expressions of Reverence

As well as the obligations of spiritual children which we have so far considered, we might anticipate that if living in places and at times when
society was punctilious about ceremonial observances, they would be
required to display their obedience and submission by means of outward
expressions of reverence. This, indeed, is precisely what our sources
reveal. Dorotheus, for instance, averred that he used to treat the door of
the cell, in which his spiritual father lived, with the same respect as one
would show to "the precious Cross."[97] The advice given by Climacus to
the disciple coming to confession reflects a similar outlook.

> At confession let your appearance and your disposition be like those of a con-
> demned criminal. Bow your head to the ground, and if possible you should
> shed tears on the feet of your judge and physician as though they were the
> feet of Christ.[98]

To state the matter in general terms, it was regarded as a matter of course
that the inward disposition required of spiritual children should receive
appropriate expression in an outward and visible manner.

Nicetas informs us that Symeon showed his respect for the Studite in
many such ways, even

> venerating as a holy of holies the place where he had seen him standing in
> prayer.[99]

Unfortunately, it is impossible to rely on the details given, since, as
Hausherr observed, Nicetas appears at this point to have been reproducing admonitions which Symeon himself gave to others.[100] We can,
nevertheless, cite some firsthand evidence, in that Symeon thanked God
that he had been "counted worthy to prostrate himself at [the Studite's]
holy feet,"[101] and it is by no means fanciful to suppose that he in fact
behaved as Nicetas stated. Why should he not have displayed to his

---

[97] *Doctrinae* IV, 56, 4–7.
[98] *Sc. Par.* 4, 708D–709A.
[99] *Life*, 12, 19–26.
[100] *Life*, p. 21, n. 1.—the source is *Ch* I, 30, 4–24, cf. Darrouzès, *SC* 51, p. 188, supplementary note 2.
[101] *Cat XXXV*, 119; cf. the prayer recommended in *Ch* I, 60, 10f.

spiritual father those outward expressions of reverence which he enjoined
on others? Since he was convinced that the Studite was a living saint, how
could he have failed to honour his person in every possible way? The
Chapter, which Nicetas used and which gives the fullest details concerning
the reverential behaviour demanded by Symeon, is as follows:

> Trust is clearly shown by one who reverences as holy the spot on which his
> guide and father stands; who fervently takes in his hands the dust from his
> father's feet and then puts it on his own head and spreads it on [his chest,
> over] his heart, to act as a remedy for passions and to purge away sins; who
> does not dare to come near his father or even to touch one of his tunics or
> one of his garments, unless bidden to do so; who, if he handles anything
> belonging to his father, does so with awe and reverence, counting himself
> unworthy not only to look at and attend to such things, but unworthy even
> to be in the same cell as his father.[102]

This calls for no comment, except to say that while it is tempting to try
to explain the last sentence as a conscious autobiographical reference, in
the light of Nicetas' statement that Symeon was at first lodged in the Studite's cell, it is probably safer to understand the words as simply an allusion to the custom of disciples acting as servants to their spiritual
fathers.[103]

Another indication of the kind of respectful behaviour considered right
by Symeon, can be found in the passage in which he portrayed the relationship between spiritual child and spiritual father as somehow parallel
to that between the disciples and Christ.

> If [your father] instructs you to sit at table, and if [he assigns you a place]
> near himself, accept it thankfully, but maintain silence and continue to
> reverence and honour him ...[104]

To this instruction he added shortly afterwards an explicit warning
against any attempt to imitate literally the conduct of the Beloved Disciple
in *St. John's Gospel*: "It is not expedient for you to lean on your father's
breast."[105] This definite exception to the general injunctions to imitate
the behaviour of Christ's disciples strikingly reveals Symeon's concern
that a spiritual child should never forget the reverence due to his father.

Students have remarked on Symeon's fondness for comparisons relating
to, and images drawn from, the imperial court, something which could
well be a consequence of his having been in the emperor's service before

---

[102] *Ch* I, 30, 14–24.
[103] Nicetas, *Life*, 11, 4–11; cf. Rousseau, *Ascetics*, p. 50: "It was often taken for
granted that a holy man's disciples would also be in some sense his servants."
[104] *Cat XX*, 99–101.
[105] *ibid.*, 125f., alluding to *St. John* 13. 23.

becoming a monk.[106] We may conjecture, then, that when he described the outward acts by which due respect should be paid to a spiritual father, he was not unmindful of court ceremonial and of the reverence manifested towards the emperor's sacred person. Although his teaching was no doubt based on tradition, one can well suppose that, given his personal devotion to the Studite, he would have felt it intolerable that courtiers should treat an emperor with greater respect than spiritual children displayed towards their father.

This emphasis of Symeon's on outward expressions of reverence may very likely prove disturbing to many in the West to-day, and it has to be admitted that, as regards both his own veneration of the Studite and what he required from spiritual children as marks of respect, he can be represented as distinctly lacking in moderation.[107] But such criticisms are beside the point when it is remembered that, as Symeon perceived the matter, this reverential behaviour was intended not for the benefit of the father but for that of the client, since he believed that it was disastrous for the latter when the proper attitude of respect was not maintained.[108] Moreover, on account of his understanding of the spiritual father as a quasi-sacramental manifestation of Christ to his disciple, he might, if he had known the modern way of putting it, have protested that his concern was that respect should be paid to the office, not to the individual holding it.

We have now examined the main areas in which a disciple can be reckoned to have duties to fulfil towards his spiritual father. In aggregate these obligations are certainly demanding, in their own way no less demanding than those which, as we saw earlier, the father must accept. In both cases it is the ideal which was being considered, and in actual daily life the ideal is seldom fully realised—though Symeon certainly claimed the Studite to have been an ideal father, and was not far from claiming to have been himself an ideal disciple.[109] Nevertheless, just as in practice he recognised that ideal fathers were few in number, so he was also well aware of the many problems caused by spiritual children who fell short of accomplishing, or even of intending to accomplish, all the obligations which the relationship imposed on them. Our investigations therefore cannot be reckoned complete until we have looked at some of the difficulties encountered by Symeon and other spiritual fathers.

---

[106] v. Darrouzès, *SC* 129, p. 166, n. 1. and cf. A. Kazhdan and G. Constable, *People and Power in Byzantium*, Dumbarton Oaks, 1982, p. 171.

[107] cf. N. Gendle, "awkward questions about Symeon's controversial views concerning ... the cult of the spiritual father ...," *Sobornost*, 7:1, (1985), p. 61.

[108] cf. chapter IX, pp. 236f.

[109] v. *Hymn LV*, 95–97, some words which he believed that he had heard God speak to him: "I have in mind the trust, the humility you have displayed before your father, and the complete renunciation of your will."

CHAPTER NINE

THE DIFFICULTIES OF SPIRITUAL FATHERHOOD

Background

In their introduction to the works of Dorotheus, Regnault and de Prèville give a brief résumé of his correspondence with his spiritual fathers, Barsanuphius and John, prefacing this by the statement that through these letters

> we are able in a sense to be present at the 'formation' of a young monk who was destined to become one of the greatest teachers of spirituality.[1]

Dorotheus, it is clear, did not find his apprenticeship easy, and the task of sustaining him must have weighed heavily on Barsanuphius and John. Nevertheless, the perseverance displayed by Dorotheus in attempting to discharge his obligations as a disciple preserved the relationship intact and resulted in the final overcoming of all difficulties. In circumstances of a different kind, however, the impediments to effective spiritual fatherhood might prove more intractable, and it is with such that we must now concern ourselves.

To assist coherent exposition, let us assume that spiritual fathers can be classified as either "conscientious" or "lax", and disciples as either "sincere" or "uncommitted". (Symeon himself, of course, will be placed in the first category, whether as father or disciple.) A "lax" father, although he can present problems for a "sincere" disciple, may not himself be conscious of difficulties in the relationship, and while he will probably be somewhat annoyed if he is abandoned by any disciple, whether "sincere" or "uncommitted", in the nature of the case he is unlikely to leave to posterity any record of his vexation. With a "conscientious" father and a "sincere" disciple, difficulties, other than those of a passing nature will not arise, unless there happens to exist between them a vast difference in spiritual temperament, of which the father, through lack of skill, remains unaware.[2] In such a case, a "sincere" disciple, if he recognises the source

---

[1] *SC* 92, intr. pp. 17–26, and cf. to similar effect D.J. Chitty, *The Desert a City*, Oxford, 1966, p. 136. Dorotheus himself later wrote of the need for an ἐπιστάτης to administer rebukes with prudence, humility and compassion, and without allowing himself to become perturbed (*Ep* 2).

[2] cf. E. Herman, 'La "stabilitas loci" nel monachismo Bizantino', *O.C.P.*, 21, (1955), p. 124: "It cannot have been a rare occurrence for a monk to find himself not getting from his hegumen the spiritual help and guidance he required."

of the trouble, may create real difficulties for his father should he humbly but persistently refuse to follow a path which for him is not the right one. As in the case of St. Teresa of Avila, however, any surviving account of the trouble will probably come from the disciple.[3] Since our attention is focused upon Symeon, who enjoyed a relationship with the Studite untroubled by difficulties of this kind, we shall concern ourselves solely with the problems faced by a "conscientious" father attempting to help an "uncommitted" disciple. This means that we shall limit ourselves to a discussion of the troubles met with by men truly qualified for spiritual fatherhood and striving to fulfil their obligations, but encountering disciples unwilling to persevere in their efforts to perform the duties pertaining to their side of the relationship.

While in some instances the difficulties and their causes can be found spelled out, at other times it is only by implication that it is possible to perceive and understand the nature of the troubles. This is especially the case when we are confronted by complaints made primarily not about spiritual children but about fathers. This can be illustrated by quoting some words from two contrasting sentences in pseudo-Basil:

> "If to spare thy body thou seekest a teacher ready to connive at thy passions ...,"

and,

> "If ... by God's grace thou hast found ... a teacher of good works ..."[4]

Now for our present purpose the qualities of the two spiritual fathers are immaterial, but we can legitimately infer that the writer knew of disciples who were free to choose their directors and who might cause grave difficulties to one who was "conscientious", by being unwilling to subject their bodies to the rigorous asceticism which he would demand of them. It is true that spiritual children of this kind would be unlikely often to attach themselves to men with a reputation for "conscientiousness", but whenever and for whatever reasons one of them might happen to do so, the father would be confronted by a dilemma: he would have to choose between either reluctantly lowering his standards in order to retain the disciple, or allowing him to depart and go perhaps to a "teacher ready to connive at [his] passions." But the "conscientious" father would feel that for a client to seek for someone "lax" was tantamount to his falling into Satan's clutches, since as pseudo-Basil put it in the same context:

---

[3] cf. G. Cunninghame Graham, *Santa Teresa*, London, 1907, p. 119: "It was the fate of this remarkable woman to struggle all her life with incompetent confessors."

[4] Pseudo-Basil, *De renuntiatione saeculi*, PG 31, 632D–633A, translation as given by W.K. Lowther Clarke, *The Ascetic Works of St. Basil*, London, 1925, p. 64.

> Whenever our wicked foe is unable to persuade us to abide in the tumult and
> destruction of the world, he hastens to persuade us ... to give ourselves ...
> to some man greedy of reputation, who justifies his own faults by a pretence
> of sympathy towards those that dwell with him.[5]

It requires little imagination to conceive of the inner conflict that would
take place in the mind of a spiritual father who feared that he might
endanger an immortal soul if he were "lax", and yet found himself in
charge of a disciple who showed signs of being "uncommitted". A consideration of pseudo-Basil's complaint about "lax" fathers has thus led us
to appreciate a difficulty which the "conscientious" might find themselves
having to face.

It was, not surprisingly, in his *Liber ad Pastorem* that Climacus indicated
most clearly his awareness of the potential difficulties of spiritual fatherhood. In the first chapter we hear about "sheep who lag behind because
they are lazy or greedy," and at whom therefore "the pastor should throw
a stone by means of a word [of reproof]."[6] Furthermore, we can readily
recognise the voice of experience in the concluding words of the tenth
chapter, which deals with the reception of novices:

> Often he who is [spiritually] more infirm, is found to be in heart more hum-
> ble, for which reason he ought to be treated more gently by spiritual asses-
> sors. And the opposite is clearly true also.[7]

Although Climacus envisaged that stern measures might occasionally be
called for, he was in general optimistic about the prospects of success in
the treatment of those inclined to be recalcitrant, as long as a hegumen
or spiritual father would follow his directions. However, towards the end
of the second chapter, in which he was writing of the father's work as a
spiritual physician, he did not fail to mention, as a last resort, the possible
necessity of "amputation", in other words expulsion, lest a diseased
member "communicate its scurvy to the rest."[8] Climacus thereby
showed himself conscious of the fact that a spiritual father, in his capacity
as hegumen, must sometimes be prepared to suffer the pain of admitting
that he has failed with an individual, whom he must proceed to expel, out
of regard for the health of the community as a whole.

In the *Scala Paradisi* Climacus hinted at another sort of difficulty, when
he referred to a spiritual child who "at one time obeys and at another dis-
obeys his father."[9] These words lead us to picture the frustration caused

---

[5] *ibid.*, 632D, translation, *ibid.*, pp. 63f.
[6] *ad Pastorem*, 1168A.
[7] *ibid.*, 1185C.
[8] *ibid.*, 1169B.
[9] *Sc. Par.* 4, 708C.

by a disciple who fails to make progress because his obedience is only sporadic, but yet—one must assume—cannot be dismissed for the very reason that he is not disobedient all the time.

To sum up, then, we may say that Climacus exhibits a realistic appreciation of the fact that a spiritual father must expect to encounter problems in his work, and sometimes to fail, the reason being that amongst his disciples he is likely to find some of the type we have classified as "uncommitted".

The *Chapter* in which the Studite forbade the abandoning of one spiritual father for another[10] testifies indirectly to his knowledge of difficulties caused by "uncommitted" disciples. Furthermore, even though we have no direct evidence, it is reasonable to assume that as a "conscientious" father he personally experienced from time to time the sorrow caused by spiritual children of this nature. We can at all events be certain that he had to contend with a difficulty of the opposite kind, the attempt made by his hegumen to detach Symeon from him. It is unfortunate that we have no account of this incident from the Studite's own pen, but we can hardly doubt that he was affected by the bitterness and hostility which preceded the enforced migration of Symeon to St. Mamas'. This conflict, we should note, probably contributed later to some of Symeon's troubles as a spiritual father, in the sense that because he knew that he himself had been able to remain loyal in spite of everything, he naturally adopted an unsympathetic attitude towards those whom he felt to be "uncommitted". At times he created difficulties for himself and for some of his spiritual children by asking too much of them, and it is likely that his tendency to do so owed something to his knowledge of what he, as a "sincere" disciple, had been strong enough to undergo.

Symeon in St. Mamas'

Symeon at the beginning of his hegumenate hoped that he and his monks would together make great spiritual progress. In the *Catechesis* apparently delivered on the very day of his installation, he appealed to his "beloved brethren in Christ" to dedicate themselves to this goal.

> Let us be eager ... to serve God and the one whom you have chosen to have the title of spiritual father, utterly unworthy though I be. So may God rejoice at your harmony and perfection, and so may I, lowly as I am, rejoice to see you advancing in godly living, continually reaching out towards higher attainments in faith, chastity, the fear of God, devoutness, compunction and tears—through all these the inner man is purified, is

---

[10] *Ch* 36, *Life*, p. L.

filled with divine light and comes to belong entirely to the Holy Spirit . . .[11]

This might be discounted as no more than the conventional rhetoric of an inaugural address, but an examination of other *Catecheses* shows how Symeon did genuinely hope, at least for some time, to inspire his whole community with his own lofty ideals. In chapter VII some passages were quoted which illustrate the hopes he entertained; these quotations were taken from *Cat XX*, which is, it will be remembered, a written document that he circulated among his monks.[12] Symeon's purpose in composing it was

> to benefit the soul and assist it in its flight from the world, in freeing itself from the passions and in acquiring love for God and perfect dispassion.[13]

Whatever may have been the case with other monastic superiors, it is clear that for Symeon there were both advantages and disadvantages in his being, by virtue of his office, spiritual father as well as hegumen. Because of his position as head of the community, he was free to use methods of training a disciple such as Arsenius which would not otherwise have been open to him;[14] on the other hand, it is easy to see that the very fact that he was the personal embodiment of authority was not calculated to endear him to those of his monks who disliked his enthusiastic efforts to encourage them to make spiritual progress.

An example of one kind of trouble caused to Symeon by monks unwilling or unable to share his ideals is found in *Cat XXXII*. In this he reminded his hearers that blasphemy against the Holy Spirit was the unforgivable sin, and then on the authority of St. Basil insisted that it was being committed by those who attributed to the devil activities inspired by the Holy Spirit.[15] He went on to explain that this is what is being done,

> when anyone sees wonders being brought about by the Holy Spirit, or some divine gift [bestowed] on one of the brethren—I mean compunction, or tears, or humility, or divine knowledge, or a word [full] of divine wisdom from above, or anything else which is bestowed by the divine Spirit on those who love God—[when anyone sees such things] and calls them deceit practised by the devil.[16]

In speaking thus, Symeon was virtually accusing one or more of his monks

---

[11] *Cat I*, 171–180, "reaching out" (ἐπεκτείνομαι) being both a reminiscence of *Philippians* 3. 13, and favourite theme of Gregory of Nyssa.
[12] v. chapter V, p. 90, and for its origin as a written document, v. *Cat XX*, 14.
[13] *ibid.*, 17–20.
[14] cf. chapter VII, pp. 131, 148f.
[15] *Cat XXXII*, 7–14, referring to Basil, *Reg. brev. tract.* 273, *PG* 31, 1272BC.
[16] *Cat XXXII*, 15–20.

of asserting that the apparent signs that some of their brethren were making spiritual progress were no more than Satanic frauds. Having both to preside over, and be a spiritual father to, men who said such things out of blindness or out of a determination not to try to follow him, Symeon could not help coming to know of the difficulties inherent in spiritual fatherhood not only from the authorities of the past and from the Studite, but also from his own experience as hegumen. At St. Mamas'

> instead of leading all his spiritual children ... along the path of Christ's love, he had to struggle resolutely against the violent opposition of a party among his monks.[17]

Symeon's personality and temperament were no doubt partly responsible for his difficulties, but we shall gain a fuller understanding of the situation if we consider the different types of monks who are likely to have been represented in his community. Some of them of course were men with a true vocation, who were eagerly striving for holiness, and whom Nicetas could describe as "living devout lives;"[18] but assuming that St. Mamas' was much the same as most contemporary Byzantine monasteries, it also contained others who were very different. Charanis has demonstrated that the monastic order included men drawn from a whole variety of social backgrounds, among them peasants who sought the tonsure simply in order to better their lot.[19] People of this kind, who would naturally appear unresponsive in the eyes of a hegumen such as Symeon, were without doubt to be found among the members of his community, for otherwise there would have been no point in his indignant diatribe addressed to an imaginary monk.

> Tell me ... did you deceitfully pretend that you wanted the bond of union with the brotherhood ... when the whole object you had in mind was never to lack food sufficient to satisfy your hunger and gluttony, while you enjoyed a carefree and painless existence? ... Your only motive in receiving the tonsure was to become a brother and get your share of goods and possessions which probably would never have been yours, had you remained in the world.[20]

While we might be inclined, from our perspective, to sympathize with

---

[17] Krivochéine, SC 96, intr. p. 53.

[18] Life, 39. 8.

[19] P. Charanis, 'The Monk in Byzantine Society' Dumbarton Oaks Papers, 25, (1971), pp. 76–79 (doubtless some, whose original motives for entering a monastery were questionable, ended by becoming saints, as for instance Paul of Latros, whom Charanis cites).

[20] Cat III, 78–107 (extracts); cf. "Denunciation of monks who did not sincerely renounce the world was probably in effect denunciation of those who had started out with little or nothing to renounce," P. Magdalino, 'The Byzantine Holy Man in the Twelfth Century,' The Byzantine Saint, London, 1981, p. 57.

those who were forced to apply for admission to a monastery because they could see no other way of escaping destitution, for Symeon they were bound to present a problem, because in all probability they would be unable to understand his appeals and would lack any intention of cultivating the virtues which he was ardently concerned to commend. It is easy to see how, faced with men of such a kind, who were at one and the same time monks whose hegumen he was, and spiritual children for whose salvation he felt a father's responsibility, Symeon would be forced to abandon the hopes with which he had entered upon his office. It appears that, for all his knowledge of the human heart and of the realities of cenobitic life, when he found himself confronted by many who were more or less incapable of sharing his ideals, his reaction was simply to re-iterate appeals and rebukes. These, it would seem, largely failed to have the desired effect, and indeed the reason for the rebellion of some of his monks should probably be ascribed to Symeon's inability or refusal, in his teaching and his conduct of monastic affairs, to make concessions to human weakness.

Certainly there is evidence in the *Hymns* that Symeon became sad and anxious because he felt that the opposition with which he was faced made it impossible for him to succeed as a spiritual father.[21] He was comforted, however, by an assurance that Christ understood the situation, supported him and was willing to allow him to lay down some part of his burden. The words, which he believed Christ spoke to him, include the following:

> If you are absolutely unwilling to become like [the unresponsive monks], and if you do not consent to be seduced by their counsels and become their partner in wicked deeds, you will face revolt, strife and unceasing war . . . It is better to be shepherded and in no way to shepherd such men, but to take thought for what concerns yourself, while praying for them and for all men that they may all be converted and attain to knowledge, while teaching and instructing only those who are willing [to be taught].[22]

If we wish to use the language of psychology rather than that of mysticism, we shall say that the above shows how Symeon to some extent came to terms with his limitations, and accepted the fact that as spiritual father he could and should only hope to be successful with those of his monks who were prepared to allow themselves to be guided by him.

But although comforted in this way, Symeon was still bound to suffer personally when he heard monks, for whatever reason, ascribing to the influence of Satan what he was convinced were manifestations of the presence and power of the Holy Spirit. For his part he was convinced that

---

[21] e.g. *Hymn XIV*, 87–89 and *Hymn XLVII*, 63–67.
[22] *Hymn XLIII*, 96–99, 111–115.

through the Studite he had indeed received the Spirit of God,[23] that he was thus qualified to be a hegumen and spiritual father, and that therefore he ought to be regarded by his children as an icon of Christ. But instead of being accepted in this way, he found himself automatically included in the charge that anyone who claimed to have received gifts "bestowed by the divine Spirit" was being duped by the devil. Those who spoke or thought thus must, from Symeon's point of view, have been "uncommitted" in the deepest sense, and it was impossible for him not to feel wounded when faced with this rejection of all that he had hoped to achieve for all the members of his community.

At this point it should be observed that although monks who lacked a real vocation may simply have been trying to excuse their spiritual torpor by uttering what sounded to Symeon like blasphemy against the Holy Spirit, many highly-placed personages were at that time questioning the possibility, and perhaps even the desirability, of a person's actually becoming a saint in the contemporary world. The prevalence of such opinions explains Symeon's discovery that everybody was sure that he could not possibly find a living saint,[24] and accounts in part for the scepticism with which he was confronted when he asserted the Studite's sanctity. The *Menologion* of Symeon Metaphrastes, produced about that time, may well have contributed something to this state of mind, for

> it has been remarked that [his] saints almost all belong to ancient times and that there are only a very few of them who date from the period of iconoclasm or of the wars with the Arabs. Is not this an instance of the same 'antiquarianising' spirit which inspires Constantine VII's undertakings?[25]

Magdalino is more definite, and specifically mentions Symeon in his assessment:

> The compilation of the Metaphrastic corpus and the Synaxarion of Constantinople, and the opposition aroused by Symeon the New Theologian in his attempt to establish a cult of his spiritual father Symeon the Studite, indicate that the official Church was tending, from the end of the tenth century, to conceive of the communion of saints as a closed society, whose numbers were now more or less complete.[26]

There is no reason to suppose that the community in St. Mamas' was insulated from this climate of contemporary opinion, which conveniently justified the recalcitrance of all those of his monks who were unwilling

---

[23] cf. *Cat VI*, 263–267 and *Cat XXXV*, 255–257, in both of which the Studite was mentioned by Symeon in connection with his own reception of the Holy Spirit.

[24] *Cat XXXV*, 78–80.

[25] Lemerle, *Premier humanisme*, p. 293, n. 77.

[26] Magdalino, *op. cit.*, p. 61.

to allow Symeon to lead them along the arduous path to sanctity.

All this provides the background to the frustration which can be detected in the language used by Symeon in some of the *Catecheses*.

> It is heresy to swerve from any of the dogmas laid down to define our orthodox faith, but it is wholly to subvert the incarnation of our God and Saviour Jesus Christ ... when one denies that there are at the present time some who love God, who are deemed worthy of [receiving] the Holy Spirit, and who by him are baptized as sons of God, so as to become gods by knowledge, by experience and by contemplation.[27]

His personal dilemma was whether to make such a claim for himself and be taxed with pride, or to follow the way of humility but then be unable to use his experience to refute what was being said by monks, his spiritual children, who were infected by a plague that he considered worse than heresy. This dilemma he openly expounded on another occasion.

> If instead of speaking openly we make an effort to conceal the gift [bestowed on us], those people take what we say as the literal truth; but if we do speak out and disclose the truth, they immediately accuse us of being arrogant, because they are themselves ignorant of the sayings of the holy apostles. What sayings? 'We have the mind of Christ.'[28]

For Symeon, accepting or rejecting the possibility of becoming a saint in the present was tantamount to accepting or rejecting the truth of Holy Scripture, for

> If ... you say that this is impossible even for someone who desires it, what are we to do with [the text], ... 'Be holy (ἅγιοι, 'saints'), for I am holy?' But if it is impossible to be [a saint] without desiring to be one, then ... you are self-condemned, since you neither desire nor choose to be this, for if you want to be [a saint], you can be one.[29]

Whatever their motives or excuses, those monks who opposed Symeon and resisted his efforts to lead them towards sanctity wounded him in a manner which he did not attempt to hide. Hausherr[30] cites a telling passage from *Tr Eth XI*, a work which was intended, not like the *Catecheses* for his monks, but for a wider public, and in which Symeon referred clearly to the sufferings inflicted on him by some members of his community.

---

[27] *Cat XXXII*, 49–56; cf. *Cat XXIX*, 137ff., cited by B. Fraigneau-Julien, *op. cit.*, p. 188.

[28] *Cat XXXIV*, 197–202, quoting *I Corinthians* 2. 16; cf. *ibid.*, 97f., ὁ τρόπος ... τῆς ἐμῆς, ὡς τινες οἴονται, μεγαλορρημοσύνης ...

[29] *ibid.*, 220–227 (extracts), with quotation taken from *I Peter* 1. 16, which itself quotes *Leviticus* 11. 44. (Symeon put γίνεσθε instead of the Biblical writers' ἔσεσθε.)

[30] Hausherr, *Life*, pp. LXX (*sic*, really LXXI)—LXXII.

If they hear it said of someone else that he has striven lawfully according to the Lord's commandments and become humble in heart and thought, that he is purifying himself from passions of every kind and proclaiming to all the mighty works of God, in other words all that God has done for him in fulfilment of his most true promises; and if that person, speaking for the benefit of his hearers, [tells of] how he was counted worthy to behold the light of God and God in the light of glory, and also of how he became conscious in himself of the indwelling and the activity of the Holy Spirit, and of how in the Holy Spirit he has himself become holy (ἅγιος)—[if they hear this], they at once bay like angry hounds at the one who utters such words, and hasten to devour him, if they can.[31]

These lines, which comprise only part of the passage quoted by Hausherr, have an obvious biographical reference; they clearly reveal Symeon's distress at being faced by men who rejected the claims to sanctity and spiritual experience which as a spiritual father he felt himself obliged to make "for the benefit of his hearers." Modern readers, who may at this point be tempted to sympathize more with the hearers than with Symeon, should recall the reasons that impelled him to adopt and maintain his seemingly arrogant stance: he had a passionate desire to lead his spiritual children to become holy (saints, ἅγιοι), believing his duty to be nothing less than this; he was convinced that he could not be successful in this, unless he, their father, was holy himself; at the same time he was confident that, in spite of his innate unworthiness, he had acquired this essential qualification through his own father, the Studite.[32] He thus met with an insurmountable obstacle when any of his monks denied the possibility of sanctity in the contemporary world, and his troubled indignation can still be felt in the words he used in some of his *Catecheses*.

Did you reproach us secretly for having spoken bombastically? did you condemn us as vainglorious?[33]

It is quite possible that not all the monks whose unresponsiveness brought sorrow to Symeon went as far as the men we have just been considering, but he was vulnerable because his temperament made him unable to rest content with anything less than a total response. Accordingly, although at one time he came to believe, as we saw, that in some cases he could legitimately abandon active efforts to win over obdurate opponents, on another occasion he felt that Christ was urging him:

Do not henceforth cease from admonishing, do not cease from lamenting,

---

[31] *Tr Eth IX*, 359–370, a passage abounding in Scriptural echoes.
[32] *Cat VI*, 263–267, and *Cat XXXII*, 79–91, where there is a mention of the reception of the Spirit by other disciples of the Studite as well as by Symeon.
[33] *Cat XXXIV*, 11–13.

and do not cease from seeking after their salvation, so that, if they obey you and are converted, you will [be able to] count them as brethren, and will win over men who are members [of your body] . . .[34]

The strength of his emotions is laid bare in his appeal to his monks,

Render to me, brethren, a love equal to mine for you, [render it] to me who am under the sway of a tyrannical love.[35]

He was deeply hurt by the failure of many in St. Mamas' to respond positively to his attempts to lead them towards holiness, and he found this unresponsiveness almost impossible to understand. Thus, addressing in the singular "each one of you who cleaves to the vanity of things present," he asked:

If you know what is better, how is it that you do what is worse, like one who lacks perception? If you know that all is shadow and that everything visible passes away, are you not ashamed to be trifling with a shadow and treasuring what is fleeting?[36]

When he spoke thus, Symeon was not concerned about members of his community who in effect totally rejected him as spiritual father, but was manifesting his impatient longing to guide along the paths of spirituality sluggish monks who, incomprehensibly as it appeared to him, preferred to dally with worthless trifles. Although such failure to respond is more passive than the type of rejection we examined earlier, it is equally the mark of an "uncommitted" disciple, and cannot fail to inflict suffering on a "conscientious" father.

A further difficulty which Symeon appears to have encountered must also be briefly mentioned. It comes to light in his complaint, "Friends easily become enemies, if they find the smallest excuse."[37] This apparently general statement occurs in a *Hymn* in which he bewailed the troubles which beset him at St. Mamas', and it suggests that amongst these troubles was the disloyalty of some monks whom he had earlier thought of as genuine disciples and well-disposed towards him.

Greater pain must have been caused to Symeon when he sensed unresponsiveness to teaching which came directly from the Studite. Thus a *Catechesis*, extolling the value of tears, begins with a description[38] of what he had noticed during the reading in church of some words written by his father, "Brother, never communicate without shedding tears." Symeon

---

[34] *Hymn XLI*, 148–151.
[35] *Cat XIX*, 80f.
[36] *ibid.*, 132f., 139–142.
[37] *Hymn XLIII*, 79f.
[38] *Cat IV*, 11–18.

stated that on hearing this many in the congregation, which included monks, had sneered and had remarked that if really faced with such a requirement, they would have to pass their whole lives as non-communicants. This incident he took as a kind of text for his *Catechesis*, and although we cannot be sure that all the mocking monks were his spiritual children,[39] the way in which Symeon here and elsewhere emphasised the divine inspiration of the Studite,[40] suggests that by no means all his brethren showed themselves eager to accept promptly everything which he passed on to them from this source.

As a loyal disciple, Symeon was quick to defend his father against attacks from whatever quarter they originated, but it seems possible to detect at some points in his utterances a special grief caused by the unresponsiveness of his own spiritual children to the example and teaching of the Studite. "Do you take the blessed Symeon for a fool, and are you ashamed to imitate his actions?" he asked in *Cat VI*,[41] addressing in the singular, as he often did, an imaginary individual member of his monastic congregation. We may suppose that Symeon had detected a resistance to his citations of the words of the Studite, a man whose heir he felt himself to be and whom he firmly believed to have been divinely inspired, and in these circumstances it was natural that he should react with wounded indignation.

While the difficulties which Symeon had to face in St. Mamas' were partly caused by his being the man he was, they were certainly increased by the fact that he held the position of spiritual father *ex officio*, as an automatic consequence of having been chosen as hegumen. Although the uniting of the two functions in a single office-bearer could facilitate the training of monastic spiritual children, it is easy to appreciate that it could also at times have the opposite effect. Christophorides discusses at some length whether in monasteries the two roles were always intended to be combined, and points out that the hegumen, as the "head" of the "body", was the natural person to be the monks' spiritual father. He indicates at the same time that there was no absolute and inflexible rule to this effect, and stresses that as long the hegumen was a genuinely spiritual man, the monks would suffer no hardship as a result of his being the only person authorised to act as their father.[42] Hausherr was more conscious of the possibility of unsatisfactory results:

---

[39] Presumably the incident occurred in St. Mamas' in the course of one of the festivals instituted by Symeon in honour of the Studite. According to Nicetas (*Life*, 73, 11–15), the congregation on these occasions included people from outside so that other monks might have been present.

[40] *Cat IV*, 5–8; cf. *Cat VI*, 188–195.

[41] *Cat VI*, 300f.

[42] Christophorides, *op. cit.*, pp. 58–63.

> When one reads the *Typika*, one gets the impression that in coenobia in which the hegumen keeps all authority in his own hands, the revealing of thoughts comes to be a mere confession of sins ... In place of the primitive system in which the initiative rested with the disciple and he resorted to the spiritual guide who inspired him with confidence, little by little regulation and control by authority were established ... The spiritual father is now no more than a purveyor of absolution and calculator of penances.[43]

It is particularly interesting to remember that the Studite showed that he was aware, though from a different angle, of the problems resulting from the same person's being both spiritual father and hegumen.

> It would be right for all to go to the hegumen for confession [of thoughts], but ... some are unwilling to reveal their thoughts to the hegumen, because of their great frailty and because they do not trust him ...[44]

On balance, one might conclude that when the two functions are combined, the disadvantages are in most cases likely to outweigh the possible benefits. This has been generally recognised in the Orthodox Churches, where the usual practice to-day is that although in newly-founded or newly-refounded monasteries[45] the hegumen acts as spiritual father of the disciples who have joined him, yet once a stable community has come into existence, the task of spiritual fatherhood is entrusted to one or more monks trained by the founder, and a line of fathers succeeding one another is thus inaugurated.

In the tenth and eleventh centuries, while it was doubtless very common for the hegumen to be also spiritual father of the monastery,[46] Symeon himself had proved that exceptions were possible by his own insistence on remaining under the direction of the Studite. In addition, the latter's views on the subject were presumably known to him. It is therefore surprising that he never appears to have been willing to allow his monks any choice in the matter, but to have insisted that having chosen him as hegumen they must also accept him as their sole spiritual father. He may, as was suggested, have done so because he did not believe that any other members of the community were qualified for the work.[47] This practical consideration is the probable cause of his being able to distinguish, in a theoretical case, between spiritual father and hegumen.[48] But, whatever

---

[43] Hausherr, *Direction spirituelle*, pp. 227f.
[44] *Ch* 36, *Life*, p. XLIX.
[45] cf. Kallistos of Diokleia (K. Ware), 'Wolves and monks: life on the Holy Mountain today,' *Sobornost*, 5:2, (1983), pp. 63f.
[46] cf. chapter IV, pp. 54f.
[47] cf. chapter VI, p. 94, for the situation while the Studite was still alive.
[48] *Cat XXVI*, 80f. *Cat XXVI*, a written work, in which Symeon addressed an imaginary novice, was presumably intended both for St. Mamas' and for other monasteries where conditions were different.

his reasons for adopting the dual role, there is nothing at all surprising in the fact that his doing so caused grave difficulties to a man such as Symeon, determined as he was to act as a "conscientious" father to a group of monks, many of who were in his eyes definitely "uncommitted". His very zeal as a reforming hegumen made it hard for him to be successful as the spiritual father of St. Mamas', whereas he probably had no difficulties of the kind we are considering when surrounded during his last years by the band of like-minded disciples who gathered round him in exile.

Another type of anxiety which troubled Symeon was caused by certain monks who, in his opinion, were ignorant of their true condition and wished to act as spiritual fathers while still far from qualified to do so. Such monks, who of course disliked being addressed or treated as spiritual children, are depicted in one of the *Hymns*.

> If someone speaks thus to them: 'Listen to me, children, and remove the veil from over your heart,' they become furious at these very words, because they were not called 'fathers' but were addressed as 'children', their hatred of the speaker being increased by his language. They are unable to recognise the passion which besets them, or rather the [many] passions which darken their mind and their thoughts, and which separate from God those whom they take captive.[49]

It is easy to picture this kind of reaction to their hegumen on the part of monks who had themselves become, or at least wished to become, spiritual fathers to men and women living in the world, and it is not improbable that the monastery of St. Mamas included such men.

> Monks frequently acted as spiritual directors, both as confessor and as more informal consultant ... The range of Theodore the Studite's correspondence shows how widely he was consulted outside monastic circles, and the same is true of John Mauropous, monk and archbishop of Euchaita in Asia Minor in the 11th century.[50]

Obviously it would have been difficult for Symeon to persuade men overanxious to be reckoned spiritual fathers to behave as teachable disciples. In *Tr Eth VI*, a work of a more general nature than the *Hymn* from which we have just quoted a few lines, Symeon approached the problems from a slightly different point of view. Since, nevertheless, he still had monks in mind, his experiences as hegumen of St. Mamas' are likely to have exerted considerable influence on what he wrote. We can observe his

---

[49] *Hymn LII*, 127–134, "veil" being an allusion to *II Corinthians* 3. 14f., and "separate from God" recalling *Wisdom* 1. 3.

[50] J.M. Hussey, 'Byzantine Monasticism,' *Cambridge Medieval History*, Cambridge, 1967, IV (ii), 183.

anxiety about the difficulty of getting the spiritually sick to acknowledge the truth of their condition.

> The health they imagine [they enjoy] is to fulfil the desires of the flesh and to do all that convetousness and appetite suggest; and . . . those who wallow in passions and are dominated by them, yet do not perceive their bondage— nobody will ever persuade them that they are in a sorry state or get them to change to anything better. They are blind, yet do not believe that anybody other than themselves can see . . .[51]

After analysing this condition at some length, Symeon adopted his usual device: he imagined himself to be addressing an individual, whom in this case he severely castigated. Part of his rebuke was conveyed through questions:

> If you confess—and you do well to do so—that you have not received a share in [God's] gift . . . why do you not maintain a praiseworthy silence and seek through repentance and tears to gain, and learn about, these [good things]— instead of wanting to talk fruitlessly about matters of which you have no true knowledge, although without [possessing] them you still love to be called a saint (ἅγιος), are sure that you are already saved, and dare to listen to others when they disclose their thoughts (λογισμοί), and to teach others? . . . Are you not afraid to be a pastor to (ποιμαίνω) your brethren, you who sit in darkness and have not even acquired that eye which beholds the true light? Are you not ashamed to act as a physician (ἰατρεύω) to others while sick yourself and not even capable of perceiving your own wounds?[52]

By his mention of receiving the disclosure of thoughts and functioning in a spiritual sense as physicians, Symeon shows that he had in mind men eager to be accepted as spiritual fathers. If, as seems reasonable, we suppose that though seeking to reach a wider public he was thinking of some of his own monks when he penned this rebuke, we shall conclude that he was himself faced with this difficulty: men whom he knew to be far from qualified to act as fathers, were intent on doing so. This eagerness of theirs meant that they were blinding themselves to the truth of their own condition, and in consequence were refusing to seek, through Symeon, for the healing and enlightenment which they really needed. Alternatively, if it be thought more likely that Symeon was writing on the basis of his knowledge about conditions in general, without reference to his experience as

---

[51] *Tr Eth VI*, 334–342; unlike the *Catecheses*, the *Treatises* are not, as such, addresses to his monks and unlike the *Hymns*, they do not directly treat of Symeon's personal experiences—cf. chapter II, p. 11, (n. 7), and Darrouzès, *SC* 122, intr. p. 13.

[52] *ibid.*, 383–401 (extracts). It is interesting that, in spite of his experience of the prevailing scepticism about the existence of contemporary saints, Symeon depicted an unworthy person as being gratified by the title. Perhaps the ambitions of such people contributed to the general unwillingness to admit the possibilty of saints actually living at that time.

hegumen of St. Mamas', our quotations still demonstrate that he was aware of the problem which at any rate some spiritual fathers had to deal with. When superficially considered, the prestige attaching to spiritual fatherhood is likely to appear attractive to some men, and it would be strange if there had been no examples known to Symeon of immature disciples anxious to act as fathers while still unqualified to do so, and through this very anxiety of theirs claiming to be the equals of their own pastors and spiritual physicians, and perhaps *de facto* independent of them.

If properly carried out, the work of a father demands, as we have seen, much labour and much expenditure of time. Symeon therefore felt that it was liable to conflict with his own need to devote himself to God in prayer. This feeling can be seen manifested in one of his *Hymns*, when he went so far as to express doubts about his own salvation, which he feared that he might have imperilled through his concern for his recalcitrant brethren.

> I exulted while I enjoyed to the full that ineffable light ... At first I was a stranger to the wickednesses of men, but as I dwelt longer among them, I took upon myself the affairs of others, and, O Master, I was carried away by contentious men. Hoping to reform them, I shared in their wickedness, and in my folly,—alas!—I participated in the darkness of the passions ... But do thou, Lover of men, make haste to have pity on me; speedily deliver me who have fallen thus for thy sake ... Yes, I know that thou, my all-pitying God, didst ordain that indeed we should deliver a brother from death and from sin's sting, yet should not through sin perish with him—but this befell me, poor wretch, and so through negligence have I fallen and through trusting in myself. Yet [thou didst ordain] that I should deliver him and myself together, but if [I could] not, that I should remain above, lament over him who fell, and strive with all my power to keep from falling with him.[53]

In this there is much interesting material, but Symeon's style is allusive, and to interpret him it is necessary to resort to conjectures. By contrasting his life when "a stranger to the wickedness of men" with his experience of taking upon himself "the affairs of others," he was apparently depicting the difference between his early days as a simple monk in St. Mamas' and the time when as hegumen he began to feel responsible for the conduct of others. His trouble had, it would seem, two aspects: first of all, through involvement in human contentiousness he had forfeited his dispassion—it may be assumed that he was not very patient when confronted by monks who quarrelled; secondly, and probably because of this, he had ceased to "enjoy to the full that ineffable light," or in other words the quality of his spiritual life had been impaired. The result was that, unless "speedily

---

[53] *Hymn XLIX*, 27–65 (extracts).

delivered,'' he feared that he might ''perish with'' the brother or brothers whom he had been attempting to save. We are led to recognise through this extract how difficulties caused by unsatisfactory monastic disciples have repercussions on the interior life of a ''conscientious'' spiritual father such as Symeon.

The primary concern of a hegumen/spiritual father ought to be the salvation of the monks for whom he is responsible, and accordingly it is in connection with their spiritual progress or lack of it that he should be most conscious of his success or failure. In fact, if he is ''conscientious,'' it is of failure that he is the more likely to be aware, and so it is not strange that Symeon had little, if anything, to say about his own successes in St. Mamas'.[54] But in reality the total picture cannot have been as gloomy as the preceding pages may have suggested, for Symeon's influence did persist, and there is no need to be completely distrustful of Nicetas' account of the virtues and achievements of some of those monks who were his ''sincere'' disciples.[55]

Problems concerning Seculars

In moving on to examine the difficulties, as Symeon saw them, which confront a spiritual father in his attempts to care for disciples who live in the world, it is obvious that we are confronted with a relationship basically different from that considered in the last section. Unlike a monk, a secular is at liberty to remain without a spiritual father, or if he decides to seek one, he is free to chose whom he will, provided the father will accept him as a spiritual child. When investigating a relationship of this nature, we shall not expect to encounter any of those continuing tensions which arise when a ''conscientious'' father is faced with ''uncommitted'' disciples belonging to his monastic flock.

On the other hand, the fact that a secular client is free to abandon a spiritual guide who displeases him means that those who incline to be ''uncommitted'' are likely to exercise this freedom, and then perhaps look for another father. Human nature being what it is, this is scarcely surprising, but it is interesting that evidence exists to show that spiritual fathers were not alone in Constantinople in having cause to complain about such fickleness. The impression gained from a study of the letters of a tenth-century Byzantine school-master was thus described by Lemerle:

---

[54] However, in *Cat XII*, 66–80, he felt able to congratulate his monks once on keeping the first week of Lent in an exemplary manner.

[55] v. *Life*, 45–58, with details of Arsenius, a bishop from the West, and others.

> The very frequent movement of pupils who come and go from one [school] to another arouses fierce competition between [the masters], competition which is not always fair.[56]

Symeon's letters reveal that spiritual fathers faced problems of somewhat the same kind with regard to their children who were living in the world.

It would, of course, be a mistake to over-emphasise the difference between conditions within monastic communities and those outside them. Climacus was writing for monks, but he thought it necessary to warn them against succumbing to the temptation to flit from one father to another.

> Deserving of every punishment at God's hands are the sick who make trial of a physician and receive some benefit from him, but before being completely cured abandon him out of preference for another.[57]

Presumably, in spite of what was prescribed in many *typika*, namely that the monks were to have the hegumen and no one else as spiritual father,[59] it was not always possible to enforce such regulations, particularly in the larger monasteries. Hence the Studite, it will be remembered, permitted a novice to choose someone other than the hegumen as his director, but found it necessary to speak in the strongest terms against the practice of changing from one to another after an initial choice had been made.[59]

To some extent, then, a "conscientious" father, who had had to deal with troubles caused by monastic spiritual children, might have anticipated similar problems when dealing with disciples living in the world. Yet in many respects the relationship between a secular person and his director was bound to be different from that between a monk living under vows and his spiritual father, who was often also his hegumen. To illustrate the difficulties which Symeon experienced, or knew about, in connection with secular spiritual children, we shall make considerable use of his still unpublished *Ep 3*, which throws much light on the subject and also at times reveals him in an extremely pessimistic mood.[60]

Symeon wrote this letter to somebody living in the world in order to exhort him to find a spiritual father of the right kind, and some scribe prefixed to it a title which includes the words, "how one can recognise a

---

[56] *Premier humanisme*, p. 279.

[57] *Sc. Par.* 4, 709D.

[58] A good example is found in 'Le *typikon* de la *Théotokos Évergétis*,' (ed. P. Gautier), *R.E.B.*, 40, (1980), p. 57.

[59] *Ch* 36, *Life*, p. XLIXf.; cf. chapter VIII, p. 213.

[60] Krivochéine in *Lumière* (especially pp. 99–101) used excerpts from *Ep 3* as examples of Symeon's teaching about the need to find a spiritual father and then submit to him.

man who is undefiled ....''[61] Amongst the various matters touched
on by Symeon, we must first notice his complaint that many who were
baptized as infants and brought up with some knowledge of the Bible
imagined that they needed nothing more than this to ensure their salvation, provided that they resorted to confession in a purely formal manner,
falling far short of a genuine relationship with a spiritual father.

> But since they were baptized as infants, they think themselves innocent,
> although subsequently they have not honoured him who regenerated them
> ...; and because from childhood they have learnt the holy Scriptures, they
> suppose that this is piety enough for them, and are of the opinion that for
> salvation it is sufficient simply to tell and confess their sins and receive
> pardon from their [spiritual] fathers, even if they possess no faith [in them],
> and even if they fail to accord them esteem and reverence as apostles of God,
> mediators and leaders.[62]

Such people must have had an attitude in some respects not unlike that
of Symeon in his early days. However, whereas he wanted to find a
spiritual father whom he could honour as a saint, and having found him
was willing to be led eventually into that class of disciples whom we have
styled "sincere", the people criticised in *Ep 3* appear never to have ceased
being "uncommitted", while at the same time conspicuously failing to
show respect to their fathers, who must have found them extremely
difficult to deal with.

It is impossible to know whether, and if so, to what extent, Symeon had
personal experience of unsatisfactory disciples of this sort, but in view of
the fact that his reputation as an enthusiast and perfectionist is likely to
have been known to many in Constantinople fairly soon after his installation as hegumen, it might be conjectured that not many persistently
"uncommitted" seculars would have approached him. In that case it
might be assumed that in his description he was drawing upon the experiences of other spiritual fathers, among them perhaps the Studite, who
were regarded as less demanding. An alternative explanation would be
that he was indulging in a general lament about the wickedness of the age,
without reference to specific instances. The latter supposition is on the
whole the more probable, to judge from the tone of much of *Ep 3*.

Lack of respect for a spiritual father could result also, Symeon perceived, in his being compelled to acquiesce in a disciple's wishes, something which would lead to disastrous consequences for both of them. On
the other hand, if he refused to acquiesce, he would be abandoned by his
client.

---

[61] *Ep 3*, 208r.
[62] *ibid.*, 219r, with reminiscence of *II Timothy* 3. 15 in "from childhood ..."

> If [his father] does not go along with him, or rather does not fall and perish with him, he leaves him . . .[63]

Symeon's reaction in this letter was to stress repeatedly the duty of spiritual children to honour their fathers. He implied that some disciples were too restrictive in their understanding of Christ's words, "He who receives you, receives me," and therefore warned the recipient of his letter:

> Do not presume to say to yourself that these words were spoken only in regard to the apostles, and that it is they alone to whom we are bound to pay heed.[64]

Later Symeon complained that in the present age nobody, whether layman, monk, priest or bishop was willing to receive anyone else as an apostle of God or disciple of Christ. On the contrary, "we monks speak evil of other monks, priests of bishops, and laymen of everybody and of one another."[65] The situation appeared to Symeon to be so full of danger that he again reverted to it, and asked indignantly how we can claim to love our neighbours or our brethren,

> when we neither love, nor esteem, nor give due honour to our fathers who have been responsible for our obtaining so many good things, and through whose agency God makes us his sons . . .[66]

His own loyalty and devotion to the Studite had brought troubles to Symeon, and the recollection of these in all likelihood made him particularly aware of the failings of those who, when there was no question of their being required to undergo any personal suffering, refused to respect their spiritual fathers and thus actually subverted the relationship. Even if he personally did not experience treatment of this kind at the hands of any of his secular disciples, it is clear that he knew of it as something which other fathers had to endure.

Moreover, although tradition forbade disciples under any circumstances to presume to judge or condemn their spiritual fathers, there were now some seculars who, according to Symeon, excused their lack of respect by saying:

> I do not observe him keeping God's commandments, and that is why I fail to honour him.

This kind of objection Symeon dismissed as "a vain excuse," and then in his indignation asked his imaginary objector:

---

[63] *ibid.*, 218v.

[64] *ibid.*, 210r, Christ's words being cited from *St. Matthew* 10. 40, and "Do not presume . . ." a reminiscence of *ibid.* 3. 9.

[65] *ibid.*, 218r.

[66] *ibid.*, 219v.

> Do you keep them any better than he does? Is that your reason for acting as his judge?[67]

One must suppose that, writing to this person who might eventually attach himself as a spiritual child to some father, Symeon was determined at the very outset to forewarn him of the abuses which he would hear of, or perhaps had already heard of, in the social circles in which he moved. Since the letter is in Symeon's normal written Greek style, the recipient must have been an educated man, and presumably therefore a member of the upper classes.[68] It is not to be wondered at if some people with such a background, conscious of their status as persons at least on an equality with their spiritual fathers from the social and educational point of view, were prone to behave towards them in an unsubmissive, and perhaps disrespectful, fashion.[69] The same motive, perhaps, played some part in leading men of this kind to claim the right to dictate to a father how they wished to be directed, and this conjecture that educated seculars could prove difficult to deal with finds some support in Symeon's complaint.

> As you can see and understand for yourself, everything is in confusion, and all order and every divine tradition stemming from the apostles has been abolished, and there is a total rejection of the commandments of Christ. And this whole terrible and deadly state of affairs has come about in this generation because all men suppose that they have been initiated into divine matters, understand God's commandments and are capable of making proof of, and discerning, what is beneficial to them.[70]

If we assume that Symeon was guilty of some natural exaggeration, and that by "all men" he in fact meant "all men who have been educated," in other words all who belonged to the same section of society as himself and the man to whom he was writing, we have in these lines striking evidence of the lack of docility which many members of the upper classes displayed and of which, as a spiritual father, he absolutely disapproved. Even if Symeon's "all men" does include others as well as the educated, these at least would have figured prominently amongst the men who laid claim to a knowledge of "divine matters" and of "God's commandments." There is thus no reason for doubting that a good many such troublesome disciples existed.

As well as complaining about difficult spiritual children, Symeon, who was certainly "conscientious", was impelled to warn the recipient of his

---

[67] *ibid.*, 220r.

[68] cf. Lemerle, *Premier humanisme*, p. 260, and Mango, *Byzantium*, p. 236.

[69] In modern times some Indian clergymen have faced similar difficulties when responsible for congregations containing lay members of a higher caste, or better educated, than themselves.

[70] *Ep 3*, 218v.

letter against fathers who in his opinion were "lax", and whom he considered unscrupulous in their efforts to attach secular disciples to themselves. (When examining the evidence about to be adduced, we shall do well to bear in mind Lemerle's remarks about Byzantine school-masters and the unfair competition which they encountered from colleagues.) There was a danger, he wrote, that one might fall into the clutches of a "false apostle and false Christ."[71] From the beginning such have been raised up by the devil, and accordingly those who

> hide themselves beneath the darkness of their own passions, lusts and wills, and walk therein as in the depth of night, find teachers of their own kind.[72]

These "teachers" were, of course, the "lax" competitors, who by pandering to their clients or potential clients created difficulties for spiritual fathers who were more demanding simply by being "conscientious".

The advice given by Symeon to the would-be disciple was what one might expect:

> When ... you see someone engaged in any of all these [wicked practices], seeking the glory that comes from men, and in order to please men relaxing the commandments of God, you must recognise him as a deceiver and not a true [father].[73]

This is not the only indication that he knew of questionable means employed by such persons in their desire to attract disciples, for in another letter he wrote of some who

> before they are [spiritually] born, and while they still do not know themselves, let alone God, lightly and boldly profess to be fathers of others and teachers, and make efforts to draw to themselves, by all kinds of means and devices, everyone who is just abandoning the world and, as I have said, is looking for a spiritual father.[74]

Symeon was not alone in noticing and being critical of such behaviour; Magdalino had occasion to refer to a twelfth-century author, Eustathios of Thessalonica, who "thought that hypocritical holy men were motivated largely by the desire to acquire spiritual children."[75] Symeon denounced persons of this kind and in effect accused them of "unfair competition," for when he called them hypocrites and lovers of luxury,[76] he was implying

---

[71] *ibid.*, 211r.

[72] *ibid.*, 212v; cf. also *Ch* I, 49, 24f., where even the monastic spiritual child is warned of the existence of "many deceivers and false teachers."

[73] *Ep 3*, 214v, previously quoted for a different purpose in chapter V, p. 88.

[74] *Ep 4*, 165–170.

[75] Magdalino, *op. cit.*, p. 58, citing in n. 42 *Eustathii Opuscula*, 96 (ed. T.L.F. Tafel, Frankfurt-am-Main, 1832).

[76] *Ep 3*, 215r.

that they unscrupulously made everything easy for wealthy secular disciples.

An interesting fact related to the foregoing is that Symeon was aware that such clients often had no illusions about the quality of the men whom they selected as their spiritual fathers.

> Because, as I have said, they consider and hold all men to be sinners, but are persuaded that the grace of God is operative even through [the ministrations of] the unworthy, they imagine that they are getting those [benefits] which are wrought in us by the Holy Spirit and those foretastes of the good things of eternity which are given to us. But the priest, through whom these things are bestowed upon them, they turn away from as being a sinner, and they have similar ideas with regard to monks.[77]

Thus, in addition to complaining of the behaviour of these spiritual children towards their fathers, Symeon was indignant because he perceived that their reasons for choosing men whom they did not respect were based on a purely mechanical idea about the way in which forgiveness is obtained and salvation secured. He could not refrain from criticising people who deliberately resorted to ''lax'' spiritual fathers whom they openly, it would seem, despised as unworthy. Excessive emphasis on the *ex opere operato* efficacy of the sacramental rites ran counter to Symeon's firm conviction of the need for personal experience of grace on the part of those who receive a sacrament, and personal sanctity in the lives of those by whom it is administered.[78] The vigour of his reaction against a mechanical outlook such as that of the seculars criticised in *Ep 3* was manifested in a different form in *Ep 1*. There, to defend the right of monks, even if unordained, to receive confessions, Symeon asserted that they had had transmitted to them ''the gift of the Spirit'' precisely on account of the unworthiness of the majority of bishops and priests, though he characteristically added that the devil had subsequently been at work in monasteries also, and that many ''monks'' were in reality ''not monks at all.''[79]

Thus, whether or not he was ever personally troubled by them in the course of his dealings with secular disciples, Symeon was very conscious that there did exist monks eager, for bad reasons, to become spiritual fathers and prepared to be unscrupulous in their attempts to reach their goal. As he saw it, these men contributed largely to the difficulties which a father must expect to encounter in his relationships with non-monastic spiritual children. Surrounded by such competitors a ''conscientious''

---

[77] *ibid.*, 218v.

[78] These themes can be found scattered throughout Symeon's works—for examples, v. *Ep 1, passim, Cat XXVIII*, 190–300, *Tr Eth XIV*, 224–247.

[79] *Ep 1*, p. 124, 1–11, ending μοναχοὶ πάμπαν ἀμόναχοι.

father would often find it hard to retain and lead to "sincere" discipleship a secular person who was at first inclined to be "uncommitted". In a monastery, the hegumen might at the very least expect to be able to dissuade a monk from attaching himself to some self-chosen and undesirable spiritual father; over men and women living in the world, neither Symeon nor any other "conscientious" father had any means of exercising control, apart from force of personality and pastoral skill. It is, of course, for this reason that in the current section, but not in the previous one, we have met with denunciations of "lax" fathers and have been confronted with the concept of "unfair competition."

It would, however, be a great mistake so to dwell on difficulties as to forget that, just because of its voluntary nature, the relationship between a spiritual father and a secular disciple is capable of being, in a true sense, successful. In spite of the gloomy tone so apparent in *Ep 3*, Symeon could write *Ep 2* without giving any hint that the spiritual child whom he was addressing was in any way disobedient or unsubmissive. It must be assumed also that the secular disciples, whom Nicetas mentions, were not people who caused Symeon anxieties of the sort to which our attention has been directed. Men, such as the patrician Genesios, the "prominent personage" Christopher Phagura, and others of similar standing, were proud to be numbered amongst Symeon's spiritual children, and while doubtless Nicetas recorded their names[80] as a method of honouring his hero, he would scarcely have done so had they been known to have proved "uncommitted" or unsatisfactory in some other way.

Symeon's Reluctance

What has emerged in the preceding sections of this chapter provides much support for the verdict of a French Roman Catholic writer:

> If true directors are rare, true spiritual children are none the less so, because there are very few persons who aspire to sanctity through the way of the cross and continually dying to themselves.[81]

There is in fact no inducement for anyone who is "conscientious" to seek to become a spiritual father. If he undertakes the work, he will do so because he sees it as a duty laid on him by God, a duty which he will most likely feel to be unwelcome. Such was certainly Symeon's attitude, for we have seen how conscious he was of being beset by many difficulties in his

---

80 *Life*, 54, 6, 55, 1f., 100, 1f., 102, 7f.

81 J.N. Grou, *Manual for Interior Souls*, (English translation), London, 1892, (reprinted 1952), p. 129.

attempts to fulfil the obligations entailed by spiritual fatherhood. Indeed, as Völker has observed, he not only regarded it as inevitable that a "conscientious" father would be hated by those who, on the basis of human and worldly wisdom, accounted themselves wise, but he also envisaged the possibility of his having to suffer a fate similar to that of Christ.[82] It was Symeon's perception of the sin involved in burying one's talent in the earth that made him willing, in spite of everything, to minister to others in this way.[83]

Evidence of Symeon's reluctance is not hard to find. From one of the *Catecheses*, for example, we can cite his complaint:

> I exhort you, but I am not listened to, I rebuke you and am rejected, I reprove you and am hated, I chasten you and am chastened and indeed pursued as though I were an enemy, and through doing all this I am unable to get any rest. I should like to give up and attend only to my own faults, but whenever I decide to cease from this [work], my heart is kindled like a fire, and I, poor wretch, am once again condemned to the same weary round ... I am amazed at how we ... rejoice to bind ourselves to our sins and how we devour those trying to set us free from such bonds.[84]

Symeon here laid bare his misery at the rejection of his efforts to do what he considered to be incumbent upon him as hegumen/spiritual father. Though he would clearly have liked to abandon the task, it was a duty from which he was unable to escape. Against his will, he felt constrained to continue doing the work, and the words he used about fire in his heart with their echo of the language of the psalmist and of Jeremiah make it clear that he felt the constraint to be of divine origin. Nothing less than this would have been strong enough to overcome his natural shrinking from being compelled to suffer at the hands of the very monks whom he was endeavouring to set free from their bondage to sin.

In another *Catechesis* we find him appealing to his flock and complaining of the burden which, as spiritual father, he had to bear.

> If you truly love me, reveal to me the purposes of your hearts. Let me know, not merely by your words, but by your deeds, that God is with you and that I have not laboured in vain. But if you will not do this, why do you go and procure a burden for me and then draw back and burden me the more? It is a burden which—most paradoxically—causes me both unspeakable joy and boundless grief: joy because I am praying for you and rejoicing in the

---

[82] Völker, *Praxis*, pp. 114–116, cf. *Cat XV*, 26–36, *Cat XX*, 130–160.

[83] "Burying one's talent," a reference to *St. Matthew* 25. 18 (cf. *St. Luke* 19. 20), is an image to which Symeon several times recurred, v. *Cat VI*, 223f., *Cat XXXIV*, 24f., 61–67, *Hymn XXVIII*, 109f., *Hymn XLIII*, 122f.

[84] *Cat III*, 48–62 (extracts), with reminiscences of *Psalm* 38. 4 (39. 3) and *Jeremiah* 20. 9.

hope of recovering you [for God], but grief because I am afraid of your being stifled by the world, being deceived and becoming false to Christ, the thought of which makes me tremble and sends me out of my wits.[85]

Here it must be admitted that Symeon manifested a certain ambivalence in admitting that his "burden" was capable of causing him joy as well as grief. But the word he employed, βάρος, is the one used by St. Paul when bidding the Galatians to "bear one another's burdens,"[86] and this, in the light of Symeon's statement that he was left to bear it alone, suggests that he mainly felt that he was being compelled to carry an unwelcome load. This interpretation is confirmed by the fact that in the final sentence of our quotation much more emphasis is laid upon fears than upon hopes. As spiritual father, Symeon felt himself responsible for the salvation of the monks, his spiritual children, and therefore he was afraid that, should they prove at the last to have been "false to Christ," he would in fact "have . . . laboured in vain." The overall impression conveyed is that in spite of recognising that given "sincere" disciples spiritual fatherhood might be a source of joy, Symeon was predominantly conscious of the unwelcome nature of the burden which it imposed on him in St. Mamas'.

Furthermore, since as pastor a father ought to lead his flock to "the spiritual mountains of mystical contemplations,"[87] he will be compelled to speak about his own spiritual experiences in the course of his efforts to guide and inspire his disciples. Symeon at times attempted to avoid self-advertisement by describing visions and revelations as though they were the experience of someone else which had been recounted to him.[88] We noticed, however, that he did not escape the obvious criticism, levelled at him by those of this monks who were unsympathetic, that he was actually depicting himself in a conceited manner. Symeon was naturally sensitive to comments charging him with boastfulness,[89] and felt the need to reply to them. On one occasion when he did this, he used language which again indicates that he was a reluctant spiritual father, only undertaking the work because he believed it to be a duty imposed on him by God. Part of his answer, made as so often to an imaginary objector, ran as follows:

The Apostles and the Fathers have spoken in terms not different from my words and have even gone further. Yet [in their case] the speakers appear

---

[85] *Cat XIX*, 82–92, with reminiscences of *I Corinthians* 4. 5, of *Philippians* 2. 16, and (more remotely) of *St. Matthew* 13. 22 / *St. Mark* 4. 19.

[86] *Galatians* 6. 2, and cf. chapter VI, p. 110.

[87] *Hymn XLIII*, 72f.—cf. chapter VI, p. 108.

[88] v. *Cat VI*, 121–131, *Cat XVI*, *Cat XXII*, and cf. the biographical note inserted at *PG* 120, 685D–688A, which states that he spoke "as if about some other person, since he was trying to conceal himself in order to avoid the glory that comes from men . . ."

[89] *Cat XXXIV*, 97f. (quoted above at n. 28), cf. *Cat VI*, 232–235.

worthy of credence, which renders what they say acceptable and trustworthy, whereas our pitiful personality causes even what is admitted by
everyone to seem false and abominable to you.[90]

He then added that there was a further reason, namely the need to combat
the prevalent error that there were no contemporary saints, which had led
him, "albeit unwillingly," to divulge what he had revealed.[91] Aware,
then, of the reaction he was inevitably provoking in some of the monks
who were his hearers, Symeon could only insist that this part of his work
as pastor was one which he found most distasteful, since he was conscious
of appearing to these critics as no more than a "pitiful personality."
Doubtless he felt differently when he knew that he was addressing "sincere" disciples, who would regard him, as he had regarded the Studite,
as Christ's "holy disciple and apostle."[92] However, as hegumen Symeon
had no choice but to minister both to those who willingly accepted his
authority and also to the others who openly showed their dislike of his
leadership, and this renders his distaste for the task easy to understand.

But there was a further reason for his reluctance. At the beginning of
Ep 4 he explained that he would prefer not to have to undertake anything
which would necessitate involvement with other people. Spiritual fatherhood cannot have been excluded from the tasks he had in mind, for he
went on to make it clear that his longing to escape such involvement had
had to give way to his knowledge that it was his duty to help his neighbour,
and for a man in Symeon's position willingness to act as a father was an
obvious way in which he might be called on to fulfil this duty.

> I could wish—he wrote—to be so utterly dead to the world, my beloved
> brother, as not to be known to anyone on earth, but in truth to pass through
> life like a dead man, and to live in obscurity that life which is hidden in Christ
> ... That is the life I longed for and am even now longing for, but since, to
> use Paul's words, we are not our own, for we were bought with a price, we
> ought not only to have regard to our own interests or to ourselves, but each
> ought [to be concerned] to please his neighbour for his good, and there is
> thus laid on me the absolute necessity to perform with all eagerness the
> injunctions of my Master and Lord Jesus Christ, who redeemed me.[93]

Here Symeon was not complaining of specific difficulties caused by recalcitrant monks or "uncommitted" secular disciples; it might perhaps be
thought that in these opening sentences of his letter he was merely paying
tribute to convention when he expressed his desire to be unknown. But

---

[90] *Cat XXXIV*, 188–192.
[91] *ibid.*, 193–196.
[92] *Cat XXXVI*, 160f.
[93] *Ep 4*, 6–17 (extracts); "hidden in Christ" is a reminiscence of *Colossians* 3. 3, and
for "Paul's words," v. *I Corinthians* 6. 19f., *Philippians* 2. 4, *Romans* 15. 2.

as against an interpretation which would tax him with artifice of this kind, there are two points to be borne in mind: first, as he showed by quoting it elsewhere, he had not forgotten the Studite's pronouncement that a monk ought to be one who "does not even make his existence known;"[94] and, secondly, it will be remembered that we have found evidence that he did feel at times the work he engaged in as a spiritual father might endanger his salvation.[95] In *Ep 4* he ascribed the overcoming of his reluctance to his acknowledgment of the duty which he owed to his neighbour, whereas at other times he was conscious of being influenced by the Scriptural warning against burying one's talent in the earth.[96] Each of these considerations will have had power to impel Symeon to act as a spiritual father, but his reluctance did not disappear.

There is no reason to be surprised at his shrinking from the work. Clearly Symeon belonged to the class of "conscientious" spiritual fathers, and such men are the very ones who will find themselves confronted by the difficulties and anxieties of the kind which we have been investigating, but which will not arise to trouble their "lax" counterparts. Furthermore, as the passage quoted from *Ep 4* suggests, the better fitted a person is to be a spiritual guide to others because of his personal experience ($\pi\varepsilon\tilde{\iota}\rho\alpha$) of divine realities, the more unwilling he will probably be to undertake a duty which is both demanding and one which he is likely to perceive as threatening to interrupt his own converse with God. Symeon clearly felt this way, and therefore this reluctance could be vanquished only by the overriding force of "the injunctions of [his] Master and Lord."

Although, as our study will have made clear, it would be going too far to claim Symeon as the embodiment of all that a spiritual father ought to be, the very fact that he was reluctant is a testimony to his having been genuinely called to, and fitted for, the task. Spiritual fatherhood is not best exercised by those who for higher or lower motives put themselves forward as volunteers; in fact, "those [directors] who are truly animated by the Spirit of God . . . do not propose themselves unless they are called in, and even so they always advance with a certain timidity."[97] The men best qualified to be spiritual fathers are those who, like Symeon, would much rather live "that life which is hidden in Christ," but who are nevertheless convinced that Christ is calling them to undertake this ministry, and who in obedience accept the vocation, which reaches them when others come

---

[94] *Cat VI*, 174.
[95] cf. above, p. 233.
[96] cf. above, p. 242.
[97] J.-P. de Caussade, *Self-Abandonment to Divine Providence*, (tr. A. Thorold, revised by J. Joyce), Fontana, 1971, p. 140.

and ask for their assistance. ''One does not become a Spiritual Father because he seeks it or wants it or desires it ... In spiritual paternity, it is the son who seeks, and the Father comes into the role of paternity only with anguish and fear.''[98]

---

[98] M.B. Pennington, *O Holy Mountain*, London, 1980, p. 98, reporting the words of a modern hegumen.

CHAPTER TEN

SYMEON AND SPIRITUAL FATHERHOOD: CONCLUDING REFLECTIONS

Through Symeon we have been introduced to a great variety of material illustrating not only the actual behaviour of spiritual fathers and of their disciples but also the various objectives underlying it. It is now necessary, in conclusion, to try to assess what Symeon, through his life and his writings, has contributed to our knowledge of the development of the theory and practice of spiritual fatherhood. The subject may fittingly be approached by briefly considering his Church's attitude towards him.

In Völker's opinion, after Symeon's death little circles of faithful devotees kept his teaching alive, with the result that the hesychast movement was later profoundly influenced by it.[1] In addition, as Krivochéine remarked, many copies of manuscripts containing his works were made, particularly in the fourteenth century and especially on Mount Athos, and Symeon has never lacked disciples and fervent admirers. On the other hand, Krivochéine could not deny that his place in the Church's calendar has always been minimal, no church has ever been dedicated in his honour, and the liturgical office to commemorate him was only composed in the eighteenth century. As for the reasons for this neglect,

> his unique kind of personality, mystical and pugnacious at the same time, his apostolic zeal in proclaiming the vision of God as open to every Christian —all this upset faint-hearted temperaments, and they preferred to forget Symeon.[2]

In this judgment Krivochéine mainly had in mind Symeon's life and teaching as a mystic, but much the same conclusion would be reached by someone considering his career as a disciple and a spiritual father. At no time, for instance, could the authorities of the Church be expected to

---

[1] Völker, *Praxis*, p. 489, cf. F. Halkin, 'Deux Vies de S. Maxime le Kausokalybe, ermite au Mont Athos (XIVe S.),' *Saints moines d'Orient*, London, (Variorum Reprints), 1973, XI, p. 38, n. 1.

[2] Krivochéine, *Lumière*, pp. 421–424, with quotation taken from p. 423; Hausherr, *Life*, p. VIII, n. 4, gives the full title of the office, and some extracts from it, while Christophorides in his bibliography (*op. cit.*, p. 150) mentions a new critical edition of it, prepared by S. Koutsa and published in Athens in 1975. Krivochéine (p. 421) remarks that even if we allow that there might have been an earlier commemorative office, the fact of its having been lost is in itself significant. Symeon died on 12 March, but because this date falls in Lent, his feast day has been transferred to 12 October, but in practice, according to Krivochéine, little notice is taken of it (p. 424, n. 5).

welcome either his strictures on unworthy bishops, priests and hegumens or his insistence on the spiritual but unordained monk's possessing the right to absolve, even though there might be willingness to recognise the orthodoxy and the value of much that he taught about spiritual fatherhood in general.

Interest in Symeon, which seems to have been recently growing, is often confined to the study of him as a mystic, and thus leads to an examination of his writings simply as source-material for this purpose. There is in this a danger that the real man, whom Krivochéine portrays, may be forgotten, and that he may become for some of his admirers what he appears as depicted by Nicetas, a somewhat unreal paragon of saintly mysticism. No such danger has attended our study of Symeon in connection with spiritual fatherhood, for here inevitably we have had to take note of his defects and faults as well as of all that was admirable in his loyalty, his understanding, his skill and his enthusiasm.

Our investigations have shown that although in one sense there may be little that is original in Symeon's approach, yet he occupies a most important place in the history of spiritual fatherhood because of the way in which he upheld and revivified the best of the tradition of the past, a tradition which continues up to the present day.[3] His concern for tradition must, of course, be seen within the perspective of what has repeatedly been stressed in preceding chapters, namely that by far the most intense influence on Symeon's practice and teaching was his personal experience of discipleship to his own spiritual father, the Studite. Through this relationship, many of his own deep needs came to be satisfied, and he was thereby enabled to develop both as a mystic and as himself a spiritual father to others. From his own writings we have observed how through being a disciple he came to revise and enrich his understanding of the purpose of spiritual fatherhood. This fact is in no way at variance with the claim that Symeon was an upholder of tradition, since it has always been a part of the tradition in Orthodox ascetical theology that the father ought to be more concerned to share his experience with his spiritual child than to exact from him conformity to external codes of behaviour.[4]

These reflections lead naturally to an attempt to answer the question: how can we assess what we have learned by attempting to study Symeon not as a mystic, but in connection with spiritual fatherhood? The reply necessarily involves some kind of a summary of the vast amount of material available in the writings of Symeon himself, the Studite and Nicetas,

---

[3] cf. M.B. Pennington, *O Holy Mountain!*, London, 1980, and S. Bolshakoff, *Russian Mystics*, Kalamazoo/London, 1977 (especially chapter XII).

[4] cf. *Cat VI*, 261–267, quoted chapter VI, p. 114.

and we begin by reminding ourselves of the many facets of the relationship between a father and his spiritual children, clients or disciples. Symeon's own development provides a case-study of a client who sought a spiritual father for inadequate reasons and was for a time a back-slider, but as a result of that father's skill came to be an intensely loyal disciple, and through their relationship was led into deep spiritual experiences in the present, without of course abandoning his hope for salvation in the next world. Hence we have a paradigm of how spiritual fatherhood might operate, and an example of what it might effect.

The career of Symeon also introduced us to an instance of how a succession of spiritual fathers may be secured, for we were led to assume that at an early stage the Studite recognised this spiritual child as a potential father, and so treated him as an heir[5] and trained him through a kind of apprenticeship. Having himself become a spiritual father, Symeon through his various writings revealed to us his opinions of other fathers, and his reactions to disciples both monastic and secular, to those who were ''sincere'' and eager for progress as well as to the recalcitrant and ''uncommitted''. We were able also to investigate in considerable detail what he understood as being included in a father's duty towards his spiritual children, this involving not only the training which he ought to give them, but also the goal which he should try to help them reach.

From Symeon's *Catecheses* and from various of his other works, it was possible to obtain an understanding of the qualifications he regarded as essential,[6] while from his *Epistles* we came to learn of the existence of men unfitted for spiritual fatherhood who competed unscrupulously in their attempts to attract disciples. The prevalence of such people formed one of the many difficulties with which ''conscientious'' fathers had to contend. Other troubles were caused by spiritual children: Symeon, when trying to urge on those among his monks who were unresponsive, found their resistance a significant part of the burden he had to bear, and if there is no direct evidence that any of his own spiritual children in the world proved a source of anxiety, he clearly knew that there were others who behaved very badly towards their fathers. All this evidence has to be taken into account if we wish to have a realistic picture of the actual life and work of a spiritual father in Byzantium at that time, and *mutatis mutandis* at other times and in other places.

It must not be forgotten that Symeon hinted also at the need not to cling indefinitely to disciples; he was not innovating when he spoke of a stage being reached at which the spiritual child in a sense no longer needs his

---

[5] cf. *Cat XVI*, 65–75, with the Elijah/Elisha *motif*, and *Cat VI*, 198–208, 223–232.
[6] cf. *Cat XX*, 197–211.

father, but in this connection he used the image of Pentecost in a striking manner, in accordance with his habit of laying stress upon the Holy Spirit's activity. Taking this in conjunction with his references to the Studite as his παιδαγωγός, we are led to recognise how well he understood that vitally important as is the part which the spiritual father must play, it is still in the last resort no more than a preparatory one. This in one way is not surprising in the light of his statement that at the very outset the intending disciple might be sent to a new father by the Holy Spirit,[7] whom Symeon always accepted as the final arbiter. In another way, however, the idea of a disciple's becoming somehow independent of his father is not one that we might expect to discover in him, since his devotion to the Studite might well have precluded his hinting at anything of this kind. The fact that by implication he ruled out a possessive attitude towards spiritual children is an indication of Symeon's own maturity.

From our study it will have become very clear that in Symeon's relations with others, both as disciple and as spiritual father, much depended on compatibility or incompatibility of temperament and personality. This observation is not as platitudinous as it might at first sight appear, for it testifies to an essential difference between sacramental confession and spiritual fatherhood: in the former, because the bishop or priest is acting as the appointed minister of a sacrament, the kind of person he is should be capable of being disregarded, although it cannot be altogether ignored if, as is customary, he is a source of counsel as well as of absolution for a penitent; the spiritual father, on the other hand, is involved in a different type of relationship, and though there is a sense in which this relationship might be called sacramental, it cannot escape being profoundly influenced by the personal interaction between himself and his disciple. Symeon received immense benefit from the Studite because their personalities were mutually sympathetic; the same could be said in respect of the disciples, whether monastic or secular, who proved responsive to Symeon, while it is plain that there were some amongst his monks with whom he was temperamentally so incompatible that he could not hope to be a true spiritual father to them.

It would be tempting to assert that this somehow proves that Symeon was less successful than the Studite, but about the latter, who in any case was never a hegumen, we really do not know enough to be able to compare their failures or successes in any meaningful way. From our knowledge of Symeon, on the other hand, we have certainly received the impression that his enthusiastic temperament did incapacitate him from being an

---

[7] *ibid.*, 54f.

acceptable spiritual father to the *moyen sensuel* element in the community of which he was hegumen. It has been well said that "Love is a gift or it is nothing,"[8] and in *Cat I* Symeon affirmed his desire to impart this gift to each and all of his monks. He suffered greatly through his inability to persuade them all to accept it at his hands, an inability due partly to his being as hegumen also *ex officio* spiritual father, and partly to the clash between his personality and that of those monks who in his eyes were persistently recalcitrant.

Symeon's partial failure, as well as exhibiting plainly the disadvantages of a hegumen's being the sole spiritual father of a monastery, also suggests that nobody, however skilful and experienced, ought to expect that his way of exercising this ministry will meet the needs of all potential clients. This fact, taken in conjunction with Symeon's insistence, which we have noted, that properly qualified fathers are few and far between, raises a question about his affirmation that no one who genuinely seeks will fail to find the spiritual father he needs. It would seem that, formally at least, there is an inherent contradiction in Symeon's position, but he would no doubt have claimed to have resolved it by allowing that those who have not found a father may look to Christ alone;[9] at any rate he must be given credit for affirming the truth that spiritual fathers cannot be produced to order.

The reason why Symeon held that true fathers are rare might be that he believed the work to be demanding and the necessary qualifications for it not easily acquired. But if we take account also of what we discovered concerning his own reluctance and his censure of those whom he considered too eager to act as fathers, we must not overlook the possibility that he also believed that any who were truly qualified for the role would inevitably hesitate to undertake it, and would only do so in obedience to the prompting of the Holy Spirit. Certainly, both by his faith that he was divinely guided by a vision to commit himself to the Studite, and also in his teaching about who should function as spiritual fathers, Symeon demonstrated his conviction that everything to do with this ministry ought to be seen as resting in the hands of God. In this sense, as well as in that referred to in our preliminary treatment of the subject,[10] spiritual fatherhood is a charismatic ministry and Symeon would certainly have insisted that the number of those called to exercise it cannot be increased as a result of purely human decisions.

Even if problems and difficulties feature prominently in what Symeon

---

[8] A. Jones, *Soul Making: The Desert Way of Spirituality*, London, 1986, p. 131.
[9] *Ep 3*, 211r–212r; *Tr Eth VII*, 402–405.
[10] cf. chapter IV, p. 56.

had to say on the subject of spiritual fatherhood, it must not be forgotten that his works testify also to the realisation in some cases of his splendid ideals: provided that both father and disciple were of the right type, he expected that their relationship would be the means of the latter's being transformed and enlightened by the Holy Spirit, and even made divine.[11] He entertained this expectation because of what he himself and others had experienced. Symeon deserves our gratitude because from his writings we are enabled to understand why it is only infrequently that all he hoped for from spiritual fatherhood is actually achieved, but are also assured that given the right conditions the goal can be, and has been, reached.

In studying Symeon we have thus been in contact with a man who, although a genuine representative of tradition, and indeed one who strove hard to re-establish it, was never a slavish follower of precedent but one who was receptive both to the riches of the past and also to the riches he acquired through his own experience in the present. With regard to spiritual fatherhood he exemplifies some words of a woman of our own day:

> Whoever does such work must needs do it in his own way. Not that he inter-prets the tradition in his own individual manner but, applying the generally accepted interpretation to a unique case, he gives to it the colouring of his own personality. This colouring he is free to give, indeed cannot avoid giving; but this requires of him humility, courage and tact, if his guidance is to remain true to the spirit of the tradition.[12]

By and large such a description, apart from the word, "tact", fits St. Symeon the New Theologian, and our study of him justifies, it is hoped, the claim that he ought to be recognised as a most significant contributor to the tradition of spiritual fatherhood and to the understanding of that tradition at the present time.

---

[11] *Cat XX*, 165–186.

[12] Iulia de Beausobre, quoted in C. Babington Smith, *Iulia de Beausobre—A Russian Christian in the West*, London, 1983, p. 69.

INDEX

* Indicates persons/subjects closely connected with St. Symeon the New Theologian or
composite entries which include items having some particular reference to him.